PEARSON ALWAYS LEARNING

Keith Mulbery • Cynthia Krebs • Lynn Hogan
Eric Cameron • Jason Davidson • Linda K. Lau
Rebecca Lawson • Jerri Williams • Amy Rutledge

Series Editor
Mary Anne Poatsy

Series Created by
Dr. Robert T. Grauer

Exploring Microsoft® Office 2016

Volume 1

Access

Custom Edition for Camden County College

Taken from:
Exploring Microsoft® Office 2016, Volume 1
by Keith Mulbery, Cynthia Krebs, Lynn Hogan, Eric Cameron,
Jason Davidson, Linda K. Lau, Rebecca Lawson,
Jerri Williams, and Amy Rutledge
Series Editor: Mary Anne Poatsy
Series Created by Dr. Robert T. Grauer

Cover Art: Courtesy of Photodisc/Getty Images.

Taken from:

Exploring Microsoft® Office 2016, Volume 1
by Keith Mulbery, Cynthia Krebs, Lynn Hogan, Eric Cameron, Jason Davidson, Linda K. Lau, Rebecca Lawson, Jerri Williams, and Amy Rutledge
Series Editor: Mary Anne Poatsy
Series Created by Dr. Robert T. Grauer

New York, New York 10013

This special edition published in cooperation with Pearson Education, Inc.

Pearson Education, Inc., 330 Hudson Street, New York, New York 10013
A Pearson Education Company
www.pearsoned.com

Printed in the United States of America

000200010272044629

JK

ISBN 10: 1-323-50888-0
ISBN 13: 978-1-323-50888-6

13 2019

Dedications

For my husband, Ted, who unselfishly continues to take on more than his share to support me throughout the process; and for my children, Laura, Carolyn, and Teddy, whose encouragement and love have been inspiring.

Mary Anne Poatsy

I dedicate this book in memory to Grandpa Herman Hort, who dedicated his life to his family and to the education field as a teacher and administrator. He inspired a daughter and several grandchildren to become passionate educators and provide quality curriculum to students.

Keith Mulbery

For my children for all of believing in me, encouraging me, and supporting me. Thank you Marshall Krebs, Jaron Krebs, Jenalee Krebs Behle, and Michelle Krebs. To my writing mentor, Dr. Keith Mulbery, for the same reasons.

Cynthia Krebs

I dedicate this work to my wonderful family—my husband, Paul, and my daughters, Jenn and Alli. You have made this adventure possible with your support, encouragement, and love. You inspire me!

Lynn Hogan

I dedicate this book to my wife Anny, for supporting me through the writing process, to my nieces Daniela and Gabriela, who someday will be old enough to think it is cool their names are in a book, and to my students, who make a career in teaching fulfilling. May you all go forward, change the world and inspire others.

Eric Cameron

I dedicate this book in loving memory of my grandfather Laurence L. Leggett. A passionate lifelong educator, gifted musician, and incredible role model. I will never forget our time together. I strive every day to make you proud.

Jason Davidson

I dedicate this book to my only child, Catherine Shen, who taught me that there is another wonderful life outside of my work. My life has been more fulfilling and exciting with her in it. I also dedicate this book to the loving memory of my dog, Harry, who was by my side, through thick and thin, for 16 years. I miss him dearly every day.

Linda K. Lau

This book is dedicated to my children and to my students to inspire them to never give up and to always keep reaching for their dreams.

Rebecca Lawson

I offer thanks to my family and colleagues who have supported me on this journey. I would like to dedicate the work I have performed toward this undertaking to my little grandson, Yonason Meir (known for now as Mei-Mei), who as his name suggests, is the illumination in my life.

Jerri Williams

To my husband Dan, whose encouragement, patience, and love helped make this endeavor possible. Thank you for taking on the many additional tasks at home so that I could focus on writing.

Amy Rutledge

About the Authors

Mary Anne Poatsy, Series Editor, Windows 10 Author

Mary Anne is a senior faculty member at Montgomery County Community College, teaching various computer application and concepts courses in face-to-face and online environments. She holds a B.A. in Psychology and Education from Mount Holyoke College and an M.B.A. in Finance from Northwestern University's Kellogg Graduate School of Management.

Mary Anne has more than 12 years of educational experience. She is currently adjunct faculty at Gwynedd-Mercy College and Montgomery County Community College. She has also taught at Bucks County Community College and Muhlenberg College, as well as conducted personal training. Before teaching, she was Vice President at Shearson Lehman in the Municipal Bond Investment Banking Department.

Dr. Keith Mulbery, Excel Author

Dr. Keith Mulbery is the Department Chair and a Professor in the Information Systems and Technology Department at Utah Valley University (UVU), where he currently teaches systems analysis and design, and global and ethical issues in information systems and technology. He has also taught computer applications, C# programming, and management information systems. Keith served as Interim Associate Dean, School of Computing, in the College of Technology and Computing at UVU.

Keith received the Utah Valley State College Board of Trustees Award of Excellence in 2001, School of Technology and Computing Scholar Award in 2007, and School of Technology and Computing Teaching Award in 2008. He has authored more than 17 textbooks, served as Series Editor for the Exploring Office 2007 series, and served as developmental editor on two textbooks for the Essentials Office 2000 series. He is frequently asked to give presentations and workshops on Microsoft Office Excel at various education conferences.

Keith received his B.S. and M.Ed. in Business Education from Southwestern Oklahoma State University and earned his Ph.D. in Education with an emphasis in Business Information Systems at Utah State University. His dissertation topic was computer-assisted instruction using Prentice Hall's Train and Assess IT program (the predecessor to MyITLab) to supplement traditional instruction in basic computer proficiency courses.

Cynthia Krebs, PowerPoint Author

Cynthia Krebs is the Program Director of Business and Marketing Education at Utah Valley University. She is a tenured professor in the Information Systems and Technology Department at UVU where she teaches the Methods of Teaching Business, Marketing, and Digital Technology course to future teachers, as well as classes in basic computer applications and business proficiency applications. She holds a B.S and M.S. in Business Education with an emphasis in Economic Education. Cynthia has received numerous awards, and has presented extensively at the local, regional, and national levels as well as consulting with government organizations and businesses.

Cynthia lives by a peaceful creek I in Springville, Utah. When she isn't teaching or writing, she enjoys spending time with her children, spoiling her grandchildren Ava, Bode, Solee, Morgan, and Preslee. She loves traveling and reading.

Lynn Hogan, Word Author

Lynn Hogan teaches at the University of North Alabama, providing instruction in the area of computer applications. With over 30 years of educational experience at the community college and university level, Lynn has taught applications, programming, and concepts courses in both online and classroom environments. She received an M.B.A. from the University of North Alabama and a Ph.D. from the University of Alabama.

Lynn is a co-author of Practical Computing and has served on the authoring team of Your Office as well as the Exploring Office 2010 series. She resides in Alabama with her husband and two daughters.

Eric Cameron, Access Author

Eric Cameron is a tenured Associate Professor at Passaic County Community College, where he has taught in the Computer and Information Sciences department since 2001. He holds an M.S. in Computer Science and a B.S. degree in Computer Science with minors in Mathematics and Physics, both from Montclair State University. He currently co-chairs the College's General Education committee and served as a member of the College's Academic Assessment, College Writing, and Educational Technology committees at various points. Eric has also developed degrees in Graphic Design and Medical Informatics for the College. Eric previously worked as a software engineer both as a full-time employee and contractor, most recently for ITT/Exelis (now part of Harris Corporation).

This is Eric's fourth publication for Pearson, after authoring Web 2.0 and Windows 8 books in the Your Office series and co-authoring the Exploring Access 2013 text.

Jason Davidson, Excel Author

Jason Davidson is a faculty member in the College of Business at Butler University, where he teaches Advanced Web Design, Data Networks, Data Analysis and Business Modeling, and introductory information systems courses. He is the co-author of Exploring Microsoft Excel 2013 Comprehensive, Exploring Microsoft Office 2013 Volume 2, Exploring Microsoft Office 2013 Plus, and Exploring VBA for Microsoft Office 2013.

With a background in media development, prior to joining the faculty at Butler, he worked in the technical publishing industry. Along with teaching, he currently serves as an IT consultant for regional businesses in the Indianapolis area. He holds a B.A. in Telecommunication Arts from Butler University and an M.B.A. from Morehead State University. He lives in Indianapolis, Indiana, and in his free time enjoys road biking, photography, and spending time with his family.

Dr. Linda K. Lau, Word Author

Since 1994, Dr. Linda K. Lau is a Management Information Systems (MIS) faculty at the College of Business and Economics, Longwood University, located in Farmville, Virginia. She received the Outstanding Academic Advisor Award in 2006. Besides teaching and advising, Linda has authored and co-authored numerous journal and conference articles and textbooks, edited two books, and sat on several editorial boards. Her current research interest focuses on cyber security and forensics, and she is the associate editor for the Journal of Digital Forensics, Security and Law (JDFSL). Linda earned her Ph.D. from Rensselaer Polytechnic Institute in 1993, and her MBA and Bachelor of Science from Illinois State University in 1987 and 1986, respectively. In her younger days, Linda worked as a flight attendant for Singapore International Airlines for six years before coming to America to pursue her academic dream. She also worked as a financial consultant with Salomon Smith Barney from 1999–2000 before returning to the academic world. Linda resides in Richmond with her family.

Rebecca Lawson, PowerPoint Author

Rebecca Lawson is a professor in the Computer Information Technologies program at Lansing Community College. She coordinates the curriculum, develops the instructional materials, and teaches for the E-Business curriculum. She also serves as the Online Faculty Coordinator at the Center for Teaching Excellence at LCC. In that role, she develops and facilitates online workshops for faculty learning to teach online. Her major areas of interest include online curriculum quality assurance, the review and development of printed and online instructional materials, the assessment of computer and Internet literacy skill levels to facilitate student retention, and the use of social networking tools to support learning in blended and online learning environments.

Jerri Williams, Access Author

Jerri Williams is a Senior Instructor at Montgomery County Community College in Pennsylvania. Jerri also works as an independent corporate trainer, technical editor, and content developer. She is interested in travel, cooking, movies, and tending to her colonial farmhouse. Jerri is married, and is the mother of two daughters, Holly (an Accounting graduate and full-time mother to an adorable son, Meir) and Gwyneth (a corporate defense attorney). Jerri and Gareth live in the suburbs of Philadelphia. They enjoy their home and garden, and spending time with family and good friends.

Amy Rutledge, Common Features Author

Amy Rutledge is a Special Instructor of Management Information Systems at Oakland University in Rochester, Michigan. She coordinates academic programs in Microsoft Office applications and introductory management information systems courses for the School of Business Administration. Before joining Oakland University as an instructor, Amy spent several years working for a music distribution company and automotive manufacturer in various corporate roles including IT project management. She holds a B.S. in Business Administration specializing in Management Information Systems, and a B.A. in French Modern Language and Literature. She holds an M.B.A from Oakland University. She resides in Michigan with her husband, Dan and daughters Emma and Jane.

Dr. Robert T. Grauer, Creator of the Exploring Series

Bob Grauer is an Associate Professor in the Department of Computer Information Systems at the University of Miami, where he is a multiple winner of the Outstanding Teaching Award in the School of Business, most recently in 2009. He has written numerous COBOL texts and is the vision behind the Exploring Office series, with more than three million books in print. His work has been translated into three foreign languages and is used in all aspects of higher education at both national and international levels. Bob Grauer has consulted for several major corporations including IBM and American Express. He received his Ph.D. in Operations Research in 1972 from the Polytechnic Institute of Brooklyn.

Brief Contents

Access

Application Capstone Exercises

Contents

Microsoft Office Access 2016

CHAPTER ONE **Introduction to Access:** Finding Your Way Through an Access Database 662

CHAPTER TWO **Tables and Queries in Relational Databases:** Designing Databases and Extracting Data 732

Acknowledgments

The Exploring team would like to acknowledge and thank all the reviewers who helped us throughout the years by providing us with their invaluable comments, suggestions, and constructive criticism.

Adriana Lumpkin
Midland College

Alan S. Abrahams
Virginia Tech

Alexandre C. Probst
Colorado Christian University

Ali Berrached
University of Houston–Downtown

Allen Alexander
Delaware Technical & Community College

Andrea Marchese
Maritime College, State University of New York

Andrew Blitz
Broward College; Edison State College

Angel Norman
University of Tennessee, Knoxville

Angela Clark
University of South Alabama

Ann Rovetto
Horry-Georgetown Technical College

Astrid Todd
Guilford Technical Community College

Audrey Gillant
Maritime College, State University of New York

Barbara Stover
Marion Technical College

Barbara Tollinger
Sinclair Community College

Ben Brahim Taha
Auburn University

Beverly Amer
Northern Arizona University

Beverly Fite
Amarillo College

Biswadip Ghosh
Metropolitan State University of Denver

Bonita Volker
Tidewater Community College

Bonnie Homan
San Francisco State University

Brad West
Sinclair Community College

Brian Powell
West Virginia University

Carol Buser
Owens Community College

Carol Roberts
University of Maine

Carolyn Barren
Macomb Community College

Carolyn Borne
Louisiana State University

Cathy Poyner
Truman State University

Charles Hodgson
Delgado Community College

Chen Zhang
Bryant University

Cheri Higgins
Illinois State University

Cheryl Brown
Delgado Community College

Cheryl Hinds
Norfolk State University

Cheryl Sypniewski
Macomb Community College

Chris Robinson
Northwest State Community College

Cindy Herbert
Metropolitan Community College–Longview

Craig J. Peterson
American InterContinental University

Dana Hooper
University of Alabama

Dana Johnson
North Dakota State University

Daniela Marghitu
Auburn University

David Noel
University of Central Oklahoma

David Pulis
Maritime College, State University of New York

David Thornton
Jacksonville State University

Dawn Medlin
Appalachian State University

Debby Keen
University of Kentucky

Debra Chapman
University of South Alabama

Debra Hoffman
Southeast Missouri State University

Derrick Huang
Florida Atlantic University

Diana Baran
Henry Ford Community College

Diane Cassidy
The University of North Carolina at Charlotte

Diane L. Smith
Henry Ford Community College

Dick Hewer
Ferris State College

Don Danner
San Francisco State University

Don Hoggan
Solano College

Don Riggs
SUNY Schenectady County Community College

Doncho Petkov
Eastern Connecticut State University

Donna Ehrhart
State University of New York at Brockport

Elaine Crable
Xavier University

Elizabeth Duett
Delgado Community College

Erhan Uskup
Houston Community College–Northwest

Eric Martin
University of Tennessee

Erika Nadas
Wilbur Wright College

Floyd Winters
Manatee Community College

Frank Lucente
Westmoreland County Community College

G. Jan Wilms
Union University

Gail Cope
Sinclair Community College

Gary DeLorenzo
California University of Pennsylvania

Gary Garrison
Belmont University

Gary McFall
Purdue University

George Cassidy
Sussex County Community College

Gerald Braun
Xavier University

Gerald Burgess
Western New Mexico University

Gladys Swindler
Fort Hays State University

Hector Frausto
California State University
Los Angeles

Heith Hennel
Valencia Community College

Henry Rudzinski
Central Connecticut State University

Irene Joos
La Roche College

Iwona Rusin
Baker College; Davenport University

J. Roberto Guzman
San Diego Mesa College

Jacqueline D. Lawson
Henry Ford Community College

Jakie Brown Jr.
Stevenson University

James Brown
Central Washington University

James Powers
University of Southern Indiana

Jane Stam
Onondaga Community College

Janet Bringhurst
Utah State University

Jean Welsh
Lansing Community College

Jeanette Dix
Ivy Tech Community College

Jennifer Day
Sinclair Community College

Jill Canine
Ivy Tech Community College

Jill Young
Southeast Missouri State University

Jim Chaffee
The University of Iowa Tippie College of Business

Joanne Lazirko
University of Wisconsin–Milwaukee

Jodi Milliner
Kansas State University

John Hollenbeck
Blue Ridge Community College

John Seydel
Arkansas State University

Judith A. Scheeren
Westmoreland County Community College

Judith Brown
The University of Memphis

Juliana Cypert
Tarrant County College

Kamaljeet Sanghera
George Mason University

Karen Priestly
Northern Virginia Community College

Karen Ravan
Spartanburg Community College

Karen Tracey
Central Connecticut State University

Kathleen Brenan
Ashland University

Ken Busbee
Houston Community College

Kent Foster
Winthrop University

Kevin Anderson
Solano Community College

Kim Wright
The University of Alabama

Kristen Hockman
University of Missouri–Columbia

Kristi Smith
Allegany College of Maryland

Laura Marcoulides
Fullerton College

Laura McManamon
University of Dayton

Laurence Boxer
Niagara University

Leanne Chun
Leeward Community College

Lee McClain
Western Washington University

Linda D. Collins
Mesa Community College

Linda Johnsonius
Murray State University

Linda Lau
Longwood University

Linda Theus
Jackson State Community College

Linda Williams
Marion Technical College

Lisa Miller
University of Central Oklahoma

Lister Horn
Pensacola Junior College

Lixin Tao
Pace University

Loraine Miller
Cayuga Community College

Lori Kielty
Central Florida Community College

Lorna Wells
Salt Lake Community College

Lorraine Sauchin
Duquesne University

Lucy Parakhovnik
California State University, Northridge

Lynn Keane
University of South Carolina

Lynn Mancini
Delaware Technical Community College

Mackinzee Escamilla
South Plains College

Marcia Welch
Highline Community College

Margaret McManus
Northwest Florida State College

Margaret Warrick
Allan Hancock College

Marilyn Hibbert
Salt Lake Community College

Mark Choman
Luzerne County Community College

Maryann Clark
University of New Hampshire

Mary Beth Tarver
Northwestern State University

Mary Duncan
University of Missouri–St. Louis

Melissa Nemeth
Indiana University-Purdue University Indianapolis

Melody Alexander
Ball State University

Michael Douglas
University of Arkansas at Little Rock

Michael Dunklebarger
Alamance Community College

Michael G. Skaff
College of the Sequoias

Michele Budnovitch
Pennsylvania College of Technology

Mike Jochen
East Stroudsburg University

Mike Michaelson
Palomar College

Mike Scroggins
Missouri State University

Mimi Spain
Southern Maine Community College

Muhammed Badamas
Morgan State University

NaLisa Brown
University of the Ozarks

Nancy Grant
Community College of Allegheny County–South Campus

Nanette Lareau
University of Arkansas Community College–Morrilton

Nikia Robinson
Indian River State University

Pam Brune
Chattanooga State Community College

Pam Uhlenkamp
Iowa Central Community College

Patrick Smith
Marshall Community and Technical College

Paul Addison
Ivy Tech Community College

Paula Ruby
Arkansas State University

Peggy Burrus
Red Rocks Community College

Peter Ross
SUNY Albany

Philip H. Nielson
Salt Lake Community College

Philip Valvalides
Guilford Technical Community College

Ralph Hooper
University of Alabama

Ranette Halverson
Midwestern State University

Richard Blamer
John Carroll University

Richard Cacace
Pensacola Junior College

Richard Hewer
Ferris State University

Richard Sellers
Hill College

Rob Murray
Ivy Tech Community College

Robert Banta
Macomb Community College

Robert Dušek
Northern Virginia Community College

Robert G. Phipps Jr.
West Virginia University

Robert Sindt
Johnson County Community College

Robert Warren
Delgado Community College

Rocky Belcher
Sinclair Community College

Roger Pick
University of Missouri at Kansas City

Ronnie Creel
Troy University

Rosalie Westerberg
Clover Park Technical College

Ruth Neal
Navarro College

Sandra Thomas
Troy University

Sheila Gionfriddo
Luzerne County Community College

Sherrie Geitgey
Northwest State Community College

Sherry Lenhart
Terra Community College

Sophia Wilberscheid
Indian River State College

Sophie Lee
California State University, Long Beach

Stacy Johnson
Iowa Central Community College

Stephanie Kramer
Northwest State Community College

Stephen Z. Jourdan
Auburn University at Montgomery

Steven Schwarz
Raritan Valley Community College

Sue A. McCrory
Missouri State University

Sumathy Chandrashekar
Salisbury University

Susan Fuschetto
Cerritos College

Susan Medlin
UNC Charlotte

Susan N. Dozier
Tidewater Community College

Suzan Spitzberg
Oakton Community College

Suzanne M. Jeska
County College of Morris

Sven Aelterman
Troy University

Sy Hirsch
Sacred Heart University

Sylvia Brown
Midland College

Tanya Patrick
Clackamas Community College

Terri Holly
Indian River State College

Terry Ray Rigsby
Hill College

Thomas Rienzo
Western Michigan University

Tina Johnson
Midwestern State University

Tommy Lu
Delaware Technical Community College

Troy S. Cash
Northwest Arkansas Community College

Vicki Robertson
Southwest Tennessee Community

Vickie Pickett
Midland College

Weifeng Chen
California University of Pennsylvania

Wes Anthony
Houston Community College

William Ayen
University of Colorado at Colorado Springs

Wilma Andrews
Virginia Commonwealth University

Yvonne Galusha
University of Iowa

Special thanks to our content development and technical team:

Barbara Stover
Julie Boyles
Lisa Bucki
Lori Damanti
Sallie Dodson
Patti Hammerle
Jean Insigna
Elizabeth Lockley
Joyce Nielsen
Janet Pickard
Linda Pogue
Steven Rubin
Mara Zebest

Preface

The Exploring Series and You

Exploring is Pearson's Office Application series that requires students like you to think "beyond the point and click." In this edition, we have worked to restructure the Exploring experience around the way you, today's modern student, actually use your resources.

The goal of Exploring is, as it has always been, to go farther than teaching just the steps to accomplish a task—the series provides the theoretical foundation for you to understand when and why to apply a skill. As a result, you achieve a deeper understanding of each application and can apply this critical thinking beyond Office and the classroom.

The How & Why of This Revision

Outcomes matter. Whether it's getting a good grade in this course, learning how to use Excel so students can be successful in other courses, or learning a specific skill that will make learners successful in a future job, everyone has an outcome in mind. And outcomes matter. That is why we revised our chapter opener to focus on the outcomes students will achieve by working through each Exploring chapter. These are coupled with objectives and skills, providing a map students can follow to get everything they need from each chapter.

Critical Thinking and Collaboration are essential 21st century skills. Students want and need to be successful in their future careers—so we used motivating case studies to show relevance of these skills to future careers and incorporated Soft Skills, Collaboration, and Analysis Cases with Critical Thinking steps in this edition to set students up for success in the future.

Students today read, prepare, and study differently than students used to. Students use textbooks like a tool—they want to easily identify what they need to know and learn it efficiently. We have added key features such as Tasks Lists (in purple), Step Icons, Hands-On Exercise Videos, and tracked everything via page numbers that allow efficient navigation, creating a map students can easily follow.

Students are exposed to technology. The new edition of Exploring moves beyond the basics of the software at a faster pace, without sacrificing coverage of the fundamental skills that students need to know.

Students are diverse. Students can be any age, any gender, any race, with any level of ability or learning style. With this in mind, we broadened our definition of "student resources" to include physical Student Reference cards, Hands-On Exercise videos to provide a secondary lecture-like option of review; and MyITLab, the most powerful and most ADA-compliant online homework and assessment tool around with a direct 1:1 content match with the Exploring Series. Exploring will be accessible to all students, regardless of learning style.

Providing You with a Map to Success to Move Beyond the Point and Click

All of these changes and additions will provide students an easy and efficient path to follow to be successful in this course, regardless of where they start at the beginning of this course. Our goal is to keep students engaged in both the hands-on and conceptual sides, helping achieve a higher level of understanding that will guarantee success in this course and in a future career.

In addition to the vision and experience of the series creator, Robert T. Grauer, we have assembled a tremendously talented team of Office Applications authors who have devoted themselves to teaching the ins and outs of Microsoft Word, Excel, Access, and PowerPoint. Led in this edition by series editor Mary Anne Poatsy, the whole team is dedicated to the Exploring mission of moving students **beyond the point and click**.

Key Features

The **How/Why Approach** helps students move beyond the point and click to a true understanding of how to apply Microsoft Office skills.

- **White Pages/Yellow Pages** clearly distinguish the theory (white pages) from the skills covered in the Hands-On Exercises (yellow pages) so students always know what they are supposed to be doing and why.
- **Case Study** presents a scenario for the chapter, creating a story that ties the Hands-On Exercises together.
- **Hands-On Exercise Videos** are tied to each Hands-On Exercise and walk students through the steps of the exercise while weaving in conceptual information related to the Case Study and the objectives as a whole.

The **Outcomes focus** allows students and instructors to know the higher-level learning goals and how those are achieved through discreet objectives and skills.

- **Outcomes** presented at the beginning of each chapter identify the learning goals for students and instructors.
- **Enhanced Objective Mapping** enables students to follow a directed path through each chapter, from the objectives list at the chapter opener through the exercises at the end of the chapter.
    - **Objectives List:** This provides a simple list of key objectives covered in the chapter. This includes page numbers so students can skip between objectives where they feel they need the most help.
    - **Step Icons:** These icons appear in the white pages and reference the step numbers in the Hands-On Exercises, providing a correlation between the two so students can easily find conceptual help when they are working hands-on and need a refresher.
    - **Quick Concepts Check:** A series of questions that appear briefly at the end of each white page section. These questions cover the most essential concepts in the white pages required for students to be successful in working the Hands-On Exercises. Page numbers are included for easy reference to help students locate the answers.
    - **Chapter Objectives Review:** Appears toward the end of the chapter and reviews all important concepts throughout the chapter. Newly designed in an easy-to-read bulleted format.

- **MOS Certification Guide** for instructors and students to direct anyone interested in prepping for the MOS exam to the specific locations to find all content required for the test.

End-of-Chapter Exercises offer instructors several options for assessment. Each chapter has approximately 11–12 exercises ranging from multiple choice questions to open-ended projects.

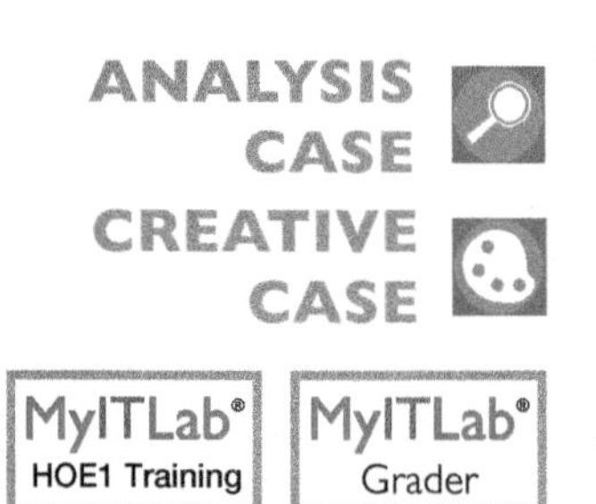

- **Multiple Choice, Key Terms Matching, Practice Exercises, Mid-Level Exercises, Beyond the Classroom Exercises, and Capstone Exercises** appear at the end of all chapters.
    - **Enhanced Mid-Level Exercises** include a **Creative Case** (for PowerPoint and Word), which allows students some flexibility and creativity, not being bound by a definitive solution, and an **Analysis Case** (for Excel and Access), which requires students to interpret the data they are using to answer an analytic question, as well as **Discover Steps**, which encourage students to use Help or to problem-solve to accomplish a task.
- **Application Capstone** exercises are included in the book to allow instructors to test students on the entire contents of a single application.

Resources

Instructor Resources

The Instructor's Resource Center, available at www.pearsonhighered.com, includes the following:

- **Instructor Manual** provides one-stop-shop for instructors, including an overview of all available resources, teaching tips, as well as student data and solution files for every exercise.
- **Solution Files with Scorecards** assist with grading the Hands-On Exercises and end-of-chapter exercises.
- **Prepared Exams** allow instructors to assess all skills covered in a chapter with a single project.
- **Rubrics** for Mid-Level Creative Cases and Beyond the Classroom Cases in Microsoft Word format enable instructors to customize the assignments for their classes.
- **PowerPoint Presentations** with notes for each chapter are included for out-of-class study or review.
- **Multiple Choice, Key Term Matching, and Quick Concepts Check Answer Keys**
- **Test Bank** provides objective-based questions for every chapter.
- **Scripted Lectures** offer an in-class lecture guide for instructors to mirror the Hands-On Exercises.
- **Syllabus Templates**
  - Outcomes, Objectives, and Skills List
  - Assignment Sheet
  - File Guide

Student Resources

Student Data Files

Access your student data files needed to complete the exercises in this textbook at www.pearsonhighered.com/exploring.

Available in MyITLab

- **Hands-On Exercise Videos** allow students to review and study the concepts taught in the Hands-On Exercises.
- **Audio PowerPoints** provide a lecture review of the chapter content, and include narration.
- **Multiple Choice quizzes** enable you to test concepts you have learned by answering auto-graded questions.
- **Book-specific 1:1 Simulations** allow students to practice in the simulated Microsoft Office 2016 environment using hi-fidelity, HTML5 simulations that directly match the content in the Hands-On Exercises.
- **eText** available in some MyITLab courses and includes links to videos, student data files, and other learning aids.
- **Book-specific 1:1 Grader Projects** allow students to complete end of chapter Capstone Exercises live in Microsoft Office 2016 and receive immediate feedback on their performance through various reports.

Access

Introduction to Access

LEARNING OUTCOME You will demonstrate understanding of relational database concepts.

OBJECTIVES & SKILLS: After you read this chapter, you will be able to:

CASE STUDY | Managing a Business in the Global Economy

Northwind Traders is an international gourmet food distributor that imports and exports specialty foods from around the world. Keeping track of customers, vendors, orders, and inventory is a critical task. The owners of Northwind have just purchased an order-processing database created with Microsoft Access 2016 to help manage their customers, suppliers, products, and orders.

You have been hired to learn, use, and manage the database. Northwind's owners are willing to provide training about their business and Access. They expect the learning process to take about three months. After three months, your job will be to support the order-processing team as well as to provide detail and summary reports to the sales force as needed. Your new job at Northwind Traders will be a challenge, but it is also a good opportunity to make a great contribution to a global company. Are you up to the task?

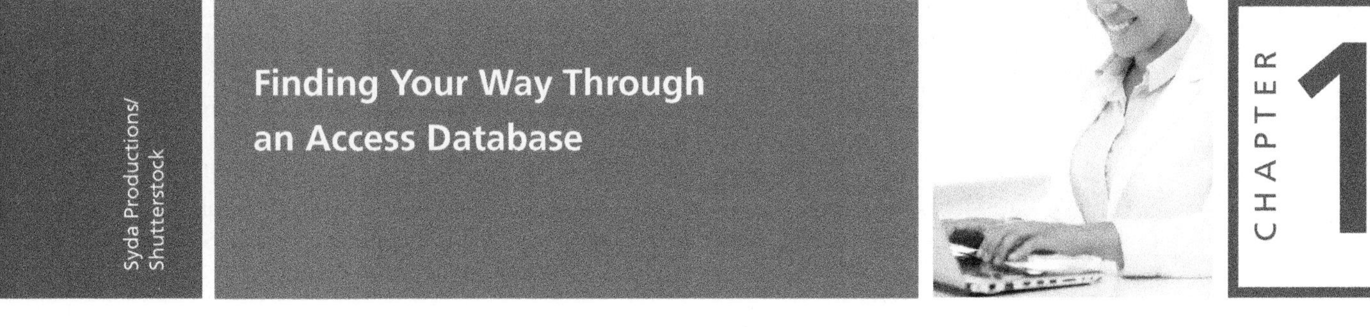

Finding Your Way Through an Access Database

Customer ID	Company Name	Contact Name	Contact Title	Address	City	Region	Postal Co
ALFKI	Alfreds Futterkiste	Maria Anders	Sales Representative	Obere Str. 57	Berlin		12209
ANATR	Ana Trujillo Emparedados y helados	Ana Trujillo	Owner	Avda. de la Constitución 2222	México D.F.		05021
ANTON	Antonio Moreno Taquería	Antonio Moreno	Owner	Mataderos 2312	México D.F.		05023
AROUT	Around the Horn	Thomas Hardy	Sales Representative	120 Hanover Sq.	London		WA1 1DP
BERGS	Berglund snabbköp	Christina Berglund	Order Administrator	Berguvsvägen 8	Luleå		S-958 22
BLAUS	Blauer See Delikatessen	Hanna Moos	Sales Representative	Forsterstr. 57	Mannheim		68306
BLONP	Blondel père et fils	Frédérique Citeaux	Marketing Manager	24, place Kléber	Strasbourg		67000
BOLID	Bólido Comidas preparadas	Martín Sommer	Owner	C/ Araquil, 67	Madrid		28023
BONAP	Bon app'	Laurence Lebihan	Owner	12, rue des Bouchers	Marseille		13008
BOTTM	Bottom-Dollar Markets	Elizabeth Lincoln	Accounting Manager	23 Tsawassen Blvd.	Tsawassen	BC	T2F 8M4
BSBEV	B's Beverages	Victoria Ashworth	Sales Representative Trainee	Fauntleroy Circus	London		EC2 5NT
CACTU	Cactus Comidas para llevar	Patricio Simpson	Sales Agent	Cerrito 333	Buenos Aires		1010
CENTC	Centro comercial Moctezuma	Francisco Chang	Marketing Manager	Sierras de Granada 9993	México D.F.		05022
CHOPS	Chop-suey Chinese	Yang Wang	Owner	Hauptstr. 29	Bern		3012
COMMI	Comércio Mineiro	Pedro Afonso	Sales Associate	Av. dos Lusíadas, 23	São Paulo	SP	05432-043
CONSH	Consolidated Holdings	Elizabeth Brown	Sales Representative	Berkeley Gardens	London		WX1 6LT
DRACD	Drachenblut Delikatessen	Sven Ottlieb	Order Administrator	Walserweg 21	Aachen		52066

Access 2016, Windows 10, Microsoft Corporation

FIGURE 1.1 Northwind Traders Database

Access 2016, Windows 10, Microsoft Corporation

FIGURE 1.2 Northwind Traders Contacts Database

CASE STUDY | Managing a Business in the Global Economy

Starting File	Files to be Submitted
a01h1Traders	**a01h1Traders_LastFirst_*CurrentDate*** **a01h2Traders_LastFirst** **a01h3Contacts_LastFirst**

Databases Are Everywhere!

A ***database*** is a collection of data organized as meaningful information that can be accessed, managed, stored, queried, sorted, and reported. You probably participate in data collection and are exposed to databases on a regular basis. Your college or university stores your personal and registration data. When you registered for this course, your data was entered into a database. If you have a bank account, have a Social Security card, have a medical history, or have booked a flight with an airline, your information is stored in a database.

You use databases online without realizing it, such as when you shop or check your bank statement. Even when you type a search phrase into Google and click Search, you are using Google's massive database with all of its stored webpage references and keywords. Look for something on Amazon, and you are searching Amazon's database to find a product that you might want to buy. Figure 1.3 shows the results of searching for a term on Pearson's website. The search has accessed the Pearson database, and the results are displayed in a webpage.

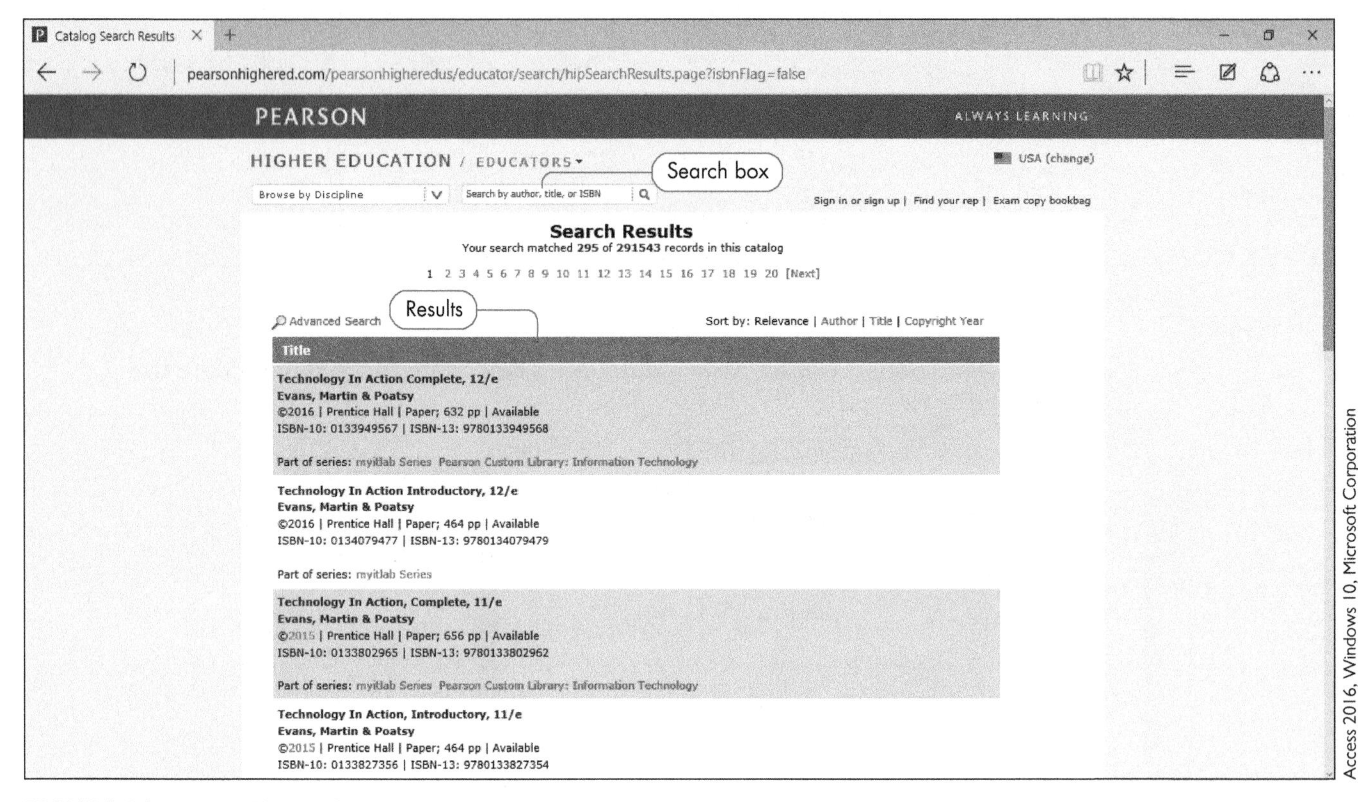

FIGURE 1.3 Pearson Website Search

A ***database management system (DBMS)*** is a software system that provides the tools needed to create, maintain, and use a database. Database management systems make it possible to access and control data and display the information in a variety of formats. ***Access*** is the database management system included in professional editions of the Office 2016 suite. Access is a valuable decision-making tool used by many organizations. More advanced DBMS packages include Microsoft SQL Server, MySQL, and Oracle.

Organizations from all industries rely on data to conduct daily operations. Businesses maintain and analyze data about their students, customers, employees, orders, volunteers, activities, and facilities. Data and information are two terms that are often used interchangeably. However, when it comes to databases, the two terms mean different things. Data is what is entered into a database. Information is the finished product that is produced by the database. Data is converted to information by selecting, performing calculations, and sorting. Decisions in an organization are usually based on information produced by a database, rather than raw data. For example, the number 55 is just data, because it could mean anything. Only when a label is attached to it (for example, as someone's age) does it take on meaning and become information.

In this section, you will learn the fundamentals of organizing data in a database, explore Access database objects and the purpose of each object, and examine the Access interface.

Opening, Saving, and Enabling Content in a Database

As you work through the material in this book, you will frequently be asked to open a database, save it with a new name, and enable content. You can also start by creating a new database if appropriate.

If you have been provided a database, open the file to get started. When you open any database for the first time, you will be presented with a warning that it might contain harmful code. By enabling the content, the database file will be trusted on the computer you are working on. All content from this publisher and associated with this book can be trusted.

To open an existing Access database and enable content, complete the following steps:

1. Start Access 2016. Backstage view displays. (Note: If Access is already open, click the File tab to display Backstage view).
2. Click Open Other Files.
3. Click Browse to open the Open dialog box.
4. Locate and select the database and click Open.
5. Click Enable Content on the message bar (see Figure 1.4). Access will close and reopen the database, and the security warning disappears and will not appear again for this database.

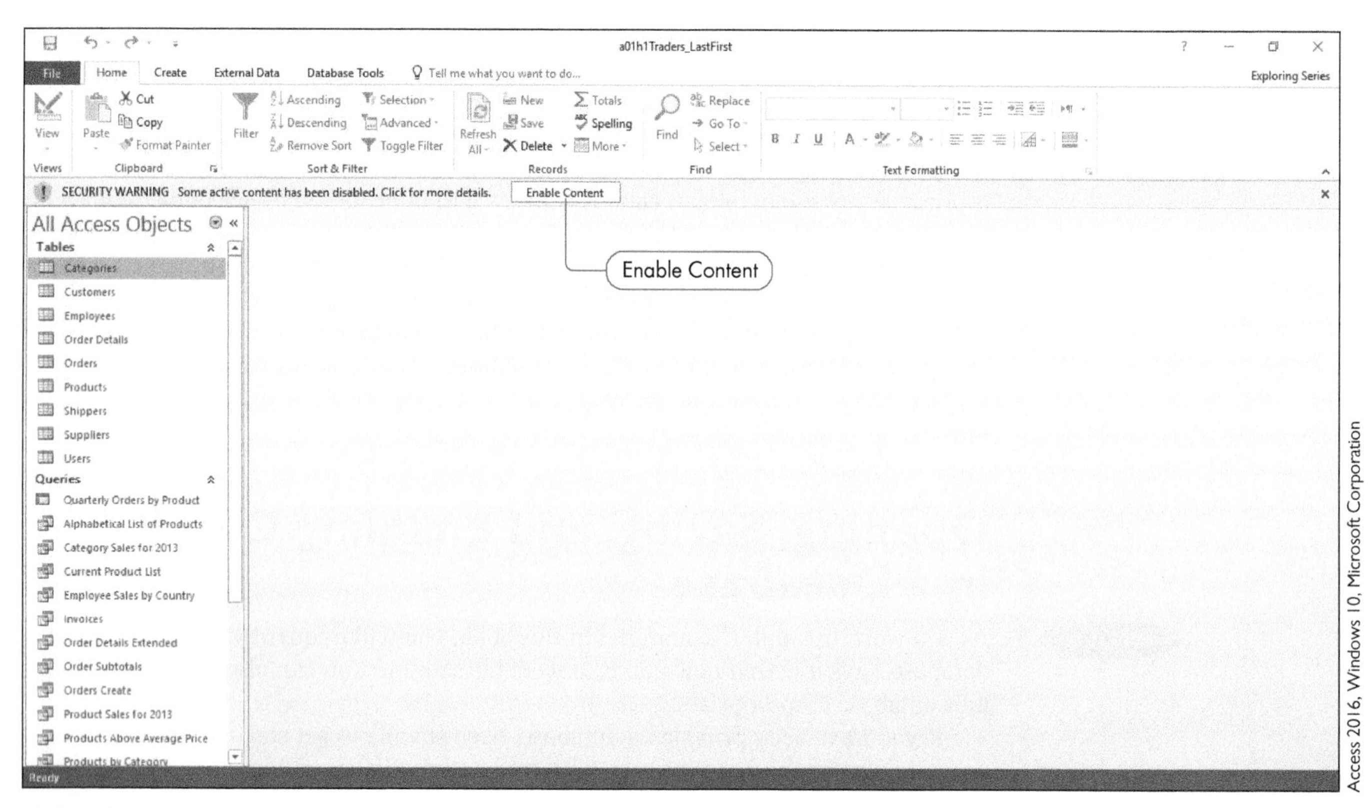

FIGURE 1.4 Access Security Warning

Backstage view gives you access to the Save As command. Most assignments will have you save the starting database file with a new name.

To save the database with a new name, complete the following steps:

1. Click the File tab.
2. Select Save As.
3. Ensure Save Database As is selected (see Figure 1.5).
4. Click Save As.
5. Type the new name for your database, and click Save.

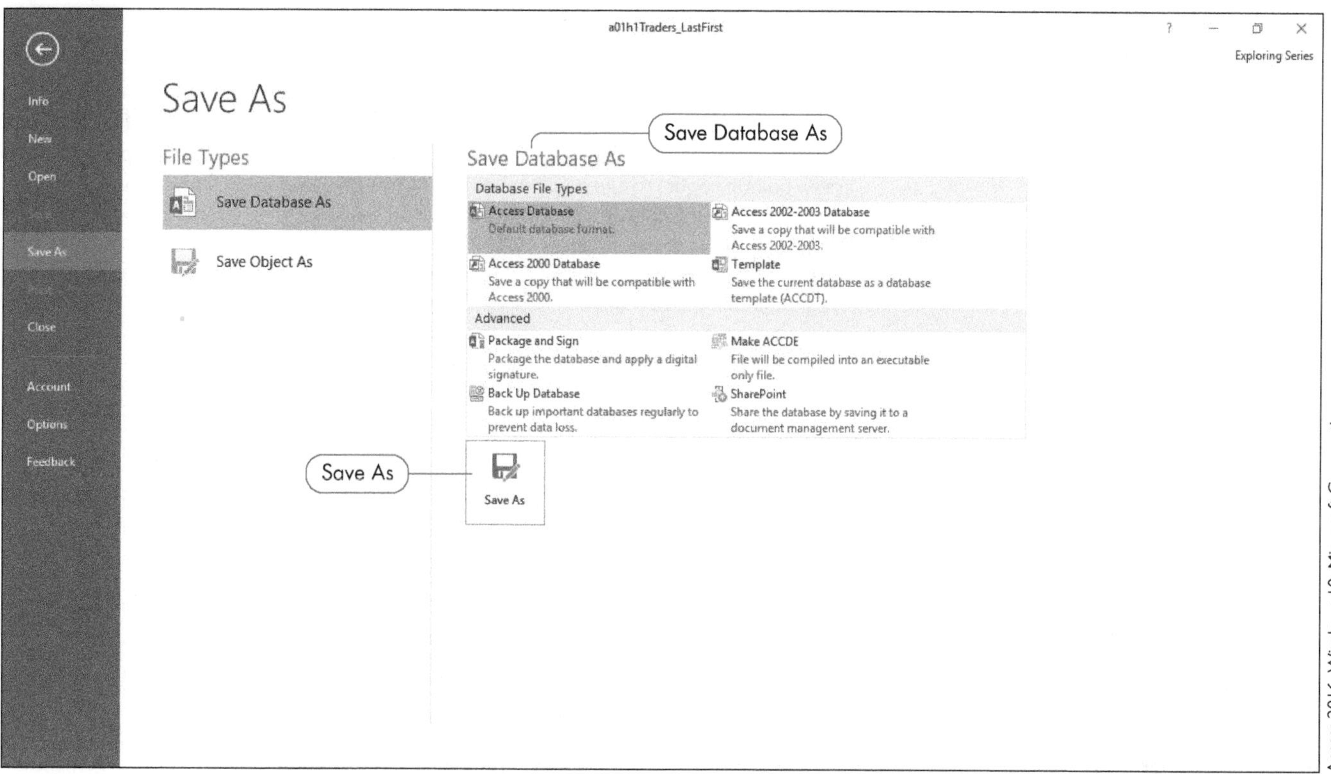

FIGURE 1.5 Access Save As Options

> **TIP: ALTERNATIVE SAVE FORMAT: ACCESS DATABASE EXECUTABLE**
>
> Creating an Access Database Executable (ACCDE) file allows users to enter data, but not add, modify, or delete objects. In other words, the only task they can do is data entry. This file format protects against users changing designs or deleting objects.
>
> To create an Access Database Executable, click the File tab, click Save As, and double-click Make ACCDE. Click Save to save as an Access Database Executable.

Recognizing Database Object Types

Databases must be carefully managed to keep information accurate. Data need to be changed, added, and deleted. Managing a database also requires that you understand when data is saved and when you need to use the Save commands.

In Access, each component created and used to make the database function is known as an ***object***. Objects include tables, queries, forms, and reports, and can be found in the ***Navigation Pane***. The Navigation Pane is an Access interface element that organizes and lists the objects in an Access database. The Navigation Pane appears on the left side of the screen, and displays all objects. You can open any object by double-clicking the object's name in the list.

TIP: NAVIGATION PANE DISPLAY

You can toggle the display of the Navigation Pane by clicking the Shutter Bar Open/Close button at the top-right corner of the pane. The Shutter Bar Open/Close button appears as a double arrow. If the Navigation Pane is shown, the button will appear as a double arrow pointing left « and it will hide the Navigation Pane when clicked. If the Navigation Pane is hidden, the button appears as a double arrow pointing right » and it will show the Navigation Pane when clicked. You can collapse the contents of an object group by clicking the group heading or the double arrows to the right of the group heading. To expand the contents of an object group that has been hidden, click the heading again or click the double arrows to the right of the group heading again. To change the way objects are grouped in the Navigation Pane, click the list arrow on the Navigation Pane title bar and select your preferred configuration of the available options. Refer to Figure 1.6 to see the features of the Navigation Pane.

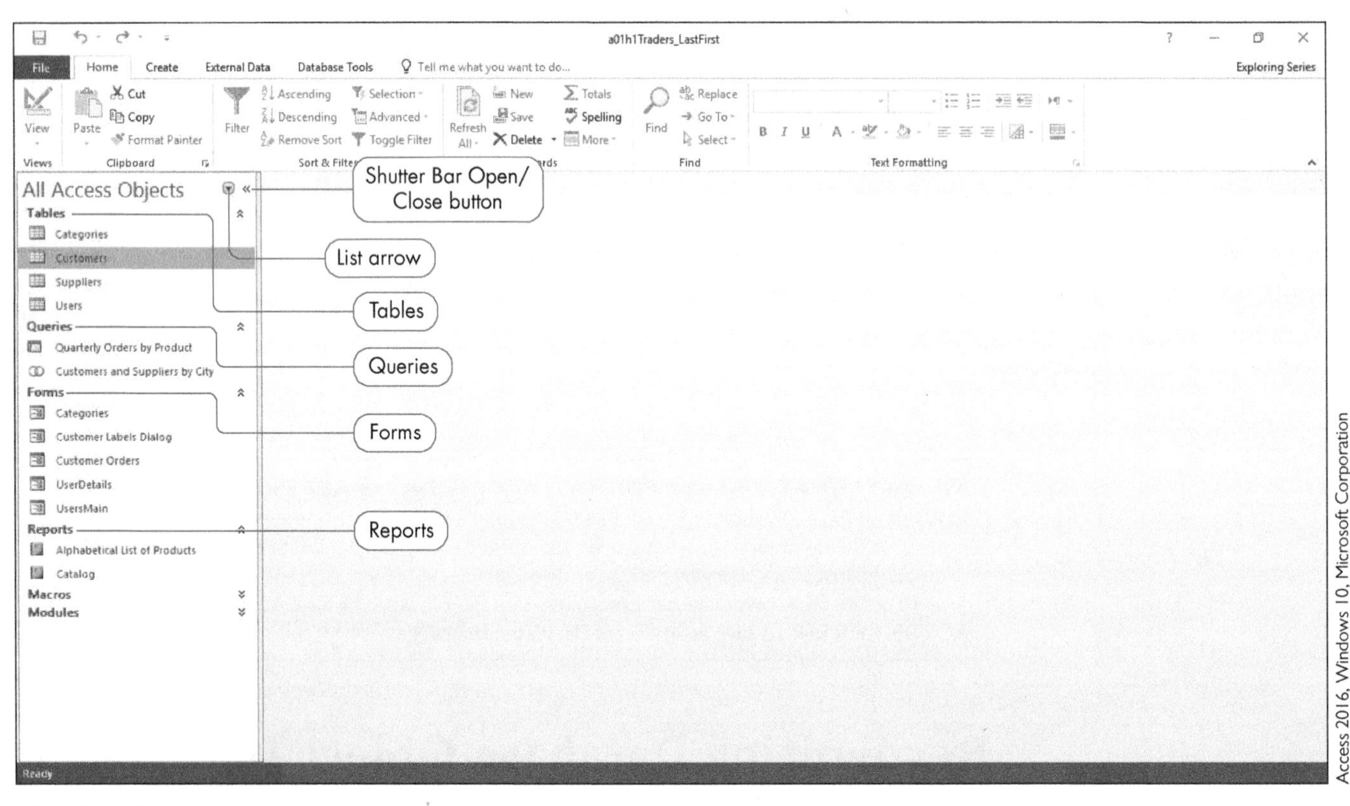

FIGURE 1.6 Navigation Pane Features

Most databases contain multiple tables. By default, the objects display in groups by object type in the Navigation Pane. In other words, you will see a list of tables, followed by queries, followed by forms, followed by reports. The purpose of each of these objects is described below.

- A ***table*** is where all data is stored in your database, and thus can be said to be the foundation of each database. Tables organize data into columns and rows. Each column represents a ***field***, a category of information we store in a table. For example, in the Northwind database, a table containing customer information would include fields such as Customer ID, Company Name, and City. Each row in a table contains a ***record***, a complete set of all the fields about one person, place, event, or concept. A customer record, for example, would contain all of the fields about a single customer, including the Customer ID, the Company Name, Contact Name, Contact Title, Address, City, etc. Figure 1.7 shows both fields and records. The ***primary key*** is a field (or combination of fields) that uniquely identifies each record in a table. Common primary keys are driver's license number, government

ID number (such as a Social Security number), passport number, and student ID. Many of these primary keys are generated by a database. Your college or university's database likely assigns a unique identifier to a student as soon as they apply, for example.

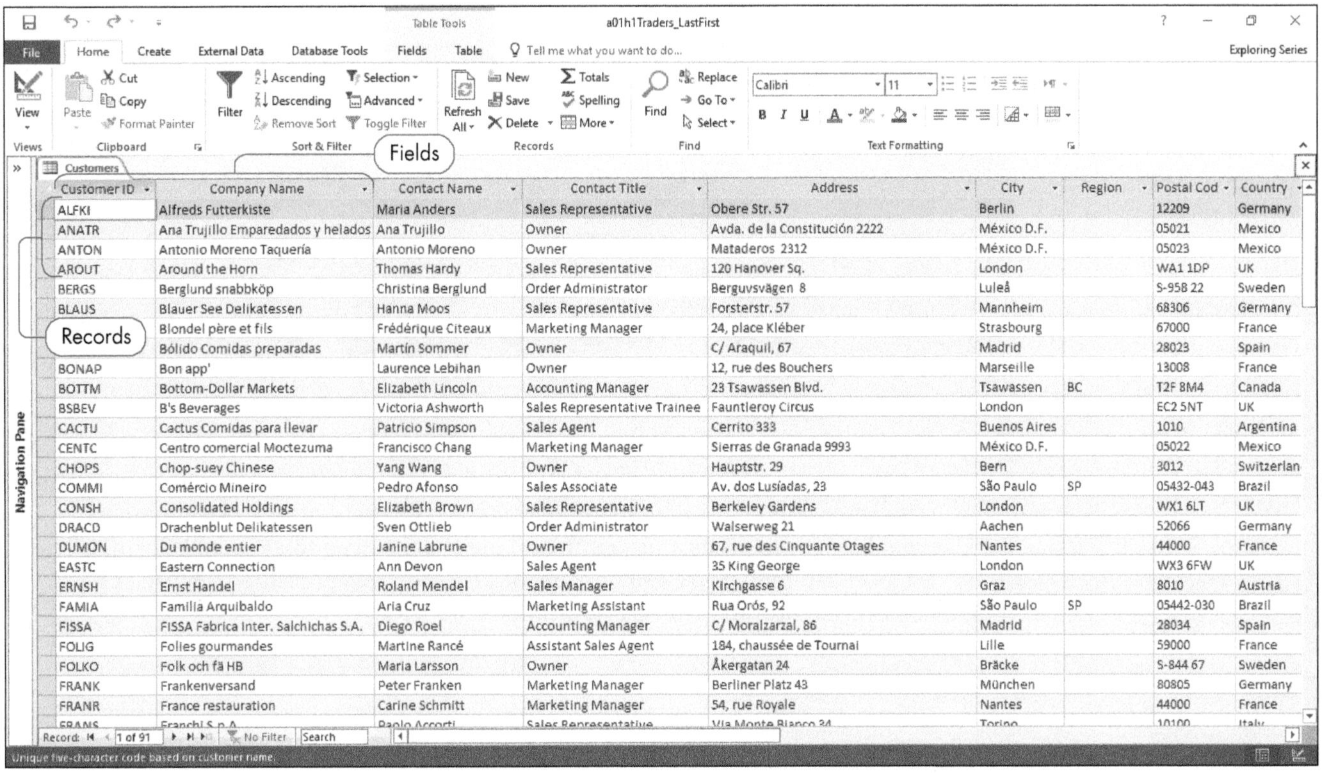

Fields

Records

Customers

Customer ID	Company Name	Contact Name	Contact Title	Address	City	Region	Postal Cod	Country
ALFKI	Alfreds Futterkiste	Maria Anders	Sales Representative	Obere Str. 57	Berlin		12209	Germany
ANATR	Ana Trujillo Emparedados y helados	Ana Trujillo	Owner	Avda. de la Constitución 2222	México D.F.		05021	Mexico
ANTON	Antonio Moreno Taquería	Antonio Moreno	Owner	Mataderos 2312	México D.F.		05023	Mexico
AROUT	Around the Horn	Thomas Hardy	Sales Representative	120 Hanover Sq.	London		WA1 1DP	UK
BERGS	Berglund snabbköp	Christina Berglund	Order Administrator	Berguvsvägen 8	Luleå		S-958 22	Sweden
BLAUS	Blauer See Delikatessen	Hanna Moos	Sales Representative	Forsterstr. 57	Mannheim		68306	Germany
	Blondel père et fils	Frédérique Citeaux	Marketing Manager	24, place Kléber	Strasbourg		67000	France
	Bólido Comidas preparadas	Martín Sommer	Owner	C/ Araquil, 67	Madrid		28023	Spain
BONAP	Bon app'	Laurence Lebihan	Owner	12, rue des Bouchers	Marseille		13008	France
BOTTM	Bottom-Dollar Markets	Elizabeth Lincoln	Accounting Manager	23 Tsawassen Blvd.	Tsawassen	BC	T2F 8M4	Canada
BSBEV	B's Beverages	Victoria Ashworth	Sales Representative Trainee	Fauntleroy Circus	London		EC2 5NT	UK
CACTU	Cactus Comidas para llevar	Patricio Simpson	Sales Agent	Cerrito 333	Buenos Aires		1010	Argentina
CENTC	Centro comercial Moctezuma	Francisco Chang	Marketing Manager	Sierras de Granada 9993	México D.F.		05022	Mexico
CHOPS	Chop-suey Chinese	Yang Wang	Owner	Hauptstr. 29	Bern		3012	Switzerlan
COMMI	Comércio Mineiro	Pedro Afonso	Sales Associate	Av. dos Lusíadas, 23	São Paulo	SP	05432-043	Brazil
CONSH	Consolidated Holdings	Elizabeth Brown	Sales Representative	Berkeley Gardens	London		WX1 6LT	UK
DRACD	Drachenblut Delikatessen	Sven Ottlieb	Order Administrator	Walserweg 21	Aachen		52066	Germany
DUMON	Du monde entier	Janine Labrune	Owner	67, rue des Cinquante Otages	Nantes		44000	France
EASTC	Eastern Connection	Ann Devon	Sales Agent	35 King George	London		WX3 6FW	UK
ERNSH	Ernst Handel	Roland Mendel	Sales Manager	Kirchgasse 6	Graz		8010	Austria
FAMIA	Familia Arquibaldo	Aria Cruz	Marketing Assistant	Rua Orós, 92	São Paulo	SP	05442-030	Brazil
FISSA	FISSA Fabrica Inter. Salchichas S.A.	Diego Roel	Accounting Manager	C/ Moralzarzal, 86	Madrid		28034	Spain
FOLIG	Folies gourmandes	Martine Rancé	Assistant Sales Agent	184, chaussée de Tournai	Lille		59000	France
FOLKO	Folk och fä HB	Maria Larsson	Owner	Åkergatan 24	Bräcke		S-844 67	Sweden
FRANK	Frankenversand	Peter Franken	Marketing Manager	Berliner Platz 43	München		80805	Germany
FRANR	France restauration	Carine Schmitt	Marketing Manager	54, rue Royale	Nantes		44000	France
FRANS	Franchi S.p.A.	Paolo Accorti	Sales Representative	Via Monte Bianco 34	Torino		10100	Italy

Record: 1 of 91 No Filter Search

Unique five-character code based on customer name.

FIGURE 1.7 An Access Table

- A ***query*** (or queries, plural) is a question you ask about the data in your database. Notice the word query is similar to the word inquiry, which means question. It produces a subset of data that provides information about the question you have asked. For example, a query may display a list of which customers live in a specific town, or a list of children registered for a specific after-school program. You can double-click a query in the Navigation Pane and you will notice the interface is similar to that of a table, as shown in Figure 1.8.

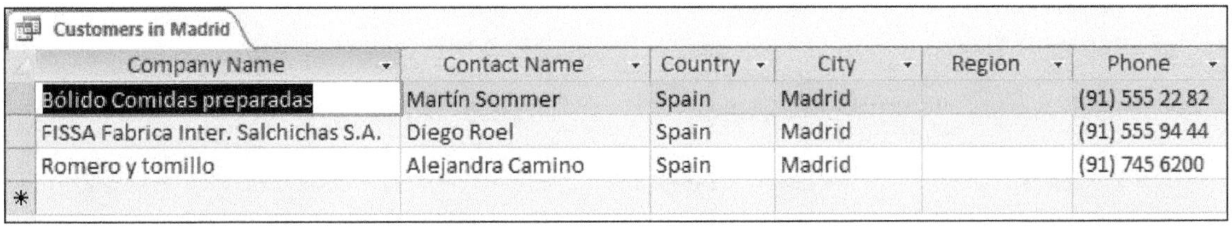

Customers in Madrid

Company Name	Contact Name	Country	City	Region	Phone
Bólido Comidas preparadas	Martín Sommer	Spain	Madrid		(91) 555 22 82
FISSA Fabrica Inter. Salchichas S.A.	Diego Roel	Spain	Madrid		(91) 555 94 44
Romero y tomillo	Alejandra Camino	Spain	Madrid		(91) 745 6200

FIGURE 1.8 An Access Query

- A ***form*** allows simplified entry and modification of data. Much like entering data on a paper form, a database form enables you to add, modify, and delete table data. Most forms display one record at a time, which helps prevent data entry errors. Forms are typically utilized by the users of the database, while the database designer creates and edits the form structure. Figure 1.9 shows a form. Notice a single record is displayed.

Customers

Customers

Customer ID: ALFKI

Company Name: Alfreds Futterkiste

Contact Name: Maria Anders Title: Sales Representative

Address: Obere Str. 57

City: Berlin Region:

Postal Code: 12209 Country: Germany

Phone: 030-0074321 Fax: 030-0076545

Access 2016, Windows 10, Microsoft Corporation

FIGURE 1.9 An Access Form

- A ***report*** contains professional-looking formatted information from underlying tables or queries. Much like a report you would prepare for a class, a report enables you to perform research and put the results into a readable format. The report can then be viewed on-screen, saved to a file, or printed. Figure 1.10 shows a report in Print Preview mode.

Customer Contacts

Customer Contacts

Contact Name	Company Name	Contact Title	Phone	City	Region	Country
Alejandra Camino	Romero y tomillo	Accounting Manager	(91) 745 6200	Madrid		Spain
Alexander Feuer	Morgenstern Gesundkost	Marketing Assistant	0342-023176	Leipzig		Germany
Ana Trujillo	Ana Trujillo Emparedados y helados	Owner	(5) 555-4729	México D.F.		Mexico
Anabela Domingues	Tradição Hipermercados	Sales Representative	(11) 555-2167	São Paulo	SP	Brazil
André Fonseca	Gourmet Lanchonetes	Sales Associate	(11) 555-9482	Campinas	SP	Brazil
Ann Devon	Eastern Connection	Sales Agent	(171) 555-0297	London		UK
Annette Roulet	La maison d'Asie	Sales Manager	61.77.61.10	Toulouse		France
Antonio Moreno	Antonio Moreno Taquería	Owner	(5) 555-3932	México D.F.		Mexico
Aria Cruz	Familia Arquibaldo	Marketing Assistant	(11) 555-9857	São Paulo	SP	Brazil
Art Braunschweiger	Split Rail Beer & Ale	Sales Manager	(307) 555-4680	Lander	WY	USA
Bernardo Batista	Que Delícia	Accounting Manager	(21) 555-4252	Rio de Janeiro	RJ	Brazil
Carine Schmitt	France restauration	Marketing Manager	40.32.21.21	Nantes		France
Carlos González	LILA-Supermercado	Accounting Manager	(9) 331-6954	Barquisimeto	Lara	Venezuela
Carlos Hernández	HILARIÓN-Abastos	Sales Representative	(5) 555-1340	San Cristóbal	Táchira	Venezuela
Catherine Dewey	Maison Dewey	Sales Agent	(02) 201 24 67	Bruxelles		Belgium
Christina Berglund	Berglund snabbköp	Order Administrator	0921-12 34 65	Luleå		Sweden
Daniel Tonini	La corne d'abondance	Sales Representative	30.59.84.10	Versailles		France

Page: 1 No Filter

Access 2016, Windows 10, Microsoft Corporation

FIGURE 1.10 An Access Report

Figure 1.11 displays the different object types in Access with the foundation object—the table—in the center of the illustration. The purpose each object serves is explained underneath the object name. The flow of information between objects is indicated by single-arrowhead arrows if the flow is one direction only. Two-arrowhead arrows indicate that the flow goes both directions. For example, you can use forms to view, add, delete, or modify data from tables.

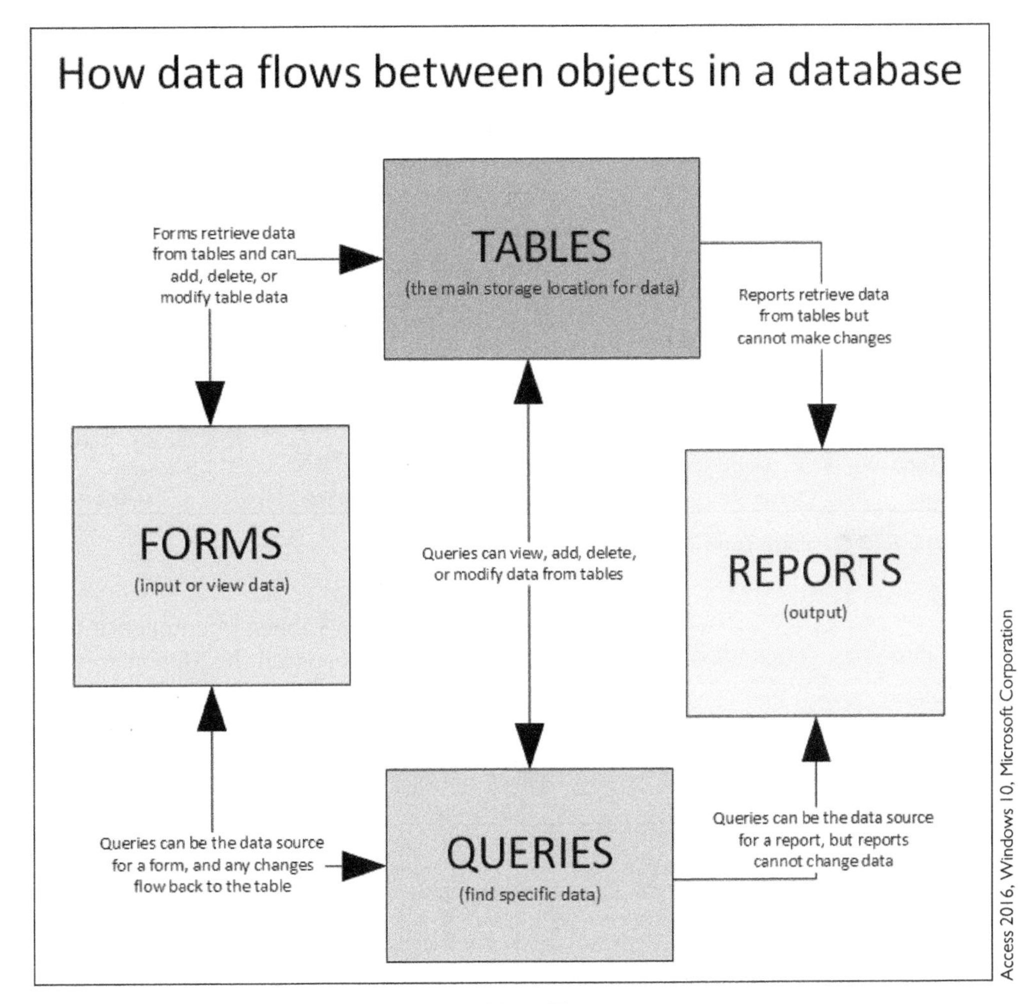

FIGURE 1.11 Flow of Information Between Object Types

Two other object types, macros and modules, are rarely used by beginning Access users. A ***macro*** object is a stored series of commands that carry out an action. Macros are often used to automate tasks. A ***module*** is an advanced object written using the VBA (Visual Basic® for Applications) programming language. Modules provide more functionality than macros, but are not generally required for even intermediate users.

Examine the Access Interface

While Access includes the standard elements of the Microsoft Office applications interface such as the title bar, the Ribbon, the Home tab, Backstage view, and scroll bars, it also includes elements unique to Access.

The Access Ribbon has five tabs that always display, as well as tabs that appear only when particular objects are open. The two tabs that are unique to Access are:

- External Data tab: Contains all of the operations used to facilitate data import and export. See Figure 1.12.

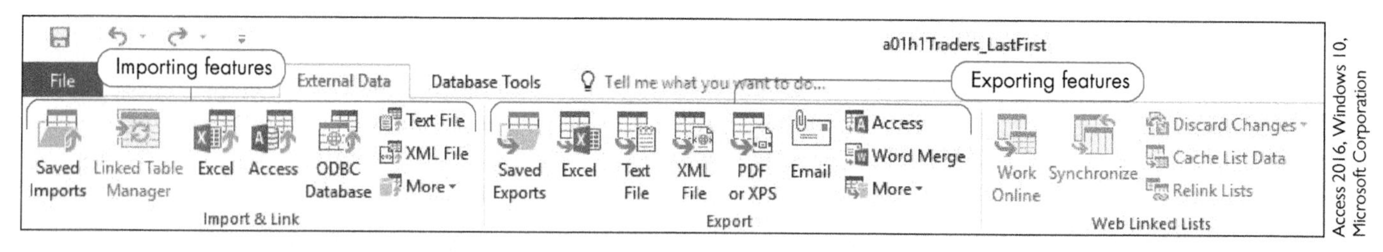

FIGURE 1.12 External Data Tab

- Database Tools tab: Contains the feature that enables users to create relationships between tables and enables use of more advanced features of Access. Figure 1.13 shows the Database Tools tab.

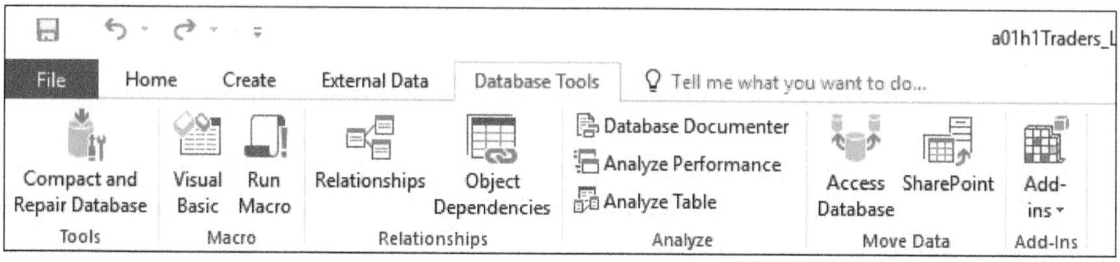

FIGURE 1.13 Database Tools Tab

By default, Access uses a Tabbed Documents interface. That means that each object that is open has its own tab beneath the Ribbon and to the right of the Navigation Pane. You can switch between open objects by clicking a tab to make that object active, similar to the way an Excel worksheet has tabs at the bottom of the screen. Figure 1.14 shows the Access interface with multiple objects open.

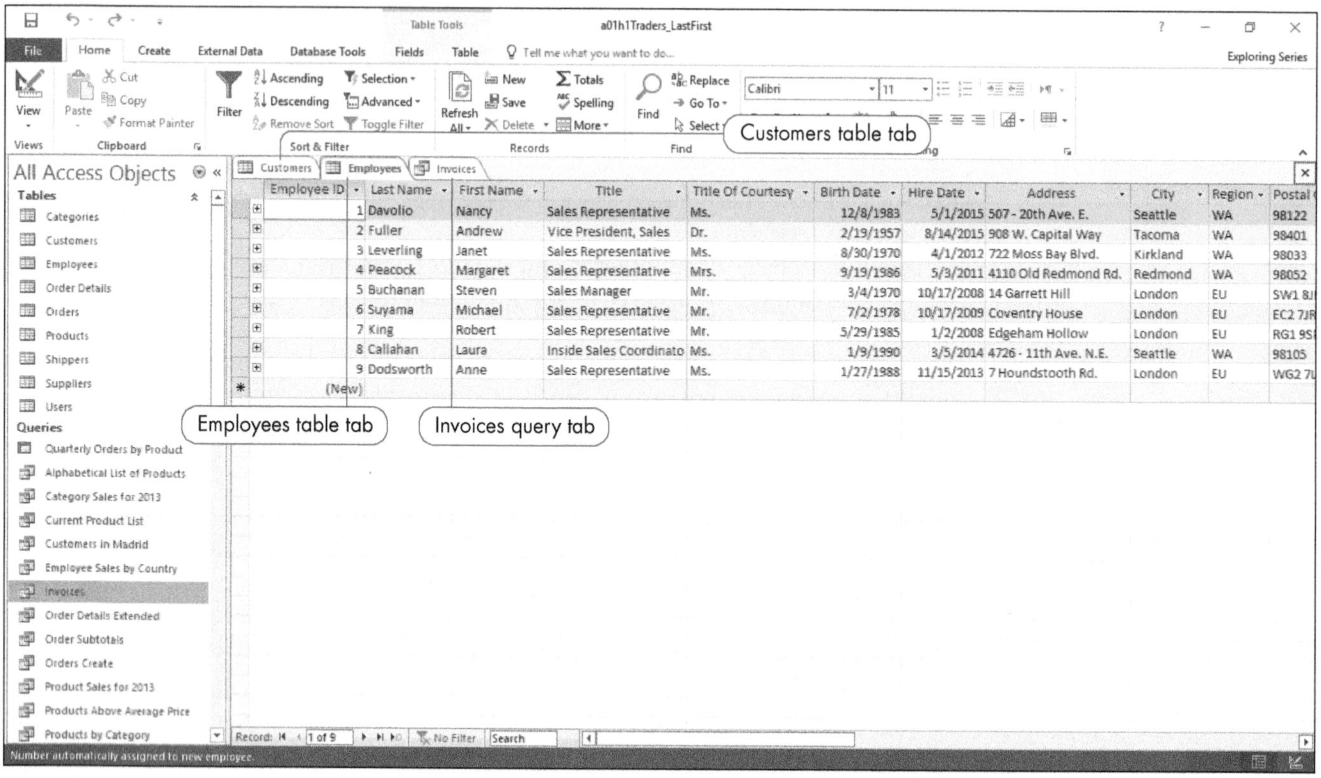

FIGURE 1.14 Access Database with Multiple Objects Open

Explore Table Datasheet View

Access provides two different ways to view a table: Datasheet view and Design view. When you double-click a table, Datasheet view displays by default. ***Datasheet view*** is a grid containing fields (columns) and records (rows). You can view, add, edit, and delete records in Datasheet view. Figure 1.15 shows the Customers table in Datasheet view. Each row contains a record for a specific customer. Click the record selector, or row heading, at the beginning of a row to select the record. Each column represents a field, or one attribute about a customer. Click the field selector, or column heading, to select a field.

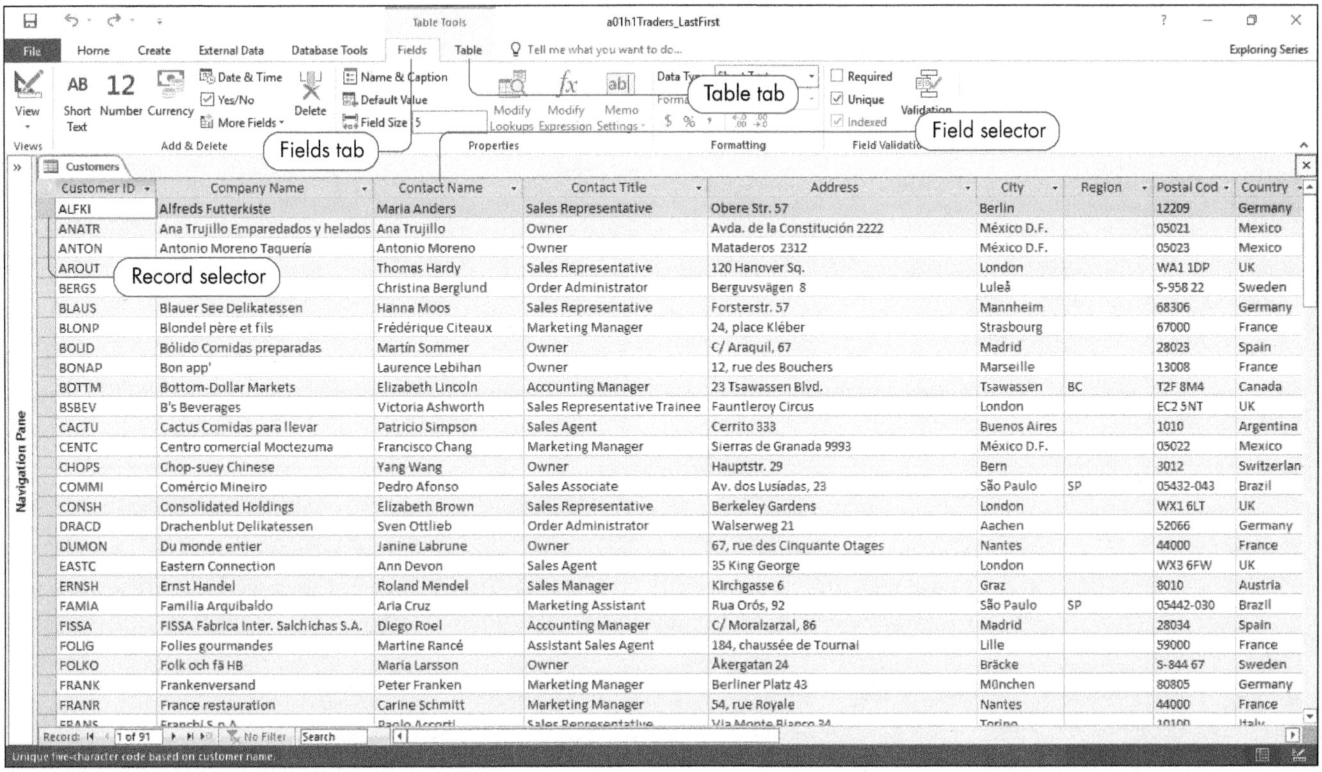

Access 2016, Windows 10, Microsoft Corporation

FIGURE 1.15 Datasheet View for Customers Table

Notice the Customers table shows records for 91 employees. The customer records contain multiple fields about each customer, including the Company Name, Contact Name, and so on. Occasionally a field does not contain a value for a particular record. For example, many customers do not have a Region assigned. Access shows a blank cell when data is missing.

Navigate Through Records

The navigation bar at the bottom of Figure 1.16 shows that the Customers table has 91 records and that record number 18 is the current record. The pencil symbol to the left of record 18 indicates that the data in that record is being edited and that changes have not yet been saved. The pencil icon disappears when you move to another record. Access saves data automatically as soon as you move from one record to another. This may seem counterintuitive at first because other Office applications, such as Word and Excel, do not save changes and additions automatically. The navigation arrows enable you to go to the first record, the previous record, the next record, or the last record. Click the right arrow with a yellow asterisk to add a new (blank) record.

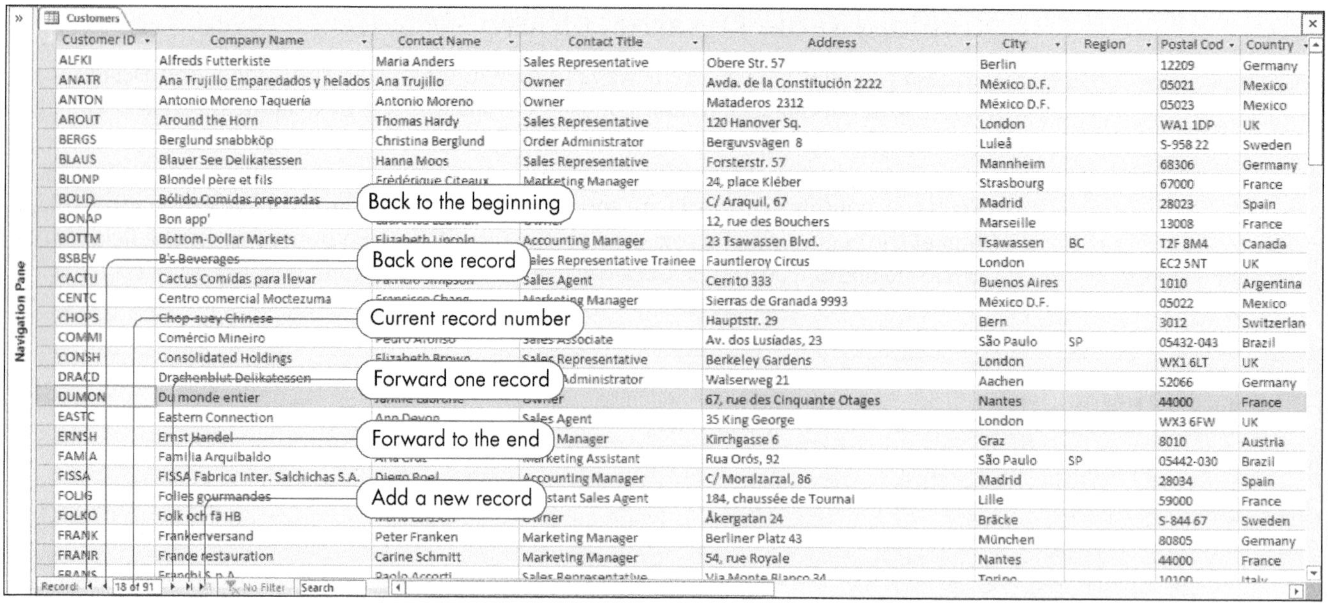

Access 2016, Windows 10, Microsoft Corporation

FIGURE 1.16 Navigation Arrows in a Table

Navigation works for more than just tables. Navigation arrows are also available in queries and forms. Figure 1.17 shows the same navigation arrows appearing in forms.

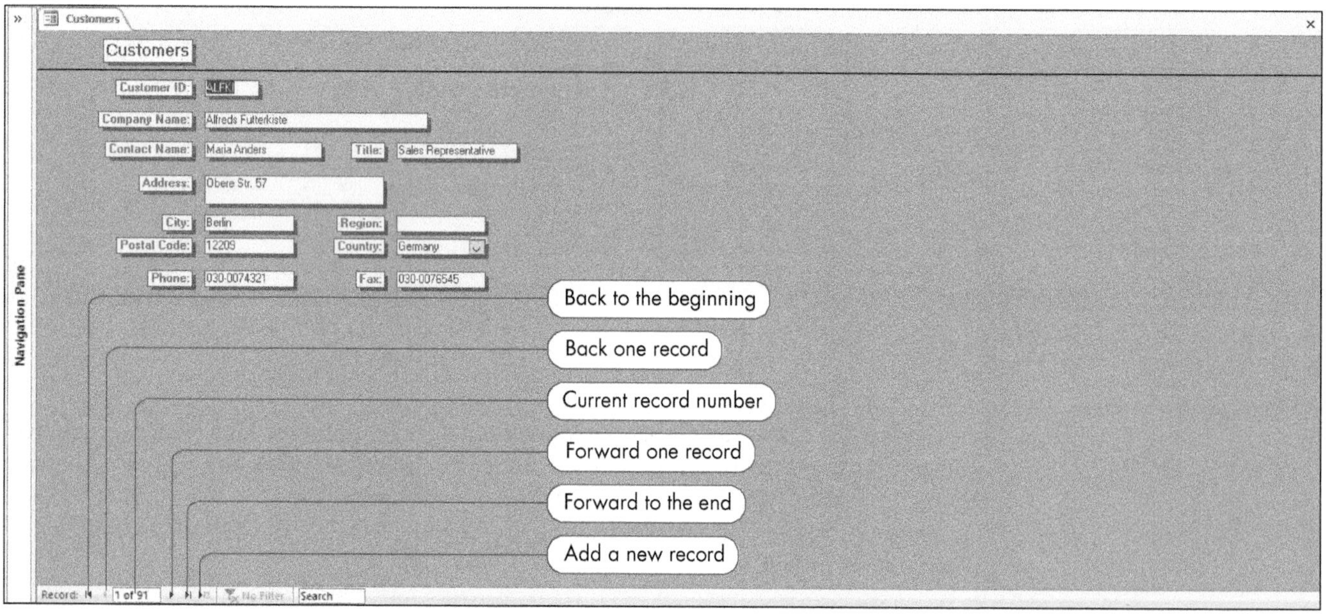

Access 2016, Windows 10, Microsoft Corporation

FIGURE 1.17 Navigation Arrows in a Form

In addition to navigating, you also have access to the Find command. The Find command is located in the Find group on the Home tab, and can be used to locate specific records. You can search for a single field or the entire record, match all or part of the selected field(s), move forward or back in a table, or specify a case-sensitive search.

To find a record using the Find command, complete the following steps:

1. Open the table that contains the data you are searching for. Note that if you want to search a query, form, or report, you can follow the same steps, except open the appropriate object instead of the table.
2. Click any cell within the field you want to search. For example, if you want to search the City field in the Customers table, as shown in Figure 1.18, click any City value.
3. Ensure the Home tab is selected.
4. Click Find in the Find group.
5. Type the value you are searching for in the Find What box. Note that the entry is not case sensitive.
6. Click Find Next to find the next matching value.

Customers

Customer ID	Company Name	Contact Name	Contact Title	Address	City	Region	Postal Code	Country	Phone	
ALFKI	Alfreds Futterkiste	Maria Anders	Sales Representative	Obere Str. 57	Berlin		12209	Germany	030-007432	030
ANATR	Ana Trujillo Emparedados y helados	Ana Trujillo	Owner	Avda. de la Constitución 2222	México D.F.		05021	Mexico	(5) 555-472	(5)
ANTON	Antonio Moreno Taquería	Antonio Moreno	Owner	Mataderos 2312	México D.F.		05023	Mexico	(5) 555-393	
AROUT	Around the Horn	Thomas Hardy	Sales Representative	120 Hanover Sq.	London		WA1 1DP	UK	(171) 555-7	(17
BERGS	Berglund snabbköp	Christina Berglund	Order Administrator	Berguvsvägen 8	Luleå		S-958 22	Sweden	0921-12 34	092
BLAUS	Blauer See Delikatessen	Hanna Moos	Sales Representative	Forsterstr. 57	Mannheim		68306	Germany	0621-08460	062
BLONP	Blondel père et fils	Frédérique Citeaux	Marketing Manager	24, place Kléber	Strasbourg		67000	France	88.60.15.31	88.
BOLID	Bólido Comidas preparadas	Martín Sommer	Owner	C/ Araquil, 67	Madrid		28023	Spain	(91) 555 22	(91
BONAP	Bon app'	Laurence Lebihan	Owner	12, rue des Bouchers	Marseille		13008	France	91.24.45.40	91.
BOTTM	Bottom-Dollar Markets	Eliza			ssen	BC	T2F 8M4	Canada	(604) 555-4	(60
BSBEV	B's Beverages	Victo			n		EC2 5NT	UK	(171) 555-1	
CACTU	Cactus Comidas para llevar	Patri			s Aires		1010	Argentina	(1) 135-555	(1)
CENTC	Centro comercial Moctezuma	Fran			o D.F.		05022	Mexico	(5) 555-339	(5)
CHOPS	Chop-suey Chinese	Yang					3012	Switzerland	0452-07654	
COMMI	Comércio Mineiro	Pedr			ulo	SP	05432-043	Brazil	(11) 555-76	
CONSH	Consolidated Holdings	Eliza			n		WX1 6LT	UK	(171) 555-2	(17
DRACD	Drachenblut Delikatessen	Sven			n		52066	Germany	0241-03912	024
DUMON	Du monde entier	Janin			s		44000	France	40.67.88.88	40.
EASTC	Eastern Connection	Ann			n		WX3 6FW	UK	(171) 555-0	(17
ERNSH	Ernst Handel	Rola					8010	Austria	7675-3425	767
FAMIA	Familia Arquibaldo	Aria Cruz	Marketing Assistant	Rua Orós, 92	São Paulo	SP	05442-030	Brazil	(11) 555-98	
FISSA	FISSA Fabrica Inter. Salchichas S.A.	Diego Roel	Accounting Manager	C/ Moralzarzal, 86	Madrid		28034	Spain	(91) 555 94	(91
FOLIG	Folies gourmandes	Martine Rancé	Assistant Sales Agent	184, chaussée de Tournai	Lille		59000	France	20.16.10.16	20.
FOLKO	Folk och fä HB	Maria Larsson	Owner	Åkergatan 24	Bräcke		S-844 67	Sweden	0695-34 67	
FRANK	Frankenversand	Peter Franken	Marketing Manager	Berliner Platz 43	München		80805	Germany	089-087731	089
FRANR	France restauration	Carine Schmitt	Marketing Manager	54, rue Royale	Nantes		44000	France	40.32.21.21	40.
FRANS	Franchi S.p.A.	Paolo Accorti	Sales Representative	Via Monte Blanco 34	Torino		10100	Italy	011-498826	011

Record: 1 of 91 No Filter Search

Find and Replace
Searching for Berlin
Find Replace
Find What: Berlin
Find Next
Cancel
Look In: Current field
Match: Whole Field
Search: All
Match Case Search Fields As Formatted

Access 2016, Windows 10, Microsoft Corporation

FIGURE 1.18 Find Command

Explore Table Design View

Design view gives you a detailed view of the table's structure and is used to create and modify a table's design by specifying the fields it will contain, the fields' data types, and their associated properties. When you double-click a table in the Navigation Pane, it will open in Datasheet view, as the design of a table typically does not change frequently.

To switch between Datasheet and Design view, complete the following steps:

1. Click the Home tab.
2. Click View in the Views group to toggle between the current view and the previous view. See Figure 1.19.

FIGURE 1.19 View Button

Also notice the arrow that allows you to select either Design or Datasheet view. Either way of performing this task is correct.

Data types define the type of data that will be stored in a field, such as short text, numeric, currency, date/time, etc. For example, if you need to store the hire date of an employee, you would input a field name and select the Date/Time data type. A ***field property*** defines the characteristics of a field in more detail. For example, for the field OrderDate, you could set add validation (the OrderDate must be today's date or later), or choose whether the field is required or not. Though some changes can be made to the field properties in Datasheet view, Design view gives you access to more properties.

Figure 1.20 shows Design view for the Orders table. In the top portion, each row contains the field name the data type, and an optional description for each field in the table. In the bottom portion, the Field Properties pane contains the properties (details) for a field. Click a field, and the properties for that field display in the Field Properties section of Design view window. Depending on a field's data type, the available properties will change.

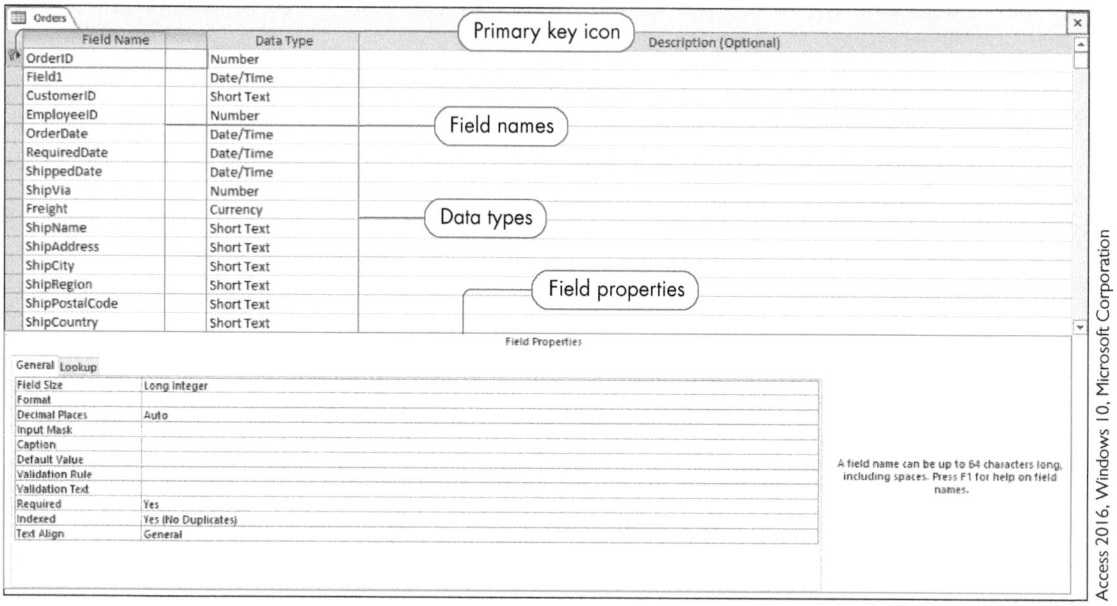

Access 2016, Windows 10, Microsoft Corporation

FIGURE 1.20 Orders Table Design View

Notice the key icon next to the OrderID field; this denotes this field is the primary key in the Orders table; it ensures that each record in the table is unique and can be distinguished from every other record. You may have multiple orders from the same customer, but you can tell they are different because there are two separate OrderIDs. This is why many companies ask for you to include your account number when you pay a bill. The account number, similar to an OrderID, uniquely identifies you and helps ensure that the payment is not applied to the wrong customer.

In Figure 1.20, the OrderID field has an AutoNumber data type—a number that is generated by Access and is automatically incremented each time a record is added. Each field's data type determines the type of input accepted. Data types will be discussed further in a later chapter.

Rename and Describe Tables

To make a table easy to use, Access includes a few properties you can modify. Tables default to a name of Table1 (or Table2, etc.) if you do not specify otherwise. As you can imagine, this would be very difficult to navigate.

To rename a table, complete the following steps:

1. Verify that the table is closed. If it is not closed, right-click the table tab and select Close. A table cannot be renamed while it is open.
2. Right-click the table name in the Navigation Pane.
3. Select Rename on the shortcut menu.
4. Type the new name over the selected text and press Enter.

Tables also include a description, which can be useful to provide documentation about the contents of a table. For example, most tables in the Northwind database are straightforward. However, just in case, the database comes with predefined descriptions for most tables. This can provide a user with additional clarification regarding the purpose of a table if they know where to look. By default, descriptions are not shown unless you right-click the table and select Table Properties. If you are working with a complex database, adding descriptions can be extremely helpful for new users. Figure 1.21 shows a table description.

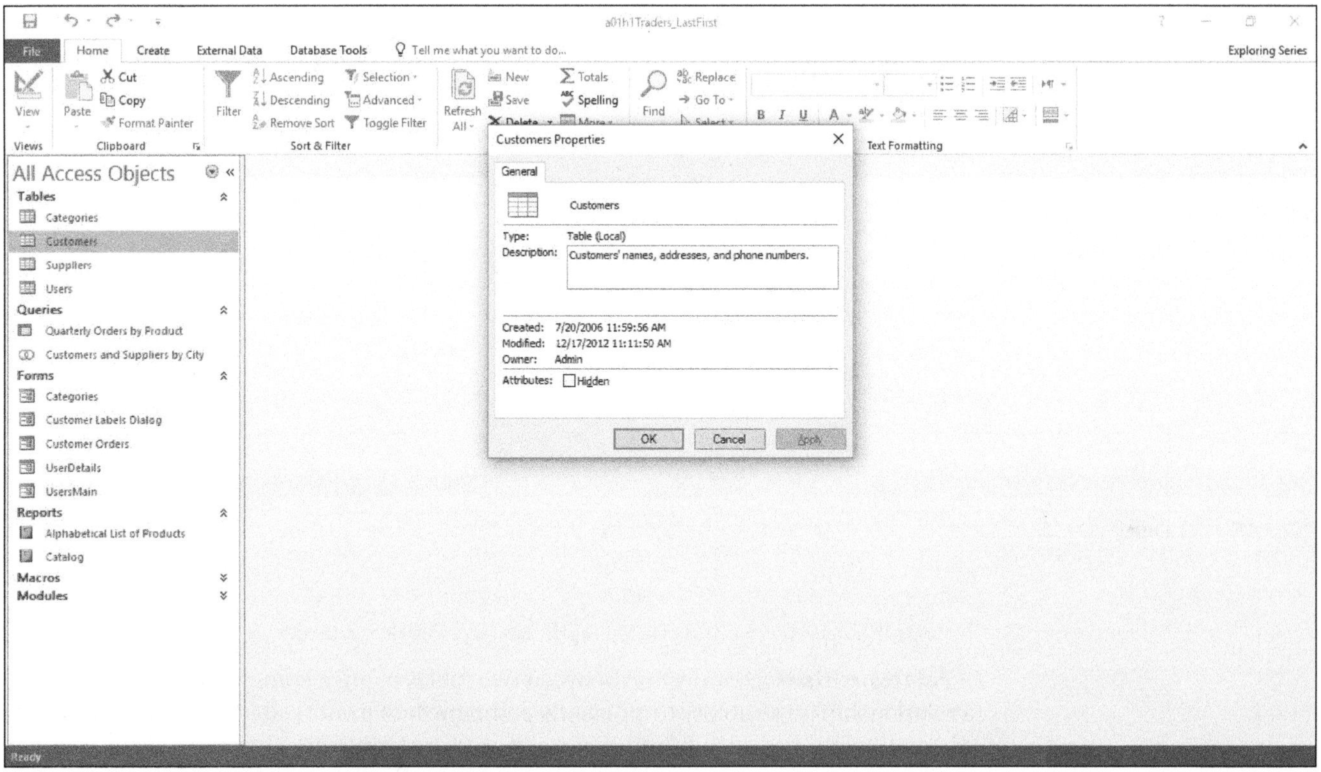

Access 2016, Windows 10, Microsoft Corporation

FIGURE 1.21 Previewing a Table Description

To enter a table description, complete the following steps:

1. Right-click the table name in the Navigation Pane.
2. Select Table Properties on the shortcut menu.
3. Type the description in the Table Properties dialog box and click OK.

> **TIP: SHOWING OBJECT DETAILS**
> Most users will not need to see a description frequently. However, if necessary, you can change the Navigation Pane to display details by default. The details include the creation date, modification date, and description of the object. You may need to increase the size of the Navigation Pane to see the full description, so this works better on wider screens.
>
> To show object details, right-click All Access Objects in the Navigation Pane and click View By. Select Details to display the full details. Resize the Navigation Pane so you can view the complete descriptions, if necessary. Figure 1.22 shows a view of objects with descriptions.

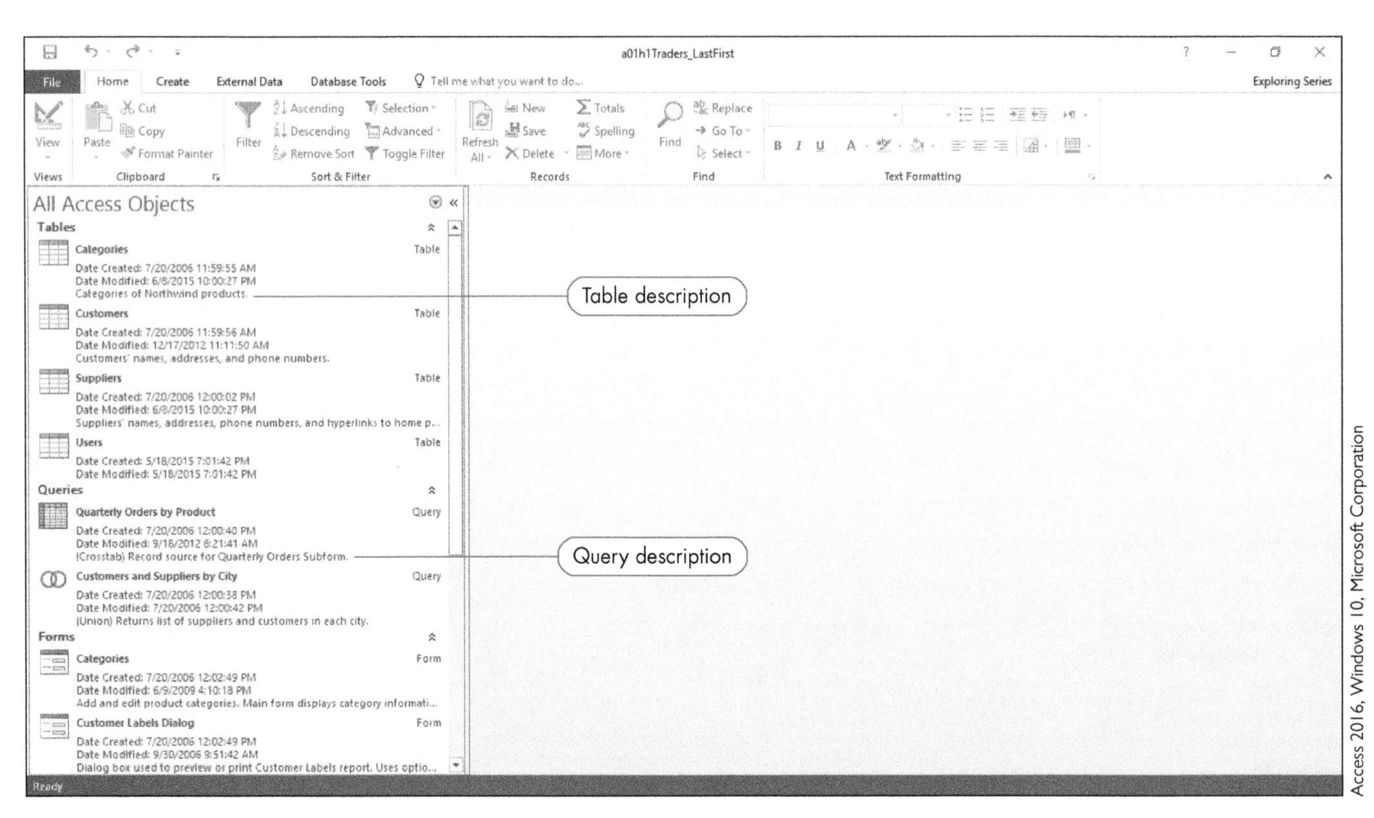

FIGURE 1.22 Detail View of Objects

Understand Relationships Between Tables

A ***relationship*** is a connection between two tables using a common field. The benefit of a relationship is the ability to efficiently combine data from related tables for the purpose of creating queries, forms, and reports. If you are using an existing database, relationships are likely created already. The design of the Northwind database, which contains multiple tables, is illustrated in Figure 1.23. The tables have been created, the field names have been added, and the data types have been set. The diagram shows the relationships that were created between tables using join lines. Join lines enable you to create a relationship between two tables using a common field. For example, the Suppliers table is joined to the Products table using the common field SupplierID. These table connections enable you to query the database for information stored in multiple tables. This feature gives the manager the ability to ask questions like "What products are produced by the supplier Exotic Liquids?" In this case, the name of the supplier (Exotic Liquids) is stored in the Supplier table, but the products are stored in the Products table. Notice in Figure 1.24, you can tell there is a table related to the Supplier table, because a plus sign ⊞ appears to the left of each Supplier. If you click the plus sign, you will see a list of products produced by this company.

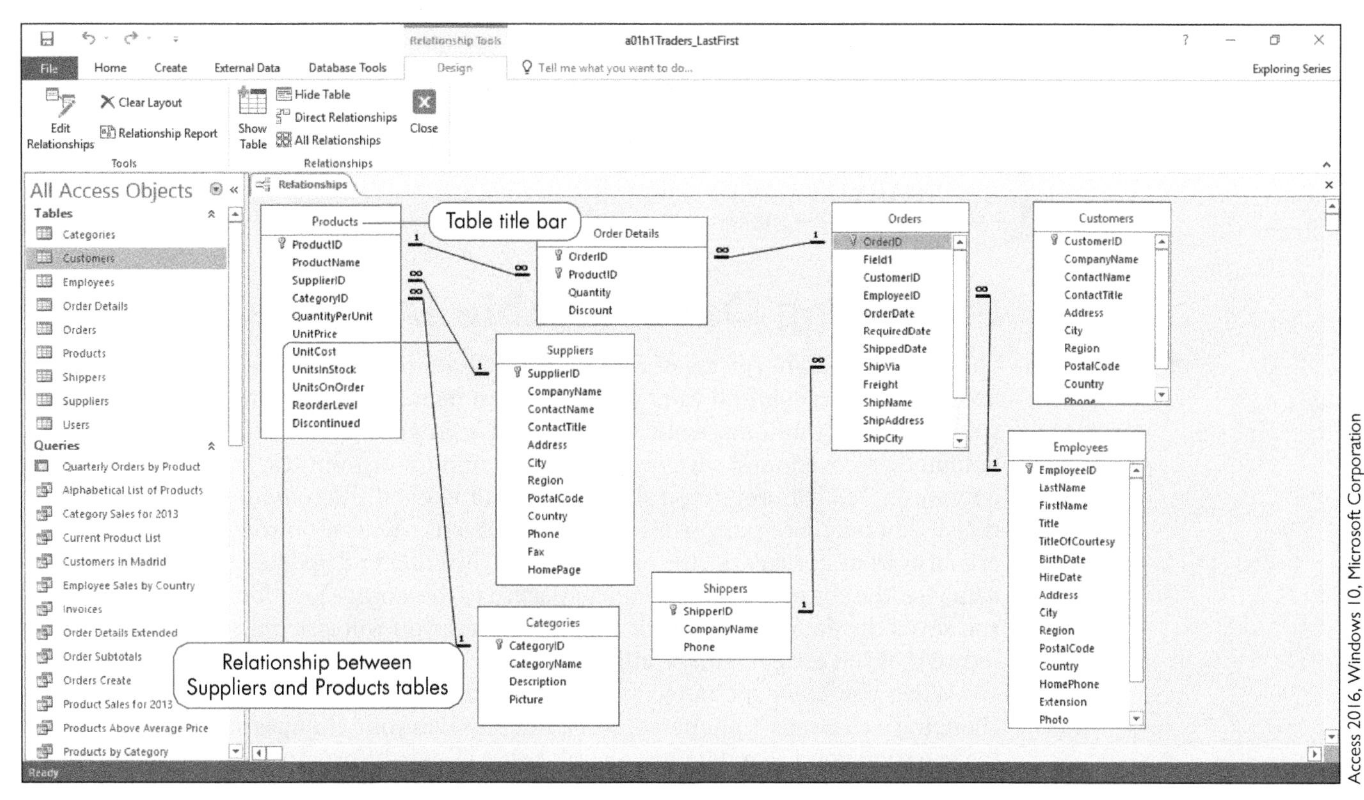

FIGURE 1.23 Northwind Database Relationships

Table Tools
a01h1Traders_LastFirst
File | Home | Create | External Data | Database Tools | Fields | Table | Tell me what you want to do... | Exploring Series
View | Paste | Cut | Copy | Format Painter | Filter | Ascending | Descending | Remove Sort | Selection | Advanced | Toggle Filter | Refresh All | New | Save | Delete | Totals | Spelling | More | Find | Replace | Go To | Select | Calibri | 11
Views | Clipboard | Sort & Filter | Records | Find | Text Formatting

+ sign
Records in another table

All Access Objects
Tables: Categories, Customers, Employees, Order Details, Orders, Products, Shippers, Suppliers, Users
Queries: Quarterly Orders by Product, Alphabetical List of Products, Category Sales for 2013, Current Product List, Customers in Madrid, Employee Sales by Country, Invoices, Order Details Extended, Order Subtotals, Orders Create, Product Sales for 2013, Products Above Average Price, Products by Category

Suppliers

Supplier ID	Company Name	Contact Name	Contact Title	Address	City	Regio	Postal
1	Exotic Liquids	Charlotte Cooper	Purchasing Manager	49 Gilbert St.	London		EC1 4S
2	New Orleans Cajun Delights	Shelley Burke	Order Administrator	P.O. Box 78934	New Orleans	LA	70117
3	Grandma Kelly's Homestead	Regina Murphy	Sales Representative	707 Oxford Rd.	Ann Arbor	MI	48104

Product ID	Product Name	Category	Quantity Per Unit	Unit Price	UnitCost	Units In Stock	Units On Order	Reorder Lev
6	Grandma's Boysenberry Spread	Condiments	12 - 8 oz jars	$25.00	$10.50	120	0	
7	Uncle Bob's Organic Dried Pears	Produce	12 - 1 lb pkgs.	$30.00	$18.00	15	0	
8	Northwoods Cranberry Sauce	Condiments	12 - 12 oz jars	$40.00	$12.00	6	0	
(New)				$0.00	$0.00	0	0	

Supplier ID	Company Name	Contact Name	Contact Title	Address	City	Regio	Postal
4	Tokyo Traders	Yoshi Nagase	Marketing Manager	9-8 Sekimai	Tokyo		100
	Cooperativa de Quesos 'Las Cabras'	Antonio del Valle Saavedra	Export Administrator	Calle del Rosal 4	Oviedo	Asturias	33007
6	Mayumi's	Mayumi Ohno	Marketing Representative	92 Setsuko	Osaka		545
7	Pavlova, Ltd.	Ian Devling	Marketing Manager	74 Rose St.	Melbourne	Victoria	3058
8	Specialty Biscuits, Ltd.	Peter Wilson	Sales Representative	29 King's Way	Manchester		M14 G
9	PB Knäckebröd AB	Lars Peterson	Sales Agent	Kaloadagatan 13	Göteborg		S-345
10	Refrescos Americanas LTDA	Carlos Diaz	Marketing Manager	Av. das Americanas 12.890	São Paulo		5442
11	Heli Süßwaren GmbH & Co. KG	Petra Winkler	Sales Manager	Tiergartenstraße 5	Berlin		10785
12	Plutzer Lebensmittelgroßmärkte AG	Martin Bein	International Marketing Mg	Bogenallee 51	Frankfurt		60439
13	Nord-Ost-Fisch Handelsgesellschaft mb	Sven Petersen	Coordinator Foreign Market	Frahmredder 112a	Cuxhaven		27478
14	Formaggi Fortini s.r.l.	Elio Rossi	Sales Representative	Viale Dante, 75	Ravenna		48100
15	Norske Meierier	Beate Vileid	Marketing Manager	Hatlevegen 5	Sandvika		1320
16	Bigfoot Breweries	Cheryl Saylor	Regional Account Rep.	3400 - 8th Avenue	Bend	OR	97101
17	Svensk Sjöföda AB	Michael Björn	Sales Representative	Brovallavägen 231	Stockholm		S-123
18	Aux joyeux ecclésiastiques	Guylène Nodier	Sales Manager	203, Rue des Francs-Bourgeois	Paris		75004
19	New England Seafood Cannery	Robb Merchant	Wholesale Account Agent	Order Processing Dept.	Boston	MA	02134
20	Leka Trading	Chandra Leka	Owner	471 Serangoon Loop, Suite #402	Singapore		0512
21	Lyngbysild	Niels Petersen	Sales Manager	Lyngbysild	Lyngby		2800

Record: 1 of 3 | No Filter | Search
Number automatically assigned to new product.

FIGURE 1.24 Related Tables

Relationships will be discussed further in a later chapter. However, you can view the existing relationships in any database to familiarize yourself with the way tables work together.

To view existing database relationships, complete the following steps:

1. Click Relationships in the Relationships group on the Database Tools tab.
2. Reposition tables by dragging the table's title bar (as shown above in Figure 1.23) to a new location so all relationships are visible. This is not required, but doing so may make the relationships easier to follow.
3. Click Close in the Relationships group of the Design tab to close the Relationships window.

Modifying Data in Table Datasheet View

The Save function in Access works differently than the other Office applications. Word, Excel, and PowerPoint all work primarily from memory (RAM). In those applications, your work is not automatically saved to your storage location. Office may perform an automatic recovery and save every specified amount of minutes; however, you should not rely on that feature, so you should save your work. If the computer crashes or power is lost, you may lose part or all of your document. Access, on the other hand, works primarily from storage (i.e., the hard drive). As you enter and update the data in an Access database, the changes are automatically saved to the storage location you specified when you saved the database. If a power failure occurs, you will lose only the changes to the record that you are currently editing.

When you make a change to a record's content in an Access table (for example, changing a customer's phone number), Access saves your changes as soon as you move the insertion point to a different record. You will only be prompted to save if you make changes to the design of the table (such as changing the font or background color). Editing data is done similarly in queries and forms. Recall that reports cannot change data, so changes to data cannot be done there.

To edit a record, tab to the field you want to modify and type the new data. When you start typing, you erase all existing data in the field because the entire field is selected.

TIP: UNDO WORKS DIFFERENTLY

You can click Undo to reverse the most recent change (the phone number you just modified, for example) to a single record immediately after making changes to that record. However, unlike other Office programs that enable multiple Undo steps, you cannot use Undo to reverse multiple edits in Access. Undo (and Redo) are found on the Quick Access Toolbar.

Adding Records to a Table

STEP 4

Data in a database will be constantly changing. You should expect new data to be added. If you are working with a Customer database, you would expect new customers to be added constantly. If you are dealing with a Restaurant database, new menu items could be added daily.

To add a new record to a table, complete the following steps:

1. Open the table in Datasheet view (if it is not already open) by double-clicking it in the Navigation Pane.
2. Click New in the Records group on the Home tab.
3. Begin typing. If you are unable to type, you have probably selected a field with a data type of AutoNumber, which Access assigns for you. If this is the case, click in a different field and begin typing. The asterisk record indicator changes to a pencil symbol to show that you are in editing mode (see Figure 1.25). Note: you can follow the same process to add a record in a form (shown in Figure 1.26) or query.
4. Press Tab to move to the following field and enter data, and repeat this step until you have input all required data for this record.
5. Move to another record by clicking elsewhere or pressing Tab in the last field in a record. As soon as you move to another record, Access automatically saves the changes to the record you created or changed.

New record

Customer ID	Company Name	Contact Name	Contact Title	Address	City	Region	Postal Cod	Country
SUPRD	Suprêmes délices	Pascale Cartrain	Accounting Manager	Boulevard Tirou, 255	Charleroi		B-6000	Belgium
THEBI	The Big Cheese	Liz Nixon	Marketing Manager	89 Jefferson Way	Portland	OR	97201	USA
THECR	The Cracker Box	Liu Wong	Marketing Assistant	55 Grizzly Peak Rd.	Butte	MT	59801	USA
TOMSP	Toms Spezialitäten	Karin Josephs	Marketing Manager	Luisenstr. 48	Münster		44087	Germany
TORTU	Tortuga Restaurante	Miguel Angel Paolino	Owner	Avda. Azteca 123	México D.F.		05033	Mexico
TRADH	Tradição Hipermercados	Anabela Domingues	Sales Representative	Av. Inês de Castro, 414	São Paulo	SP	05634-030	Brazil
TRAIH	Trail's Head Gourmet Provisioners	Helvetius Nagy	Sales Associate	722 DaVinci Blvd.	Kirkland	WA	98034	USA
VAFFE	Vaffeljernet	Palle Ibsen	Sales Manager	Smagsløget 45	Århus		8200	Denmark
VICTE	Victuailles en stock	Mary Saveley	Sales Agent	2, rue du Commerce	Lyon		69004	France
VINET	Vins et alcools Chevalier	Paul Henriot	Accounting Manager	59 rue de l'Abbaye	Reims		51100	France
WANDK	Die Wandernde Kuh	Rita Müller	Sales Representative	Adenauerallee 900	Stuttgart		70563	Germany
WARTH	Wartian Herkku	Pirkko Koskitalo	Accounting Manager	Torikatu 38	Oulu		90110	Finland
WELLI	Wellington Importadora	Paula Parente	Sales Manager	Rua do Mercado, 12	Resende	SP	08737-363	Brazil
WHITC	White Clover Markets	Karl Jablonski	Owner	305 - 14th Ave. S.	Seattle	WA	98128	USA
WILMK	Wilman Kala	Matti Karttunen	Owner/Marketing Assistant	Keskuskatu 45	Helsinki		21240	Finland
WOLZA	Wolski Zajazd	Zbyszek Piestrzeniewicz	Owner	ul. Filtrowa 68	Warszawa		01-012	Poland
ABCDE								

Pencil icon

Record: 92 of 92

Unique five-character code based on customer name.

Access 2016, Windows 10, Microsoft Corporation

FIGURE 1.25 Adding a Record Using a Table

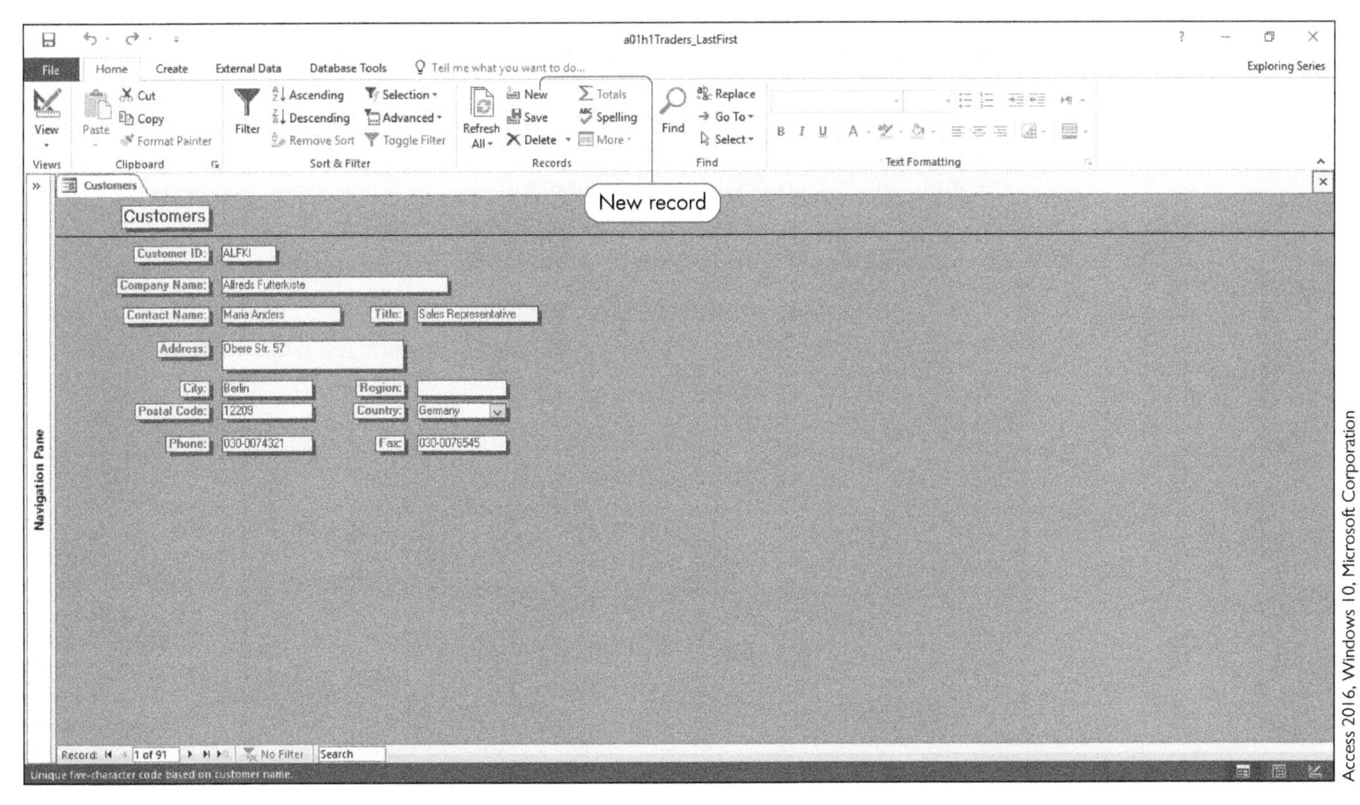

FIGURE 1.26 Adding a Record Using a Form

As with most of Office, there are a number of ways to perform the same task. Data entry is the same. See Table 1.1 for a list of some shortcuts you can use when performing data entry.

TABLE 1.1 Keyboard Shortcuts for Entering Data

Keystroke	Result
Up arrow (↑)	Moves insertion point up one row.
Down arrow (↓)	Moves insertion point down one row.
Left arrow (←)	Moves insertion point left one field in the same row.
Right arrow (→)	Moves insertion point right one field in the same row.
Tab or Enter	Moves insertion point right one field in the same row.
Shift+Tab	Moves insertion point left one field in the same row.
Home	Moves insertion point to the first field in the current row.
End	Moves insertion point to the last field in the current row.
Esc	Cancels any changes made in the current field while in Edit mode.
Ctrl+Z	Reverses the last unsaved edit.

Deleting Records from a Table

Deciding to delete records is not a simple decision. Many times, deleting records is a bad idea. Say you are working in the database for an animal shelter. Once an animal has been adopted, you may be tempted to delete the animal from the database. However, you would then lose any record of the animal ever existing, and if the owner calls asking if the animal has had its shots, or how old the animal is, you would no longer be able to provide that information. Often, instead of deleting information, you would create a yes/no field indicating that a record is no longer relevant. For example, the shelter database might have a check box for adopted. If the adopted box is checked yes, the animal is no longer at the shelter, but the information is still available. That said, sometimes you will certainly find it appropriate to delete a record.

To delete a record from a table, complete the following steps:

1. Click the record selector for the record you want to delete (see Figure 1.27).
2. Click Delete in the Records group on the Home tab. Click Yes in the warning dialog box. Note that you can take similar steps in queries and forms.

Delete

Record selector

Customer ID	Company Name	Contact Name	Contact Title	Address	City	Region	Postal Cod	Country
ALFKI	Alfreds Futterkiste	Maria Anders	Sales Representative	Obere Str. 57	Berlin		12209	Germany
ANATR	Ana Trujillo Emparedados y helados	Ana Trujillo	Owner	Avda. de la Constitución 2222	México D.F.		05021	Mexico
ANTON	Antonio Moreno Taquería	Antonio Moreno	Owner	Mataderos 2312	México D.F.		05023	Mexico
AROUT	A	Thomas Hardy	Sales Representative	120 Hanover Sq.	London		WA1 1DP	UK
BERGS	Be	Christina Berglund	Order Administrator	Berguvsvägen 8	Luleå		S-958 22	Sweden
BLAUS	Blauer See Delikatessen	Hanna Moos	Sales Representative	Forsterstr. 57	Mannheim		68306	Germany
BLONP	Blondel père et fils	Frédérique Citeaux	Marketing Manager	24, place Kléber	Strasbourg		67000	France
BOLID	Bólido Comidas preparadas	Martín Sommer	Owner	C/ Araquil, 67	Madrid		28023	Spain
BONAP	Bon app'	Laurence Lebihan	Owner	12, rue des Bouchers	Marseille		13008	France
BOTTM	Bottom-Dollar Markets	Elizabeth Lincoln	Accounting Manager	23 Tsawassen Blvd.	Tsawassen	BC	T2F 8M4	Canada
BSBEV	B's Beverages	Victoria Ashworth	Sales Representative Trainee	Fauntleroy Circus	London		EC2 5NT	UK
CACTU	Cactus Comidas para llevar	Patricio Simpson	Sales Agent	Cerrito 333	Buenos Aires		1010	Argentina
CENTC	Centro comercial Moctezuma	Francisco Chang	Marketing Manager	Sierras de Granada 9993	México D.F.		05022	Mexico
CHOPS	Chop-suey Chinese	Yang Wang	Owner	Hauptstr. 29	Bern		3012	Switzerlan
COMMI	Comércio Mineiro	Pedro Afonso	Sales Associate	Av. dos Lusíadas, 23	São Paulo	SP	05432-043	Brazil
CONSH	Consolidated Holdings	Elizabeth Brown	Sales Representative	Berkeley Gardens	London		WX1 6LT	UK
DRACD	Drachenblut Delikatessen	Sven Ottlieb	Order Administrator	Walserweg 21	Aachen		52066	Germany
DUMON	Du monde entier	Janine Labrune	Owner	67, rue des Cinquante Otages	Nantes		44000	France
EASTC	Eastern Connection	Ann Devon	Sales Agent	35 King George	London		WX3 6FW	UK
ERNSH	Ernst Handel	Roland Mendel	Sales Manager	Kirchgasse 6	Graz		8010	Austria
FAMIA	Familia Arquibaldo	Aria Cruz	Marketing Assistant	Rua Orós, 92	São Paulo	SP	05442-030	Brazil
FISSA	FISSA Fabrica Inter. Salchichas S.A.	Diego Roel	Accounting Manager	C/ Moralzarzal, 86	Madrid		28034	Spain
FOLIG	Folies gourmandes	Martine Rancé	Assistant Sales Agent	184, chaussée de Tournai	Lille		59000	France
FOLKO	Folk och fä HB	Maria Larsson	Owner	Åkergatan 24	Bräcke		S-844 67	Sweden
FRANK	Frankenversand	Peter Franken	Marketing Manager	Berliner Platz 43	München		80805	Germany
FRANR	France restauration	Carine Schmitt	Marketing Manager	54, rue Royale	Nantes		44000	France
FRANS	Franchi S.p.A.	Paolo Accorti	Sales Representative	Via Monte Bianco 34	Torino		10100	Italy

Record: 2 of 91 No Filter Search

Unique five-character code based on customer name.

FIGURE 1.27 Deleting a Record

If you attempt to delete a record, you may get an error message. For example, if you try to delete a customer who has adopted pets, you may get a message stating *You cannot delete this record because another table has related records.* Even though the customer may have moved, they cannot be deleted because related records exist in another table, in this case, animals the customer has adopted.

Using Database Utilities

Database administrators spend a lot of time maintaining databases. Software utility programs make this process simpler. As Access is a database management utility, there are a number of tools that can be used to protect, maintain, and improve performance of a database.

Back Up a Database

Back Up Database is a utility that creates a duplicate copy of the entire database to protect from loss or damage. Imagine what would happen to a firm that loses track of orders placed, a charity that loses the list of donor contributions, or a hospital that loses the digital records of its patients. Making backups is especially important when you have multiple users working with the database. When you use the Back Up Database utility, Access provides a file name for the backup that uses the same file name as the database you are backing up, an underscore, and the current date. This makes it easy for you to keep track of databases by the date they were created.

Keep in mind, backing up a database on the same storage device as the original database can leave you with no protection in the event of hardware failure. Backups are typically stored on a separate device, such as an external hard drive or network drive.

To back up a database, complete the following steps:

1. Click the File tab.
2. Click Save As.
3. Click Back Up Database under the Advanced group (see Figure 1.28).
4. Click Save As. Revise the location and file name if you want to change either and click Save.

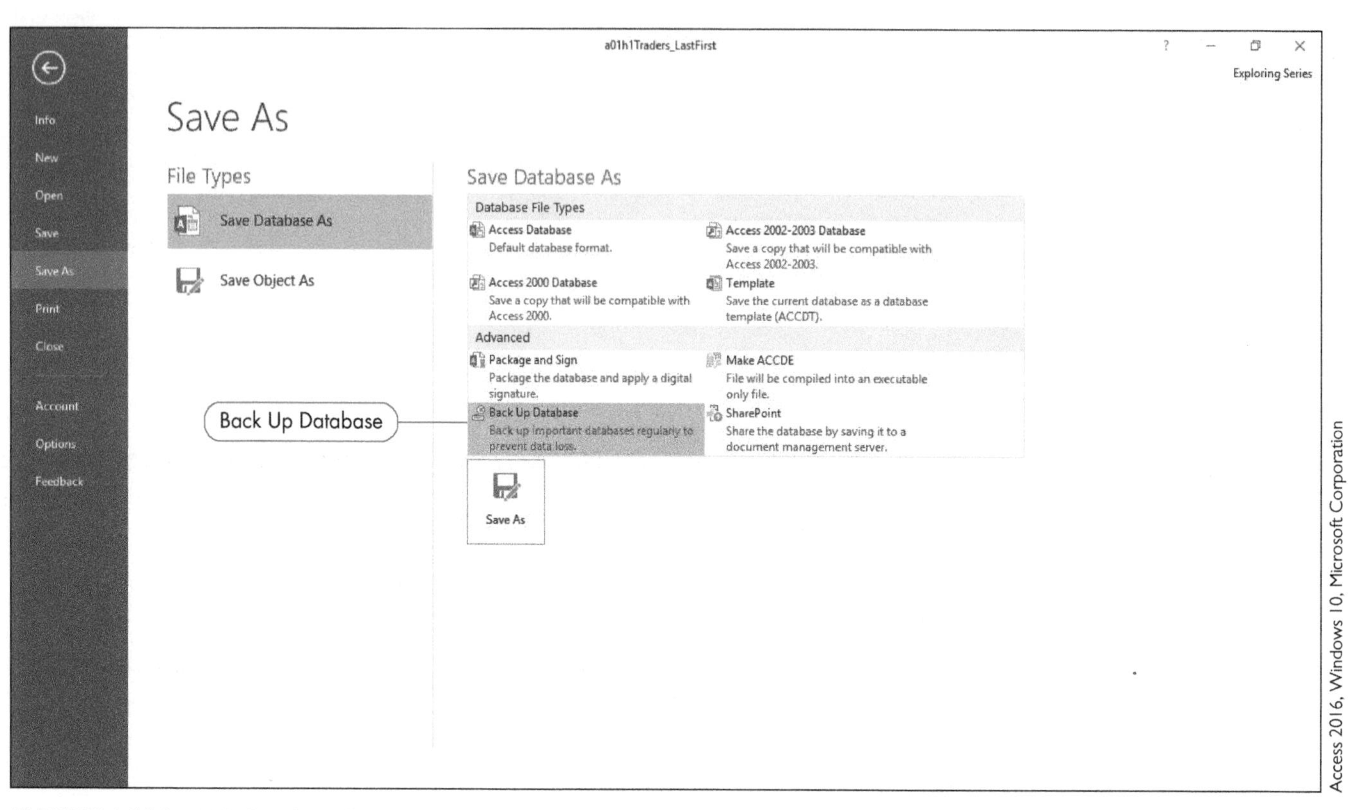

FIGURE 1.28 Back Up Database Option

Compact and Repair a Database

Databases have a tendency to expand with everyday use and may become corrupt, so Access provides the ***Compact and Repair Database*** utility. Compact and Repair Database reduces the size of a database and fixes any errors that may exist in the file.

To compact and repair an open database, complete the following steps:

1. Click the File tab.
2. Click Compact and Repair Database in the Info options. If you have any unsaved design changes, you will be prompted to save before the compact and repair can complete.

Alternately, you can have Access perform a Compact and Repair automatically.

To have Access compact and repair a database each time you close the database, complete the following steps:

1. Click the File tab.
2. Click Options.
3. Click Current Database.
4. Click the Compact on Close check box under Application Options in the Options for the current database pane.
5. Click OK.

TIP: SPLIT DATABASES

Another utility built into Access is the ***Database Splitter*** tool, which puts the tables in one file (the back-end database), and the queries, forms, and reports in a second file (the front-end database). This way, each user can create their own queries, forms, and reports without potentially changing an object someone else needs.

To split a database, click the Database Tools tab and click Access Database in the Move Data group. Click Split Database and click OK.

Encrypt a Database

To protect a database from unauthorized access, you can encrypt the database, which enables you to password-protect the stored information. Adding a password requires that the database be opened in exclusive mode. Open Exclusive mode guarantees that you are the only one currently using the database.

To open a database in exclusive mode, complete the following steps:

1. Ensure that the database is closed. You cannot open a database with exclusive access unless it is currently closed.
2. Click the File tab.
3. Click Open.
4. Click Browse to display the Open dialog box.
5. Locate and click the database you want to open, and click the Open arrow at the bottom of the dialog box. Make sure you click the arrow next to the word Open, and not the Open button.
6. Select Open Exclusive from the list. The database opens in exclusive mode.

To add a password once the database has been opened in exclusive mode, complete the following steps:

1. Click the File tab.
2. Click Encrypt with Password. The Set Database Password dialog box opens.
3. Type a password, and re-enter the password in the Verify box. Click OK.

Print Information

Though Access is primarily designed to store data electronically, you may want to produce a print copy of your data.

To print information from any object (table, query, form, report) in your database, complete the following steps:

1. Click the File tab.
2. Click Print. The right panel display changes to enable you to choose a print option.
3. Click Print.
4. Change any settings that may need changing (for example, the print range or number of copies).
5. Click OK.

It is good practice to preview your work before printing a document. This way, if you notice an error, you can fix it and not waste paper.

To preview your work before printing, complete the following steps:

1. Click the File tab.
2. Click Print.
3. Click Print Preview.
4. Click Close Print Preview on the Print Preview tab to exit without printing, or click Print to open the Print dialog box (see Figure 1.29).

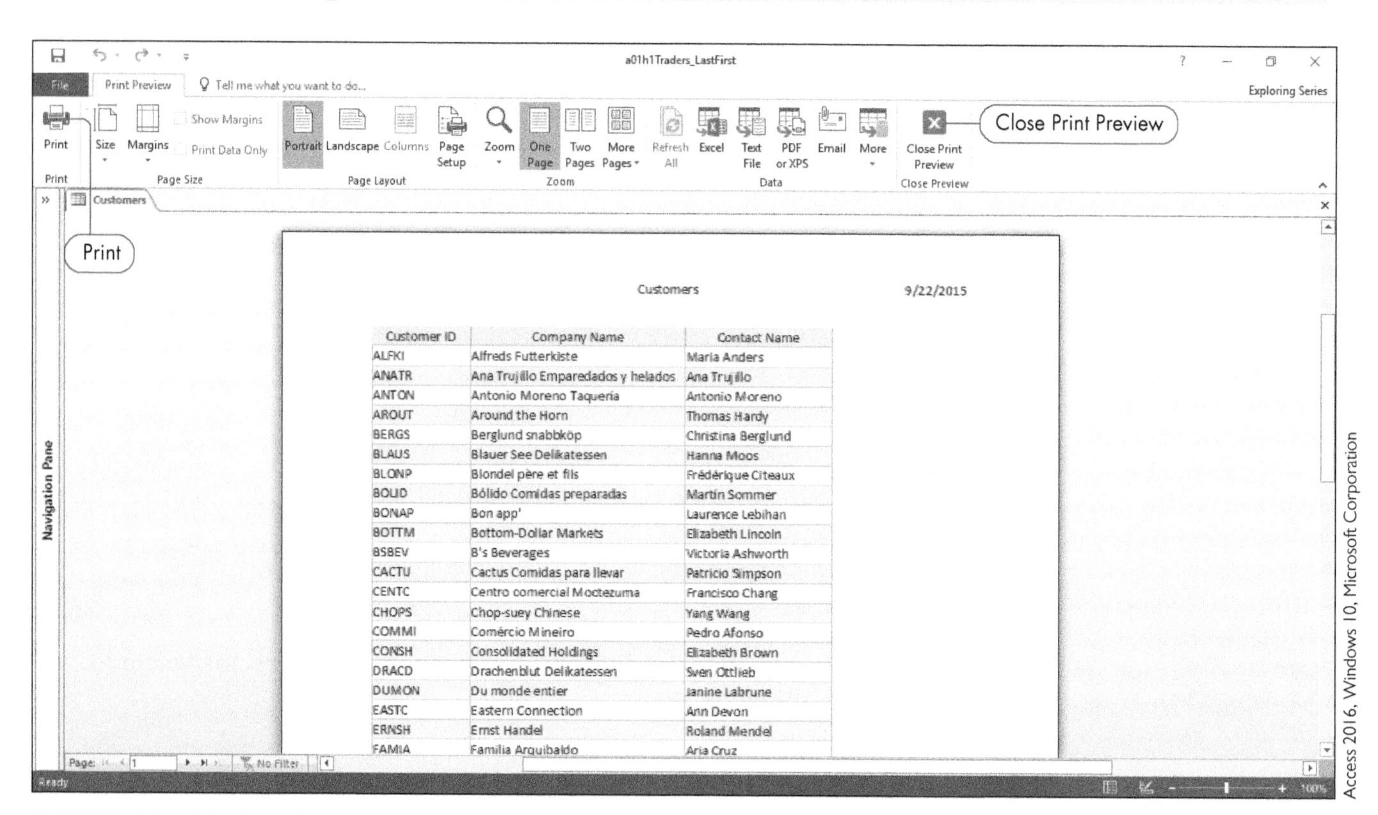

FIGURE 1.29 Table Print Preview

Quick Concepts

1. Name the four main types of objects in an Access database and briefly describe the purpose of each. ***pp. 668–670***
2. What is the difference between Datasheet view and Design view in a table? ***pp. 673, 675***
3. How does Access handle saving differently than other Office programs such as Excel? ***p. 680***
4. How do relationships benefit a database user? ***p. 678***

Hands-On Exercises

Watch the Video for this Hands-On Exercise!
MyITLab®
HOE1 Training

Skills covered: Open a Database • Save a Database with a New Name • Enable Content in a Database • Examine the Access Interface • Explore Table Datasheet View • Navigate Through Records • Explore Table Design View • Rename and Describe Tables • Understand Relationships Between Tables • Understand the Difference Between Working in Storage And Memory • Change Data in Table Datasheet View • Add Records to a Table • Delete Records from A Table • Back Up a Database • Compact and Repair a Database • Encrypt a Database • Print Information

1 Databases Are Everywhere!

Northwind purchases food items from suppliers around the world and sells them to restaurants and specialty food shops. Northwind depends on the data stored in its Access database to process orders and make daily decisions. You will open the Northwind database, examine the Access interface, review the existing objects in the database, and explore Access views. You will add, edit, and delete records using both tables and forms. Finally, you will back up the database.

STEP 1 » OPEN, SAVE, AND ENABLE CONTENT IN A DATABASE

As you begin your job, you first will become familiar with the Northwind database. This database will help you learn the fundamentals of working with database files. Refer to Figure 1.30 as you complete Step 1.

Step c: Enable Content

FIGURE 1.30 Northwind Database

a. Open Access, click **Open Other Files**, and click **Browse**. Navigate to the folder location designated by your instructor. Click *a01h1Traders* and click **Open**.

> **TROUBLESHOOTING:** If you make any major mistakes in this exercise, you can close the file, open *a01h1Traders* again, and then start this exercise over.

b. Click the **File tab** and click **Save As.** Click **Save As** and save the file as **a01h1Traders_LastFirst**.

When you save files, use your last and first names. For example, as the Access author, I would save my database as "a01h1Traders_CameronEric."

The Security Warning message bar appears below the Ribbon, indicating that some database content is disabled.

c. Click **Enable Content** on the Security Warning message bar.

When you open an Access file, you should enable the content.

STEP 2 » RECOGNIZE DATABASE OBJECT TYPES

Now that you have opened the Northwind database, you examine the Navigation Pane, objects, and views to become familiar with these fundamental Access features. Refer to Figure 1.31 as you complete Step 2.

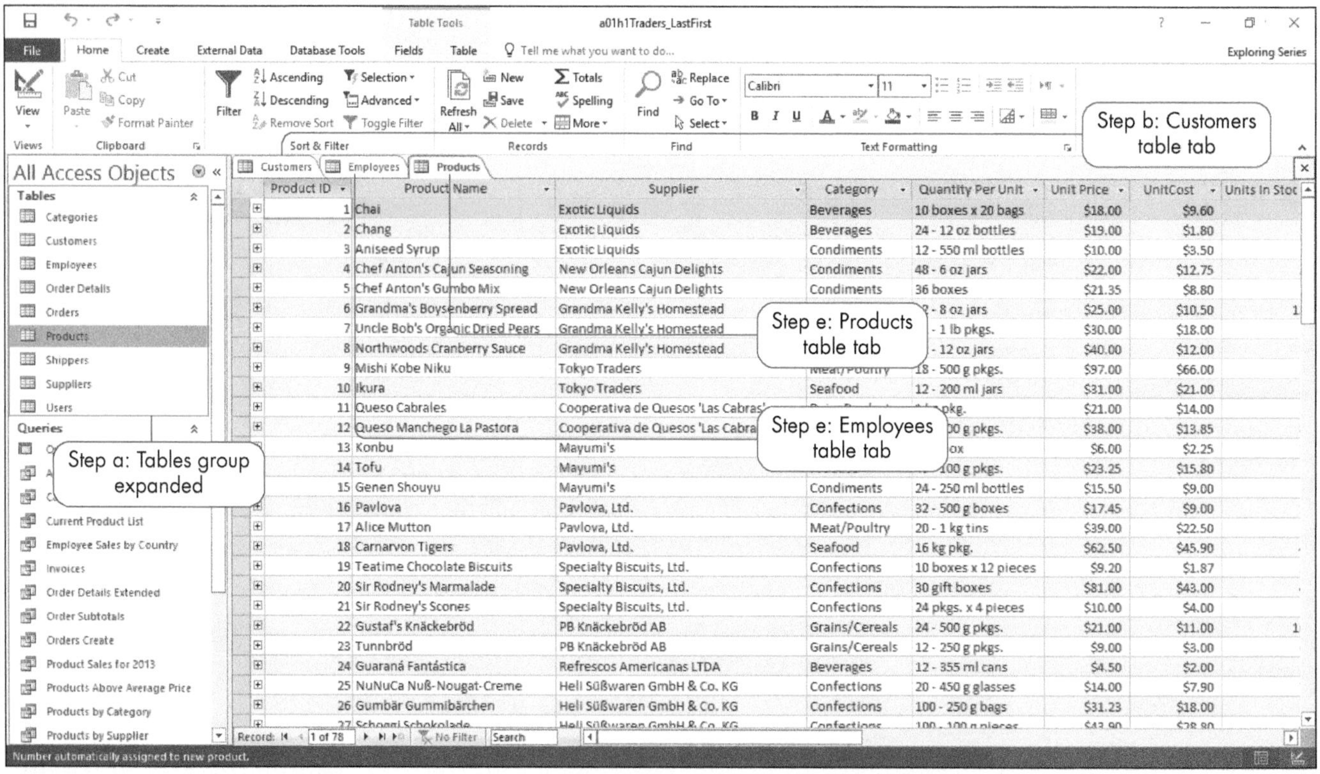

FIGURE 1.31 Northwind Objects

Access 2016, Windows 10, Microsoft Corporation

a. Scroll through the Navigation Pane and notice the Access objects listed under each expanded group.

The Tables group and the Forms group are expanded, displaying all of the table and form objects. The Queries, Reports, Macros, and Modules groups are collapsed so that the objects in those groups are not displayed.

b. Double-click the **Customers table** in the Navigation Pane.

The Customers table opens in Datasheet view, showing the data contained in the table. The Customers tab displays below the Ribbon indicating the table object is open. Each customer's record displays on a table row. The columns of the table display the fields that comprise the records.

c. Click **View** in the Views group on the Home tab.

The view of the Customers table switches to Design view. The top portion of Design view displays each field that comprises a customer record, the field's data type, and an optional description of what the field should contain. The bottom portion of Design view displays the field properties (details) for the selected field.

d. Click **View** in the Views group on the Home tab again.

Because the View button is a toggle, your view returns to Datasheet view, which shows the data stored in the table.

e. Double-click **Employees** in the Tables group of the Navigation Pane. Double-click **Products** in the same location.

The Employees and Products tables open. The tabs for three table objects display below the Ribbon: Customers, Employees, and Products.

f. Click **Shutter Bar Open/Close** « on the title bar of the Navigation Pane to hide the Navigation Pane. Click again to » show the Navigation Pane.

Shutter Bar Open/Close toggles to allow you to view more in the open object window, or to enable you to view your database objects.

g. Scroll down in the Navigation Pane and click **Reports**.

The Reports group expands, and all report objects display.

h. Scroll up until you can see Forms. Click **Forms** in the Navigation Pane.

The Forms group collapses and individual form objects no longer display.

STEP 3 » MODIFY DATA IN TABLE DATASHEET VIEW

You want to learn to edit the data in the Northwind database, because data can change. For example, employees will change their address and phone numbers when they move, and customers will change their order data from time to time. Refer to Figure 1.32 as you complete Step 3.

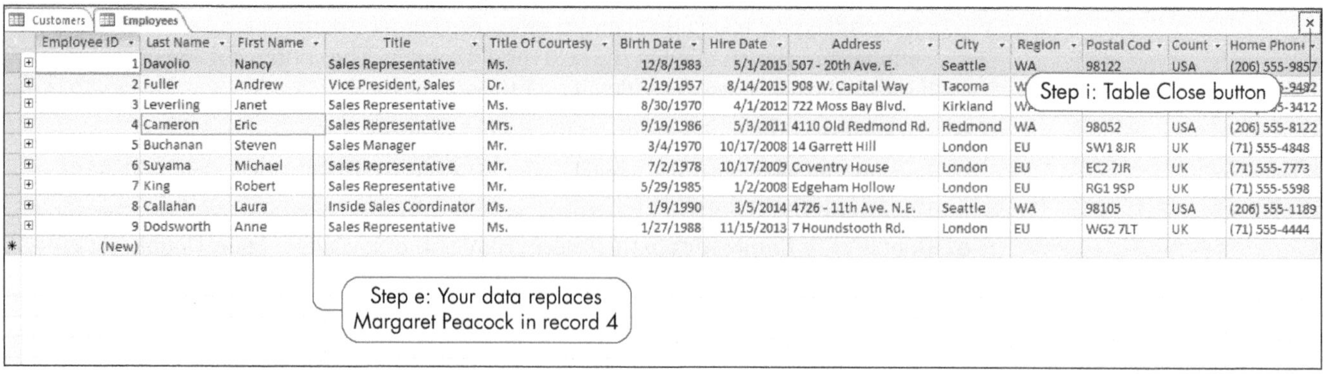

Customers | Employees

Employee ID	Last Name	First Name	Title	Title Of Courtesy	Birth Date	Hire Date	Address	City	Region	Postal Cod	Count	Home Phone
1	Davolio	Nancy	Sales Representative	Ms.	12/8/1983	5/1/2015	507 - 20th Ave. E.	Seattle	WA	98122	USA	(206) 555-9857
2	Fuller	Andrew	Vice President, Sales	Dr.	2/19/1957	8/14/2015	908 W. Capital Way	Tacoma	W[illegible]	[illegible]	[illegible]	[illegible]-9482
3	Leverling	Janet	Sales Representative	Ms.	8/30/1970	4/1/2012	722 Moss Bay Blvd.	Kirkland	WA	[illegible]	[illegible]	[illegible]5-3412
4	Cameron	Eric	Sales Representative	Mrs.	9/19/1986	5/3/2011	4110 Old Redmond Rd.	Redmond	WA	98052	USA	(206) 555-8122
5	Buchanan	Steven	Sales Manager	Mr.	3/4/1970	10/17/2008	14 Garrett Hill	London	EU	SW1 8JR	UK	(71) 555-4848
6	Suyama	Michael	Sales Representative	Mr.	7/2/1978	10/17/2009	Coventry House	London	EU	EC2 7JR	UK	(71) 555-7773
7	King	Robert	Sales Representative	Mr.	5/29/1985	1/2/2008	Edgeham Hollow	London	EU	RG1 9SP	UK	(71) 555-5598
8	Callahan	Laura	Inside Sales Coordinator	Ms.	1/9/1990	3/5/2014	4726 - 11th Ave. N.E.	Seattle	WA	98105	USA	(206) 555-1189
9	Dodsworth	Anne	Sales Representative	Ms.	1/27/1988	11/15/2013	7 Houndstooth Rd.	London	EU	WG2 7LT	UK	(71) 555-4444
(New)												

Step i: Table Close button

Step e: Your data replaces Margaret Peacock in record 4

FIGURE 1.32 Northwind Employees Table

a. Click the **Employees tab** to view the Employees table.

b. Double-click **Peacock** (the value of the Last Name field in the fourth row); the entire name highlights. Type your last name to replace Peacock.

The pencil symbol in the record selector box indicates that the record is being edited but has not yet been saved.

c. Press **Tab** to move to the next field in the fourth row. Replace Margaret with your first name and press **Tab**.

You have made changes to two fields in the same record.

d. Click **Undo** on the Quick Access Toolbar.

Your first and last names revert back to Margaret Peacock because you have not yet left the record.

e. Type your first and last names again to replace Margaret Peacock. Press **Tab**.

You should now be in the title field and the title, Sales Representative, is selected. The record has not been saved, as indicated by the pencil symbol in the record selector box.

f. Click anywhere in the third row where Janet Leverling's data is stored.

The pencil symbol disappears, indicating that your changes have been saved.

g. Click the **Address field** in the first row, Nancy Davolio's record. Select the entire address and then type **4004 East Morningside Dr.** Click anywhere on the second record, Andrew Fuller's record.

h. Click **Undo**.

Nancy Davolio's address reverts back to 507 - 20th Ave. E. However, the Undo command is now faded. You can no longer undo the change that you made replacing Margaret Peacock's name with your own.

i. Click **Close** [X] at the top of the table to close the Employees table.

The Employees table closes. You are not prompted to save your changes; they have already been saved for you because Access works in storage, not memory. If you reopen the Employees table, you will see your name in place of Margaret Peacock's name.

STEP 4 ›› ADD RECORDS TO A TABLE

You have been asked to add new information about a new line of products to the Northwind database. Refer to Figure 1.33 as you complete Step 4.

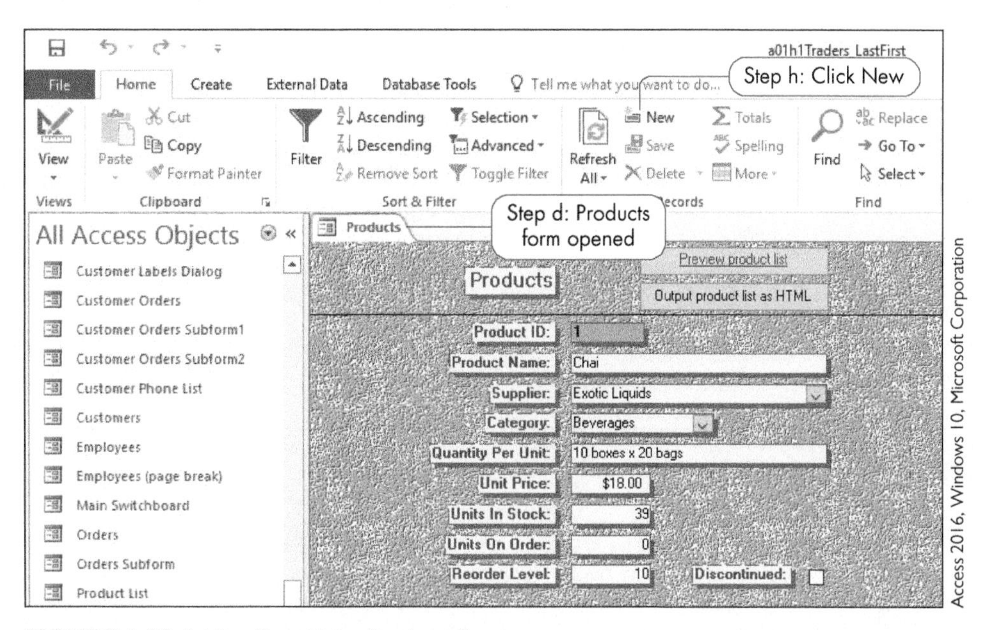

FIGURE 1.33 Adding Data Using Products Form

a. Right-click the **Customers tab** and click **Close All**.

b. Click the **Tables group** in the Navigation Pane to collapse it. Click the **Reports group** in the Navigation Pane to collapse it as well.

c. Click the **Forms group** in the Navigation Pane to expand the list of available forms.

d. Double-click the **Products form** to open it.

e. Click the **Next record** arrow. Click **Last record**, click **Previous record**, and then click **First record**.

f. Click **Find** in the Find group on the Home tab, type **Grandma** in the **Find box**, click the **Match arrow**, and then select **Any Part of Field**. Click **Find Next**.

You should see the data for Grandma's Boysenberry Spread. Selecting the Any Part of Field option will return a match even if it is contained in the middle of a word.

g. Close the Find dialog box.

h. Click **New** in the Records group of the Home tab.

i. Type the following information for a new product. Click, or press **Tab**, to move into the next cell. Notice as soon as you begin typing, Access will assign a ProductID to this product.

Field Name	Value to Type
Product Name	***Your names* Pecan Pie** (replacing Your name with your last name)
Supplier	**Grandma Kelly's Homestead** (click the arrow to select from the list of Suppliers)
Category	**Confections** (click the arrow to select from the list of Categories)
Quantity Per Unit	**1**
Unit Price	**15.00**
Units in Stock	**18**
Units on Order	**50**
Reorder Level	**20**
Discontinued	**No** (leave the check box unchecked)

j. Click anywhere on the Pecan Pie record you just typed. Click the **File tab**, click **Print**, and then click **Print Preview**.

The first four records display in the Print Preview.

k. Click **Last Page** in the navigation bar and click **Previous Page** to show the new record you entered.

The beginning of the Pecan Pie record is now visible. The record continues on the next page.

l. Click **Close Print Preview** in the Close Preview group.

m. Close the Products form.

STEP 5 » DELETE RECORDS FROM A TABLE

To help you understand how Access stores data, you verify that the new product is in the Products table. You also attempt to delete a record. Refer to Figure 1.34 as you complete Step 5.

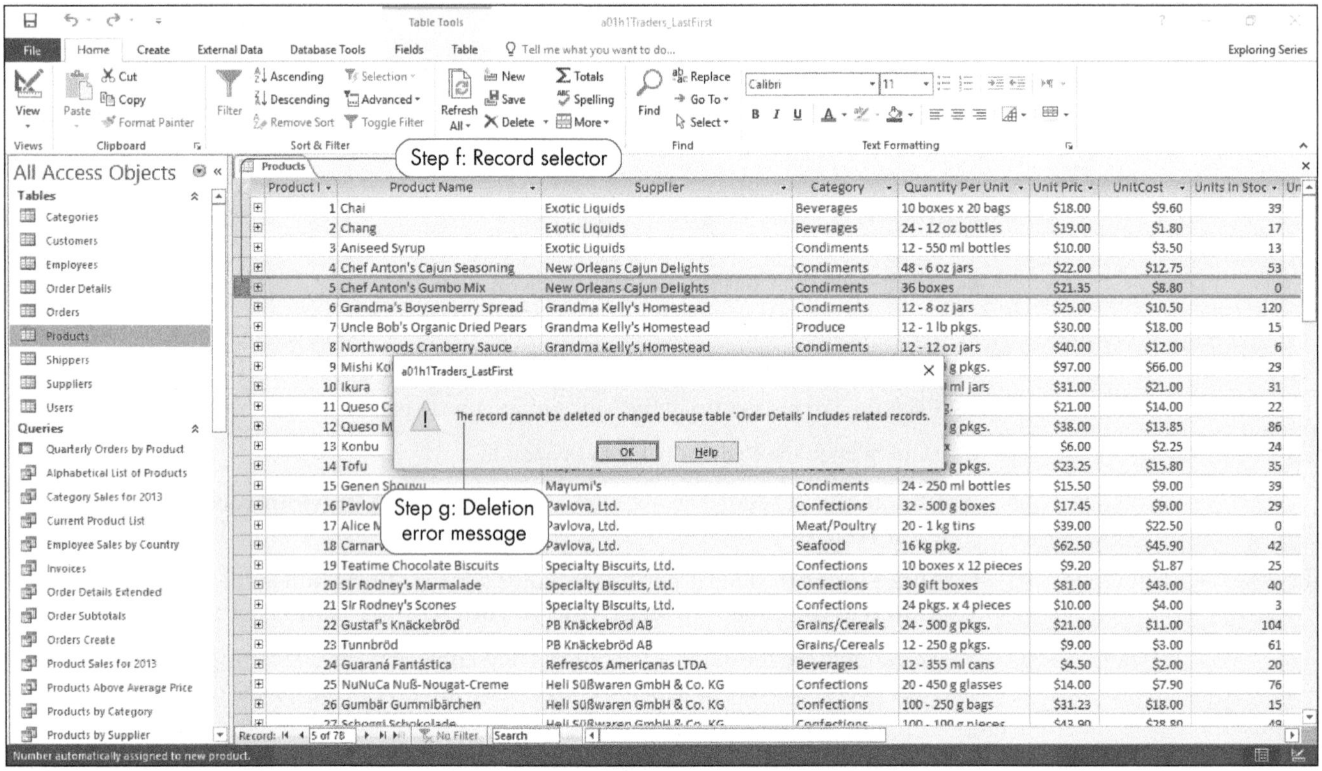

Product I	Product Name	Supplier	Category	Quantity Per Unit	Unit Pric	UnitCost	Units In Stoc
1	Chai	Exotic Liquids	Beverages	10 boxes x 20 bags	$18.00	$9.60	39
2	Chang	Exotic Liquids	Beverages	24 - 12 oz bottles	$19.00	$1.80	17
3	Aniseed Syrup	Exotic Liquids	Condiments	12 - 550 ml bottles	$10.00	$3.50	13
4	Chef Anton's Cajun Seasoning	New Orleans Cajun Delights	Condiments	48 - 6 oz jars	$22.00	$12.75	53
5	Chef Anton's Gumbo Mix	New Orleans Cajun Delights	Condiments	36 boxes	$21.35	$8.80	0
6	Grandma's Boysenberry Spread	Grandma Kelly's Homestead	Condiments	12 - 8 oz jars	$25.00	$10.50	120
7	Uncle Bob's Organic Dried Pears	Grandma Kelly's Homestead	Produce	12 - 1 lb pkgs.	$30.00	$18.00	15
8	Northwoods Cranberry Sauce	Grandma Kelly's Homestead	Condiments	12 - 12 oz jars	$40.00	$12.00	6
9	Mishi Ko			g pkgs.	$97.00	$66.00	29
10	Ikura			ml jars	$31.00	$21.00	31
11	Queso C				$21.00	$14.00	22
12	Queso M			g pkgs.	$38.00	$13.85	86
13	Konbu				$6.00	$2.25	24
14	Tofu			g pkgs.	$23.25	$15.80	35
15	Genen Shouyu	Mayumi's	Condiments	24 - 250 ml bottles	$15.50	$9.00	39
16	Pavlov	Pavlova, Ltd.	Confections	32 - 500 g boxes	$17.45	$9.00	29
17	Alice M	Pavlova, Ltd.	Meat/Poultry	20 - 1 kg tins	$39.00	$22.50	0
18	Carnar	Pavlova, Ltd.	Seafood	16 kg pkg.	$62.50	$45.90	42
19	Teatime Chocolate Biscuits	Specialty Biscuits, Ltd.	Confections	10 boxes x 12 pieces	$9.20	$1.87	25
20	Sir Rodney's Marmalade	Specialty Biscuits, Ltd.	Confections	30 gift boxes	$81.00	$43.00	40
21	Sir Rodney's Scones	Specialty Biscuits, Ltd.	Confections	24 pkgs. x 4 pieces	$10.00	$4.00	3
22	Gustaf's Knäckebröd	PB Knäckebröd AB	Grains/Cereals	24 - 500 g pkgs.	$21.00	$11.00	104
23	Tunnbröd	PB Knäckebröd AB	Grains/Cereals	12 - 250 g pkgs.	$9.00	$3.00	61
24	Guaraná Fantástica	Refrescos Americanas LTDA	Beverages	12 - 355 ml cans	$4.50	$2.00	20
25	NuNuCa Nuß-Nougat-Creme	Heli Süßwaren GmbH & Co. KG	Confections	20 - 450 g glasses	$14.00	$7.90	76
26	Gumbär Gummibärchen	Heli Süßwaren GmbH & Co. KG	Confections	100 - 250 g bags	$31.23	$18.00	15
27	Schoggi Schokolade	Heli Süßwaren GmbH & Co. KG	Confections	100 - 100 g pieces	$43.90	$28.80	49

FIGURE 1.34 Deleting Data

a. Click the **Forms group** in the Navigation Pane to collapse it. Expand the **Tables group**.

b. Double-click the **Products table** to open it.

c. Click **Last record** in the navigation bar.

The Pecan Pie record you entered in the Products form is listed as the last record in the Products table. The Products form was created from the Products table. Your newly created record, Pecan Pie, is stored in the Products table even though you added it using the form.

d. Navigate to the fifth record in the table, Chef Anton's Gumbo Mix.

e. Use the horizontal scroll bar to scroll right until you see the Discontinued field.

The check mark in the Discontinued check box tells you that this product has been discontinued.

f. Click the **record selector** to the left of the fifth record.

   A border surrounds the record and the record is shaded, indicating it is selected.

g. Click **Delete** in the Records group and read the error message.

   The error message that displays tells you that you cannot delete this record because the table 'Order Details' has related records. (Customers ordered this product in the past.) Even though the product is now discontinued and no stock remains, it cannot be deleted from the Products table because related records exist in the Order Details table.

h. Click **OK**.

i. Navigate to the last record and click the **record selector** to highlight the entire row.

   The Pecan Pie record you added earlier is displayed.

j. Click **Delete** in the Records group. Read the warning.

   The warning box that displays tells you that this action cannot be undone. Although this product can be deleted because it was just entered and no orders were created for it, you do not want to delete the record.

k. Click **No**. You do not want to delete this record. Close the Products table.

TROUBLESHOOTING: If you clicked Yes and deleted the record, return to Step 4d. Re-open the form and re-enter the information for this record. This will be important later in this lesson.

STEP 6 » USE DATABASE UTILITIES

You will protect the Northwind database by using the Back Up Database utility. Refer to Figure 1.35 as you complete Step 6.

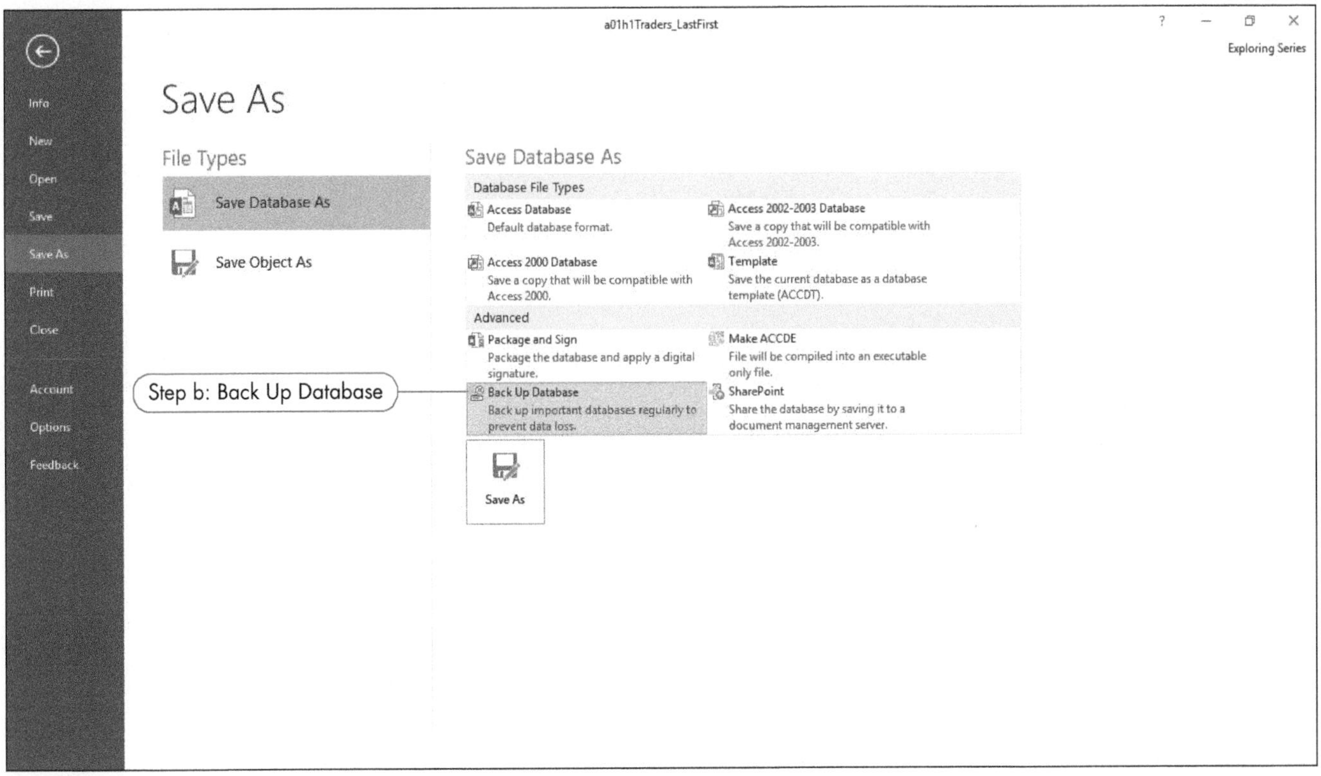

FIGURE 1.35 Backing Up a Database

a. Click the **File tab** and click **Save As**.

b. Double-click **Back Up Database** under the Advanced section to open the Save As dialog box.

   The backup utility assigns the default name by adding a date to your file name.

c. Verify that the Save in folder displays the location where you want your file saved and click **Save**.

   You just created a backup of the database after completing Hands-On Exercise 1. The original database file remains onscreen.

d. Keep the database open if you plan to continue with Hands-On Exercise 2. If not, close the database and exit Access.

Filters and Sorts

Access provides you with many tools that you can use to change the order of information and to identify and extract only the data needed at the moment. You may want to find specific information, such as which suppliers are located in Denton, TX, or which customers have placed orders in the last seven days. There may be other times you simply want to sort information rather than extract information.

In this section, you will learn how to sort information and to isolate records in a table based on criteria.

Working with Filters

Suppose you wanted to see a list of the products in the Confections category in the Northwind database. To obtain this list, you would open the Products table in Datasheet view and create a filter. A ***filter*** allows you to specify conditions to display only those records that meet those conditions. These conditions are known as criteria (or criterion, singular), and are a number, a text phrase, or an expression (such as >50) used to select records from a table. Therefore, to view a list of all Confections, you would filter the Products table, displaying only records with a Category value of Confections. In this case, Category being equal to Confections is the criterion.

You can use filters to analyze data quickly. Applying a filter does not delete any records; filters only hide records that do not match the criteria. Two types of filters are discussed in this section: Selection filter and Filter By Form.

Use a Selection Filter to Find Exact Matches

STEP 1 »» A ***Selection filter*** displays only the records that match a criterion you select. You can use a Selection filter to find records that equal a criterion. For example, if you filter a name field and you select "equals Eric", you would only find customers who have a name of Eric (but not any other variation). Selection filters are not case sensitive, so any variation of capitalization (ERIC, eric) would also appear in the search results.

To use a Selection filter to find an exact match, complete the following steps:

1. Click in any field that contains the criterion on which you want to filter.
2. Click Selection in the Sort & Filter group on the Home tab.
3. Select Equals "criterion" from the list of options (*criterion* will be replaced by the value of the field).

Figure 1.36 displays a Customers table with 91 records. The records in the table are displayed in sequence according to the CustomerID. The navigation bar at the bottom indicates that the active record is the second row in the table. Owner in the Job Title field is selected.

Selection filter options

Equals "Owner"

Does Not Equal "Owner"

Contains "Owner"

Does Not Contain "Owner"

Customer ID	Company Name	Contact Name	Contact Title	Address	City	Countr
ALFKI	Alfreds Futterkiste	Maria Anders	Sales Representative	Obere Str. 57	Berlin	Germa
ANATR	Ana Trujillo Emparedados y helados	Ana Trujillo	Owner	Avda. de la Constitución 2222	México D.F.	Mexico
ANTON	Antonio Moreno Taquería	Antonio Moreno	Owner	Mataderos 2312	México D.F.	Mexico
AROUT	Around the Horn	Eric Cameron	Sales Representative	120 Hanover Sq.	London	UK
BERGS	Berglund snabbköp	Christina Berglund	Order Administrator	Berguvsvägen 8	Luleå	Swede
BLAUS	Blauer See Delikatessen	Hanna Moos	Sales Representative	Forsterstr. 57	Mannheim	Germa
BLONP	Blondel père et fils	Frédérique Citeaux	Marketing Manager	24, place Kléber	Strasbourg	France
BOLID	Bólido Comidas preparadas	Martín Sommer	Owner	C/ Araquil, 67	Madrid	Spain
BONAP	Bon app'	Laurence Lebihan	Owner	12, rue des Bouchers	Marseille	France
BOTTM	Bottom-Dollar Markets	Elizabeth Lincoln	Accounting Manager	23 Tsawassen Blvd.	Tsawassen	Canada
BSBEV	B's Beverages	Victoria Ashworth	Sales Representative Trainee	Fauntleroy Circus	London	UK
CACTU	Cactus Comidas para llevar	Patricio Simpson	Sales Agent	Cerrito 333	Buenos Aires	Argent
CENTC	Centro comercial Moctezuma	Francisco Chang	Marketing Manager	Sierras de Granada 9993	México D.F.	Mexico
CHOPS	Chop-suey Chinese	Yang Wang	Owner	Hauptstr. 29	Bern	Switzer
COMMI	Comércio Mineiro	Pedro Afonso	Sales Associate	Av. dos Lusíadas, 23	São Paulo	Brazil
CONSH	Consolidated Holdings	Elizabeth Brown	Sales Representative	Berkeley Gardens	London	UK
DRACD	Drachenblut Delikatessen	Sven Ottlieb	Order Administrator	Walserweg 21	Aachen	Germa
DUMON	Du monde entier	Janine Labrune	Owner	67, rue des Cinquante Otages	Nantes	France
EASTC	Eastern Connection	Ann Devon	Sales Agent	35 King George	London	UK
ERNSH	Ernst Handel	Roland Mendel	Sales Manager	Kirchgasse 6	Graz	Austria
FAMIA	Familia Arquibald[illegible]	[illegible]	Marketing Assistant	Rua Orós, 92	São Paulo	Brazil
FISSA	FISSA Fabrica Inter[illegible]	[illegible]	Accounting Manager	C/ Moralzarzal, 86	Madrid	Spain
FOLIG	Folies gourmandes	Martine Rancé	Assistant Sales Agent	184, chaussée de Tournai	Lille	France
FOLKO	Folk och fä HB	Maria Larsson	Owner	Åkergatan 24	Bräcke	Swede
FRANK	Frankenversand	Peter Franken	Marketing Manager	Berliner Platz 43	München	Germa
FRANR	France restauration	Carine Schmitt	Marketing Manager	54, rue Royale	Nantes	France

Record: 2 of 91 Unfiltered

91 records shown

Access 2016, Windows 10, Microsoft Corporation

FIGURE 1.36 Unfiltered Customers Table

Figure 1.37 displays a filtered view of the Customers table, showing records with the job title Owner. The navigation bar shows that this is a filtered list containing 17 records matching the criterion. The Customers table still contains the original 91 records, but only 17 records are visible with the filter applied.

Toggle Filter

Customer ID	Company Name	Contact Name	Contact Title	Address	City	Country
ANATR	Ana Trujillo Emparedados y helados	Ana Trujillo	Owner	Avda. de la Constitución 2222	México D.F.	Mexico
ANTON	Antonio Moreno Taquería	Antonio Moreno	Owner	Mataderos 2312	México D.F.	Mexico
BOLID	Bólido Comidas preparadas	Martín Sommer	Owner	C/ Araquil, 67	Madrid	Spain
BONAP	Bon app'	Laurence Lebihan	Owner	12, rue des Bouchers	Marseille	France
CHOPS	Chop-suey Chinese	Yang Wang	Owner	Hauptstr. 29	Bern	Switzerla
DUMON	Du monde entier	Janine Labrune	Owner	67, rue des Cinquante Otages	Nantes	France
FOLKO	Folk och fä HB	Maria Larsson	Owner	Åkergatan 24	Bräcke	Sweden
GROSR	GROSELLA-Restaurante	Manuel Pereira	Owner	5ª Ave. Los Palos Grandes	Caracas	Venezuel
LETSS	Let's Stop N Shop	Jaime Yorres	Owner	87 Polk St.	San Francisco	USA
LINOD	LINO-Delicateses	Felipe Izquierdo	Owner	Ave. 5 de Mayo Porlamar	I. de Margarita	Venezuel
OTTIK	Ottilies Käseladen	Henriette Pfalzheim	Owner	Mehrheimerstr. 369	Köln	Germany
PARIS	Paris spécialités	Marie Bertrand	Owner	265, boulevard Charonne	Paris	France
SANTG	Santé Gourmet	Jonas Bergulfsen	Owner	Erling Skakkes gate 78	Stavern	Norway
SIMOB	Simons bistro	Jytte Petersen	Owner	Vinbæltet 34	København	Denmark
TORTU	Tortuga Restaurante	Miguel Angel Paolino	Owner	Avda. Azteca 123	México D.F.	Mexico
WHITC	White Clover Markets	Karl Jablonski	Owner	305 - 14th Ave. S.	Seattle	USA
WOLZA	Wolski Zajazd	Zbyszek Piestrzeniewicz	Owner	ul. Filtrowa 68	Warszawa	Poland

Job titles are all Owner

17 records shown

Record: 1 of 17 Filtered

Access 2016, Windows 10, Microsoft Corporation

FIGURE 1.37 Filtered Customers Table

You can click Toggle Filter (refer to Figure 1.37) at any time to remove all filters and display all the records in the table. Filters are a temporary method for examining table data. If you close the filtered table and reopen it, the filter will be removed and all of the records will be visible again. You can at any point click Toggle Filter to display the results of the last saved filter.

Use a Selection Filter to Find Records Containing a Value

You can also use a Selection filter to find records that contain a criterion. For example, if you filter a name field and you select "contains Eric", it would find Eric, as well as names containing Eric (such as Erica, Erich, Erick, and even Broderick, Frederick, and Frederica). As with the exact match, this is not case sensitive, as shown in the results in Figure 1.38.

Customer ID	Company Name	Contact Name	Contact Title	Address	City	Country	Region	Postal Code
ANATR	Ana Trujillo Emparedados y helados	Erich Trujillo	Owner	Avda. de la Constitución 2222	México D.F.	Mexico		05021
AROUT	Around the Horn	Eric Cameron	Sales Representative	120 Hanover Sq.	London	UK		WA1 1DP
BOTTM	Bottom-Dollar Markets	Elizabeth Erickson	Accounting Manager	23 Tsawassen Blvd.	Tsawassen	Canada	BC	T2F 8M4
COMMI	Comércio Mineiro	Broderick Afonso	Sales Associate	Av. dos Lusíadas, 23	São Paulo	Brazil	SP	05432-043

Record contains Eric

Record matches Eric

FIGURE 1.38 Finding Records Containing a Value

> **To use a Selection filter to find all values containing certain text, complete the following steps:**
>
> 1. Click in any field that contains the criterion on which you want to filter.
> 2. Click Selection in the Sort & Filter group on the Home tab.
> 3. Select Contains "criterion" from the list of options (*criterion* will be replaced by the value of the field).

Your results will show all records containing a partial or full match.

Use Filter By Form

Filter By Form is a more versatile method of selecting data because it enables you to display records based on multiple criteria. When you use Filter By Form, all of the records are hidden and Access creates a blank form in a design grid. You see only field names with an arrow in the first field. Figure 1.39 shows Filter By Form in Datasheet view, and Figure 1.40 shows Filter By Form in a form view.

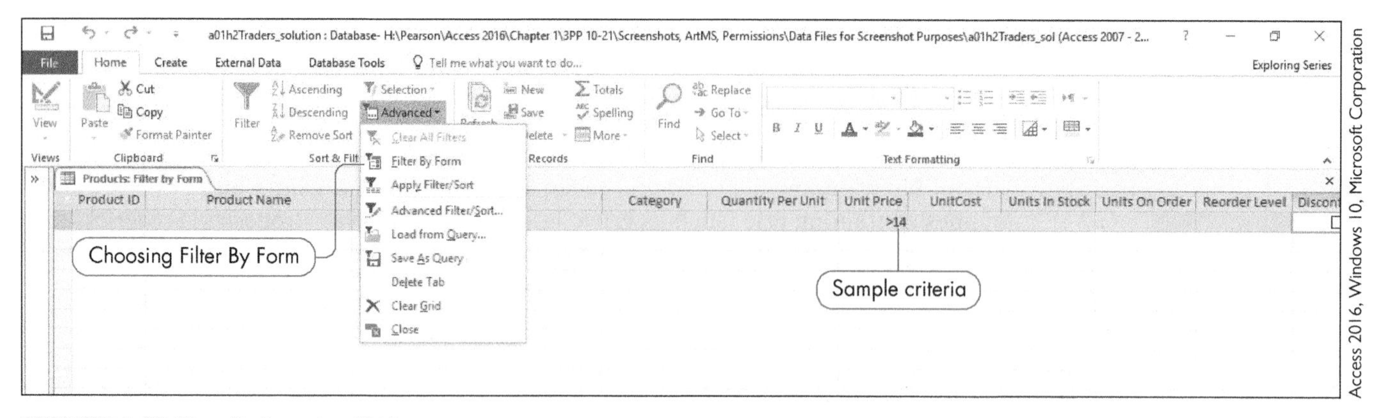

FIGURE 1.39 Filter By Form in a Table

FIGURE 1.40 Filter By Form in a Form

An advantage of using this filter method is that you can specify AND and OR logical operators. If you use the AND operator, a record is included in the results if all the criteria are true. If you use the OR operator, a record is included if at least one criterion is true. Another advantage of Filter By Form is that you can use a comparison operator such as equal (=), not equal (<>), greater than (>), less than (<), greater than or equal to (>=), and less than or equal to (<=).

To use Filter By Form, complete the following steps:

1. Click Advanced in the Sort & Filter group on the Home tab.
2. Click Filter By Form.
3. Click in the field you want to use as a criterion. Click the arrow to select the criterion from existing data.
4. Add additional criterion and comparison operators as required.
5. Click Toggle Filter in the Sort & Filter group on the Home tab to apply the filter.

Performing Sorts

You can change the order of information by sorting one or more fields. A ***sort*** lists records in a specific sequence, such as alphabetically by last name or by ascending EmployeeID.

Sort Table Data

STEP 4 »» Ascending sorts a list of text data in alphabetical order or a numeric list in lowest to highest order. Descending sorts a list of text data in reverse alphabetical order or a numeric list in highest to lowest order. You can equate this to these terms outside of a database. When you are coming down from a high place (such as the top of a ladder), you are said to be descending, and when you are climbing a ladder, you are ascending. Figure 1.41 shows the Customers table sorted in ascending order by city name.

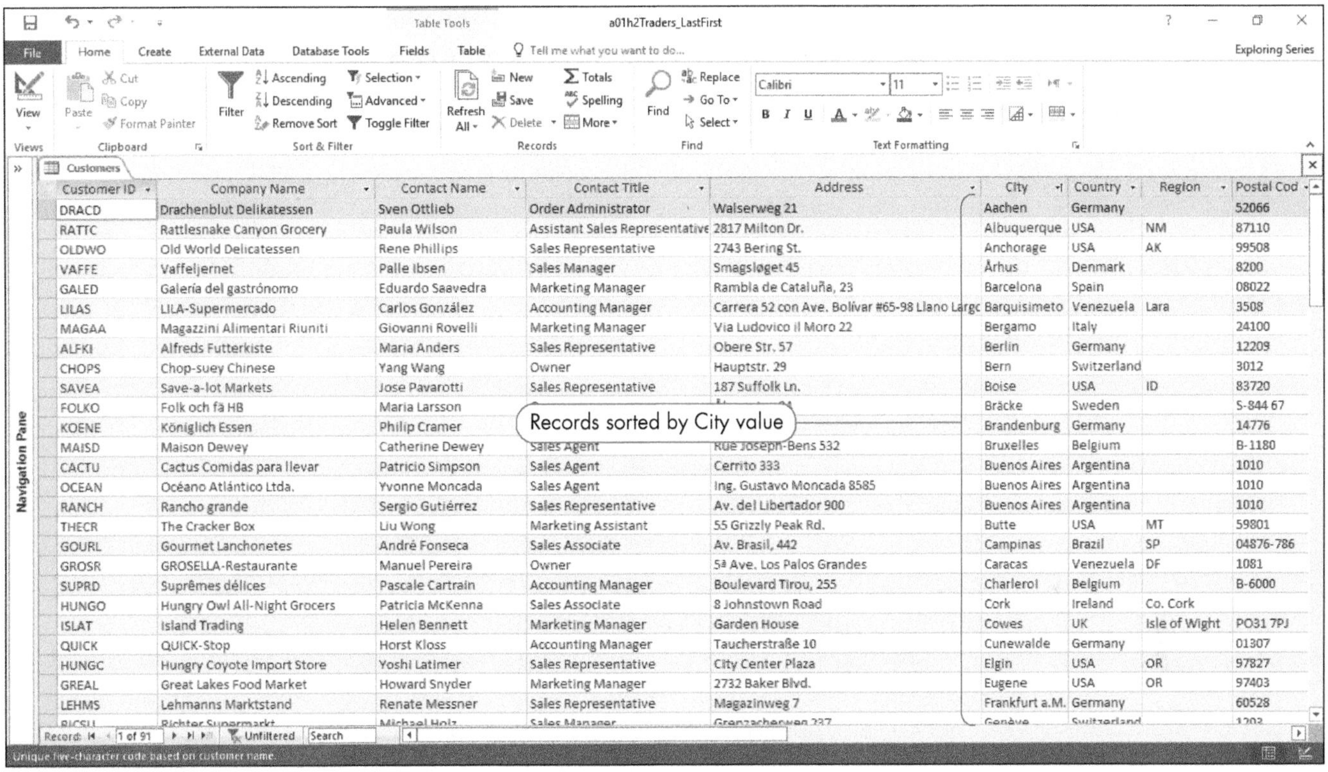

Customer ID	Company Name	Contact Name	Contact Title	Address	City	Country	Region	Postal Cod
DRACD	Drachenblut Delikatessen	Sven Ottlieb	Order Administrator	Walserweg 21	Aachen	Germany		52066
RATTC	Rattlesnake Canyon Grocery	Paula Wilson	Assistant Sales Representative	2817 Milton Dr.	Albuquerque	USA	NM	87110
OLDWO	Old World Delicatessen	Rene Phillips	Sales Representative	2743 Bering St.	Anchorage	USA	AK	99508
VAFFE	Vaffeljernet	Palle Ibsen	Sales Manager	Smagsløget 45	Århus	Denmark		8200
GALED	Galería del gastrónomo	Eduardo Saavedra	Marketing Manager	Rambla de Cataluña, 23	Barcelona	Spain		08022
LILAS	LILA-Supermercado	Carlos González	Accounting Manager	Carrera 52 con Ave. Bolívar #65-98 Llano Larg	Barquisimeto	Venezuela	Lara	3508
MAGAA	Magazzini Alimentari Riuniti	Giovanni Rovelli	Marketing Manager	Via Ludovico il Moro 22	Bergamo	Italy		24100
ALFKI	Alfreds Futterkiste	Maria Anders	Sales Representative	Obere Str. 57	Berlin	Germany		12209
CHOPS	Chop-suey Chinese	Yang Wang	Owner	Hauptstr. 29	Bern	Switzerland		3012
SAVEA	Save-a-lot Markets	Jose Pavarotti	Sales Representative	187 Suffolk Ln.	Boise	USA	ID	83720
FOLKO	Folk och fä HB	Maria Larsson			Bräcke	Sweden		S-844 67
KOENE	Königlich Essen	Philip Cramer			Brandenburg	Germany		14776
MAISD	Maison Dewey	Catherine Dewey	Sales Agent	Rue Joseph-Bens 532	Bruxelles	Belgium		B-1180
CACTU	Cactus Comidas para llevar	Patricio Simpson	Sales Agent	Cerrito 333	Buenos Aires	Argentina		1010
OCEAN	Océano Atlántico Ltda.	Yvonne Moncada	Sales Agent	Ing. Gustavo Moncada 8585	Buenos Aires	Argentina		1010
RANCH	Rancho grande	Sergio Gutiérrez	Sales Representative	Av. del Libertador 900	Buenos Aires	Argentina		1010
THECR	The Cracker Box	Liu Wong	Marketing Assistant	55 Grizzly Peak Rd.	Butte	USA	MT	59801
GOURL	Gourmet Lanchonetes	André Fonseca	Sales Associate	Av. Brasil, 442	Campinas	Brazil	SP	04876-786
GROSR	GROSELLA-Restaurante	Manuel Pereira	Owner	5ª Ave. Los Palos Grandes	Caracas	Venezuela	DF	1081
SUPRD	Suprêmes délices	Pascale Cartrain	Accounting Manager	Boulevard Tirou, 255	Charleroi	Belgium		B-6000
HUNGO	Hungry Owl All-Night Grocers	Patricia McKenna	Sales Associate	8 Johnstown Road	Cork	Ireland	Co. Cork	
ISLAT	Island Trading	Helen Bennett	Marketing Manager	Garden House	Cowes	UK	Isle of Wight	PO31 7PJ
QUICK	QUICK-Stop	Horst Kloss	Accounting Manager	Taucherstraße 10	Cunewalde	Germany		01307
HUNGC	Hungry Coyote Import Store	Yoshi Latimer	Sales Representative	City Center Plaza	Elgin	USA	OR	97827
GREAL	Great Lakes Food Market	Howard Snyder	Marketing Manager	2732 Baker Blvd.	Eugene	USA	OR	97403
LEHMS	Lehmanns Marktstand	Renate Messner	Sales Representative	Magazinweg 7	Frankfurt a.M.	Germany		60528

Records sorted by City value

Access 2016, Windows 10, Microsoft Corporation

FIGURE 1.41 Sorted Customers Table

To sort a table on one criterion, complete the following steps:

1. Click in the field that you want to use to sort the records.
2. Click Ascending or Descending in the Sort & Filter group on the Home tab.

Access can sort records by more than one field. When sorting by multiple criteria, Access first sorts by the field located on the left. It is important to understand that in order to sort by multiple fields, you must arrange your columns in this order. This may lead to moving a field to the left so it is sorted first.

To move a field, complete the following steps:

1. Click the column heading and hold down the left mouse button. A thick line appears to the left of the column.
2. Drag the field to the appropriate position.

Once the column has been moved, you can perform a sort by selecting the field to the left, sorting, and then doing the same for the secondary sort column.

5. What is the purpose of creating a filter? *p. 695*
6. What is the difference between a Selection filter and a Filter By Form? *pp. 695, 697*
7. What is a comparison operator and how is it used in a filter? *p. 698*
8. What are the benefits of sorting records in a table? *p. 699*

Hands-On Exercises

Watch the Video
for this Hands-On
Exercise!

MyITLab®
HOE2 Training

Skills covered: Use a Selection Filter to Find Exact Matches • Use a Selection Filter to Find Records Containing a Value • Use Filter By Form • Sort Table Data

2 Filters and Sorts

The sales manager at Northwind Traders wants quick answers to her questions about customer orders. You use the Access database to filter tables to answer these questions, then sort the records based on the manager's requirements.

STEP 1 » USE A SELECTION FILTER TO FIND EXACT MATCHES

The sales manager asks for a list of customers who live in London. You use a Selection filter with an equal condition to locate these customers. Refer to Figure 1.42 as you complete Step 1.

Table Tools a01h2Traders_LastFirst

File Home Create External Data Database Tools Fields Table Tell me what you want to do... Exploring Series

View | Paste | Cut | Copy | Format Painter | Filter | Ascending | Descending | Remove Sort | Selection | New | Totals | Spelling | More | Find | Replace | Go To | Select | Calibri | 11

Views | Clipboard | Sort & Filter | Find | Text Formatting

Selection menu: Equals "London" / Does Not Equal "London" / Contains "London" / Does Not Contain "London"

Step e: Choose an equals condition

Customers — Navigation Pane

Customer I	Company Name	Contact Name	Contact Title	Address	City	Country	Region	Postal Cod
ALFKI	Alfreds Futterkiste	Maria Anders	Sales Representative	Obere Str. 57	Berlin	Germany		12209
ANATR	Ana Trujillo Emparedados y helados	Ana Trujillo	Owner	Avda. de la Constitución 2222	México D.F.	Mexico		05021
ANTON	Antonio Moreno Taquería	Antonio Moreno	Owner	Mataderos 2312	México D.F.	Mexico		05023
AROUT	Around the Horn	Eric Cameron	Sales Representative	120 Hanover Sq.	London	UK		WA1 1DP
BERGS	Berglund snabbköp	Christina Berglund	Order Administrator	Berguvsvägen 8	Luleå	Sweden		S-958 22
BLAUS	Blauer See Delikatessen	Hanna Moos	Sales Representative	Forsterstr. 57	Mannheim	Germany		68306
BLONP	Blondel père et fils	Frédérique Citeaux	Marketing Manager	24, place Kléber	Strasbourg	France		67000
BOLID	Bólido Comidas preparadas	Martín Sommer	Owner	C/ Araquil, 67	Madrid	Spain		28023
BONAP	Bon app'	Laurence Lebihan	Owner	12, rue des Bouchers	Marseille	France		13008
BOTTM	Bottom-Dollar Markets	Elizabeth Lincoln	Accounting Manager	23 Tsawassen Blvd.	Tsawassen	Canada	BC	T2F 8M4
BSBEV	B's Beverages	Victoria Ashworth	Sales Representative Trainee	Fauntleroy Circus	London	UK		EC2 5NT
CACTU	Cactus Comidas para llevar	Patricio Simpson	Sales Agent	Cerrito 333	Buenos Aires	Argentina		1010
CENTC	Centro comercial Moctezuma	Francisco Chang	Marketing Manager	Sierras de Granada 9993	México D.F.	Mexico		05022
CHOPS	Chop-suey Chinese	Yang Wang	Owner	Hauptstr. 29	Bern	Switzerland		3012
COMMI	Comércio Mineiro	Pedro Afonso	Sales Associate	Av. dos Lusíadas, 23	São Paulo	Brazil	SP	05432-043
CONSH	Consolidated Holdings	Elizabeth Brown	Sales Representative	Berkeley Gardens	London	UK		WX1 6LT
DRACD	Drachenblut Delikatessen	Sven Ottlieb	Order Administrator	Walserweg 21	Aachen	Germany		52066
DUMON	Du monde entier	Janine Labrune	Owner	67, rue des Cinquante Otages	Nantes	France		44000
EASTC	Eastern Connection	Ann Devon	Sales Agent	35 King George	London	UK		WX3 6FW
ERNSH	Ernst Handel	Roland Mendel	Sales Manager	Kirchgasse 6	Graz	Austria		8010
FAMIA	Familia Arquibaldo	Aria Cruz	Marketing Assistant	Rua Orós, 92	São Paulo	Brazil	SP	05442-030
FISSA	FISSA Fabrica Inter. Salchichas S.A.	Diego Roel	Accounting Manager	C/ Moralzarzal, 86	Madrid	Spain		28034
FOLIG	Folies gourmandes	Martine Rancé	Assistant Sales Agent	184, chaussée de Tournai	Lille	France		59000
FOLKO	Folk och fä HB	Maria Larsson	Owner	Åkergatan 24	Bräcke	Sweden		S-844 67
FRANK	Frankenversand	Peter Franken	Marketing Manager	Berliner Platz 43	München	Germany		80805
FRANR	France restauration	Carine Schmitt	Marketing Manager	54, rue Royale	Nantes	France		44000
FRANS	Franchi S.p.A.	Paolo Accorti	Sales Representative	Via Monte Bianco 34	Torino	Italy		10100

Record: 4 of 91 Unfiltered Search

Datasheet View

FIGURE 1.42 Filtering the Customers Table

a. Open the *a01h1Traders_LastFirst* database if you closed it after the last Hands-On Exercise and save it as **a01h2Traders_LastFirst**, changing h1 to h2. Click **Enable Content**.

b. Double-click the **Customers table** in the Navigation Pane, navigate to record 4, and then replace Thomas Hardy with your name in the Contact Name field.

c. Scroll right until the City field is visible. The fourth record has a value of London in the City field. Click the field to select it.

d. Click **Selection** in the Sort & Filter group on the Home tab.

e. Select **Equals "London"** from the menu. Six records are displayed.

The navigation bar display shows that six records that meet the London criterion are available. The other records in the Customers table are hidden. The Filtered icon also displays on the navigation bar and column heading, indicating that the Customers table has been filtered.

f. Click **Toggle Filter** in the Sort & Filter group to remove the filter.

g. Click **Toggle Filter** again to reset the filter.

STEP 2 » USE A SELECTION FILTER TO FIND RECORDS CONTAINING A VALUE

The sales manager asks you to narrow the list of London customers so that it displays only Sales Representatives. To accomplish this task, you add a second layer of filtering using a Selection filter. Refer to Figure 1.43 as you complete Step 2.

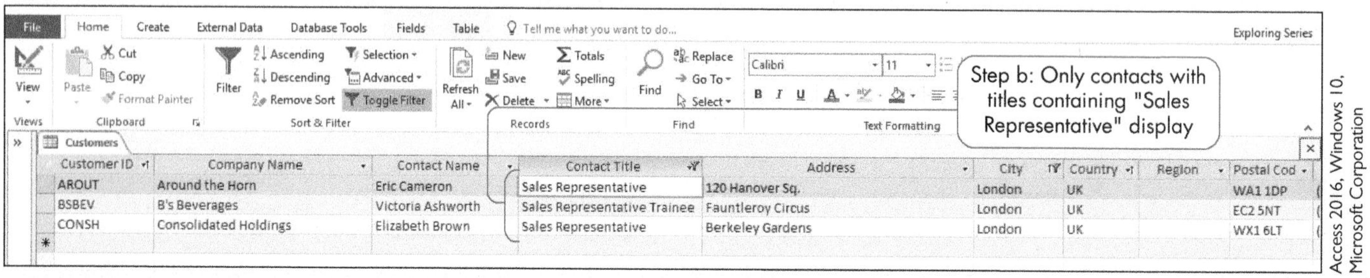

Step b: Only contacts with titles containing "Sales Representative" display

Customer ID	Company Name	Contact Name	Contact Title	Address	City	Country	Region	Postal Cod
AROUT	Around the Horn	Eric Cameron	Sales Representative	120 Hanover Sq.	London	UK		WA1 1DP
BSBEV	B's Beverages	Victoria Ashworth	Sales Representative Trainee	Fauntleroy Circus	London	UK		EC2 5NT
CONSH	Consolidated Holdings	Elizabeth Brown	Sales Representative	Berkeley Gardens	London	UK		WX1 6LT

Access 2016, Windows 10, Microsoft Corporation

FIGURE 1.43 Filtered Customers

a. Click in any field value in the Contact Title field that contains the value **Sales Representative**.

b. Click **Selection** in the Sort & Filter group, click **Contains "Sales Representative"**, and compare your results to those shown in Figure 1.43.

Three records match the criteria you set. You have applied a second layer of filtering to the customers in London. The second layer further restricts the display to only those customers who have the words Sales Representative contained in their titles. Because you chose Contains as your filter, any representatives with the phrase Sales Representative appear. This includes Victoria Ashworth, who is a Sales Representative Trainee.

> **TROUBLESHOOTING:** If you do not see the record for Victoria Ashworth, you selected Equals "Sales Representative" instead of Contains "Sales Representative". Repeat Steps a and b, making sure you select Contains "Sales Representative".

c. Close the Customers table. Click **Yes** when prompted to save the design changes to the Customers table.

STEP 3 » USE FILTER BY FORM

You are asked to provide a list of records that do not match just one set of criteria. You will provide a list of all extended prices less than $50 for a specific sales representative. Use Filter By Form to provide the information when two or more criteria are necessary. You also preview the results in Print Preview to see how the list would print. Refer to Figure 1.44 as you complete Step 3.

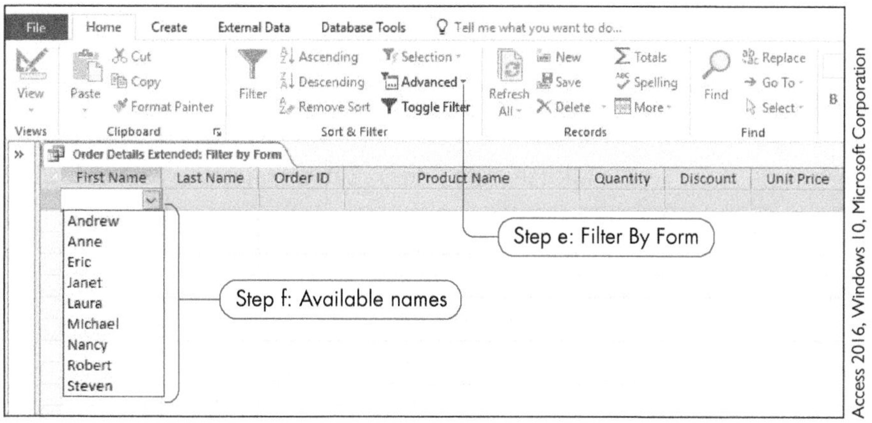

FIGURE 1.44 Using Filter By Form

a. Click the **Tables group** in the Navigation Pane to collapse the listed tables.

b. Click the **Queries group** in the Navigation Pane to expand the list of available queries.

c. Locate and double-click **Order Details Extended** to open it.

This query contains information about orders. It has fields containing information about the sales person, the Order ID, the product name, the unit price, quantity ordered, the discount given, and an extended price. The extended price is a field used to total order information.

d. Click **Advanced** in the Sort & Filter group and select **Filter By Form** from the list. The first field, First Name, is active by default.

All of the records are now hidden, and you see only field names and an arrow in the first field. Although you are applying Filter By Form to a query, you can use the same process as applying Filter By Form to a table. You are able to input more than one criterion using Filter By Form.

e. Click the **First Name arrow**.

A list of all available first names appears. Your name should be on the list. Figure 1.44 shows *Eric Cameron*, which replaced Margaret Peacock in Hands-On Exercise 1.

TROUBLESHOOTING: If you do not see your name and you do see Margaret on the list, you probably skipped steps in Hands-On Exercise 1. Close the query without saving changes, return to the first Hands-On Exercise, and then rework it, making sure not to omit any steps. Then you can return to this location and work the remainder of this Hands-On Exercise.

f. Select your first name from the list.

g. Click in the first row under the Last Name field to reveal the arrow. Locate and select your last name by clicking it.

h. Scroll right until you see the Extended Price field. Click in the first row under the Extended Price field and type **<50**.

This will select all of the items that you ordered where the total was less than 50.

i. Click **Toggle Filter** in the Sort & Filter group.

You have specified which records to include and have executed the filtering by clicking Toggle Filter.

j. Click the **File tab**, click **Print**, and then click **Print Preview**.

You instructed Access to preview the filtered query results. The preview displays the query title as a heading. The current filter is applied, as well as page numbers.

k. Click **Close Print Preview** in the Close Preview group.

l. Close the Order Details Extended query. Click **Yes** when prompted to save your changes.

STEP 4 » SORT TABLE DATA

The Sales Manager is pleased with your work; however, she would like some of the information to appear in a different order. You will now sort the records in the Customers table using the manager's new criteria. Refer to Figure 1.45 as you complete Step 4.

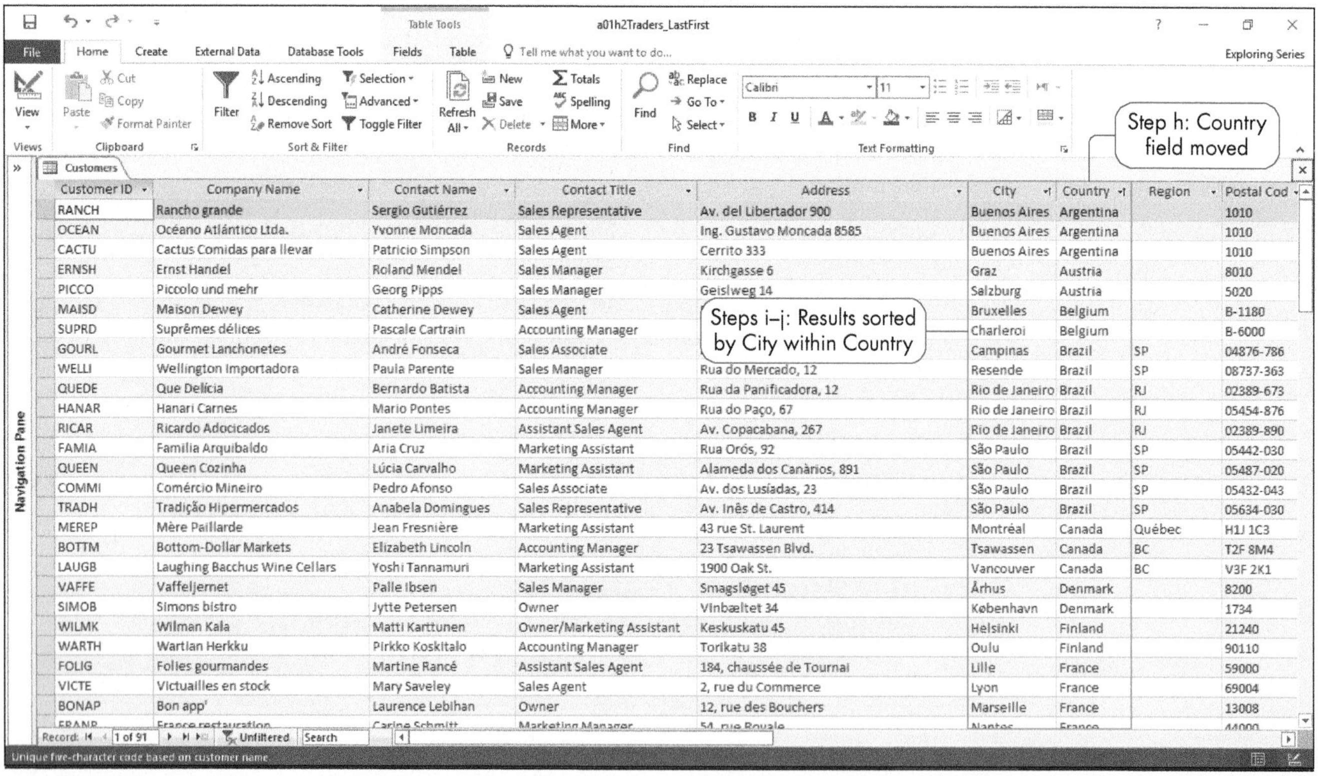

Customer ID	Company Name	Contact Name	Contact Title	Address	City	Country	Region	Postal Cod
RANCH	Rancho grande	Sergio Gutiérrez	Sales Representative	Av. del Libertador 900	Buenos Aires	Argentina		1010
OCEAN	Océano Atlántico Ltda.	Yvonne Moncada	Sales Agent	Ing. Gustavo Moncada 8585	Buenos Aires	Argentina		1010
CACTU	Cactus Comidas para llevar	Patricio Simpson	Sales Agent	Cerrito 333	Buenos Aires	Argentina		1010
ERNSH	Ernst Handel	Roland Mendel	Sales Manager	Kirchgasse 6	Graz	Austria		8010
PICCO	Piccolo und mehr	Georg Pipps	Sales Manager	Geislweg 14	Salzburg	Austria		5020
MAISD	Maison Dewey	Catherine Dewey	Sales Agent		Bruxelles	Belgium		B-1180
SUPRD	Suprêmes délices	Pascale Cartrain	Accounting Manager		Charleroi	Belgium		B-6000
GOURL	Gourmet Lanchonetes	André Fonseca	Sales Associate		Campinas	Brazil	SP	04876-786
WELLI	Wellington Importadora	Paula Parente	Sales Manager	Rua do Mercado, 12	Resende	Brazil	SP	08737-363
QUEDE	Que Delícia	Bernardo Batista	Accounting Manager	Rua da Panificadora, 12	Rio de Janeiro	Brazil	RJ	02389-673
HANAR	Hanari Carnes	Mario Pontes	Accounting Manager	Rua do Paço, 67	Rio de Janeiro	Brazil	RJ	05454-876
RICAR	Ricardo Adocicados	Janete Limeira	Assistant Sales Agent	Av. Copacabana, 267	Rio de Janeiro	Brazil	RJ	02389-890
FAMIA	Familia Arquibaldo	Aria Cruz	Marketing Assistant	Rua Orós, 92	São Paulo	Brazil	SP	05442-030
QUEEN	Queen Cozinha	Lúcia Carvalho	Marketing Assistant	Alameda dos Canàrios, 891	São Paulo	Brazil	SP	05487-020
COMMI	Comércio Mineiro	Pedro Afonso	Sales Associate	Av. dos Lusíadas, 23	São Paulo	Brazil	SP	05432-043
TRADH	Tradição Hipermercados	Anabela Domingues	Sales Representative	Av. Inês de Castro, 414	São Paulo	Brazil	SP	05634-030
MEREP	Mère Paillarde	Jean Fresnière	Marketing Assistant	43 rue St. Laurent	Montréal	Canada	Québec	H1J 1C3
BOTTM	Bottom-Dollar Markets	Elizabeth Lincoln	Accounting Manager	23 Tsawassen Blvd.	Tsawassen	Canada	BC	T2F 8M4
LAUGB	Laughing Bacchus Wine Cellars	Yoshi Tannamuri	Marketing Assistant	1900 Oak St.	Vancouver	Canada	BC	V3F 2K1
VAFFE	Vaffeljernet	Palle Ibsen	Sales Manager	Smagsløget 45	Århus	Denmark		8200
SIMOB	Simons bistro	Jytte Petersen	Owner	Vinbæltet 34	København	Denmark		1734
WILMK	Wilman Kala	Matti Karttunen	Owner/Marketing Assistant	Keskuskatu 45	Helsinki	Finland		21240
WARTH	Wartian Herkku	Pirkko Koskitalo	Accounting Manager	Torikatu 38	Oulu	Finland		90110
FOLIG	Folies gourmandes	Martine Rancé	Assistant Sales Agent	184, chaussée de Tournai	Lille	France		59000
VICTE	Victuailles en stock	Mary Saveley	Sales Agent	2, rue du Commerce	Lyon	France		69004
BONAP	Bon app'	Laurence Lebihan	Owner	12, rue des Bouchers	Marseille	France		13008

FIGURE 1.45 Updated Customers Table

a. Click the **Queries group** in the Navigation Pane to collapse the listed queries.

b. Click the **Tables group** in the Navigation Pane to expand the list of available tables and double-click the **Customers table** to open it.

This table contains information about customers. The table is sorted in alphabetical order by Company Name.

c. Click **Shutter Bar Open/Close** in the Navigation Pane to hide the Navigation Pane.

   It will be easier to locate fields in the Customer table if the Navigation Pane is hidden.

d. Click any entry in the Customer ID field. Click **Descending** in the Sort & Filter group on the Home tab.

   Sorting in descending order on a text field produces a reverse alphabetical order.

e. Scroll right until you can see both the Country and City fields.

f. Click the **Country column heading**.

   The entire field is selected.

g. Click the **Country column heading** again and hold down the **left mouse button**.

   A thick line displays on the left edge of the Country field.

h. Check to make sure that you see the thick line. Drag the **Country field** to the left until the thick line moves between the City and Region fields. Release the mouse button and the Country field position moves to the right of the City field.

   You moved the Country field next to the City field so that you can easily sort the table based on both fields.

i. Click any city name in the City field and click **Ascending** in the Sort & Filter group.

   The City field displays the cities in alphabetical order.

j. Click any country name in the Country field and click **Ascending**.

   The countries are sorted in alphabetical order. The cities within each country also are sorted alphabetically. For example, the customer in Graz, Austria, is listed before the customer in Salzburg, Austria.

k. Close the Customers table. Click **Yes** to save the changes to the design of the table.

l. Click **Shutter Bar Open/Close** in the Navigation Pane to show the Navigation Pane.

STEP 5 » VIEW RELATIONSHIPS

To further familiarize yourself with the database, you examine the connections between the tables in the Northwind database. Refer to Figure 1.46 as you complete Step 5.

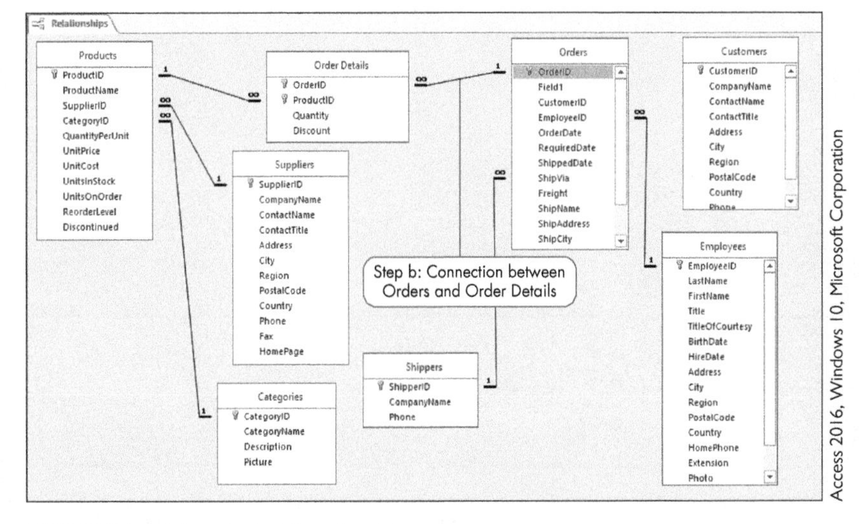

FIGURE 1.46 Northwind Relationships

a. Click the **Database Tools tab** and click **Relationships** in the Relationships group.

b. Examine the join lines showing the relationships that connect the various tables. For example, the Orders table is connected to the Order Details table using the OrderID field as the common field.

c. Close the Relationships.

d. Close the database. You will submit this file to your instructor at the end of the last Hands-On Exercise.

Access Database Creation

Now that you have examined the fundamentals of an Access database and explored the power of databases, it is time to create one! In this section, you explore the benefits of creating a database using each of the methods discussed in the next section.

Creating a Database

When you first start Access, Backstage view opens and provides you with three methods for creating a new database. These methods are:

- Create a blank desktop database
- Create a database from a template (note: there will be many templates shown)
- Create a custom web app

Creating a blank desktop database lets you create a database specific to your requirements. Rather than starting from scratch by creating a blank desktop database, you may want to use a template to create a new database. An Access ***template*** is a predefined database that includes professionally designed tables, forms, reports, and other objects that you can use to jumpstart the creation of your database. Creating a ***custom web app*** enables you to create a database that you can build and then use and share with others through the Web.

Figure 1.47 shows the options for creating a custom web app, a blank desktop database, and multiple templates from which you can select the method for which you want to create a database.

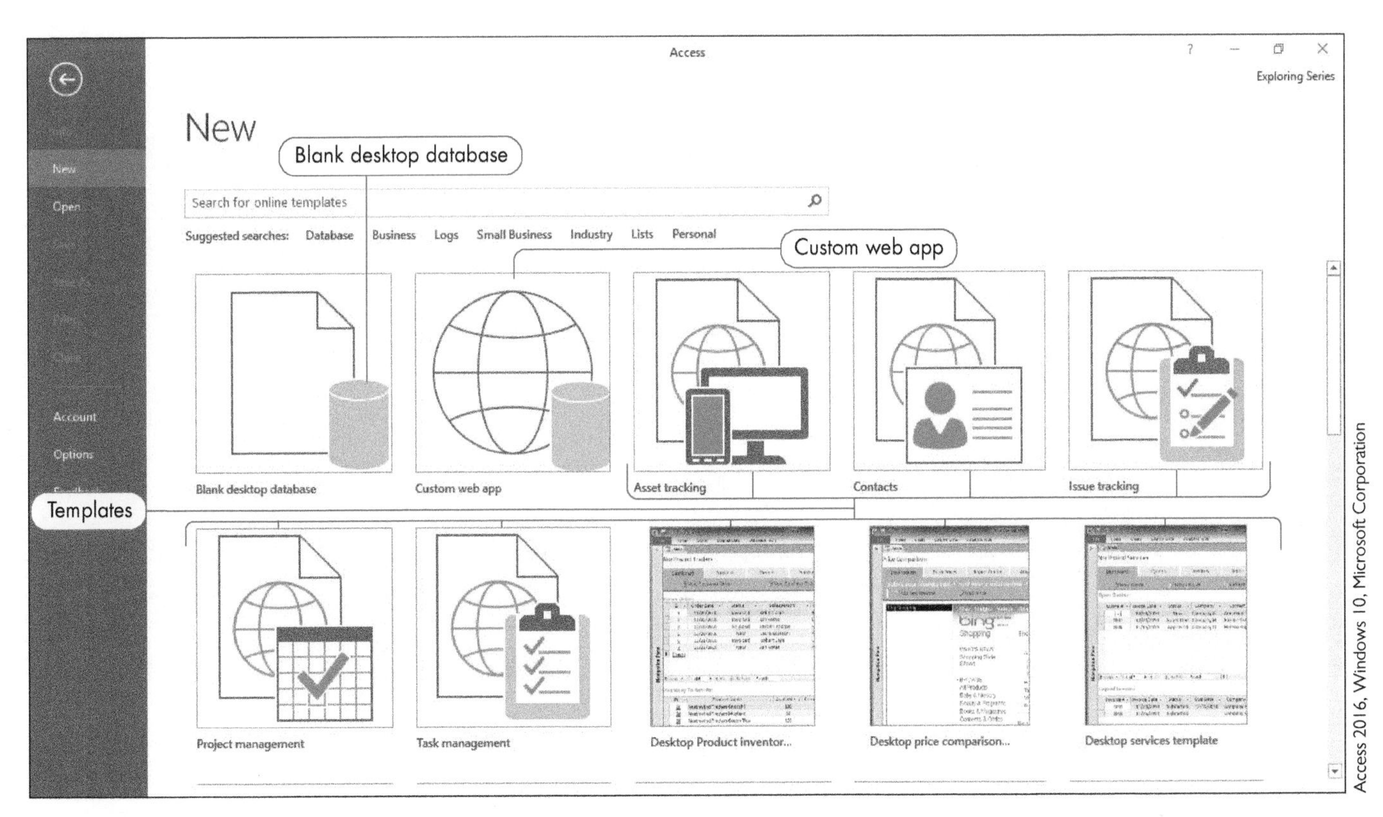

FIGURE 1.47 Options for Creating a New Database

Create a Blank Desktop Database

Often, if you are migrating from Excel to Access, you would start by creating a blank desktop database. At that point, you could import your existing structure and data into a new table. Another time you might use a blank desktop database is when you are starting a project and want to design your own tables.

When you create a blank desktop database, Access opens to a blank table in Datasheet view where you can add fields or data. You can also refine the table in Design view. You would then create additional tables and objects as necessary. Obviously, this task requires some level of Access knowledge, so unless you have requirements to follow, you may be better served using a template.

To create a blank desktop database, complete the following steps:

1. Open Access. (If Access is already open, click the File tab to open Backstage view and click New.)
2. Click the Blank desktop database tile.
3. Type the file name for the file in the text box, click Browse to navigate to the folder where you want to store the database file, and then click OK.
4. Click Create (see Figure 1.48).
5. Type data in the empty table that displays.

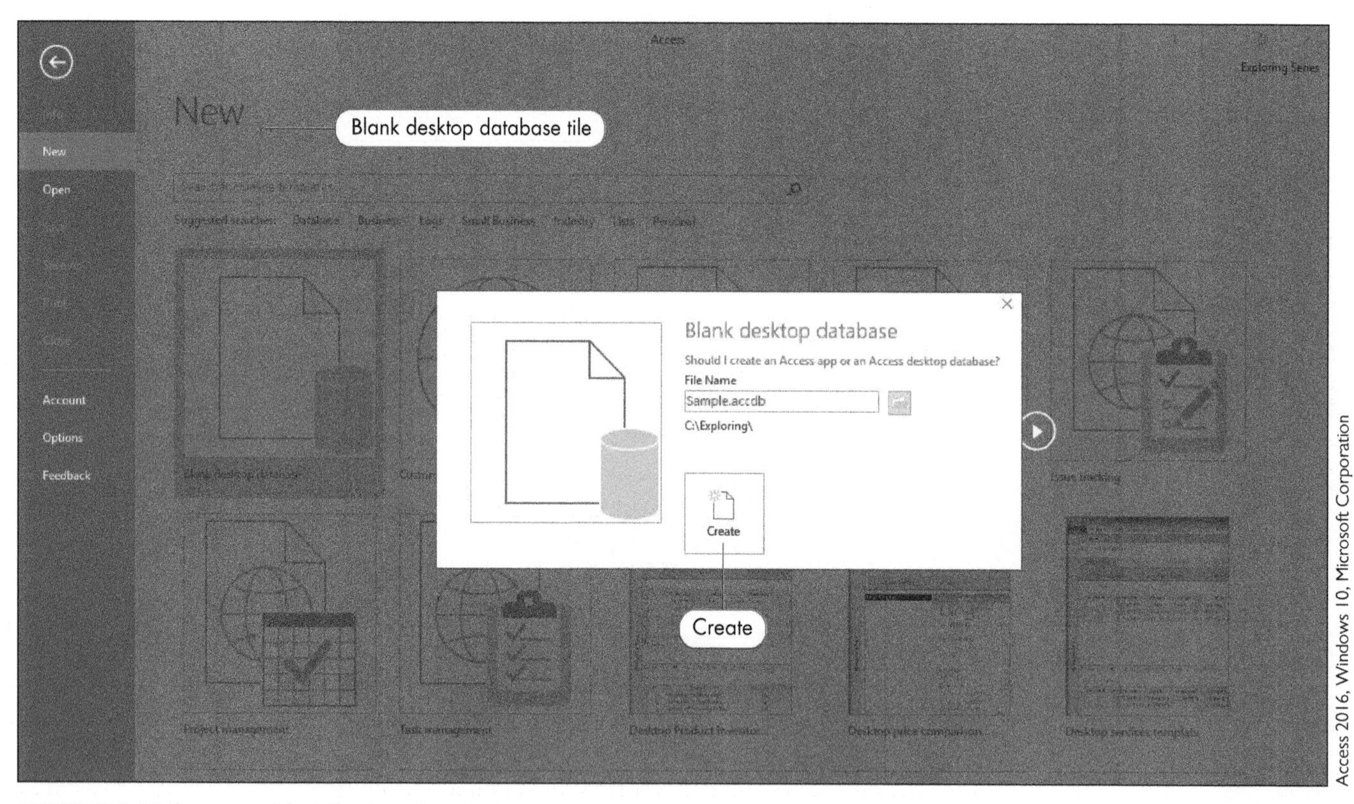

FIGURE 1.48 Creating a Blank Desktop Database

Create a Desktop Database Using a Template

STEP 1 Using a template to start a database saves you a great deal of creation time. Working with a template can also help a new Access user become familiar with database design. Templates are available from Backstage view, where you can select from a variety of templates or search online for more templates.

Access also provides templates for desktop use.

To create a desktop database from a template, complete the following steps:

1. Open Access. (If Access is already open, click the File tab to open Backstage view and click New.)
2. Click the desktop database template you want to use, or use the search box at the top of the page. Figure 1.49 shows some examples of templates.
3. Type the file name for the file in the text box, click Browse to navigate to the folder where you want to store the database file, and then click OK.
4. Click Create to download the template.

   The database will be created and will open.
5. Click Enable Content in the Security Warning message bar.

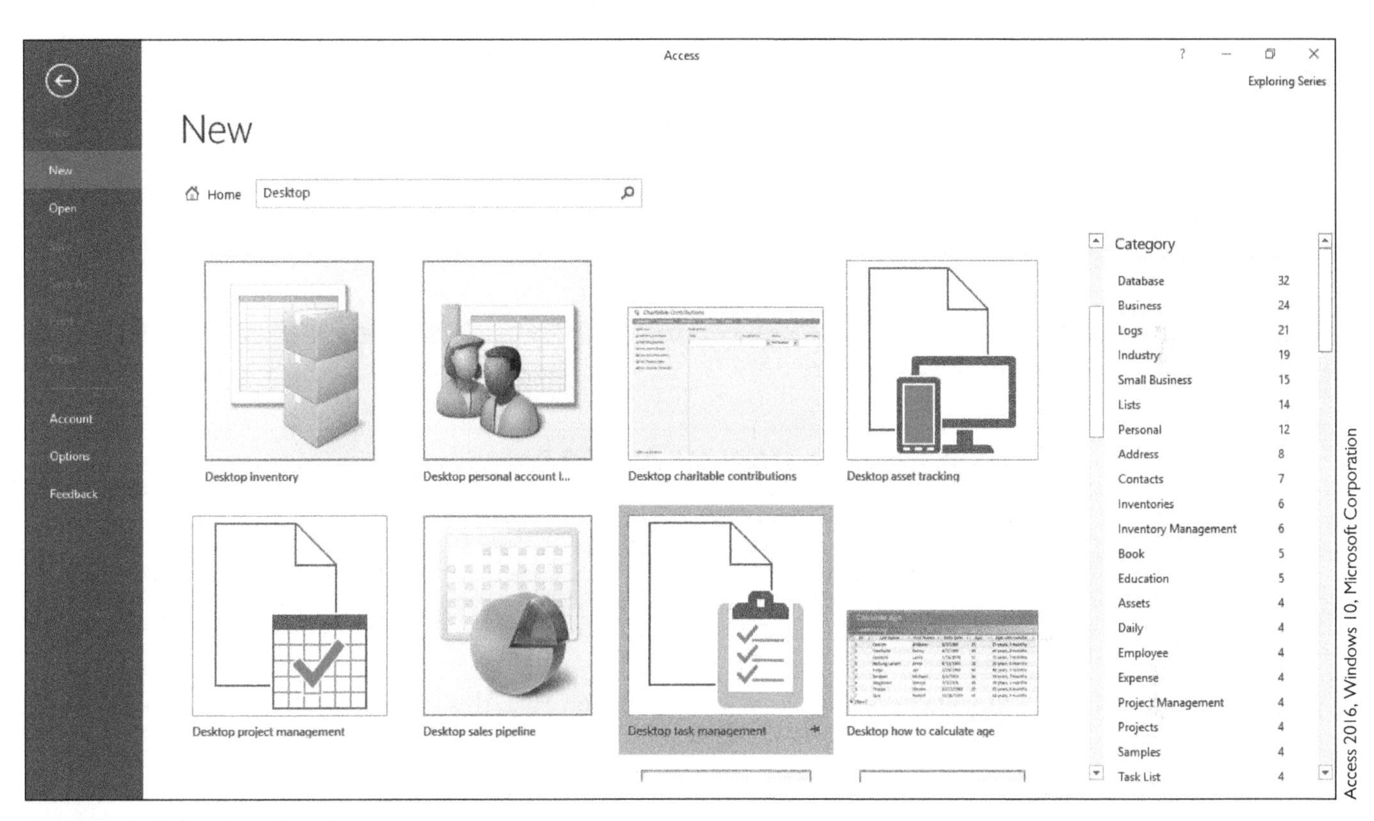

FIGURE 1.49 Database Templates

Once the database is open, you may see a Getting Started page that includes links you can use to learn more about the database. When finished reviewing the learning materials, close the Getting Started page to view the database. Figure 1.50 displays the Getting Started page included with the Desktop task management template. Notice the hyperlink to import contacts from Microsoft Outlook. If you use Outlook, this is a nice feature. Close the Getting Started page to return to the database. Because you downloaded a template, some objects will have already been created. You can work with these objects just as you did in the first three sections of this chapter. Edit any object to meet your requirements.

FIGURE 1.50 Getting Started Page for a Template

> **TIP: CREATE A TEMPLATE FROM A DATABASE**
>
> If you have a database you may want to reuse in the future, you can save it as a template. Doing so will enable you to create new databases with the same tables, queries, forms, and reports as the one you have created. You can also reuse parts of the database as application parts.
>
> To create a template from an existing database, click the File tab, click Save As, and then double-click Template. Set options such as the name and description and click OK.

If you check the option for Application Part, this template will also be available under User Templates on the Application Parts menu on the Create tab.

Add Records to a Downloaded Desktop Database

Once a desktop database template has been downloaded, you can use it as you would use any Access database. Figure 1.51 shows the Desktop Task Management template. Review the objects listed in the Navigation Pane. Once you are familiar with the database design, you can enter your data using a table or form.

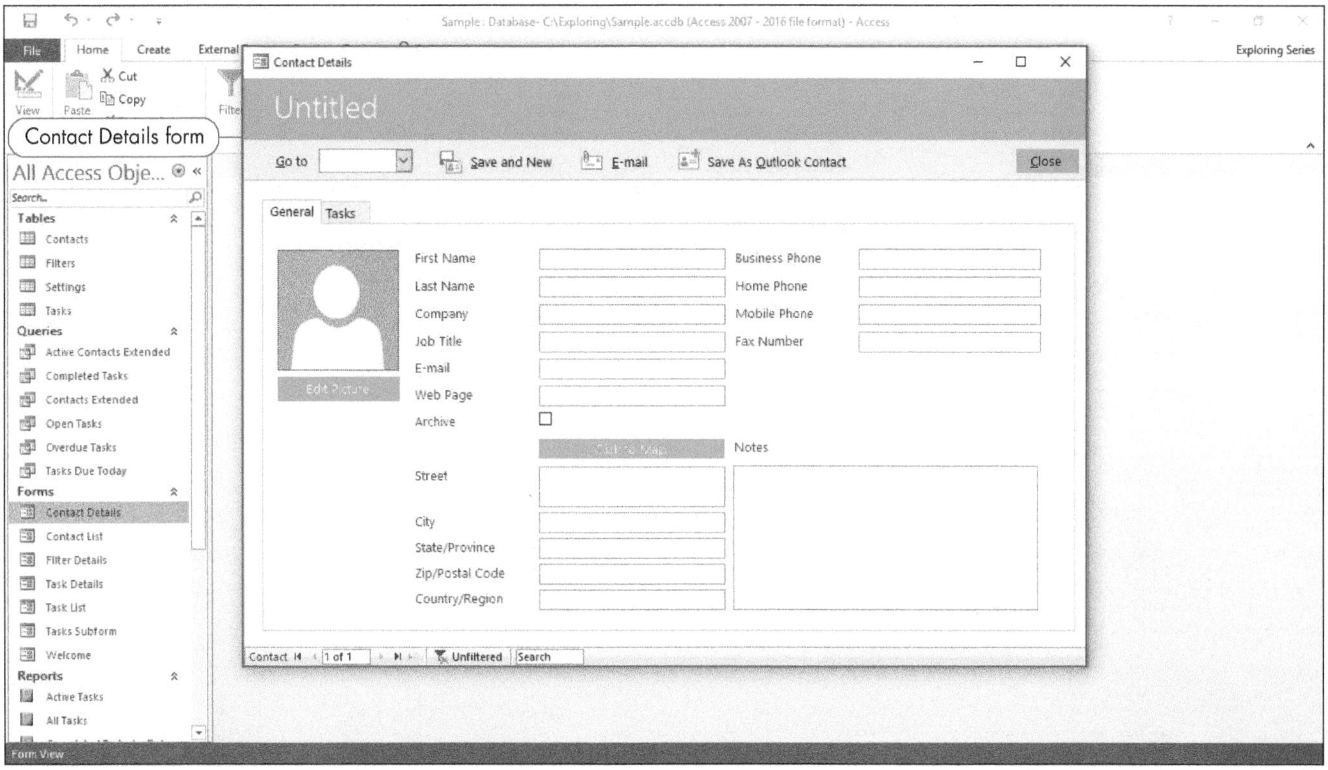

FIGURE 1.51 Desktop Task Management Database

Explore the Database Objects in a Downloaded Desktop Database Template

One of the reasons to use a template is so you do not have to create any of the objects. Therefore, you will notice each template comes with a varying amount of predefined queries, forms, and reports. Familiarize yourself with the unique features of a template; as they are professionally designed, they are typically well thought out.

Create a Table Using an Application Part

An ***application part*** enables you to add a set of common Access components to an existing database, such as a table, a form, and a report for a related task. These are provided by Microsoft and offer components (for example, a Contacts table) you can add to an existing database, rather than creating an entirely new database, as shown in Figure 1.52.

To add an application part to a database, complete the following steps:

1. Click Application Parts in the Templates group on the Create tab.
2. Select one of the options from the list.
3. Respond to the dialog boxes. For example, if you insert an Issues application part, you may be prompted to create a relationship between Issues and an existing table (such as Customers). Setting up a relationship is not required, but may be appropriate.
4. Check the Navigation Pane to verify that the new components were created.

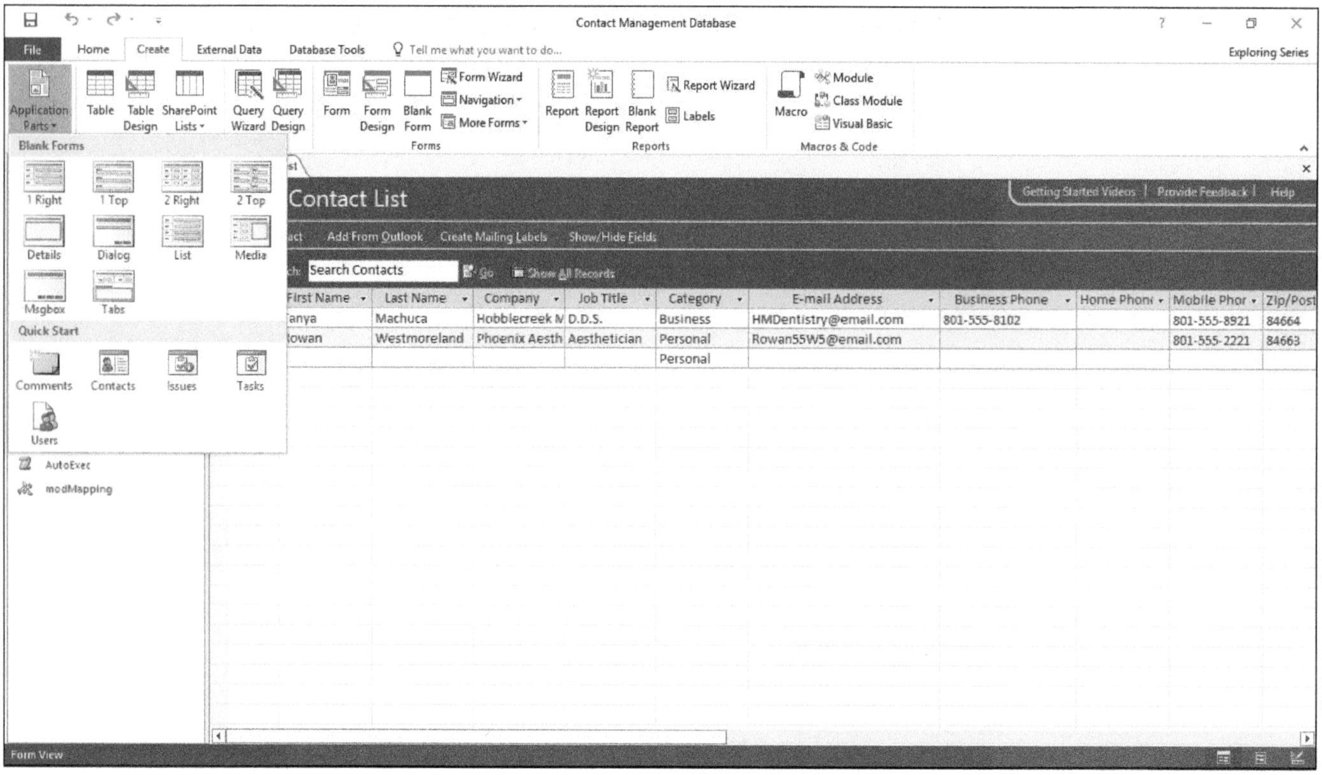

Access 2016, Windows 10, Microsoft Corporation

FIGURE 1.52 Adding an Application Part

Create a Web App Using a Template

An Access Web app (or application) is a type of database that lets you build a browser-based database app. You can create a database in the cloud that you and others can access and use simultaneously. This requires that you use a host server such as SharePoint (a Web app platform developed by Microsoft) or Office 365 (a cloud service edition of SharePoint).

Before creating a Web app, ensure that you have access to a host server. In a business environment, this would likely be set up and maintained by your Information Technology department. Your college or university may not give students access to this server. If they do, your professor can give you the information you will need.

To create a Web app using SharePoint, complete the following steps:

1. Click the File tab.
2. Click New.
3. Click Custom web app.
4. Type an App Name.
5. Input the web location (which will be provided by your company's technology professionals or by your professor, if available).
6. Click Create.
7. Create tables. This can be done manually, from a template, or from an existing data source.

In a business environment (and on the Microsoft Office Specialist examination for Access) you may need to migrate the database you have created to a SharePoint server. Doing so is similar to the Save operation covered earlier in the chapter.

To migrate an existing database to a SharePoint server, complete the following steps:

1. Click the File tab.
2. Click Save As.
3. Click SharePoint.
4. Click Save As.
5. Select the location on the SharePoint server where you wish to save your database, and click Save.

As mentioned earlier, SharePoint is typically used more in a corporate environment, so you may not have a SharePoint server available at your college or university.

9. What is a custom web app, and what is required to build a custom web app? ***p. 707***
10. What are two benefits of using a template to create a database? ***p. 708***
11. If you want to add a component to an existing database (such as a Contacts table), what would you use? ***p. 711***

Hands-On Exercises

Skills covered: Create a Database Using a Template • Add Records to a Downloaded Desktop Database • Explore the Database Objects in a Downloaded Desktop Database Template

3 Access Database Creation

After working with the Northwind database on the job, you decide to use Access to create a personal contact database. Rather than start from a blank table, you use an Access Contact Manager desktop template to make your database creation simpler.

STEP 1 » CREATE A DATABASE USING A TEMPLATE

You locate an Access desktop template that you can use to create your personal contact database. This template not only allows you to store names, addresses, telephone numbers, and other information, but also lets you categorize your contacts, send email messages, and create maps of addresses. You download and save the template. Refer to Figure 1.53 as you complete Step 1.

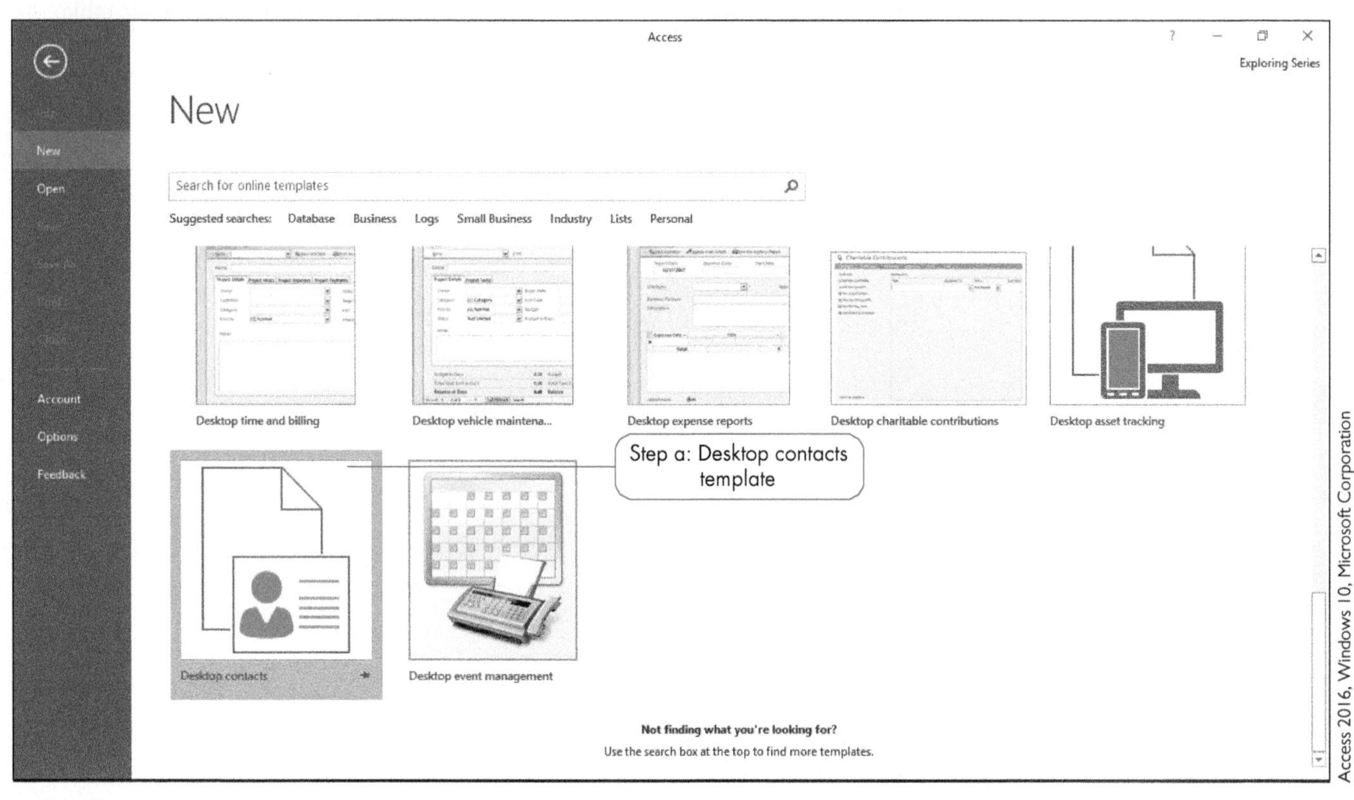

FIGURE 1.53 Database Templates

a. Open Access. Scroll down and click the **Desktop contacts** template tile.

> **TROUBLESHOOTING:** If the Desktop contacts template is not visible, you can use the search box at the top of the screen.

b. Click **Browse** to navigate to the folder where you are saving your files, type **a01h3Contacts_LastFirst** as the file name, and then click **OK**.

c. Click **Create** to download the template.

d. Click the *Show Getting Started when this database is opened* check box to deselect it, and close the Getting Started with Contacts page.

The database displays the Contact List form.

e. Click **Enable Content** on the Security Warning message bar.

STEP 2 » ADD RECORDS TO A DOWNLOADED DESKTOP DATABASE

Because the database opens in the Contact List form, you decide to begin by entering a contact in the form. Refer to Figure 1.54 as you complete Step 2.

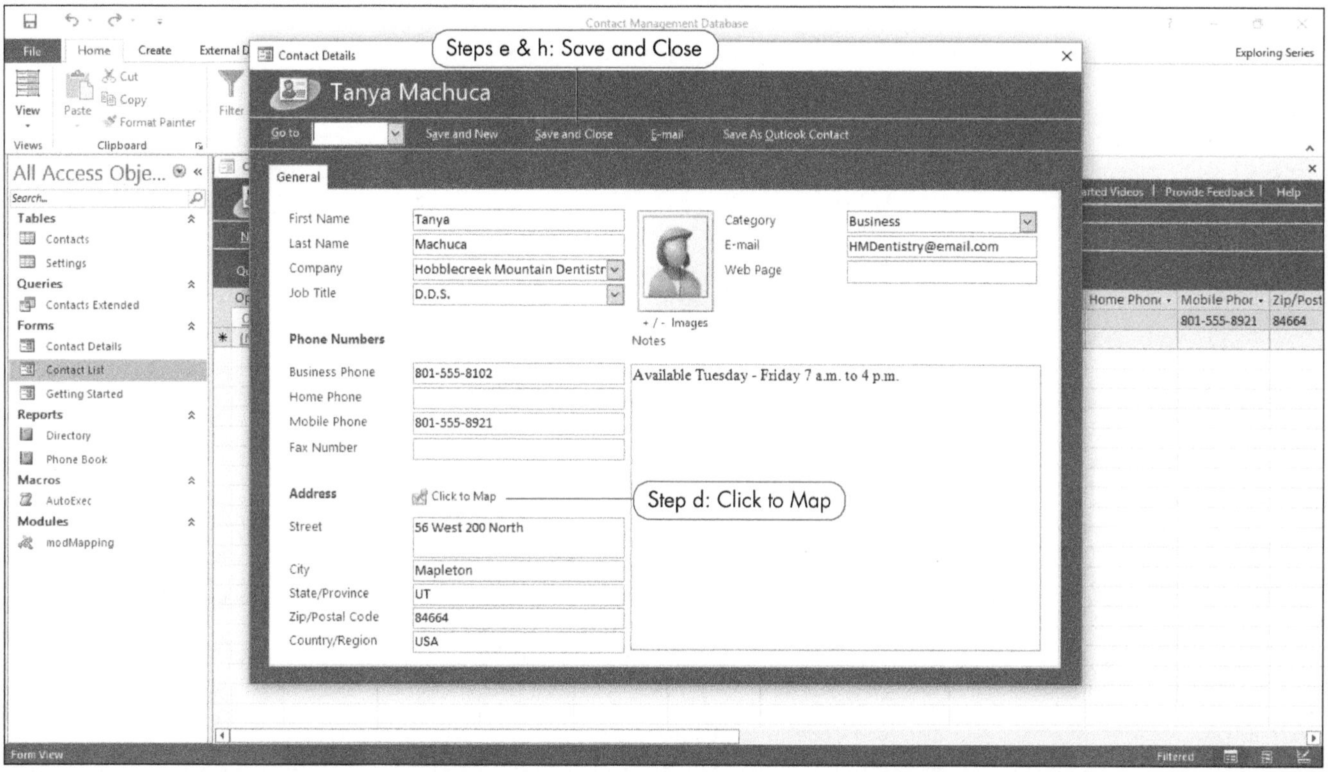

FIGURE 1.54 Contact Details for Tanya Machuca

a. Click in the First Name field of the first record. Type the following information, pressing **Tab** between each entry. Do not press Tab after entering the ZIP/Postal Code.

Field Name	Value to Type
First Name	**Tanya**
Last Name	**Machuca**
Company	**Hobblecreek Mountain Dentistry**
Job Title	**D.D.S.**
Category	**Business** (select from list)
E-mail	**HMDentistry@email.com**
Business Phone	**801-555-8102**
Home Phone	(leave blank)
Mobile Phone	**801-555-8921**
Zip/Postal Code	**84664**

b. Click **Open** in the first field of Dr. Machuca's record.

Open is a hyperlink to a different form in the database. The Contact Details form opens, displaying Dr. Machuca's information. More fields are available for you to use to store information. (Note that this form could also be opened from the Navigation Pane.)

c. Type the following additional information to the record:

Field Name	Value to Type
Street	**56 West 200 North**
City	**Mapleton**
State/Province	**UT**
Country/Region	**USA**
Notes	**Available Tuesday - Friday 7 a.m. to 4 p.m.**

d. Click the **Click to Map** hyperlink to view a map to Dr. Machuca's office.

Bing displays a map to the address in the record. You can get directions, locate nearby businesses, and use many other options.

TROUBLESHOOTING: You may be prompted to choose an application. Select any Web browser such as Microsoft Edge from the list.

e. Close the map. Click **Save and Close** in the top center of the form to close the Contact Details form.

The record is saved.

f. Click **New Contact** beneath the Contact List title bar.

The Contact Details form opens to a blank record.

g. Type the following information for a new record, pressing **Tab** to move between fields. Some fields will be blank.

Field Name	Value to Type
First Name	**Rowan**
Last Name	**Westmoreland**
Company	**Phoenix Aesthetics**
Job Title	**Aesthetician**
Mobile Phone	**801-555-2221**
Street	**425 North Main Street**
City	**Springville**
State/Province	**UT**
Zip/Postal Code	**84663**
Category	**Personal**
E-mail	**Rowan55W5@email.com**
Notes	**Recommended by Michelle**

h. Click **Save and Close**.

STEP 3 » EXPLORE THE DATABASE OBJECTS IN A DOWNLOADED DESKTOP DATABASE TEMPLATE

You explore the objects created by the template so that you understand the organization of the database. Refer to Figure 1.55 as you complete Step 3.

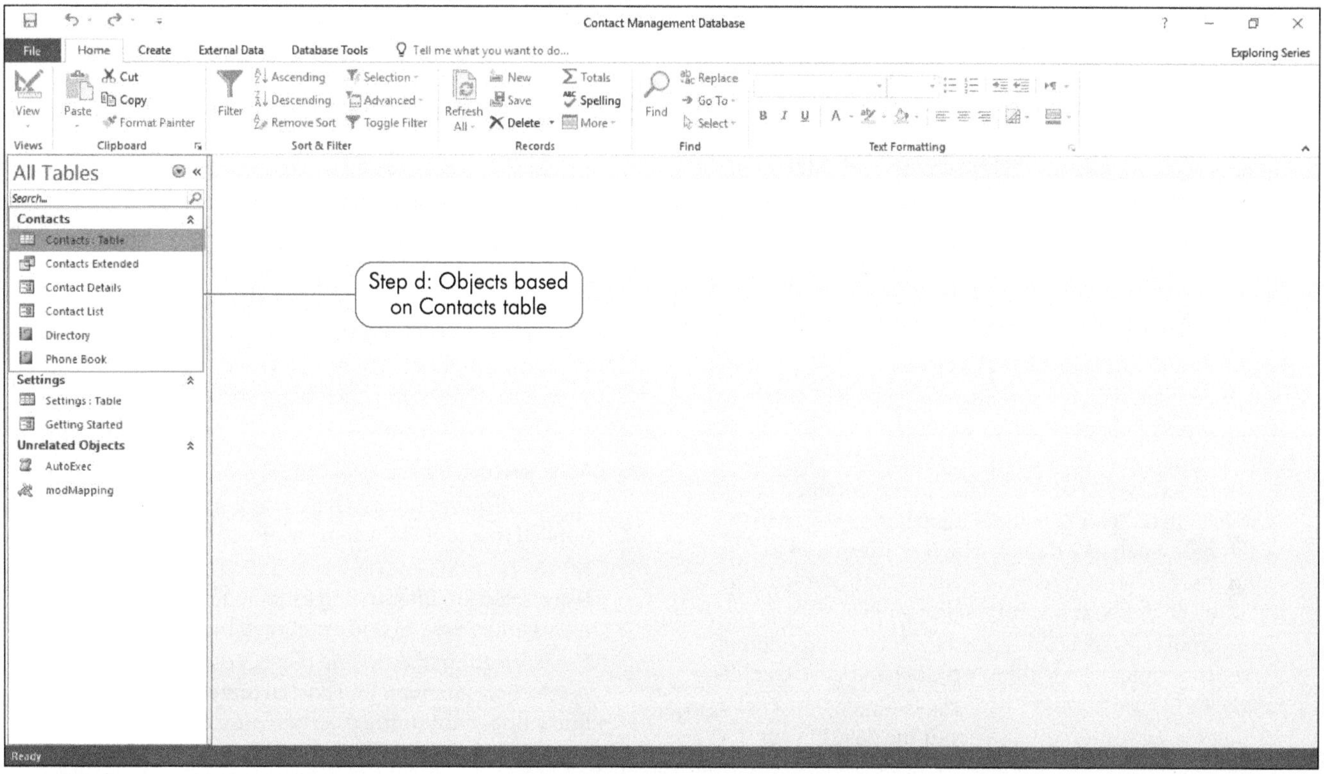

Step d: Objects based on Contacts table

Access 2016, Windows 10, Microsoft Corporation

FIGURE 1.55 Tables and Related Views

a. Double-click the **Contacts table** in the Navigation Pane.

The information you entered using the Contact List form and the Contact Details form displays in the Contacts table.

b. Double-click the **Phone Book report** in the Navigation Pane.

The Phone Book report opens displaying the contact name and phone information organized by category.

c. Double-click the **Directory report** in the Navigation Pane.

The Directory report opens, displaying a full alphabetical contact list. The Directory report was designed to display more fields than the Phone Book, but it is not organized by category.

d. Click **All Access Objects** on the Navigation Pane and select **Tables and Related Views**.

You can now see the objects that are based on the Contacts table.

e. Right-click the **Directory report tab** and select **Close All**.

f. Close the database and exit Access. Based on your instructor's directions, submit the following:

a01h1Traders_LastFirst_*CurrentDate*

a01h2Traders_LastFirst

a01h3Contacts_LastFirst

Chapter Objectives Review

After reading this chapter, you have accomplished the following objectives:

1. Open, save, and enable content in a database.

- A database is a collection of data organized as meaningful information that can be accessed, managed, stored, queried, sorted, and reported.
- A database management system (DBMS) is a software system that provides the tools to create, maintain, and use a database. Access is the database management system found in business versions of Microsoft Office.
- When a database is first opened, Access displays a message bar with a security warning. Click Enable Content if you trust the database's source.

2. Recognize database object types.

- An Access database is a structured collection of four major types of objects—tables, forms, queries, and reports.
- The foundation of a database is its tables, the objects in which data is stored. Each table in the database has a collection of fields (a piece of information stored in a database, such as a name), which are displayed as columns. Each row is referred to as a record, which is a set of all fields about an entry in the table.
- The primary key in a table is the field (or combination of fields) that uniquely identifies a record in a table (such as a driver's license number).
- A query is a question you ask about the data in your database.
- A form enables simplified entry and modification of data.
- A report contains professional-looking formatted information from underlying tables or queries.
- Examine the Access interface: Objects are organized and listed in the Navigation Pane. Access also uses a Tabbed Documents interface in which each object that is open has its own tab.
- Explore table Datasheet view: Datasheet view is a grid containing fields (columns) and records (rows).
- Navigate through records: Navigation arrows enable you to move through records, with arrows for the first, previous, next, and last records, as well as one to add a new record.
- Explore table Design view: Design view gives you a detailed view of the table's structure and is used to create and modify a table's design by specifying the fields it will contain, the fields' data types, and their associated properties.
- Rename and describe tables: Tables can be renamed as necessary and a description can be added. The description gives the user more information about what an object does.

3. Modify data in table Datasheet view.

- Access works primarily from storage. Records can be added, modified, or deleted in the database, and as the information is entered, it is automatically saved. Undo cannot reverse edits made to multiple records.

4. Add records to a table.

- A pencil symbol displays in the record selector box to indicate when you are in editing mode. Moving to another record saves the changes.

5. Delete records from a table.

- To delete a record, click the record selector and click Delete in the Records group on the Home tab.

6. Use database utilities.

- Back up a database: The Back Up Database utility creates a duplicate copy of the database. This may enable users to recover from failure.
- The Compact and Repair utility reduces the size of a database and fixes any errors that may exist in the file.
- Encrypt a database: Encrypting databases enables you to add a password to a database.
- Print information: Access can create a print copy of your data. Previewing before printing is a good practice to avoid wasting paper.

7. Work with filters.

- A filter displays records based on a set of criteria that is applied to a table to display a subset of records in that table.
- Use a selection filter to find exact matches: A selection filter can be used to find exact matches.
- Use a selection filter to find records containing a value: A selection filter can find partial matches, for example, find values containing a certain phrase.
- Use filter by form: Filter By Form displays records based on multiple criteria and enables the user to apply logical operators and use comparison operators.

8. Perform sorts.

- Sort table data: Sorting changes the order of information, and information may be sorted by one or more fields.
- Data can be sorted ascending (low to high) or descending (high to low).

9. Create a database.

- Creating a blank desktop database: Creating a blank desktop database enables you to create a database specific to your requirements.
- Create a desktop database using a template: A template is a predefined database that includes professionally designed tables, forms, reports, and other objects that you can use to jumpstart the creation of your database.
- Add records to a downloaded desktop database: Once a database has been created, it can be used as any other database is.
- Explore the database objects in a downloaded database template: Once you create a database using a template, explore it and become familiar with the contents.
- Create a table using an application part: If you require a certain type of table (such as Contacts) you can add them using an application part.
- Create a Web app using a template: Creating a custom web app enables you to create a database that you can build and use and share with others through the Web.

Key Terms Matching

Match the key terms with their definitions. Write the key term letter by the appropriate numbered definition.

- **a.** Application part
- **b.** Database
- **c.** Database Management System (DBMS)
- **d.** Datasheet view
- **e.** Design view
- **f.** Field
- **g.** Filter
- **h.** Filter By Form
- **i.** Form
- **j.** Navigation Pane
- **k.** Object
- **l.** Primary key
- **m.** Query
- **n.** Record
- **o.** Relationship
- **p.** Report
- **q.** Selection filter
- **r.** Sort
- **s.** Table
- **t.** Template

1. ______ A filtering method that displays only records that match selected criteria. **p. 695**

2. ______ A filtering method that displays records based on multiple criteria. **p. 697**

3. ______ A main component that is created and used to make a database function, such as a table or form. **p. 667**

4. ______ A method of listing records in a specific sequence (such as alphabetically). **p. 699**

5. ______ A predefined database that includes professionally designed tables, forms, reports, and other objects. **p. 707**

6. ______ A question you ask about the data in your database. **p. 669**

7. ______ An Access interface element that organizes and lists database objects in a database. **p. 667**

8. ______ An Access object that simplifies entering, modifying, and deleting table data. **p. 669**

9. ______ A set of common Access components that can be added to an existing database. **p. 711**

10. ______ An object that contains professional-looking formatted information from underlying tables or queries. **p. 670**

11. ______ An object used to store data, organizing data into columns and rows. **p. 668**

12. ______ Complete set of all the fields about one person, place, event, or concept. **p. 668**

13. ______ The field (or combination of fields) that uniquely identifies each record in a table. **p. 668**

14. ______ View that enables you to create and modify a table design. **p. 675**

15. ______ A collection of data organized as meaningful information that can be accessed, managed, stored, queried, sorted, and reported. **p. 664**

16. ______ A connection between two tables using a common field. **p. 678**

17. ______ A grid that enables you to add, edit, and delete the records of a table. **p. 673**

18. ______ A piece of information stored in a table, such as a company name or city. **p. 668**

19. ______ A software system that provides the tools needed to create, maintain, and use a database. **p. 664**

20. ______ Enables you to specify conditions to display only those records that meet certain conditions. **p. 695**

Multiple Choice

1. Which of the following is an example of an Access object?
   (a) Database
   (b) Field
   (c) Form
   (d) Record

2. Where is data in a database stored?
   (a) Form
   (b) Query
   (c) Report
   (d) Table

3. You edit several records in an Access table. When should you execute the Save command?
   (a) Immediately after you edit a record
   (b) Once at the end of the session
   (c) Records are saved automatically; the save command is not required
   (d) When you close the table

4. Which of the following is *not* true of an Access database?
   (a) Each field has a data type that establishes the kind of data that can be entered.
   (b) Every record in a table has the same fields as every other record.
   (c) Every table in a database contains the same number of records as every other table.
   (d) A primary key uniquely identifies a record.

5. Which of the following is true regarding table views?
   (a) You can add, edit, and delete records using Design view.
   (b) Datasheet view shows a detailed view of the table design.
   (c) Datasheet view provides access to more field properties than Design view.
   (d) Changes made in Datasheet view are automatically saved when you move the insertion point to a different record.

6. Which of the following utilities is used to recover in the event of loss or damage?
   (a) Back Up Database
   (b) Compact and Repair Database
   (c) Database Splitter
   (d) Encrypt Database

7. Which of the following would be matched if you use a Selection filter's exact match option for the name Ann?
   (a) Ann, ANN, and ann
   (b) Danny, Ann, and Anny
   (c) Ann (but not ANN)
   (d) Both a and b

8. Which of the following conditions is available through a Selection filter?
   (a) Equal condition
   (b) Delete condition
   (c) AND condition
   (d) OR condition

9. All of the following statements are true about creating a database *except*:
   (a) Creating a custom web app requires that you use a server (such as SharePoint).
   (b) When creating a blank desktop database, Access opens to a blank table in Datasheet view.
   (c) Using a template to create a database saves time because it includes predefined objects.
   (d) The objects provided in a template cannot be modified.

10. To add a predefined table to an existing database, you should use which of the following?
   (a) Application part
   (b) Blank desktop database
   (c) Custom web app
   (d) Database template

Practice Exercises

1 Replacement Parts

As a recent hire at Replacement Parts, you are tasked with performing updates to the customer database. You have been asked to open the company's database, save it with a new name, and then modify, add, and delete records. You will then back up the database, apply filters and sorts, and use an application part to add a new table that will be used to track customer shipping and receiving complaints. Refer to Figure 1.56 as you complete the exercise.

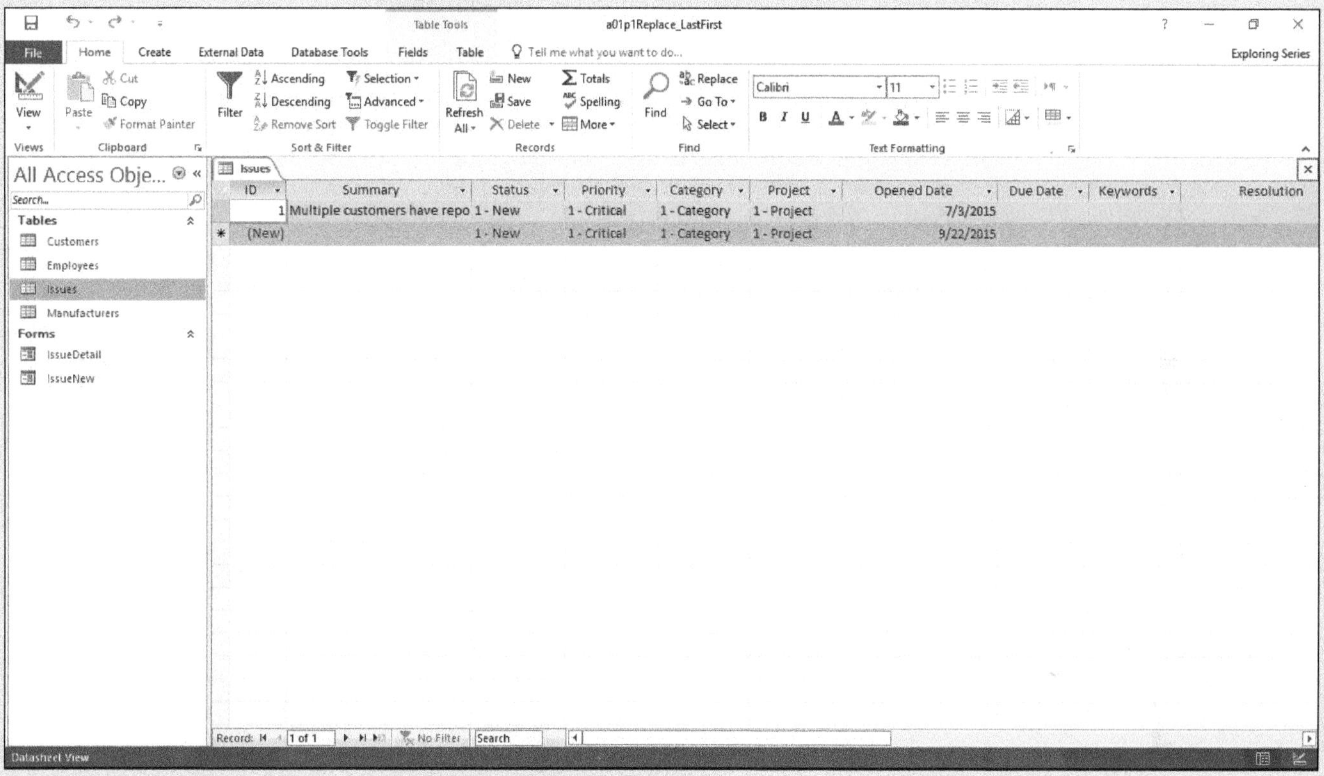

Access 2016, Windows 10, Microsoft Corporation

FIGURE 1.56 Issues Table Added to Replacement Parts Database

a. Open the *a01p1Replace* file. Save the database as **a01p1Replace_LastFirst**. Click **Enable Content** on the message bar.

b. Double-click the **Manufacturers table** to open the table in Datasheet view. Locate record 800552 (Haas). Change the name to **Haas International** and the CountyOfOrigin to **Austria**.

c. Type the following new records:

MfgID	ManufacturerName	CountryOfOrigin	EmployeeID
801411	Bolshoy Fine China	Russia	817080
801422	Tejada and Sons	Dominican Republic	816680
801433	Lubitz UK	England	817580

d. Delete record **800661** (John Bradshaw).

e. Close the Manufacturers table.

f. Click the **File tab**, click **Save As**, and then double-click **Back Up Database**. Accept the default backup file name and click **Save**.

g. Double-click the **Customers table** to open the table in Datasheet view.

h. Click the **State field** for the first record (Diego Martinez). Click **Selection** in the Sort & Filter group, and then click **Equals "OR"** to display the two customers in Oregon. Close the table, selecting **Save** when prompted.

i. Double-click the **Employees table** to open the table in Datasheet view.

j. Click the **plus sign** [+] next to Alfonso Torres. Notice he is assigned as the representative for the manufacturer Antarah.

   This information is available due to the relationship already created in the database between Employees and Manufacturers.

k. Click **Advanced** in the Sort & Filter group on the Home tab, and select **Filter By Form.** Click in the Salary field. Type **>60000** and click **Toggle Filter** in the Sort & Filter group on the Home tab to apply the filter. Six employees are displayed. Close the table, selecting **Save** when prompted.

l. Double-click the **Manufacturers table** to open the table in Datasheet view.

m. Click any value in the Manufacturer Name field. Click **Ascending** in the Sort & Filter group to sort the table by the name of the manufacturer. Close the table, selecting **Save** when prompted.

n. Click **Application Parts** in the Templates group on the Create tab. Select **Issues**. Select the option for "There is no relationship." Click **Create**.

o. Double-click the **Issues table** to open the table in Datasheet view.

p. Add a new record, typing **Multiple customers have reported damaged goods received in Denton, Texas.** in the Summary field. Leave all other fields as the default values. Compare your results to Figure 1.56.

q. Close the database and exit Access. Based on your instructor's directions, submit the following:

   a01p1Replace_LastFirst

   a01p1Replace_LastFirst_*CurrentDate*

2 Custom Coffee

The Custom Coffee Company provides coffee, tea, and snacks to offices in Miami. Custom Coffee also provides and maintains the equipment for brewing the beverages. To improve customer service, the owner recently had an Access database created to keep track of customers, orders, and products. This database will replace the Excel spreadsheets currently maintained by the office manager. The company hired you to verify and input all the Excel data into the Access database. Refer to Figure 1.57 as you complete the exercise.

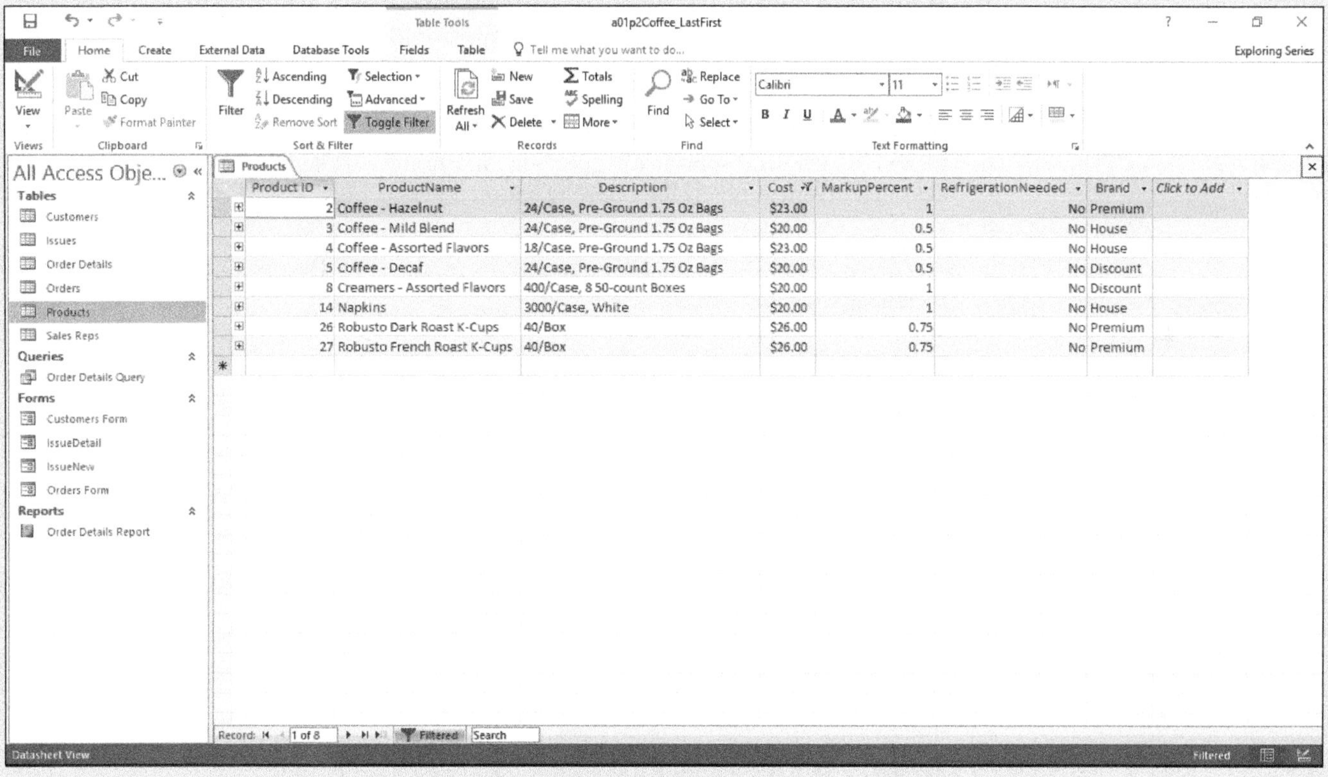

Access 2016, Windows 10, Microsoft Corporation

FIGURE 1.57 Filtered Products Table

a. Open the *a01p2Coffee* file and save the database as **a01p2Coffee_LastFirst**. Click **Enable Content** on the message bar.

b. Click the **Database Tools tab** and click **Relationships** in the Relationships group. Review the table relationships. Notice the join line between the Customers and Orders tables.

c. Click **Close** in the Relationships group.

d. Double-click the **Sales Reps table** to open it in Datasheet view. For rep number 2, replace **YourFirstName** and **YourLastName** with your first and last names. For example, as the Access author, I would type *Eric* in place of YourFirstName and *Cameron* in place of YourLastName. Close the table by clicking **Close** on the right side of the Sales Reps window.

e. Double-click the **Customers table** to open it in Datasheet view. Click **New** in the Records group. Add a new record by typing the following information; press **Tab** after each field:

Customer Name:	**Bavaro Driving School**
Contact:	**Ricky Watters**
Address1:	**1 Clausen Way**
Address2:	**Floor 2**
City:	**South Bend**

State: **IN**
Zip Code: **46614**
Phone: **(857) 519-6661**
Credit Rating: **A**
Sales Rep ID: **2**

Notice the pencil symbol in the record selector for the new row. This symbol indicates the new record has not been saved. Press **Tab**. The pencil symbol disappears, and the new customer is automatically saved to the table.

f. Click the **City field** for the second record (South Bend). Click **Selection** in the Sort & Filter group, and select **Equals "South Bend"** to display the four customers located in the town of South Bend.

g. Save and close the table by clicking **Close** on the right side of the Customers window, and clicking **Yes** when asked if you want to save the changes.

h. Double-click the **Products** table to open it in Datasheet view. Click **New** in the Records group. Add a new record by typing the following information:

Product ID: **26**
ProductName: **Robusto Dark Roast K-Cups**
Description: **40/Box**
Cost: **26**
MarkupPercent: **.75**
RefrigerationNeeded **No**
Brand **Premium**

i. Add a second product using the following information:

Product ID: **27**
ProductName: **Robusto French Roast K-Cups**
Description: **40/Box**
Cost: **26**
MarkupPercent: **.75**
RefrigerationNeeded **No**
Brand **Premium**

j. Click **Advanced** in the Sort & Filter group and select **Filter By Form**. Type **>=20** in the Cost field and click **Toggle Filter** in the Sort & Filter group.

All products costing $20 or more (there will be 8) display. See Figure 1.57.

k. Save and close the table by clicking **Close** on the right side of the Products window, and clicking Yes when asked if you want to save the changes.

l. Click the **File tab**, click **Save As**, and then double-click **Back Up Database**. Accept the default backup file name and click **Save.**

m. Click **Application Parts** in the Templates group of the Create tab. Select **Issues**. Click **Next** to accept the default relationship. Select **CustomerName** as the Field from 'Customers', select **Sort Ascending** from Sort this field, and then type **Customer** as the name for the lookup column. Click Create.

n. Double-click the **Issues table** to open it in Datasheet view.

o. Select **Advantage Sales** for the Customer and type **Customer reports hazelnut coffee delivered instead of decaf.** in the Summary field. Leave all other fields as the default values.

p. Close the database and exit Access. Based on your instructor's directions, submit the following:

a01p2Coffee_LastFirst

a01p2Coffee_LastFirst_*CurrentDate*

3 Healthy Living

You and two friends from your gym have decided to use Access to help you reach your weight goals. You decide to use the Access Nutrition template to help you get organized. Refer to Figure 1.58 as you complete this exercise.

ID	TipDescription	TipCategory	Click to Add
150	Walk, jog, skate, or cycle.	Activity	
147	Replace a coffee break with a brisk 10-minute walk. Ask a friend to go with y	Activity	
146	Get off the bus or subway one stop early and walk or skate the rest of the way	Activity	
141	Walk, skate, or cycle more, and drive less.	Activity	
139	Walk the dog—don't just watch the dog walk.	Activity	
138	Walk up and down the soccer or softball field sidelines while watching the kid	Activity	
135	Join a walking group in the neighborhood or at the local shopping mall. Recruit	Activity	
(New)			

FIGURE 1.58 Filtered Tips Table

a. Open Access and click the **Desktop Nutrition tracking** template in Backstage view.

b. Type **a01p3Nutrition_LastFirst** in the File name box. Click **Browse**. Navigate to the location where you are saving your files in the File New Database dialog box, click **OK** to close the dialog box, and then click **Create** to create the new database.

c. Click **Enable Content** on the message bar. Double-click the **My Profile** table in the Navigation Pane to open it in Datasheet view.

d. Delete the existing record.

e. Type the following information in as a new record, pressing **Tab** between each field:

Sex:	**Male**
Height:	**64**
Weight:	**190**
Age:	**48**
Lifestyle:	**Lightly Active**
Goal:	**Lose weight**

f. Click **New** in the Records group. Type the following information, pressing **Tab** between each field:

Sex:	**Male**
Height:	**69**
Weight:	**140**
Age:	**45**
Lifestyle:	**Moderately Active**
Goal:	**Gain weight**

g. Click **New** in the Records group. Type the following information, pressing **Tab** between each field:

Sex:	**Female**
Height:	**66**
Weight:	**140**
Age:	**40**
Lifestyle:	**Moderately Active**
Goal:	**Maintain my weight**

h. Close the table by clicking **Close** on the right side of the My Profile window.

i. Double-click the **Foods table**. Click **Advanced** in the Records group and then select **Filter By Form**.

j. Click the **Calories field** for the first record. Type **<200** in the Calories field and **>=15** in the Fiber [grams] field. Click **Toggle Filter** in the Sort & Filter group.

   You will have a list of all high = fiber, low = calorie foods in the database (there are three).

k. Save and close the table by clicking **Close** on the right side of the Foods window, and clicking **Yes** when asked if you want to save the changes.

l. Double-click the **Tips table** to open it in Datasheet view.

m. Click in the first **TipCategory**. Click **Ascending** in the Sort & Filter group to sort the tips in alphabetical order.

n. Highlight the word **Walk** in the fifth record (ID #138). Make sure you do not highlight the space after the word Walk when you highlight. Click **Selection** in the Sort & Filter group, and select **Contains "Walk"**.

   Seven tips appear that contain the word walk. See Figure 1.58.

o. Save and close the table by clicking **Close** on the right side of the Tips window, and clicking **Yes** when asked if you want to save the changes.

p. Click the **File tab**, click **Save As**, and then double-click **Back Up Database**. Use the default backup file name.

q. Close the database and exit Access. Based on your instructor's directions, submit the following:

   a01p3Nutrition_LastFirst

   a01p3Nutrition _LastFirst_*CurrentDate*

Mid-Level Exercises

1 Sunshine Mental Health Services

Sunshine Mental Health Services provides counseling and medication services. They have recently expanded their database to include patients in addition to the staff. You were hired to replace their former Information Technology support staff member. You will work to update the data in the database, familiarize yourself with the table relationships, filter and sort a table, and add a table to keep track of user accounts.

a. Open the *a01m1Sunshine* file and save the database as **a01m1Sunshine_LastFirst**. Click **Enable Content** on the Security Warning message bar.

b. Open the **Staff table** in Datasheet view.

c. Locate the record for Kovit Ang (StaffID 80073). Replace his Address with **11 Market Street**, replace his City with **Harrison**, and his ZIPCode with **04040**. Leave all other fields with their current values.

d. Add yourself as a new staff member. Type a StaffID of **99999** and type your name in the FullName field. Type **1 Clinton Terrace** for your Address, **Harrison** as your City, **ME** as your State, and **04040** as your ZIP. Type a JobCode of **300**, a Salary of **48500**, and a 401k contribution of **0.02**. Click the box in the Active field so a check box appears in the box.

e. Delete record **80399** (Stan Marsh).

f. Sort the table by Salary in descending order. Save and close the table.

g. Click **Relationships** in the Relationships group on the Database Tools tab and notice the relationship between the Position table and the Staff table, and the relationship between the Staff table and Patients table. Each position has staff associated with it, and staff members have patients associated with them. Close the Relationships window.

h. Rename the **Pos table** to **Position**. Add a description to the table stating **This table contains a list of all available job titles at the company**. Click **OK**.

i. Open the **Position table** in Datasheet view. Click the **plus sign** next to JobCode 100 (Social Worker). Notice seven social workers are employed by the company. Click the **plus sign** next to JobCode 300 (IT Support). Only your name should appear. Close the table.

j. Open the **Patients table** in Datasheet view. Use a Selection filter to show all patients associated with StaffID **80073**. Save and close the table.

k. Open the **Staff table** in Datasheet view. Use Filter By Form to display all staff members who earn a salary of more than **80000**. Toggle the filter to verify the results. Save and close the table.

l. Back up the database. Accept the default file name.

m. Add a **Users application part** to the database. Change the relationship so there is One 'Staff' to many 'Users' by clicking the arrow next to Patients and selecting **Staff**. Click **Next**. Select the **FullName** field from 'Staff', choose the **Sort Ascending** option, and name the lookup column **User**. Click **Create**.

n. Open the **Users table** in Datasheet view.

o. Select **Adolfo Ortiz** in the User field. Type **aortiz@sunshinementalhealth.org** for Email and **aortiz** for Login. Leave the FullName blank. Close the table.

DISCOVER

p. Create a form based on the Patients table using the Form button in the Forms group of the Create tab. Save the form as **Patient Data Entry.**

q. Switch to Form view of the form. Delete the phone number for PatientID **1** (Minoru Kobayashi). Close the form.

r. Close the database and exit Access. Based on your instructor's directions, submit the following:

a01m1Sunshine_LastFirst

a01m1Sunshine_LastFirst_*CurrentDate*

2 National Conference

ANALYSIS CASE

The Association of Higher Education will host its National Conference on your campus next year. To facilitate the conference, the Information Technology department has replaced last year's Excel spreadsheets with an Access database containing information on the rooms, speakers, and sessions. Your assignment is to create a room itinerary that will list all of the sessions, dates, and times for each room. The list will be posted on the door of each room for the duration of the conference.

a. Open the *a01m2NatConf* file and save the database as **a01m2NatConf_LastFirst**. Click **Enable Content** on the Security Warning message bar.

b. Open **Relationships**.

c. Review the objects and relationships in the database. Notice that there is a relationship between Speakers and SessionSpeaker. Close the relationships.

d. Open the **SessionSpeaker table**. Scroll to the first blank record at the bottom of the table and type a new record using SpeakerID **99** and SessionID **09**. (Note: Speaker 99 does not exist.) How does Access respond? Press **Escape** twice to cancel your change.

e. Open the **Speakers table**. Replace *YourFirstName* with your first name and *YourLastName* with your last name. Close the Speakers table.

f. Open the **Sessions table** and use a Selection filter to identify the sessions that take place in room 101.

g. Sort the filtered results in ascending order by the **SessionTitle** field. Save and close the table.

h. Open the **Master List - Sessions and Speakers** report. Right-click the **Master List - Sessions and Speakers** tab and select **Report View**.

DISCOVER

i. Apply a filter that limits the report to sessions in **Room 101** only. The process will be similar to applying a filter to a table.

j. View the report in Print Preview. Close Print Preview and close the report.

k. Back up the database. Use the default backup file name.

★ **l.** Open the *a01m2Analysis* document in Word and save as **a01m2Analysis_LastFirst**. Use the database objects you created to answer the questions. Save and close the document.

m. Close the database and exit Access. Based on your instructor's directions, submit the following:
a01m2NatConf_LastFirst
a01m2NatConf_LastFirst_*CurrentDate*
a01m2Analysis_LastFirst

3 New Castle County Technical Services

RUNNING CASE

New Castle County Technical Services (NCCTS) provides technical support for a number of companies in the greater New Castle County, Delaware, area. They are working to move their record keeping to an Access database. You will add, update, and delete some records, add filters, and create a backup.

This project is a running case. You will use the same database file across Chapters 1 through 4.

a. Open the database *a01m3NCCTS* and save the database as **a01m3NCCTS_LastFirst**. Click **Enable Content** on the Security Warning message bar.

b. Open the **Call Types table** in Datasheet view. Type the following rates for the HourlyRate field and then close the table:

Description	HourlyRate
Hardware Support	30
Software Support	25
Network Troubleshooting	40
Network Installation	40
Training	50

Description	HourlyRate
Security Camera Maintenance	**40**
Virus Removal	**25**
Disaster Recovery	**60**
VoIP Service	**45**
Other	**35**

c. Open the **Reps table** in Datasheet view. Add a new record, filling in the value **8** for the RepID field, your last name as the rep's last name, and your first name as the rep's first name.

d. Sort the Reps table by **LastName** in ascending order. Close the table.

e. Open the **Customers table** in Datasheet view. Locate the record for **Edwin VanCleef** (PC030). Delete the entire record.

f. Click in the **City field** for SVC Pharmacy. Use the Selection filter to only show customers who are located in the city of **Newark**. Save and close the table.

g. Open the **Calls table** in Datasheet view. Use **Filter By Form** to filter the HoursLogged field so only calls with 10 or more hours logged on the call (**>=10**) are displayed. Save and close the table.

h. Back up the database, using the default name.

i. Close the database and exit Access. Based on your instructor's directions, submit the following:
a01m3NCCTS_LastFirst
a01m3NCCTS_LastFirst_*CurrentDate*

Beyond the Classroom

Creating a Student Database

Create a new blank desktop database, name the file **a01b1Students_LastFirst**, and then save the database in the location where you are saving your files. Create a new table using the Contacts application part. Delete the Company, JobTitle, BusinessPhone, HomePhone, FaxNumber, Country/Region, WebPage, Attachments, ContactName, and FileAs fields from the Company table. Save the table, then switch to Datasheet view. Enter the information about at least five students, fictional or real, including your own information. Enter their major in the Notes field. Sort the table by last name in ascending order. Create a filter to display students with your major. Delete all queries, forms, and reports. Close the database and exit Access. Based on your instructor's directions, submit a01b1Students_LastFirst.

Lugo Web Hosting

DISASTER RECOVERY

Your Access database has become corrupted and you are in the process of restoring it from a backup from two weeks ago. In the last two weeks, there have been only a few changes. All users who previously had a 900 GB quota have had their quotas increased to 1 TB. In addition, all users who were previously on the server named Aerelon have been moved to another server, Caprica. You have determined you can use filters to help fix the data in the Users table. Open the *a01b2Lugo_Backup* file and save the database as **a01b2Lugo_LastFirst**. Apply filters to show users who meet the conditions above and then manually change the data for each user. Sort the table by the server in ascending order. Close the database and exit Access. Based on your instructor's directions, submit a01b2Lugo_LastFirst.

Capstone Exercise

MyITLab® Grader

You are employed as a technical supervisor at a chain of bookstores. One of the store managers has expressed confusion about Access. You have offered to train her on the basics of Access. To avoid mistakes in the main database, you will save the file with a new name. You will then train her on the basics of the database system, including making data modifications, sorting and filtering, adding a table using an application part, and creating a backup.

Modify Data in a Table

You will open an original database file and save the database with a new name. You will then demonstrate adding, updating, and deleting information.

a. Open the *a01c1Books* file and save the database as **a01c1Books_LastFirst**.

b. Open the **Publishers table** in Datasheet view. Notice that some of the publisher city and state information is missing. Update the database with the information below and close the table.

PubID	PubName	PubCity	PubState
DC	DC Comics	New York	NY
SM	St. Martin	Boston	MA
TB	Triumph Books	Chicago	IL
TL	Time Life	Pueblo	CO

c. Change the PubCity for Pearson to **Hoboken**.

d. Close the Publishers table.

e. Open the **Author table** in Datasheet view.

f. Navigate to the last record (Author ID of XXXX01) and replace **YourFirstName** with your first name and **YourLastName** with your last name. Close the table.

g. Open the **Author table** again and notice the changes you made have been stored.

h. Click the **plus sign** next to your name. Notice the book Social Media: A Student's View is listed. Close the table again.

i. Open the **Books table** in Datasheet view. Notice the book with ISBN 9780809400775 (American Cooking: The Northwest) has no items in stock. Delete this record.

j. Close the table.

Sort a Table and Apply a Selection Filter

You will sort the publisher's table by name and then apply a filter to display only publishers located in New York.

a. Open the **Publishers table** in Datasheet view. Notice Time Life appears after Triumph Books. This is because the table is sorted by the PubID field.

b. Click in any record in the PubName field and sort the field in ascending order.

c. Apply a Selection filter to display only publishers with a PubCity equal to **New York**.

d. Close the table and save the changes.

Use Filter By Form

You will obtain a list of all books with more than 50 units in stock. This will help the management decide on what books to put on sale. You will use Filter By Form to accomplish this. You will also demonstrate how filters are saved.

a. Open the **Books table** in Datasheet view.

b. Use Filter By Form to display books with more than **50** units in stock. Save and close the table.

c. Open the **Books table** in Datasheet view. Click **Toggle Filter** in the Sort & Filter group to demonstrate that the filter is saved.

Back Up a Database and Add an Application Part

You will demonstrate adding an application part to the manager to show how tables are created. You will first back the database up to reinforce the importance of backing up the data.

a. Create a backup copy of your database, accepting the default file name.

b. Add a Comments application part, selecting the option **One 'Books' to many 'Comments'**. Select the **Title field** for the Field from Books and **Sort Ascending** for Sort this field. Name the lookup column **Book**.

c. Open the **Comments table** in Datasheet view. Add a new comment. Select **Social Media: A Student's View** for the Book. Use the current date and add **A fun and insightful book!** for the Comment field.

d. Close the database and exit Access. Based on your instructor's directions, submit the following:

a01c1Books_LastFirst
a01c1Books_LastFirst_*CurrentDate*

Access

Tables and Queries in Relational Databases

LEARNING OUTCOMES

- **You will create and modify tables for data input and organization.**
- **You will develop queries to extract and present data.**

OBJECTIVES & SKILLS: After you read this chapter, you will be able to:

CASE STUDY | Bank Audit

During a year-end review, a bank auditor uncovers mishandled funds at Commonwealth Federal Bank in Wilmington, Delaware. In order to analyze the data in more detail, the auditor asks you to create an Access database so he can review the affected customers, the compromised accounts, and the branches involved.

As you begin, you realize that some of the data are contained in external Excel and Access files that you decide to import directly into the new database. Importing from Excel and Access is fairly common, and will help to avoid errors that are associated with data entry. Once the data have been imported, you will use queries to determine exactly which records are relevant to the investigation.

This chapter introduces the Bank database case study to present the basic principles of table and query design. Once the new database is created and all the data are entered, you will help the auditor answer questions by creating and running queries. The value of that information depends entirely on the quality of the underlying data—the tables.

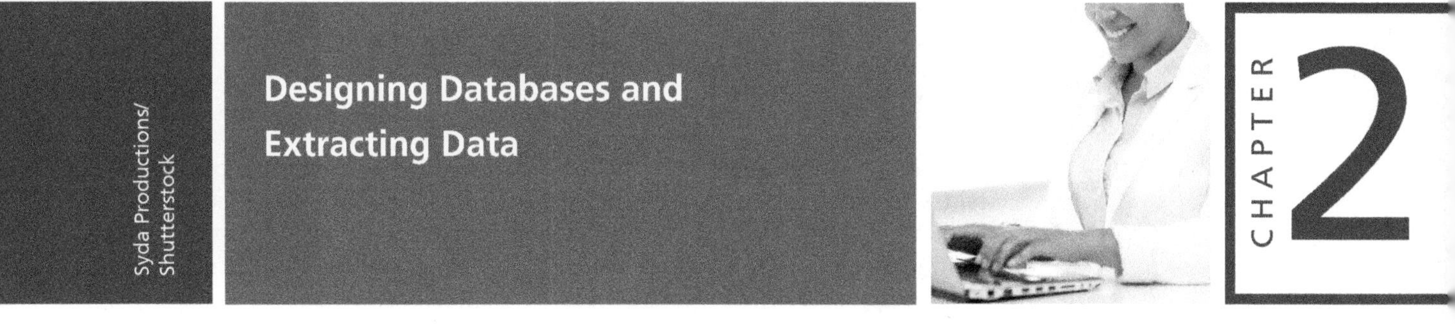

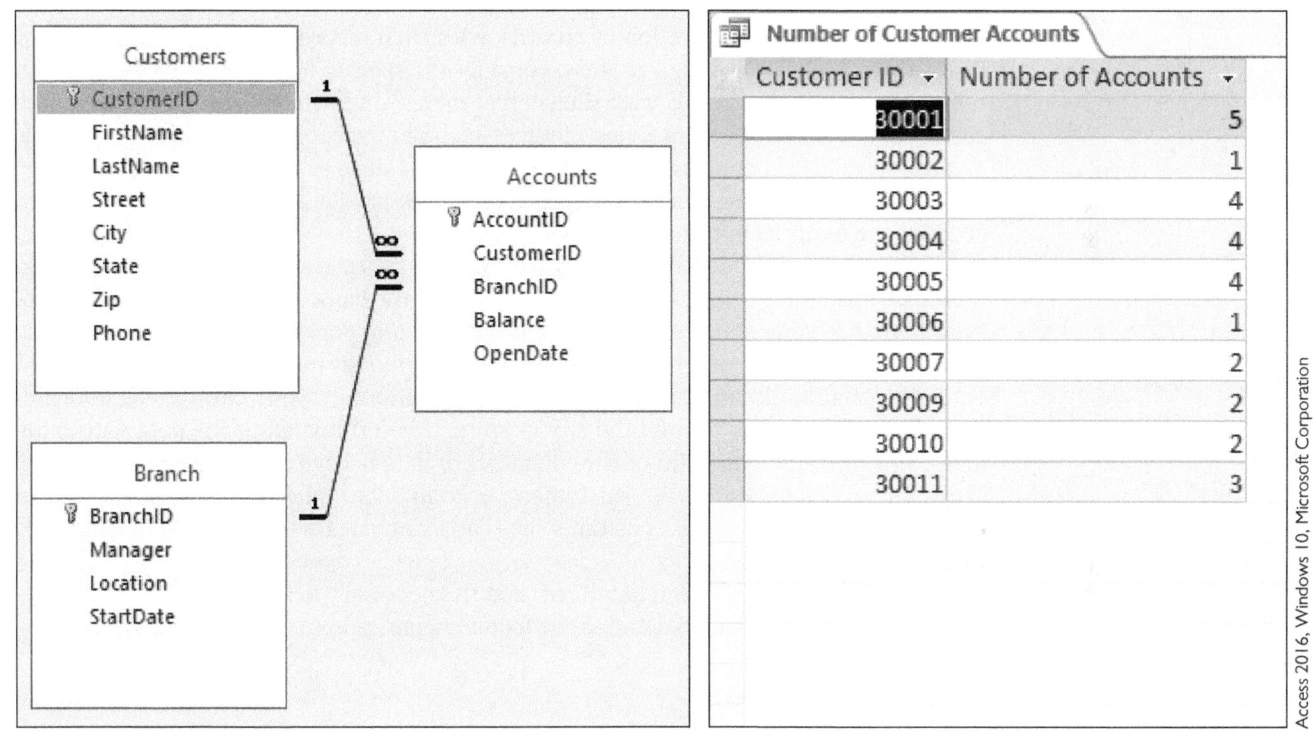

FIGURE 2.1 Bank Audit Database

CASE STUDY | Bank Audit

Starting Files	File to be Submitted
Blank desktop database **a02h2Accounts** **a02h2Customers**	**a02h4Bank_LastFirst**

Table Design, Creation, and Modification

Good database design begins with the tables. Tables provide the framework for all of the activities you perform in a database. If the framework is poorly designed, the database will not function as expected. Whether you are experienced in designing tables or are a new database designer, the process should not be done haphazardly. You should follow a systematic approach when creating tables for a database.

In this section, you will learn the essentials of good table design. After developing and analyzing the table design on paper, you will implement that design in Access. While you learned to create tables in the previous chapter, in this chapter you will learn to refine them by changing the properties of various fields.

Designing a Table

Recall that a table is a collection of records, with each record made up of a number of fields. During the table design process, consider the specific fields you will need in each table; list the proposed fields with the correct tables, and determine what type of data each field will store (numbers, dates, pictures, etc.) The order of the fields within the table and the specific field names are not significant at this stage as they can be changed later. What is important is that the tables contain all necessary fields so that the database can produce the required information later.

For example, consider the design process necessary to create a database for a bank. Most likely you have a bank account and know that the bank maintains data about you. Your bank has your name, address, phone number, and Social Security number. It also knows which accounts you have (checking, savings, money market), if you have a credit card with that bank, and what its balance is. Additionally, your bank keeps information about its branches around the city or state. If you think about the data your bank maintains, you can make a list of the categories of data needed to store that information. These categories for the bank—customers, accounts, branches—become the tables in the bank's database. A bank's customer list is an example of a table; it contains a record for each bank customer.

After the tables have been identified, add the necessary fields using these six guidelines, which are discussed in detail in the following paragraphs:

- Include the necessary data.
- Design for now and for the future.
- Store data in their smallest parts.
- Determine primary keys.
- Link tables using common fields.
- Design to accommodate calculations.

Figure 2.2 shows a customer table and two other tables found in a sample Bank database. It also lists fields that would be needed in each table.

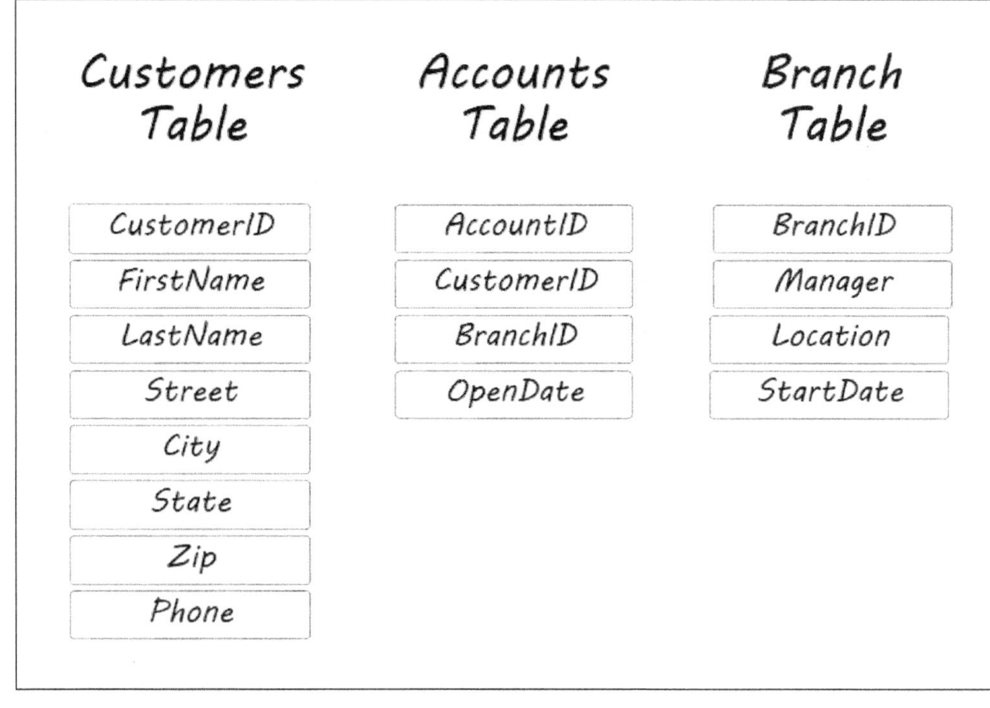

FIGURE 2.2 Rough Draft of Tables and Fields in a Sample Bank Database

Include Necessary Data

A good way to determine what data are necessary in tables is to consider the output you will need from your database. You will probably need to create professional-looking reports for others, so begin by creating a rough draft of the reports you will need. Then design tables that contain the fields necessary to create those reports. In other words, ask yourself what information will be expected from the database (output) and determine the data required (input) to produce that information. Consider, for example, the tables and fields in Figure 2.2. Is there required information that could not be generated from those tables?

- You will be able to determine how long a customer has banked with the branch because the date he or she opened the account is stored in the Accounts table, which will connect to the Customers and Branch tables.
- You will be able to determine which branch a customer uses because the Accounts table includes both the CustomerID and the BranchID. The Accounts table will eventually connect to both the Customers and Branch tables, making it possible to gather this information.
- You will not be able to generate the monthly bank statement. In order to generate a customer bank statement (showing all deposits and withdrawals for the month), you would need to add an additional table—to track activity for each account.
- You will not be able to email a customer because the Customers table does not contain an email field at this time.

If you discover a missing field, such as the email field, you can add it during the initial design process or later.

Design for Now and for the Future

As the information requirements of an organization evolve over time, the database systems that hold the data must change as well. When designing a database, try to anticipate the future needs of the system and build in the flexibility to satisfy those demands. For example, you may also decide to create additional fields for future use (such as an email or customer photo field). However, additional fields will also require more storage space, which you will need to calculate, especially when working with larger databases. Good database design must balance the data collection needs of the company with the cost associated with collection and storage. Plans must also include the frequency and cost necessary to modify and update the database.

In the Bank database, for example, you would store each customer's name, address, and home phone number. You would also want to store additional phone numbers for many customers—a cell phone number, and perhaps a work number. As a database designer, you will design the tables to accommodate multiple entries for similar data.

Store Data in Their Smallest Parts

The table design in Figure 2.2 divides a customer's name into two fields (FirstName and LastName) to store each value individually. You might think it easier to use a single field consisting of both the first and last name, but that approach is too limiting. Consider a list of customer names stored as a single field:

- Sue Grater
- Rick Grater
- Nancy Gallagher
- Harry Weigner
- Barb Shank
- Pete Shank

The first problem in this approach is the lack of flexibility: You could not easily create a salutation for a letter using the form *Dear Sue* or *Dear Ms. Gallagher* because the first and last names are not accessible individually.

A second difficulty is that the list of customers cannot be easily displayed in alphabetical order by last name because the last name begins in the middle of the field. The most common way to sort names is by the last name, which you can do more efficiently if the last name is stored as a separate field.

Think of how an address might be used. The city, state, and postal code should always be stored as separate fields. You may need to select records from a particular state or postal code, which will be easier if you store the data as separate fields.

Determine Primary Keys

When designing your database tables, it is important to determine the primary key, the field that will uniquely identify each record in a table. For example, in Figure 2.2, the CustomerID field will uniquely identify each customer in the database.

Plan for Common Fields Between Tables

As you create the tables and fields for the database, keep in mind that some tables will be joined in relationships using common fields. Creating relationships will help you to extract data from more than one table when creating queries, forms, and reports. For example, you will be able to determine which customers have which accounts by joining the Customers and Accounts tables. For now, you should name the common fields the same (although that is not a firm requirement in Access). For example, CustomerID in the Customers table will join to the CustomerID field in the Accounts table. Draw a line between common fields to indicate the joins, as shown in Figure 2.3. These join lines will be created in Access when you learn to create table relationships later in the chapter.

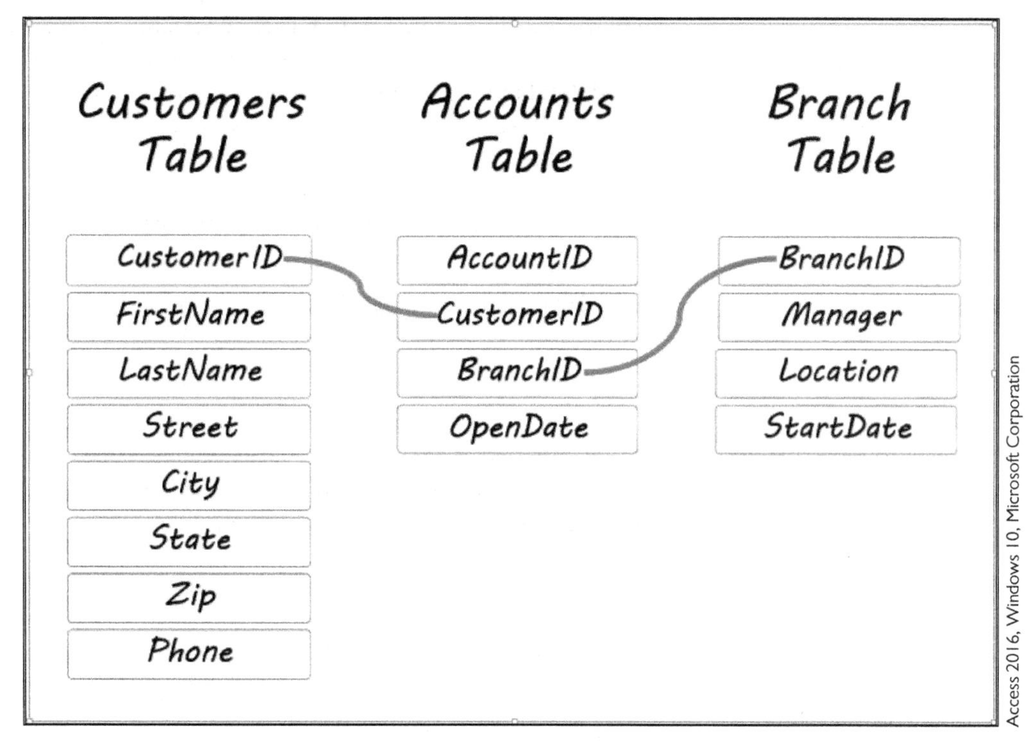

FIGURE 2.3 Determine Relationships Using Common Fields

Avoid ***data redundancy***, which is the unnecessary storing of duplicate data in two or more tables. Having redundant or duplicate data in multiple tables can lead to serious errors. Suppose the customer address data were stored in both the Customers and Accounts tables. If a customer moved to a new address, it is possible that the address would be updated in only one of the two tables. The result would be inconsistent and unreliable information. Depending on which table you would use to check an address, either the new or the old one might be given to someone requesting the information. Storing the address in only one table is more reliable; if it changes, it only needs to be updated one time (in the Customers table) and can be referenced again and again from that table.

TIP: ADD CALCULATED FIELDS TO A TABLE

A calculated field produces a value from an expression or function that references one or more existing fields. Access enables you to store calculated fields in a table using the calculated data type, and to include those fields in queries, forms, and reports. However, many Access users prefer to create calculated fields in their query designs rather than in the tables themselves.

Design to Accommodate Calculations

Calculated fields are frequently created in database objects with numeric data, such as a monthly interest field that multiplies the balance in a customer's account by 1% each month (Balance*.01). You can also create calculated fields using date/time data. For example, if you want to store the length of time a customer has had an account, you can create a calculated field that subtracts the opening date from today's date. The result will be the number of days each customer has been an account holder.

A person's age is another example of a calculated field using date arithmetic—the date of birth is subtracted from today's date and the result is divided by 365 (or 365.25 to account for leap years). It might seem easier to store a person's age as a number rather than the birth date and avoid the calculated field, but that would be a mistake because age changes over time and the field would need to be updated each time it changes. You can use date arithmetic to subtract one date from another to find out the number of days, months, or years that have elapsed between them.

Creating and Modifying Tables and Working with Data

STEP 1 Tables can be created in a new blank database or in an existing database.

To create a table, complete one of the following steps:

- Enter field names and table data directly in Datasheet view.
- Type field names in rows in Design view and then enter the data in Datasheet view.
- Import data from another database or application, such as Excel.
- Use a template.

Regardless of how a table is first created, you can always modify it later to include a new field or modify an existing field. Figure 2.4 shows a table created by entering fields in Design view.

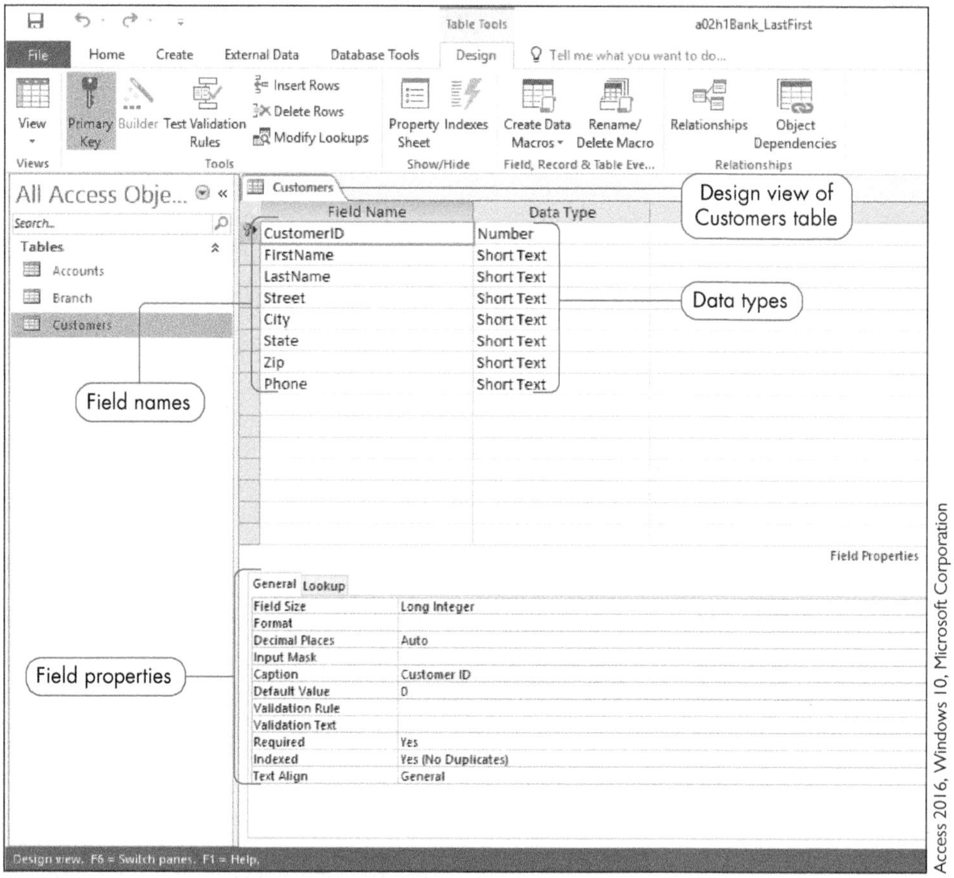

FIGURE 2.4 Customers Table Created in Design View

When you add a new field to a table, the field must be given an appropriate name to identify the data it holds. The field name should be descriptive of the data and can be up to 64 characters in length, including letters, numbers, and spaces. Field names cannot begin with a leading blank space. Database developers sometimes use Pascal Case notation for field names. Instead of spaces in multiword field names, you can use uppercase letters to distinguish the first letter of each new word, for example, ProductCost or LastName (sometimes developers use Camel Case, which is similar to Pascal Case, where the first letter of the first word is lowercase). It is sometimes preferable to avoid spaces in field names, because spaces can cause naming conflicts with other applications that may use these fields, such as Microsoft Visual Basic for Applications.

Fields can be added, deleted, or renamed either in Design view or Datasheet view. To delete a field in Datasheet view, select the field and press Delete. Click Yes in the message box.

To delete a field in Design view, complete the following steps:

1. Click the record selector of the field you want to delete to select it.
2. Click Delete Rows in the Tools group on the Design tab.
3. Click Yes in the message box that displays to confirm that you want to permanently delete the field and the data in it. Click No if you do not want to delete the field.
4. Click Yes in the second message box that displays if the selected field you are deleting is a primary key. Click No if you do not want to delete the primary key.

To rename a field, double-click the field name you want to change, type the new field name, press Enter, and then save the table.

TIP: HIDE FIELDS IN AN ACCESS DATASHEET

To hide a field in a datasheet, right-click the column selector that displays the field name and from the shortcut menu, select Hide Fields. To make the field visible again, right-click any column selector, select Unhide Fields, and select the appropriate column's check box.

Determine Data Type

Every field has an assigned ***data type*** that determines the type of data that can be entered and the operations that can be performed on that data. Access recognizes 12 data types. Table 2.1 lists these data types, their uses, and examples of each. You can change a data type after you have entered data into your table, but do so with caution. Be aware of messages from Access indicating that you may lose data when you save your changes. In some cases, changing data types is inconsequential; for example, you may want to convert a number to a currency value. This type of change would only affect the formatting displayed with the values, but not the underlying values themselves. In any case, when designing tables, choose the initial data type carefully, and be sure to back up your database before changing data types.

TABLE 2.1 Data Types and Uses

Data Type	Description	Example
Short Text	Stores alphanumeric data, such as a customer's name or address. It can contain alphabetic characters, numbers, and/or special characters (e.g., an apostrophe in O'Malley). Social Security numbers, telephone numbers, and postal codes should be designated as text fields because they are not used in calculations and often contain special characters such as hyphens and parentheses. A short text field can hold up to 255 characters.	2184 Walnut Street
Long Text	Lengthy text or combinations of text and numbers, such as several sentences or paragraphs; used to hold descriptive data. Long text controls can display up to 64,000 characters.	A description of product packaging
Number	Contains a value that can be used in a calculation, such as the number of credits a course is worth. The contents are restricted to numbers, a decimal point, and a plus or minus sign.	12
Date/Time	Stores dates or times that can be used in date or time arithmetic.	10/31/2018 1:30:00 AM
Currency	Used for fields that contain monetary values.	$1,200

TABLE 2.1 Continued

Data Type	Description	Example
AutoNumber	A special data type used to assign the next consecutive number each time you add a record. The value of an AutoNumber field is unique for each record in the table.	1, 2, 3
Yes/No	Only one of two values can be stored, such as Yes or No, True or False, or On or Off (also known as a Boolean). For example, is a student on the Dean's list: Yes or No.	Yes
OLE Object	Contains an object created by another application. OLE objects include pictures and sounds.	JPG image
Hyperlink	Stores a Web address (URL) or the path to a folder or file. Hyperlink fields can be clicked to retrieve a webpage or to launch a file stored locally.	http://www.irs.gov
Attachment	Used to store multiple images, spreadsheet files, Word documents, and other types of supported files.	An Excel workbook
Calculated	The results of an expression that references one or more existing fields.	[Price]*.05
Lookup Wizard	Creates a field that enables you to choose a value from another table or from a list of values by using a list box or a combo box.	Accounts table with a CustomerID field that looks up the customer from the records in the Customers table

Set a Table's Primary Key

STEP 2 The primary key is the field (or possibly a combination of fields) that uniquely identifies each record in a table. Access does not require that each table have a primary key. However, a good database design usually includes a primary key in each table. You should select unique and infrequently changing data for the primary key. For example, a credit card number may seem to be unique, but would not make a good primary key because it is subject to change when a new card is issued due to fraudulent activity.

You probably would not use a person's name as the primary key, because several people could have the same name. A value like CustomerID, as shown in the Customers table in Figure 2.5, is unique and is a better choice for the primary key. When no field seems to stand out as a primary key naturally, you can create a primary key field with the AutoNumber data type. The ***AutoNumber*** data type is a number that automatically increments each time a record is added.

Figure 2.6 depicts a Speakers table, where no unique field can be identified from the data itself. In this case, you can identify the SpeakerID field with an AutoNumber data type. Access automatically numbers each speaker record sequentially with a unique ID as each record is added.

Customers

Customer ID	FirstName	LastName	Street	City	State	Zip	Phone	Click to Add
30001	Allison	Millward	2732 Baker Blvd.	Greensboro	NC	27492	(555) 334-5678	
30002	Bernett	Fox	12 Orchestra Terrace	High Point	NC	27494	(555) 358-5554	
30003	Clay	Hayes	P.O. Box 555	Greensboro	NC	27492	(555) 998-4457	
30004	Cordle	Collins	2743 Bering St.	Winston-Salem	NC	27492	(555) 447-2283	
30005	Eaton	Wagner	2743 Bering St.	Greensboro	NC	27492	(555) 988-3346	
30006	Kwasi	Williams	89 Jefferson Way	High Point	NC	27494	(555) 447-5565	
30007	Natasha	Simpson	187 Suffolk Ln.	Greensboro	NC	27493	(555) 775-3389	
30008	Joy	Jones	305 - 14th Ave. S.	Winston-Salem	NC	27493	(555) 258-7655	
30009	John	Nunn	89 Chiaroscuro Rd.	Greensboro	NC	27494	(555) 998-5557	
30010	Laura	Peterson	120 Hanover Sq.	Winston-Salem	NC	27492	(555) 334-6654	
30011	YourName	YourName	800 University Ave.	High Point	NC	27494	(555) 447-1235	
* 0								

FIGURE 2.5 Customers Table with a Natural Primary Key

Speakers

SpeakerID	First Name	Last Name	Address	City	Sta	Zip Co	Phone Numl	Email	AreaOfExpertise	Click to Add
1	Jerri	Williams	10000 SW 59 Court	Miami	FL	33146	(305) 777-8888	cahsley@um.edu	Student Life	
2	Warren	Brasington	9470 SW 25 Street	Philadelphia	PA	19104	(215) 888-7654	wbrasington@up.edu	Residence Halls	
3	James	Shindell	14088 Malaga Avenue	Miami	FL	33146	(305) 773-4343	jshindell@um.edu	Administration	
		od	400 Roderigo Avenue	Gainesville	FL	32611	(352) 555-5555	ewood@uf.edu	Student Life	
			9290 NW 59 Steet	Athens	GA	30602	(706) 777-1111	kpark@ug.edu	Student Life	
		amson	108 Los Pinos Place	Tuscaloosa	AL	35487	(205) 888-4554	wwilliamson@ua.edu	Deans' Office	
7	Holly	Davis	8009 Riviera Drive	Gainesville	FL	32611	(352) 388-7676	hdavis.uf.edu	Residence Halls	
8	David	Tannen	50 Main Street	Philadelphia	PA	19104	(215) 777-2211	dtannen@up.edu	Student Life	
9	Jeffrey	Jacobsen	490 Bell Drive	Athens	GA	30602	(706) 388-9999	jjacobsen@ug.edu	Wellness	
10	Jerry	Masters	2000 Main Highway	Miami	FL	33146	(305) 777-8998	jmasters@um.edy	Wellness	
11	Kevin	Kline	2980 SW 89 Street	Gainesville	FL	32611	(352) 877-8900	kkline@uf.edu	Student Life	
			110 Center Highway	Athens	GA	30602	(706) 893-8872	jwithers@ug.edu	Wellness	
			2987 SW 14 Avenue	Philadelphia	PA	19104	(215) 558-7748	ballman@up.edu	Counseling Center	
			1008 West Marine Road	Miami	FL	33146	(305) 877-4993	mmiller@um.edu	Student Life	
15	Nancy	Vance	1878 W. 6 Street	Gainesville	FL	32611	(352) 885-4330	nvance@uf.edu	Counseling Center	
16	George	Jensen	42-15 81 Street	Elmhurst	NY	11373	(718) 555-6666	gjensen@school.edu	Residence Halls	
(New)										

FIGURE 2.6 Speakers Table with an AutoNumber Primary Key

Explore a Foreign Key

In order to share data between two tables, the tables must share a common field. The common field will generally be the primary key in one table; the same field in the adjoining table is denoted as the ***foreign key***. The CustomerID is the primary key (identified with a primary key icon) in the Customers table and uniquely identifies each customer in the database. It also displays as a foreign key in the related Accounts table. The Accounts table contains the CustomerID field to establish which customer owns the account. A CustomerID can be entered only one time in the Customers table, but it may be entered multiple times in the Accounts table because one customer may own several accounts (checking, savings, credit card, etc.). Therefore, the CustomerID is the primary key in the Customers table and a foreign key in the Accounts table, as shown in Figure 2.7.

Customers

Customer ID	FirstName	LastName	Street	City	State	Zip	Phone	Click to Add
30001	Allison	Millward	2732 Baker Blvd.	Greensboro	NC	27492	(555) 334-5678	
30002	Bernett	Fox	12 Orchestra Terrace	High Point	NC	27494	(555) 358-5554	
30003	Clay	Hayes	P.O. Box 555	Greensboro	NC	27492	(555) 998-4457	
30004	Cordle	Collins	2743 Bering St.	Winston-Salem	NC	27492	(555) 447-2283	
		Wagner	2743 Bering St.	Greensboro	NC	27492	(555) 988-3346	
		Williams	89 Jefferson Way	High Point	NC	27494	(555) 447-5565	
		Simpson	187 Suffolk Ln.	Greensboro	NC	27493	(555) 775-3389	
30008	Joy	Jones	305 - 14th Ave. S.	Winston-Salem	NC	27493	(555) 258-7655	
30009	John	Nunn	89 Chiaroscuro Rd.	Greensboro	NC	27494	(555) 998-5557	
30010	Laura	Peterson	120 Hanover Sq.	Winston-Salem	NC	27492	(555) 334-6654	
30011	YourName	YourName	800 University Ave.	High Point	NC	27494	(555) 447-1235	
0								

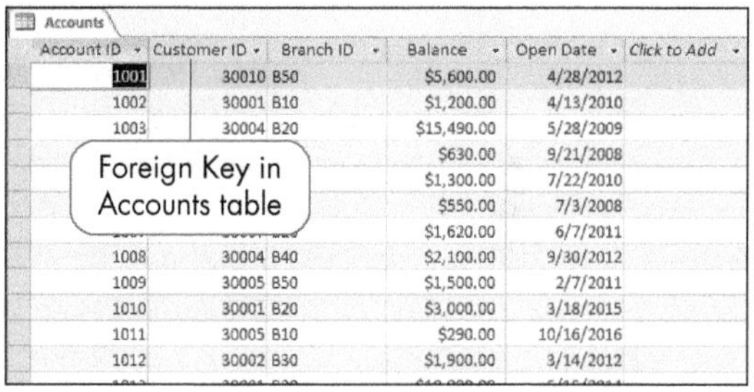

Accounts

Account ID	Customer ID	Branch ID	Balance	Open Date	Click to Add
1001	30010	B50	$5,600.00	4/28/2012	
1002	30001	B10	$1,200.00	4/13/2010	
1003	30004	B20	$15,490.00	5/28/2009	
			$630.00	9/21/2008	
			$1,300.00	7/22/2010	
			$550.00	7/3/2008	
			$1,620.00	6/7/2011	
1008	30004	B40	$2,100.00	9/30/2012	
1009	30005	B50	$1,500.00	2/7/2011	
1010	30001	B20	$3,000.00	3/18/2015	
1011	30005	B10	$290.00	10/16/2016	
1012	30002	B30	$1,900.00	3/14/2012	

FIGURE 2.7 Two Tables Illustrating Primary and Foreign Keys

> **TIP: BEST FIT COLUMNS**
>
> If a field name is cut off in Datasheet view, you can adjust the column width by positioning the pointer on the vertical border on the right side of the column. When the pointer displays as a two-headed arrow, double-click the border. You can also click More in the Records group on the Home tab, select Field Width, and then click Best Fit in the Column Width dialog box.

Work with Field Properties

STEP 3 While a field's data type determines the type of data that can be entered and the operations that can be performed on that data, its ***field properties*** determine how the field looks and behaves. The field properties are set to default values according to the data type, but you can modify them if necessary. Field properties are commonly set in Design view, as shown in Figure 2.4; however, certain properties can be set in Datasheet view, on the Table Tools Fields tab. Common property types are defined in Table 2.2.

Field Size is a commonly changed field property. The field size determines the amount of space a field uses in the database. A field with a Short Text data type can store up to 255 characters; however, you can limit the characters by reducing the field size property. For example, you might limit the State field to only two characters because all state abbreviations are two letters. When setting field sizes, you may want to anticipate any future requirements of the database that might necessitate larger values to be stored.

You can set the ***Caption property*** to create a label that is more understandable than a field name. While Pascal Case is often preferred for field names, adding a space between words is often more readable. When a caption is set, it displays at the top of a table or query column in Datasheet view (instead of the field name), and when the field is used in a report or form. For example, a field named CustomerID could have the caption *Customer Number*.

Set the Validation Rule property to restrict data entry in a field to ensure that correct data are entered. The validation rule checks the data entered when the user exits the field. If the data entered violate the validation rule, an error message displays and prevents the invalid data from being entered into the field. For example, if you have set a rule on a date field that the date entered must be on or after today, and a date in the past is entered in the field, an error message will display. You can customize the error message (validation text) when you set the validation rule.

The Input Mask property simplifies data entry by providing literal characters that are typed for every entry, such as hyphens in a Social Security number (- -), or dashes in a phone number. Input masks ensure that data in fields such as these are consistently entered and formatted.

TABLE 2.2 Common Access Table Property Types and Descriptions

Property Type	Description
Field Size	Determines the maximum number of characters of a text field or the format of a number field.
Format	Changes the way a field is displayed or printed but does not affect the stored value.
Input Mask	Simplifies data entry by providing literal characters that are typed for every entry, such as hyphens in a Social Security number (- -) or slashes in a date. It also imposes data validation by ensuring that data entered conform to the mask.
Caption	Enables an alternate (or more readable) name to be displayed other than the field name; alternate name displays in datasheets, forms, and reports.
Default Value	Enters automatically a predetermined value for a field each time a new record is added to the table. For example, if most customers live in Los Angeles, the default value for the City field could be set to Los Angeles to save data entry time and promote accurate data entry.
Validation Rule	Requires data entered to conform to a specified rule.
Validation Text	Specifies the error message that is displayed when the validation rule is violated.
Required	Indicates that a value for this field must be entered. Primary key fields always require data entry.
Allow Zero Length	Allows entry of zero length text strings ("") in a Hyperlink, or Short or Long Text fields.
Indexed	Increases the efficiency of a search on the designated field.
Expression	Used for calculated fields only. Specifies the expression you want Access to evaluate and store.
Result Type	Used for calculated fields only. Specifies the format for the calculated field results.

TIP: FREEZE FIELDS IN AN ACCESS DATABASE

To keep a field viewable while you are scrolling through a table, select the field or fields you want to freeze, right-click, and then select Freeze Fields. If you want the field(s) to remain frozen when you are finished working, save the changes when you close the table. To unfreeze all fields, right-click the field(s) and select Unfreeze All Fields.

Create a New Field in Design View

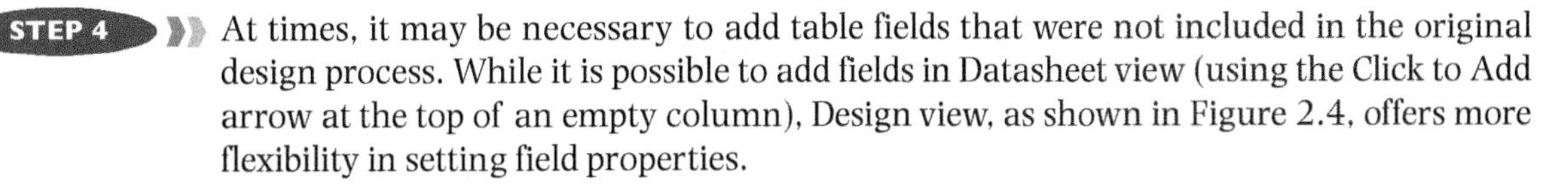

STEP 4 »» At times, it may be necessary to add table fields that were not included in the original design process. While it is possible to add fields in Datasheet view (using the Click to Add arrow at the top of an empty column), Design view, as shown in Figure 2.4, offers more flexibility in setting field properties.

To add a new field in Design view, complete the following steps:

1. Click in the first empty field row in the top pane of the table's Design view.
2. Enter the Field Name, Data Type, and Description (optional), and then set the Field Properties.
3. Click the row selector, and then click and drag the new field to place it in a different position in the table.
4. Click Save on the Quick Access Toolbar, and then switch to Datasheet view to enter or modify data.

Modify the Table in Datasheet View

STEP 5 »» Whereas Design view is commonly used to create and modify the table structure by enabling you to add and edit fields and set field properties, Datasheet view is used to add, edit, and delete records. Datasheet view of an Access table displays data in a grid format—rows represent records and columns represent fields. You can select a record by clicking the record selector on the left side of each record. Use the new blank record (marked with an asterisk) at the end of the table to add a new record, or click the New (blank) record button on the navigation bar at the bottom of the table.

Quick Concepts

1. What is meant by "Store data in its smallest parts" when designing database tables? *p. 736*
2. What is the difference between a primary key and a foreign key? *p. 741*
3. Which field property creates a more readable label that displays in the top row in Datasheet view and in forms and reports? *p. 742*

Hands-On Exercises

Watch the Video for this Hands-On Exercise!
MyITLab®
HOE1 Training

Skills covered: Create a Table in Datasheet View • Delete a Field • Set a Table's Primary Key • Work with Field Properties • Create a New Field in Design View • Modify the Table in Datasheet View

1 Table Design, Creation, and Modification

Creating a database for the bank auditor at Commonwealth Federal Bank as he investigates the mishandled funds will be a great opportunity for you to showcase your database design and Access skills.

STEP 1 » CREATE A TABLE IN DATASHEET VIEW

You create a new desktop database to store information about the mishandled funds. You enter the data for the first record (BranchID, Manager, and Location). Refer to Figure 2.8 as you complete Step 1.

Branch

ID	BranchID	Manager	Location	Click to Add
1	B10	Krebs	Uptown	
2	B20	Esposito	Eastern	
3	B30	Amoako	Western	
4	B40	Singh	Southern	
5	B50	YourLastName	Campus	
* (New)				

Step i: Save the table as Branch

Step h: Type the data directly into the datasheet

Access 2016, Windows 10, Microsoft Corporation

FIGURE 2.8 Create the Branch Table in Datasheet View

a. Start Microsoft Office Access 2016 and click **Blank desktop database**.

b. Type **a02h1Bank_LastFirst** into the File Name box.

c. Click **Browse** to find the folder location where you will store the database and click **OK**. Click **Create** to create the new database.

Access will create the new database named a02h1Bank_LastFirst and a new table will automatically open in Datasheet view. There is already an ID field in the table by default.

d. Click **Click to Add** and select **Short Text** as the Data type.

Click to Add changes to Field1. Field1 is selected to make it easier to change the field name.

e. Type **BranchID** and press **Tab**.

A list of data types for the third column opens so that you can select the data type for the third column.

f. Select Short Text in the Click to Add window, type **Manager**, and then press **Tab**.

g. Select Short Text in the Click to Add window, and then type **Location**.

h. Click in the first column (the ID field) next to the New Record asterisk, press **Tab**, and then type the data for the new table as shown in Figure 2.8, letting Access assign the ID field for each new record (using the AutoNumber data type). Replace *YourLastName* with your own last name.

i. Click **Save** on the Quick Access Toolbar. Type **Branch** in the Save As dialog box and click **OK**.

Entering field names, data types, and data directly in Datasheet view provides a simplified way to create the table initially.

STEP 2 » DELETE A FIELD AND SET A TABLE'S PRIMARY KEY

It is possible to modify tables even after data have been entered; however, be alert to potential messages from Access after you make design changes that may affect your data. In this step, you will modify the Branch table. You examine the design of the table and realize that the BranchID field is a unique identifier, making the ID field redundant. You delete the ID field and make the BranchID field the primary key field. Refer to Figure 2.9 as you complete Step 2.

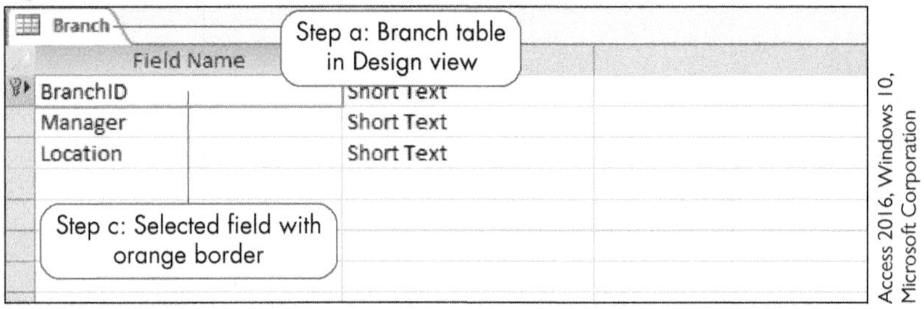

Step a: Branch table in Design view

Step c: Selected field with orange border

Access 2016, Windows 10, Microsoft Corporation

FIGURE 2.9 Branch Table in Design View

a. Click **View** in the Views group on the Home tab to switch to Design view of the Branch table.

The field name for each of the four fields displays along with the data type.

b. Ensure that the ID field selected, click **Delete Rows** in the Tools group on the Design tab. Click **Yes** to both warning messages.

Access responds with a warning that you are about to permanently delete a field and a second warning that the field is the primary key. You delete the field because you will set the BranchID field as the primary key.

c. Ensure that the BranchID field is selected, as shown in Figure 2.9.

d. Click **Primary Key** in the Tools group on the Design tab.

You set BranchID as the primary key. The Indexed property in the Field Properties section at the bottom of the design window displays Yes (No Duplicates).

e. Click **Save** on the Quick Access Toolbar to save the table.

TIP: SHORTCUT MENU

You can right-click a row selector to display a shortcut menu to copy a field, set the primary key, insert or delete rows, or access table properties. Use the shortcut menu to make these specific changes to the design of a table.

STEP 3 » WORK WITH FIELD PROPERTIES

You will modify the table design further to comply with the bank auditor's specifications. Refer to Figure 2.10 as you complete Step 3.

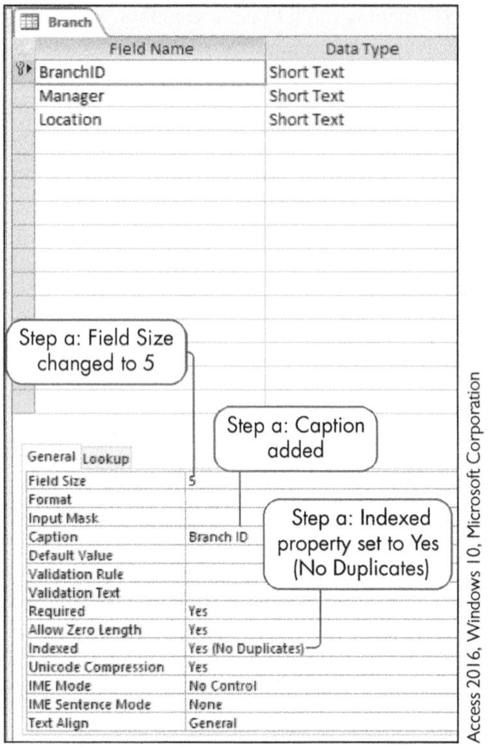

Branch

Field Name	Data Type
BranchID	Short Text
Manager	Short Text
Location	Short Text

Step a: Field Size changed to 5

Step a: Caption added

Step a: Indexed property set to Yes (No Duplicates)

General Lookup

Field Size	5
Format	
Input Mask	
Caption	Branch ID
Default Value	
Validation Rule	
Validation Text	
Required	Yes
Allow Zero Length	Yes
Indexed	Yes (No Duplicates)
Unicode Compression	Yes
IME Mode	No Control
IME Sentence Mode	None
Text Align	General

Access 2016, Windows 10, Microsoft Corporation

FIGURE 2.10 Changes to the Field Properties of the Branch Table in Design View

a. Click in the **BranchID field name**; modify the BranchID field properties by completing the following steps:

- Click in the **Field Size box** and change 255 to **5**.
- Click in the **Caption box** and type **Branch ID**. Make sure Branch and ID have a space between them.
  A caption provides a more descriptive field name. It will display as the column heading in Datasheet view.
- Check the Indexed property; confirm it is Yes (No Duplicates).

b. Click the **Manager field name**; modify the Manager field properties by completing the following steps:

- Click in the **Field Size box** in the Field Properties pane, and change 255 to **30**.
- Click in the **Caption box** in the Field Properties pane, and type **Manager's Name**.

c. Click the **Location field name** and modify the following Location field properties by completing the following steps:

- Click in the **Field Size box** and change 255 to **30**.
- Click in the **Caption box** and type **Branch Location**.

> **TIP: F6 FUNCTION KEY TO SWITCH TO FIELD PROPERTIES**
> With a field name selected in the top pane of the Design window, you can press the F6 function key to toggle to the field properties for the selected field. Continue to press F6 to cycle through the additional elements of the Access screen.

STEP 4 ›› CREATE A NEW FIELD IN DESIGN VIEW

You notify the auditor that a date field is missing in your new table. Modify the table to add the new field. Refer to Figure 2.11 as you complete Step 4.

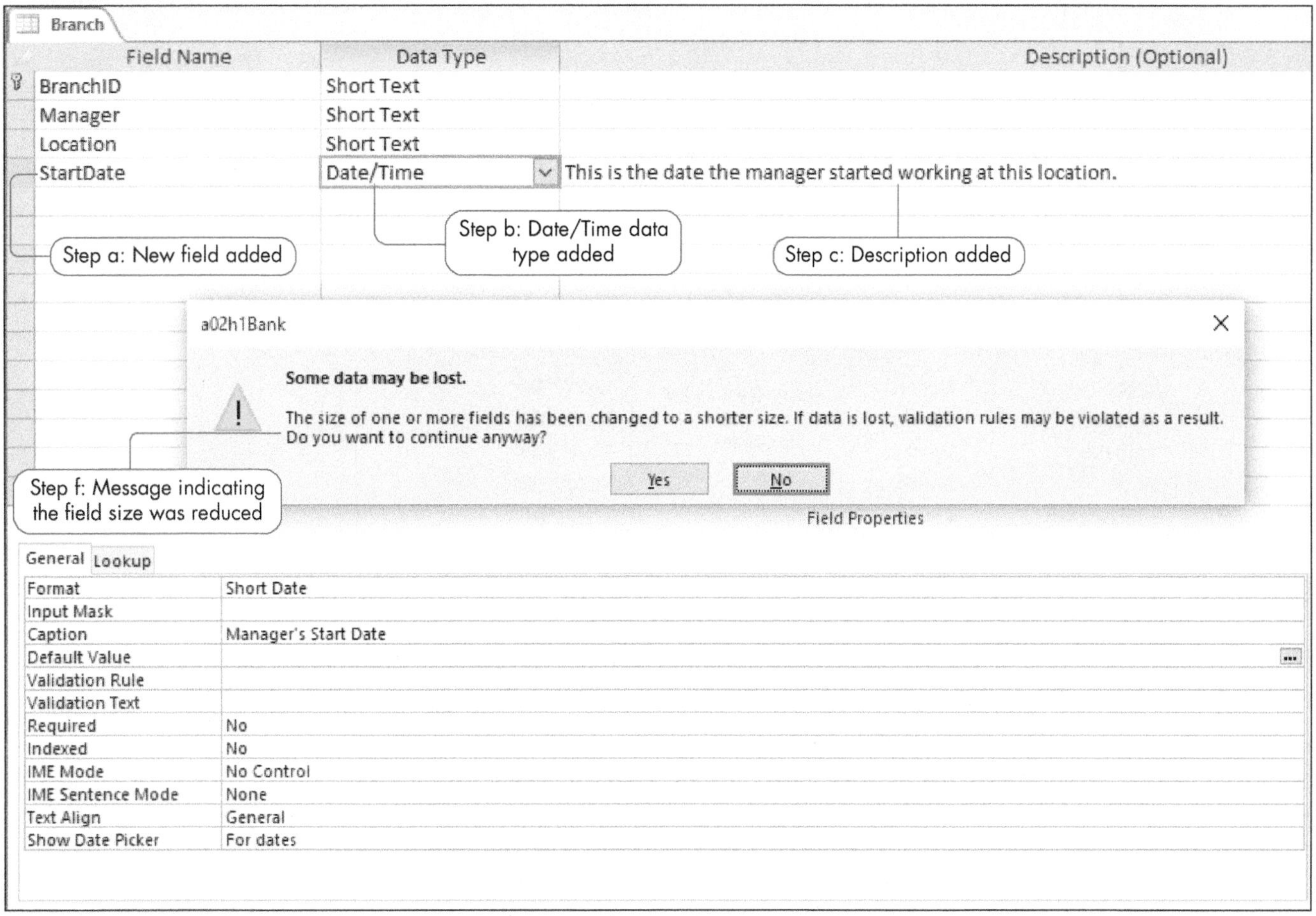

Branch
Field Name
Data Type
Description (Optional)
BranchID
Short Text
Manager
Short Text
Location
Short Text
StartDate
Date/Time
This is the date the manager started working at this location.
Step a: New field added
Step b: Date/Time data type added
Step c: Description added
a02h1Bank
Some data may be lost.
The size of one or more fields has been changed to a shorter size. If data is lost, validation rules may be violated as a result. Do you want to continue anyway?
Yes
No
Step f: Message indicating the field size was reduced
Field Properties
General
Lookup
Format
Short Date
Input Mask
Caption
Manager's Start Date
Default Value
Validation Rule
Validation Text
Required
No
Indexed
No
IME Mode
No Control
IME Sentence Mode
None
Text Align
General
Show Date Picker
For dates

Access 2016, Windows 10, Microsoft Corporation

FIGURE 2.11 Adding a New Field to the Branch Table in Design View

a. Click in the first blank field row below the Location field name and type **StartDate**.

You added a new field to the table.

b. Press **Tab** to move to the Data Type column. Click the **Data Type arrow** and select **Date/Time**.

> **TIP: KEYBOARD SHORTCUT FOR DATA TYPES**
> You also can type the first letter of the data type, such as d for Date/Time, s for Short Text, or n for Number. To use the keyboard shortcut, click in the field name and press Tab to advance to the Data Type column. Next, type the first letter of the data type.

c. Press **Tab** to move to the Description column and type **This is the date the manager started working at this location.**

d. Click in the **Format box** in the Field properties pane, click the **arrow**, and then select **Short Date** from the list of date formats.

e. Click in the **Caption box** and type **Manager's Start Date**.

f. Click **Save** on the Quick Access Toolbar.

   A warning dialog box opens to indicate that "Some data may be lost" because the size of the BranchID, Manager, and Location field properties were shortened (in the previous step). It asks if you want to continue anyway. Always read the Access warning! In this case, you can click Yes to continue because you know that the existing and anticipated data are no longer than the new field sizes.

g. Click **Yes** in the warning box.

STEP 5 » MODIFY THE TABLE IN DATASHEET VIEW

As you work with the auditor, you will modify tables in the Bank database from time to time and add and modify records. Refer to Figure 2.12 as you complete Step 5.

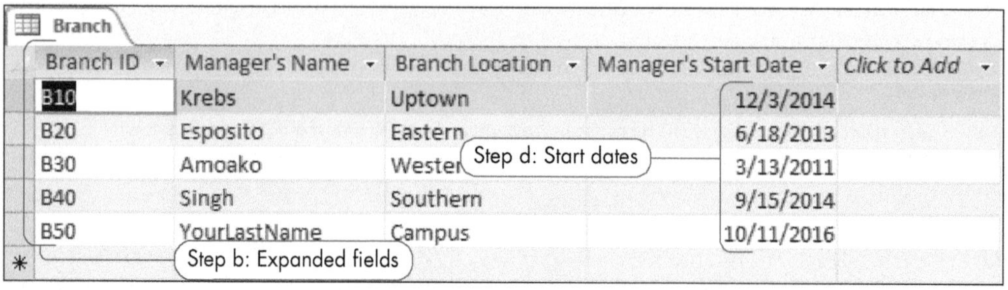

Branch

Branch ID	Manager's Name	Branch Location	Manager's Start Date	Click to Add
B10	Krebs	Uptown	12/3/2014	
B20	Esposito	Eastern	6/18/2013	
B30	Amoako	Western	3/13/2011	
B40	Singh	Southern	9/15/2014	
B50	YourLastName	Campus	10/11/2016	
*				

Step d: Start dates

Step b: Expanded fields

FIGURE 2.12 Start Dates Added to the Branch Table

a. Right-click the **Branch tab** and click **Datasheet View** from the shortcut menu.

   The table displays in Datasheet view. The field captions display at the top of the columns, but they are cut off.

b. Position the pointer over the border between Branch ID and Manager's Name so that it becomes a double-headed arrow, and double-click the border. Repeat the process for the border between Manager's Name and Branch Location, the border between Branch Location and Manager's Start Date, and the border after Manager's Start Date.

   The columns contract or expand to display the best fit for each field name.

c. Click inside the **Manager's Start Date** in the first record and click the **Date Picker** next to the date field. Use the navigation arrows to find and select **December 3, 2014** from the calendar.

   You can also enter the dates by typing them directly into the StartDate field.

d. Type the start date directly in each field for the rest of the managers, as shown in Figure 2.12.

e. Click the **Close** [X] at the top-right corner of the datasheet, below the Ribbon. Click **Yes** to save the changes.

> **TROUBLESHOOTING:** If you accidentally click Close on top of the Ribbon, you will exit Access completely. To start again, launch Access and click the first file in the Recent list.

f. Double-click the **Branch table** in the Navigation Pane to open the table. Check the start dates.

g. Click the **File tab**, click **Print**, and then click **Print Preview**.

   Occasionally, users will print an Access table. However, database developers usually create reports to print table data.

h. Click **Close Print Preview** and close the Branch table.

i. Keep the database open if you plan to continue with the Hands-On Exercise. If not, close the database and exit Access.

Multiple-Table Databases

In Figure 2.2, the sample Bank database contains three tables—Customers, Accounts, and Branch. You created one table, the Branch table, in the previous section using Datasheet view and modified the table fields in Design view. You will create the two remaining tables using different methods—by importing data from external sources.

In this section, you will learn how to import data from Excel and Access, modify tables, create indexes, create relationships between tables, and enforce referential integrity.

Sharing Data

Most companies and organizations store some type of data in Excel spreadsheets. Often, the data stored in those spreadsheets can be more efficiently managed in an Access database. At other times, importing data from Excel and other applications can reduce the data entry effort for your database.

Import Excel Data

Access provides you with a wizard that guides you through the process of importing data from Excel.

To import an Excel spreadsheet to Access, complete the following steps:

1. Click the External Data tab.
2. Click Excel in the Import & Link group. The Get External Data – Excel Spreadsheet dialog box opens, as shown in Figure 2.13.

Get External Data - Excel Spreadsheet ? ×

Select the source and destination of the data

Specify the source of the definition of the objects.

File name: C:\Users\mpoat\Documents\ Browse...

Browse to find a spreadsheet

Specify how and where you want to store the data in the current database.

Import the source data into a new table in the current database.

If the specified table does not exist, Access will create it. If the specified table already exists, Access might overwrite its contents with the imported data. Changes made to the source data will not be reflected in the database.

Append a copy of the records to the table: Branch

If the specified table exists, Access will add the records to the table. If the table does not exist, Access will create it. Changes made to the source data will not be reflected in the database.

Link to the data source by creating a linked table.

Access will create a table that will maintain a link to the source data in Excel. Changes made to the source data in Excel will be reflected in the linked table. However, the source data cannot be changed from within Access.

Options for how to store the data

OK Cancel

Access 2016, Windows 10, Microsoft Corporation

FIGURE 2.13 Import Excel Data

3. Click Browse to locate the Excel file you want to import, click the file to select it, and then click Open to specify this file as the source of the data.
4. Ensure the *Import the source data* option is selected, and click OK. The Import Spreadsheet Wizard launches.
5. Select the worksheet from the list of worksheets shown at the top of the dialog box, as shown in Figure 2.14 and then click Next.

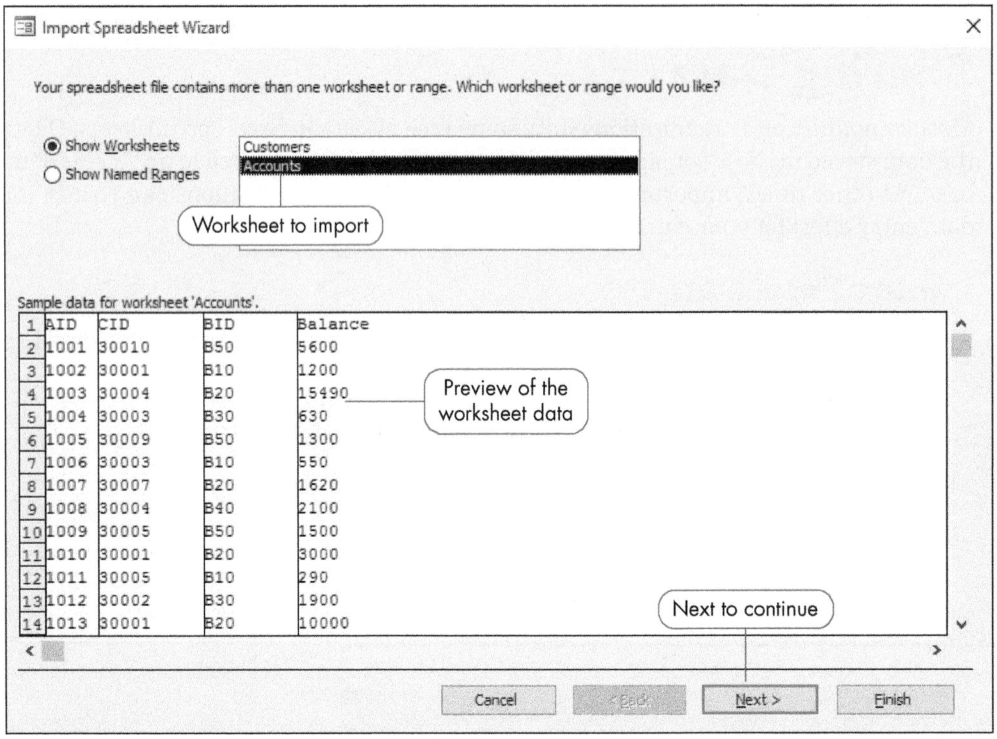

Import Spreadsheet Wizard

Your spreadsheet file contains more than one worksheet or range. Which worksheet or range would you like?

Show Worksheets
Show Named Ranges

Customers
Accounts

Worksheet to import

Sample data for worksheet 'Accounts'.

1	AID	CID	BID	Balance
2	1001	30010	B50	5600
3	1002	30001	B10	1200
4	1003	30004	B20	15490
5	1004	30003	B30	630
6	1005	30009	B50	1300
7	1006	30003	B10	550
8	1007	30007	B20	1620
9	1008	30004	B40	2100
10	1009	30005	B50	1500
11	1010	30001	B20	3000
12	1011	30005	B10	290
13	1012	30002	B30	1900
14	1013	30001	B20	10000

Preview of the worksheet data

Next to continue

Cancel | < Back | Next > | Finish

Access 2016, Windows 10, Microsoft Corporation

FIGURE 2.14 Available Worksheets and Preview of Data

6. Ensure the *First Row Contains Column Headings* check box is selected, and click Next, as shown in Figure 2.15. The column headings of the Excel spreadsheet will become the field names in the Access table.

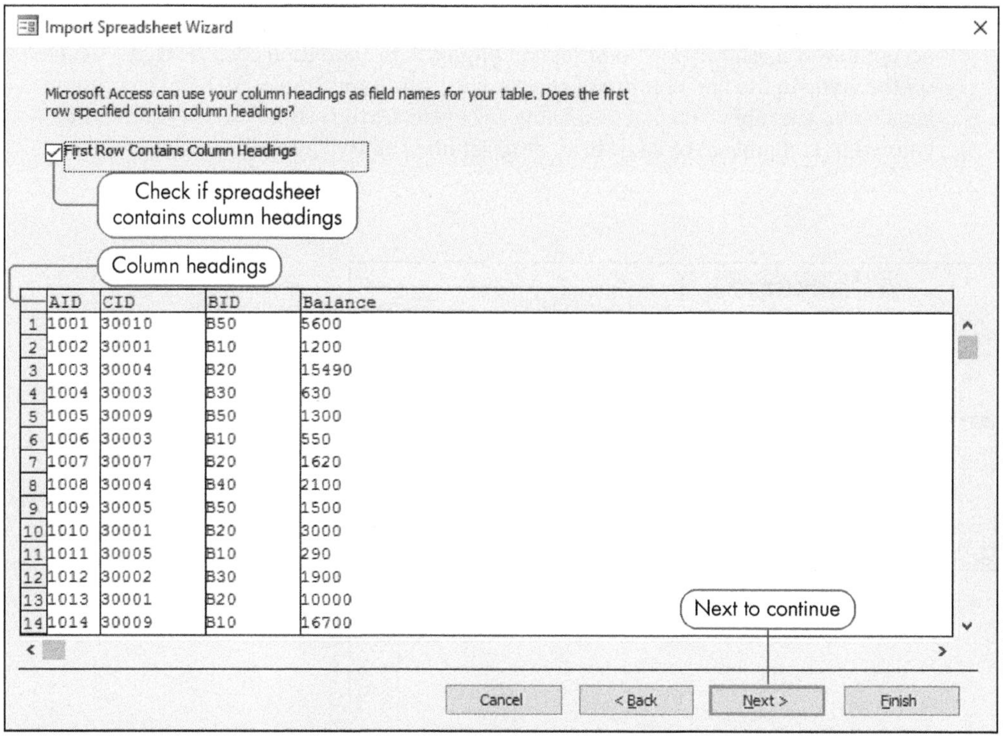

Import Spreadsheet Wizard

Microsoft Access can use your column headings as field names for your table. Does the first row specified contain column headings?

☑ First Row Contains Column Headings

Check if spreadsheet contains column headings

Column headings

	AID	CID	BID	Balance
1	1001	30010	B50	5600
2	1002	30001	B10	1200
3	1003	30004	B20	15490
4	1004	30003	B30	630
5	1005	30009	B50	1300
6	1006	30003	B10	550
7	1007	30007	B20	1620
8	1008	30004	B40	2100
9	1009	30005	B50	1500
10	1010	30001	B20	3000
11	1011	30005	B10	290
12	1012	30002	B30	1900
13	1013	30001	B20	10000
14	1014	30009	B10	16700

Next to continue

Cancel | < Back | Next > | Finish

Access 2016, Windows 10, Microsoft Corporation

FIGURE 2.15 Excel Column Headings Become Access Field Names

7. Change the field options for the imported data, as shown in Figure 2.16, and then click Next.

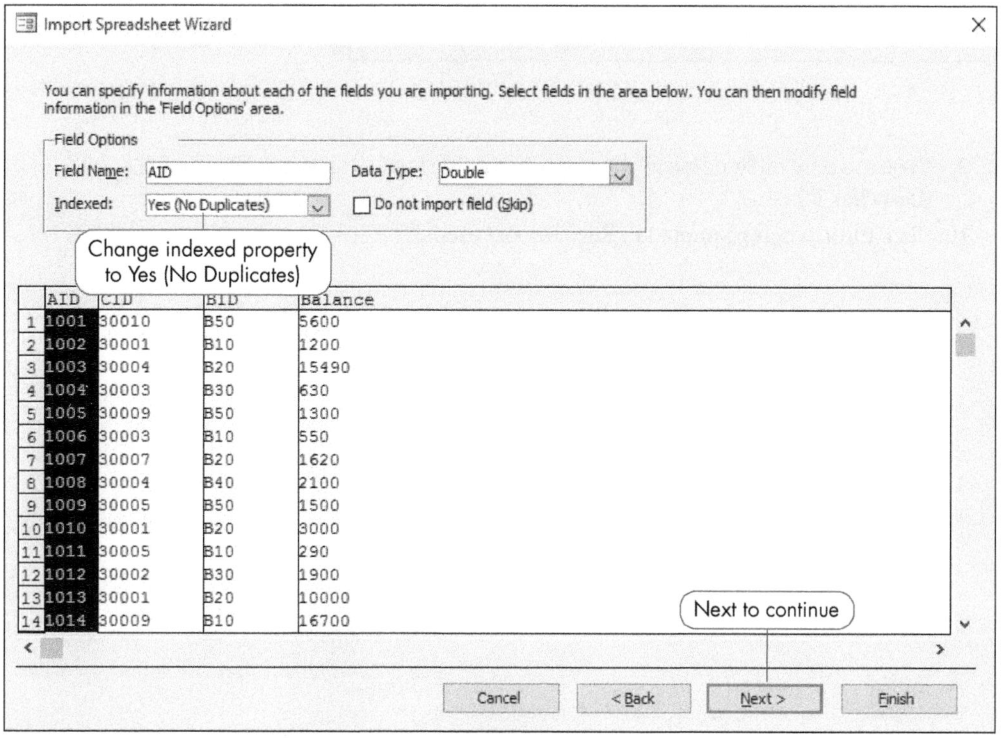

Import Spreadsheet Wizard

You can specify information about each of the fields you are importing. Select fields in the area below. You can then modify field information in the 'Field Options' area.

Field Options

Field Name: AID   Data Type: Double

Indexed: Yes (No Duplicates)   ☐ Do not import field (Skip)

Change indexed property to Yes (No Duplicates)

	AID	CID	BID	Balance
1	1001	30010	B50	5600
2	1002	30001	B10	1200
3	1003	30004	B20	15490
4	1004	30003	B30	630
5	1005	30009	B50	1300
6	1006	30003	B10	550
7	1007	30007	B20	1620
8	1008	30004	B40	2100
9	1009	30005	B50	1500
10	1010	30001	B20	3000
11	1011	30005	B10	290
12	1012	30002	B30	1900
13	1013	30001	B20	10000
14	1014	30009	B10	16700

Next to continue

Cancel | < Back | Next > | Finish

Access 2016, Windows 10, Microsoft Corporation

FIGURE 2.16 Change Field Options for Imported Data

8. Click the *Choose my own primary key* option if the imported data has a field that is acceptable as a primary key, as shown in Figure 2.17, and then click Next. Access will set the value in the first column of the spreadsheet (for example, AID) as the primary key field of the table. You can also allow Access to set the primary key if there is no value that is eligible to be a key field, or to set no primary key at all.

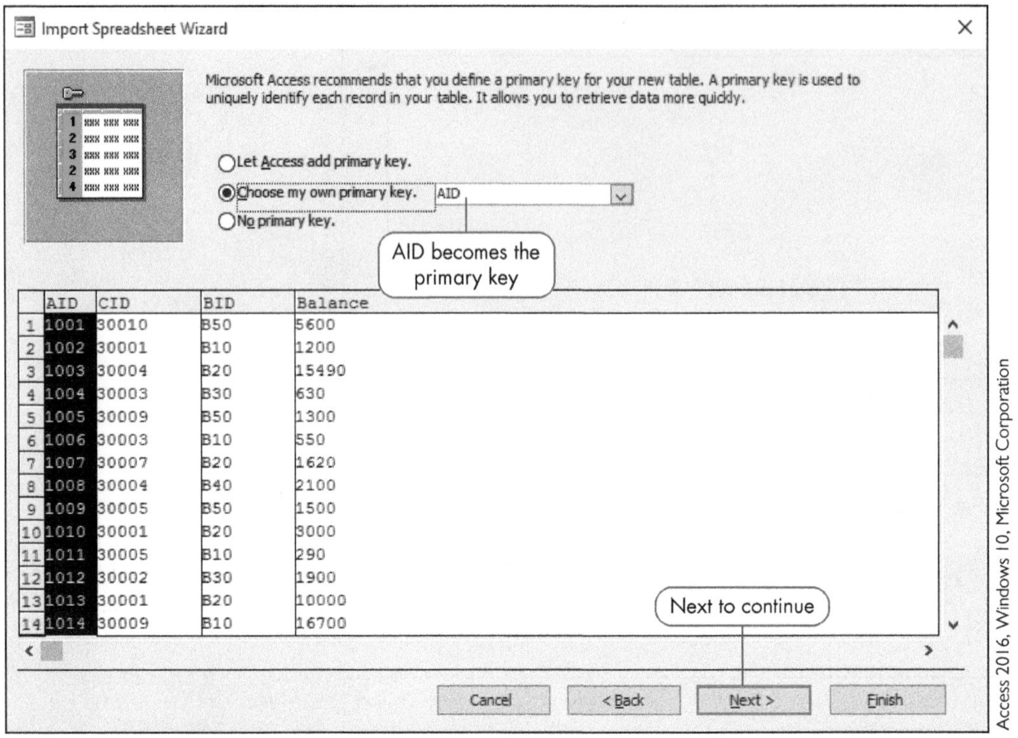

Import Spreadsheet Wizard
Microsoft Access recommends that you define a primary key for your new table. A primary key is used to uniquely identify each record in your table. It allows you to retrieve data more quickly.
Let Access add primary key.
Choose my own primary key.
AID
No primary key.
AID becomes the primary key
AID CID BID Balance
1 1001 30010 B50 5600
2 1002 30001 B10 1200
3 1003 30004 B20 15490
4 1004 30003 B30 630
5 1005 30009 B50 1300
6 1006 30003 B10 550
7 1007 30007 B20 1620
8 1008 30004 B40 2100
9 1009 30005 B50 1500
10 1010 30001 B20 3000
11 1011 30005 B10 290
12 1012 30002 B30 1900
13 1013 30001 B20 10000
14 1014 30009 B10 16700
Next to continue
Cancel
< Back
Next >
Finish
Access 2016, Windows 10, Microsoft Corporation

FIGURE 2.17 Set the Primary Key

9. Type the new table name in the Import to Table box, as shown in Figure 2.18, and then click Finish.
10. Click Close when prompted to Save Import Steps.

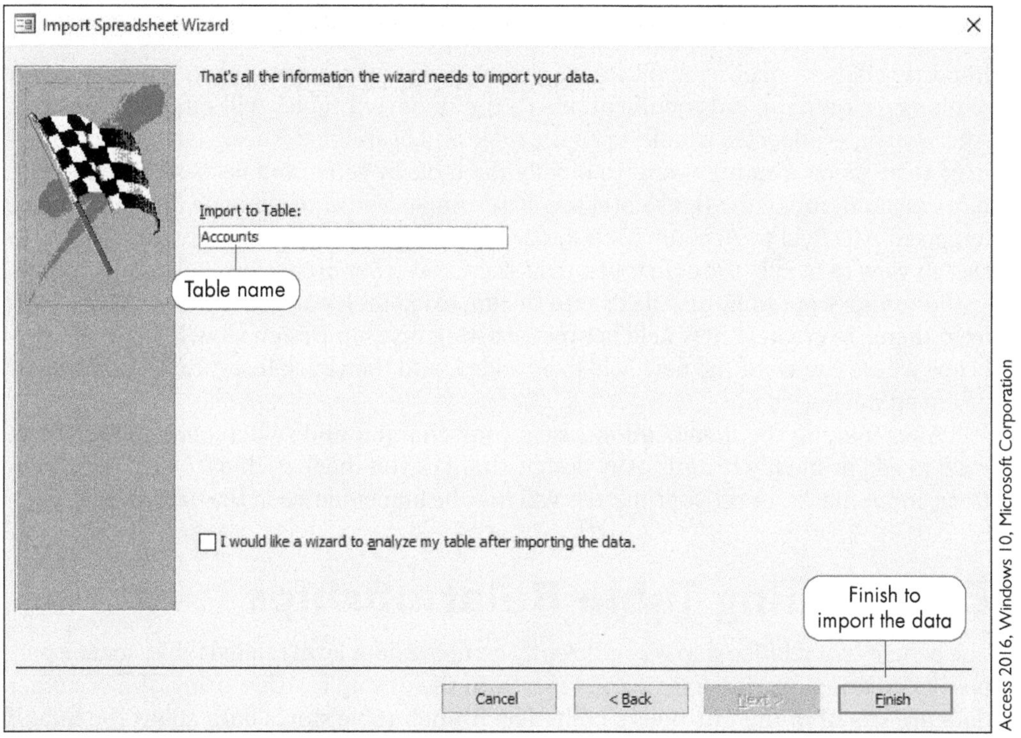

Access 2016, Windows 10, Microsoft Corporation

FIGURE 2.18 Enter a Table Name

> **TIP: LINKING TO EXTERNAL DATA**
> At times you might need to include a table in your database that already exists in another database. Instead of importing the data from this external source, you can create a link to it from within your database, and the table remains in the original database. You will be able to use the linked data as usual, without being able to modify the original table's design. You can also link to existing spreadsheets from your database without having to copy a large amount of data into your file.

Import Access Data

STEP 2 A wizard can also guide you as you import data from Access databases. You can import tables, queries, forms, reports, pages, macros, and modules from other databases. You can also modify the design of objects that are imported into your database.

To import an Access table into an existing database, complete the following steps:

1. Click the External Data tab.
2. Click Access in the Import & Link group. The Get External Data – Access Database dialog box opens.
3. Ensure that the *Import tables, queries, forms, reports, macros, and modules into the current database* option is selected.
4. Click Browse to locate the Access database you want to import.
5. Click the file to select it, and then click Open to specify this file as the source of the data.
6. Select the table you want to import, and then click OK. (Click Select All if the database contains multiple tables and you want to import all of them, and then click OK.)

Modify an Imported Table's Design and Add Data

STEP 3 Importing data from other applications saves typing and prevents errors that may occur while entering data, but modifications to the imported tables will often be required. After you have imported a table, open the table and examine the design to see if changes need to be made. You may want to modify the table by renaming fields so that they are more meaningful. In the Bank database, for example, you could change the name of the imported AID field to AccountID to make it more readable and meaningful. Switch to Design view to modify the data types, field sizes, and other properties.

You may want to fit new fields into the imported tables or delete unnecessary fields from them. To create a new field between existing fields in Design view, click in the row below where you want the new field to be added, and then click Insert Rows in the Tools group on the Design tab.

After making the modifications, save your changes and switch back to Datasheet view to add or modify records. Any design changes you made such as to field sizes, captions, input masks, or other properties will now be implemented in the datasheet.

Establishing Table Relationships

STEP 5 The benefit of a relationship is to efficiently combine data from related tables for the purpose of creating queries, forms, and reports. In the example we are using, the customer data are stored in the Customers table. The Branch table stores data about the bank's branches, management, and locations. The Accounts table stores data about account ownership and balances.

The common fields that were determined in the design phase of the tables can now be used to establish relationships between them.

To create the relationship between the common fields of two tables, complete the following steps:

1. Click the Database Tools tab.
2. Click Relationships in the Relationships group.
3. Drag the primary key field name from one table to the foreign key field name of the related table (for example, CustomerID in the Customers table to CustomerID in the Accounts table).
4. Set the desired options in the Edit Relationships dialog box, and click OK. Figure 2.19 shows the Bank database with relationships created by joining common fields.

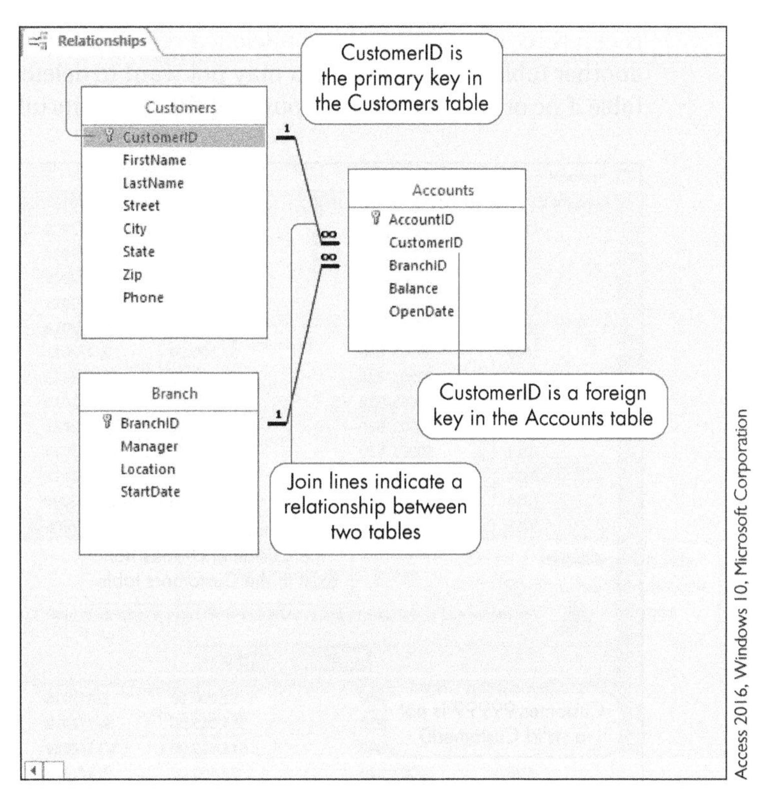

FIGURE 2.19 Relationships in the Bank Database

TIP: RETRIEVE DATA QUICKLY WITH INDEXING

When you set the primary key in Access, the Indexed property is automatically set to Yes (No Duplicates). The indexed property setting enables quick sorting in primary key order and quick retrieval based on the primary key. For non-primary key fields, it may be beneficial to set the Indexed property to Yes (Duplicates OK). Again, Access uses indexing to sort and retrieve data quickly based on the indexed field.

The primary key of a table plays a significant role when setting relationships. You cannot join two tables unless a primary key has been set in the primary table, which is one side of the relationship's join line. The other side of the relationship join line is most often the foreign key of the related table. A foreign key is a field in one table that is also the primary key and common field of another table. In the Bank database, CustomerID has been set as the primary key in the Customers table and also exists in the Accounts table. Therefore, a relationship can be set between the Customers table and the Accounts table, where CustomerID is the foreign key. Similarly, the Branch table can be joined to the Accounts table because BranchID has been set as the primary key in the Branch table, and BranchID is the foreign key in the Accounts table.

Enforce Referential Integrity

STEP 6

When you begin to create a relationship in Access, the Edit Relationships dialog box displays. The first check box, Enforce Referential Integrity, should be checked in most cases. ***Referential integrity*** enforces rules in a database that are used to preserve relationships between tables when records are changed.

When referential integrity is enforced, you cannot enter a foreign key value in a related table unless the primary key value exists in the primary table. In the case of the Bank database, the customer information is first entered into the Customers table before a customer's account information (which also includes CustomerID) can be entered into the Accounts table. If you attempt to enter an account prior to entering the customer information, an error will display, as shown in Figure 2.20. When referential integrity

Figure 2.22 displays the Relationships window for the Bank database and all the relationships created using referential integrity. The join line between the CustomerID field in the Customers table and the CustomerID field in the Accounts table indicates that a one-to-many relationship has been set. The number 1 displays on the one side of the relationship and the infinity symbol displays the many side. You can rearrange the tables by dragging the tables by the title bar. You can switch the positions of the Branch and Accounts tables in the Relationships window without changing the relationship itself.

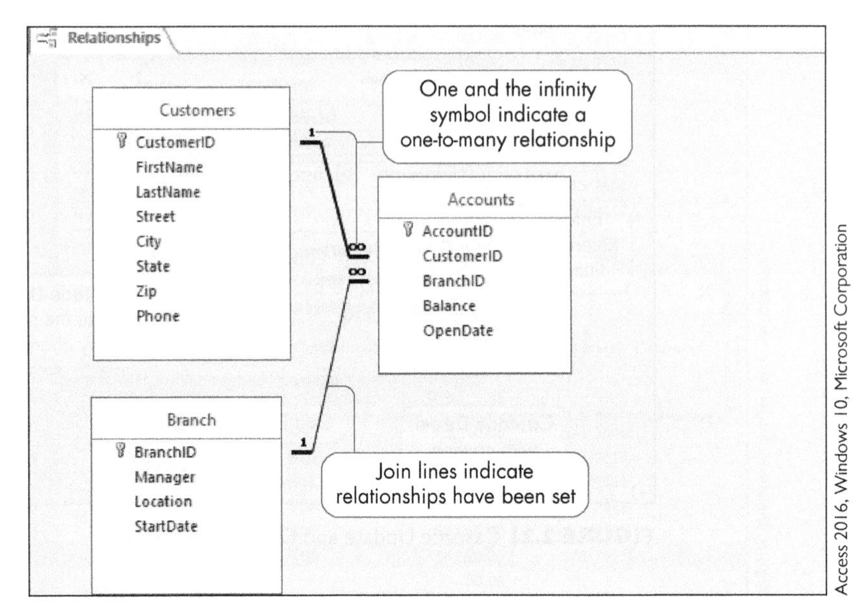

FIGURE 2.22 Relationships Window Displaying One-to-Many Relationships

TIP: NAVIGATING BETWEEN THE RELATIONSHIPS WINDOW AND A TABLE'S DESIGN

When you right-click a table's title bar in the Relationships window, the shortcut menu offers you the option to open the table in Design view. This is a convenient feature because if you want to link one table to another table, the joined fields must have the same data type. This shortcut enables you to check the fields and revise them if a table contains a field with the wrong data type.

Quick Concepts

4. Describe a scenario that may require you to import Excel data into Access. ***p. 749***
5. What is the purpose of setting a relationship between two tables? ***p. 754***
6. Why would you decide to use the Cascade Delete option (or not) when setting a relationship? ***p. 756***
7. Specify two database tables that you might design that would contain a one-to-many relationship. Describe the relationship. ***p. 756***

Hands-On Exercises

Watch the Video for this Hands-On Exercise!
MyITLab®
HOE2 Training

Skills covered: Import Excel Data • Import Data from an Access Database • Modify an Imported Table's Design • Add Data to an Imported Table • Establish Table Relationships • Enforce Referential Integrity

2 Multiple-Table Databases

You created a new Bank database, and a new Branch table. Now you are ready to import additional tables—one from an Excel spreadsheet and one from an Access database. Assume that the data are formatted correctly and are structured properly so that you can begin the import process.

STEP 1 » IMPORT EXCEL DATA

You and the auditor have discovered several of Commonwealth's files that contain customer data. These files need to be analyzed, so you decide to import the data into Access. In this step, you import an Excel spreadsheet into the Bank database. Refer to Figure 2.23 as you complete Step 1.

All Access Obje...
Search...
Tables
Branch
Customers

Step e: Imported column headings

Customers

CID	FirstName	LastName	Street	City	State	Zip	Phone	Click to Add
30001	Allison	Millward	2732 Baker Blvd.	Greensboro	NC	27492	5553345678	
30002	Bernett	Fox	12 Orchestra Terrace	High Point	NC	27494	5553585554	
30003	Clay	Hayes	P.O. Box 555	Greensboro	NC	27492	5559984457	
30004	Cordle	Collins	2743 Bering St.	Winston-Salem	NC	27492	5554472283	
30005	Eaton	Wagner	2743 Bering St.	Greensboro	NC	27492	5559883346	
30006	Kwasi	Williams	89 Jefferson Way	High Point	NC	27494	5554475565	
30007	Natasha	Simpson	187 Suffolk Ln.	Greensboro	NC	27493	5557753389	
30008	Joy	Jones	305 - 14th Ave. S.	Winston-Salem	NC	27493	5552587655	
30009	John	Nunn	89 Chiaroscuro Rd.	Greensboro	NC	27494	5559985557	
30010	Laura	Peterson	120 Hanover Sq.	Winston-Salem	NC	27492	5553346654	
*								

Access 2016, Windows 10, Microsoft Corporation

FIGURE 2.23 Imported Customers Table

a. Open *a02h1Bank_LastFirst* if you closed it at the end of Hands-On Exercise 1, and save it as **a02h2Bank_LastFirst**, changing h1 to h2.

b. Click **Enable Content** below the Ribbon to indicate that you trust the contents of the database.

c. Click the **External Data tab** and click **Excel** in the Import & Link group to launch the Get External Data – Excel Spreadsheet feature. Ensure that the *Import the source data into a new table in the current database* option is selected.

> **TROUBLESHOOTING:** Ensure that you click Excel in the Import & Link group to import the spreadsheet and not the Excel command in the Export group.

d. Click **Browse** and navigate to your student data files. Select the *a02h2Customers* workbook. Click **Open** and click **OK** to open the Import Spreadsheet Wizard.

e. Ensure that the *First Row Contains Column Headings* check box is checked to indicate to Access that column headings exist in the Excel file.

The field names CID, FirstName, LastName, Street, City, State, ZIP, and Phone will import from Excel along with the data stored in the rows in the worksheet. You will modify the field names later in Access.

f. Click **Next**.

g. Ensure that CID is displayed in the Field Name box in Field Options. Click the **Indexed arrow** and select **Yes (No Duplicates)**. Click **Next**.

The CID (CustomerID) will become the primary key in this table. It needs to be a unique identifier, so you must change the property to No Duplicates.

h. Click the **Choose my own primary key option.** Make sure that the CID field is selected. Click **Next.**

The final screen of the Import Spreadsheet Wizard asks you to name your table. The name of the Excel worksheet is Customers, and Access defaults to the worksheet name. It is an acceptable name.

i. Click **Finish** to accept Customers as the table name.

A dialog box opens prompting you to save the steps of this import to use again. If this is data that is to be collected in Excel and updated to the database on a regular basis, saving the import steps would save time. You do not need to save the import steps in this example.

j. Click **Close.**

The new table displays in the Navigation Pane of the Bank database.

k. Open the imported Customers table in Datasheet view and double-click the border between each of the field names to adjust the columns to Best Fit. Compare your table to Figure 2.23.

l. Save and close the table.

STEP 2 » IMPORT DATA FROM AN ACCESS DATABASE

The auditor asks you to import an Access database table that contains account information related to the accounts you are analyzing. You use the Import Wizard to import the database table. Refer to Figure 2.24 as you complete Step 2.

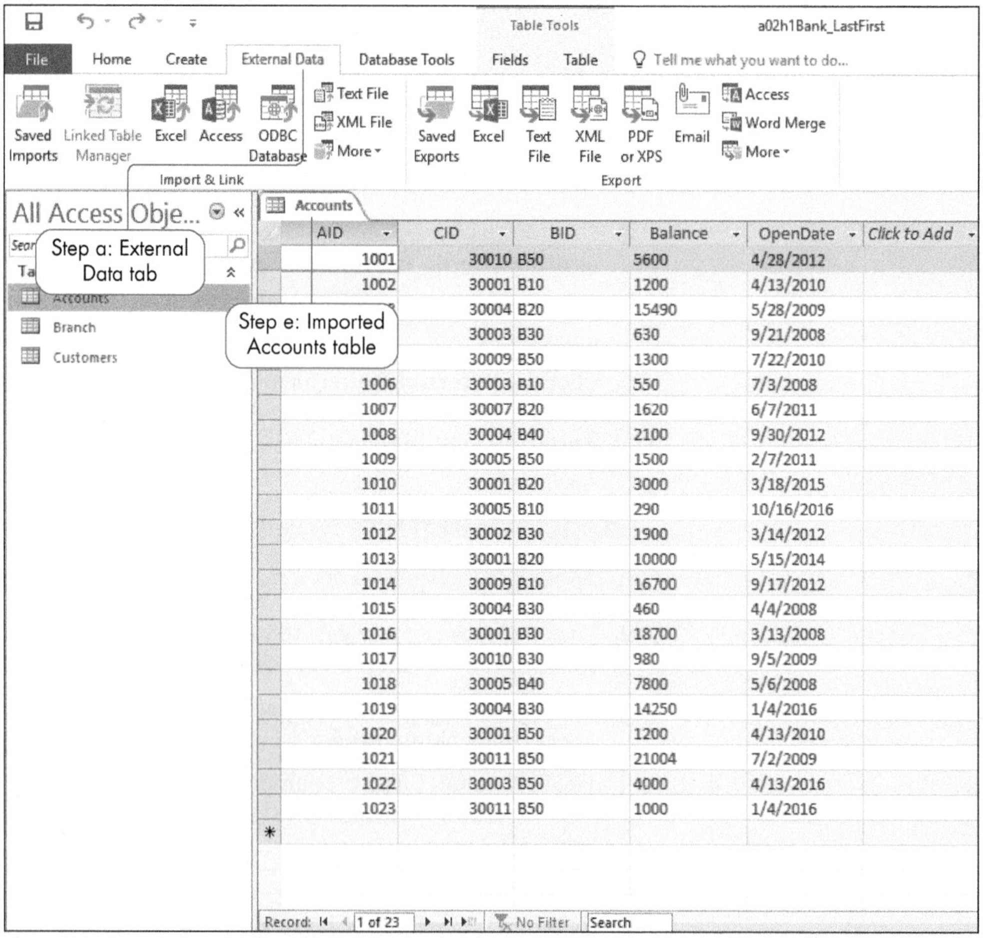

Step a: External Data tab

Step e: Imported Accounts table

AID	CID	BID	Balance	OpenDate	Click to Add
1001	30010	B50	5600	4/28/2012	
1002	30001	B10	1200	4/13/2010	
	30004	B20	15490	5/28/2009	
	30003	B30	630	9/21/2008	
	30009	B50	1300	7/22/2010	
1006	30003	B10	550	7/3/2008	
1007	30007	B20	1620	6/7/2011	
1008	30004	B40	2100	9/30/2012	
1009	30005	B50	1500	2/7/2011	
1010	30001	B20	3000	3/18/2015	
1011	30005	B10	290	10/16/2016	
1012	30002	B30	1900	3/14/2012	
1013	30001	B20	10000	5/15/2014	
1014	30009	B10	16700	9/17/2012	
1015	30004	B30	460	4/4/2008	
1016	30001	B30	18700	3/13/2008	
1017	30010	B30	980	9/5/2009	
1018	30005	B40	7800	5/6/2008	
1019	30004	B30	14250	1/4/2016	
1020	30001	B50	1200	4/13/2010	
1021	30011	B50	21004	7/2/2009	
1022	30003	B50	4000	4/13/2016	
1023	30011	B50	1000	1/4/2016	

FIGURE 2.24 Imported Accounts Table

a. Click the **External Data tab** and click **Access** in the Import & Link group to launch the Get External Data – Access Database feature. Ensure that the *Import tables, queries, forms, reports, macros, and modules into the current database* option is selected.

b. Click **Browse** and navigate to your student data files. Select the *a02h2Accounts* database. Click **Open** and click **OK** to open the Import Objects dialog box.

c. Click the **Accounts table** for importing and click **OK**.

d. Click **Close** in the Save Import Steps dialog box.

   The Navigation Pane now contains three tables: Accounts, Branch, and Customers.

e. Open the imported Accounts table in Datasheet view and compare it to Figure 2.24.

f. Close the table.

STEP 3 » MODIFY AN IMPORTED TABLE'S DESIGN

When importing tables from either Excel or Access, the fields may have different data types and property settings than required to create table relationships. You will modify the tables so that each field has the correct data type and field size. Refer to Figure 2.25 as you complete Step 3.

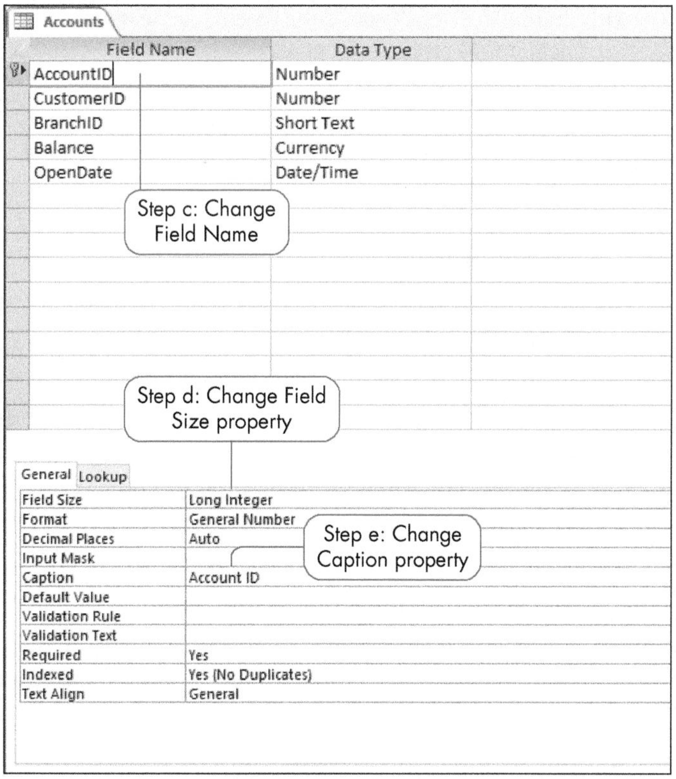

Access 2016, Windows 10, Microsoft Corporation

FIGURE 2.25 Modified Accounts Table Design

a. Right-click the **Accounts table** in the Navigation Pane.

b. Select Design view from the shortcut menu to open the table in Design view.

   The Accounts table displays with the primary key AID selected.

c. Change the AID field name to **AccountID**.

d. Change the Field Size property to **Long Integer**.

   Long Integer ensures that there will be enough numbers as the number of customers grows over time and may exceed 32,768 (the upper limit for Integer values).

e. Type **Account ID** in the Caption box for the AccountID field. The caption contains a space between Account and ID.

f. Click the **CID** field. Change the CID field name to **CustomerID**.

g. Change the Field Size property to **Long Integer**.

   You can select the Field Size option using the arrow, or you can type the first letter of the option you want. For example, type l for Long Integer or s for Single. Make sure the current option is completely selected before you type the letter.

h. Type **Customer ID** in the Caption box for the CustomerID field. The caption contains a space between Customer and ID.

i. Click the **BID field**. Change the BID field name to **BranchID**.

j. Type **5** in the Field Size property box in the Field Properties.

k. Type **Branch ID** in the Caption property box for the Branch ID field.

l. Change the Data Type of the Balance field to **Currency**.

   The Currency data type is used for fields that contain monetary values. In this case, changing the data type is not consequential; formatting the imported Balance field as Currency will not change the original data values.

m. Change the Data Type of the OpenDate field to **Date/Time** and set **Short Date** in the Format field property. Type **Open Date** in the Caption property box.

   The OpenDate field stores the date that each account was opened.

n. Click **View** in the Views group to switch to Datasheet view. Read the messages and click **Yes** to each one.

   In this case, it is OK to click Yes because the shortened fields will not cut off any data. Leave the table open.

o. Right-click the **Customers table** in the Navigation Pane and from the shortcut menu, select **Design View**.

p. Change the CID field name to **CustomerID**. Change the Field Size property of the CustomerID field to **Long Integer** and add a caption, **Customer ID**. Take note of the intentional space between Customer and ID.

   The Accounts table and the Customers table will be joined using the CustomerID field. Both fields must have the same data type.

q. Change the Field Size property to **20** for the FirstName, LastName, Street, and City fields. Change the Field Size for State to **2**.

r. Change the data type for ZIP and Phone to **Short Text**. Change the Field Size property to **15** for both fields. Remove the @ symbol from the Format property where it exists for all fields in the Customers table.

s. Click the **Phone field name** and click **Input Mask** in Field Properties. Click the **ellipsis** [...] on the right side to launch the Input Mask Wizard. Click **Yes** to save the table and click **Yes** to the *Some data may be lost* warning. Click **Finish** to apply the default phone number input mask.

   The phone number input mask enables users to enter 6105551212 in the datasheet, and Access will display it as (610) 555-1212.

t. Click **Save** to save the design changes to the Customers table.

STEP 4 » ADD DATA TO AN IMPORTED TABLE

Now that you have created the Access tables, you discover that you need to add another customer and his account records to them. Refer to Figure 2.26 as you complete Step 4.

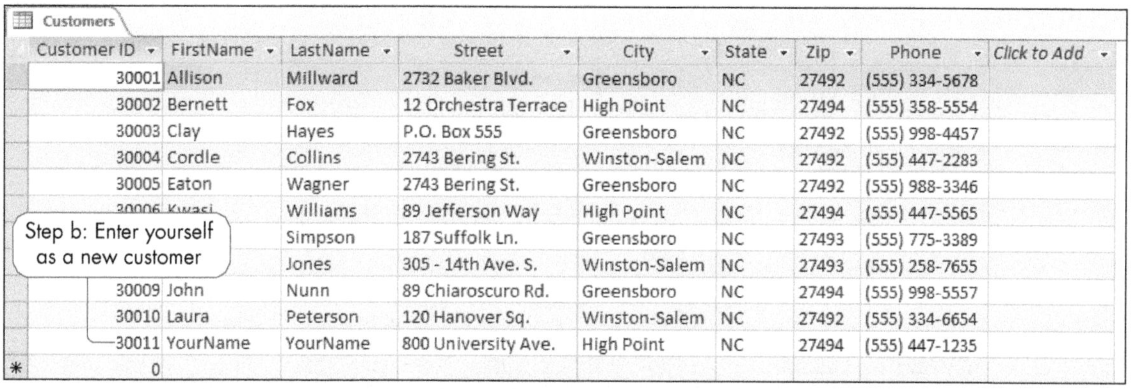

Customers

	Customer ID	FirstName	LastName	Street	City	State	Zip	Phone	Click to Add
	30001	Allison	Millward	2732 Baker Blvd.	Greensboro	NC	27492	(555) 334-5678	
	30002	Bernett	Fox	12 Orchestra Terrace	High Point	NC	27494	(555) 358-5554	
	30003	Clay	Hayes	P.O. Box 555	Greensboro	NC	27492	(555) 998-4457	
	30004	Cordle	Collins	2743 Bering St.	Winston-Salem	NC	27492	(555) 447-2283	
	30005	Eaton	Wagner	2743 Bering St.	Greensboro	NC	27492	(555) 988-3346	
	30006	Kwasi	Williams	89 Jefferson Way	High Point	NC	27494	(555) 447-5565	
			Simpson	187 Suffolk Ln.	Greensboro	NC	27493	(555) 775-3389	
			Jones	305 - 14th Ave. S.	Winston-Salem	NC	27493	(555) 258-7655	
	30009	John	Nunn	89 Chiaroscuro Rd.	Greensboro	NC	27494	(555) 998-5557	
	30010	Laura	Peterson	120 Hanover Sq.	Winston-Salem	NC	27492	(555) 334-6654	
	30011	YourName	YourName	800 University Ave.	High Point	NC	27494	(555) 447-1235	
*	0								

Step b: Enter yourself as a new customer

Access 2016, Windows 10, Microsoft Corporation

FIGURE 2.26 Customers Table Displaying the Added Customer ID 30011

a. Click **View** in the Views group to display the Customers table in Datasheet view.

The asterisk at the bottom of the table data in the row selector area is the indicator of a place to enter a new record.

b. Click next to the * in the **Customer ID field** in the new record row below 30010. Type **30011**. Fill in the rest of the data using your personal information as the customer. You may use a fictitious address and phone number.

Note the phone number format. The input mask you set formats the phone number.

c. Close the Customers table. The Accounts table tab is open.

TROUBLESHOOTING: If the Accounts table is not open, double-click Accounts in the Navigation Pane.

d. Click next to the * in the **Account ID field** in the new record row. Type **1024**. Type **30011** as the Customer ID and **B50** as the Branch ID. Type **14005** for the Balance field value. Type **8/7/2018** for the Open Date.

e. Add the following records to the Accounts table:

Account ID	Customer ID	Branch ID	Balance	Open Date
1025	30006	B40	$11,010	3/13/2018
1026	30007	B20	$7,400	5/1/2018

f. Close the Accounts table, but keep the database open.

STEP 5 » ESTABLISH TABLE RELATIONSHIPS

The tables for the bank investigation have been designed and populated. Now you will establish connections between the tables. Look at the primary and foreign keys as a guide. Refer to Figure 2.27 as you complete Step 5.

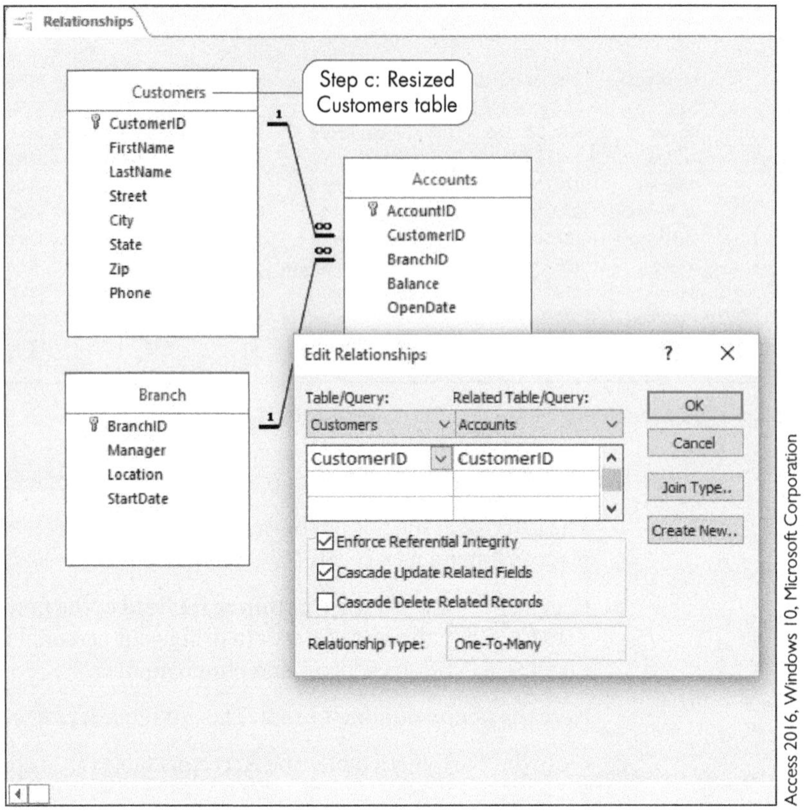

Relationships

Customers: CustomerID, FirstName, LastName, Street, City, State, Zip, Phone

Step c: Resized Customers table

Accounts: AccountID, CustomerID, BranchID, Balance, OpenDate

Branch: BranchID, Manager, Location, StartDate

Edit Relationships

Table/Query: Customers — Related Table/Query: Accounts

CustomerID — CustomerID

☑ Enforce Referential Integrity

☑ Cascade Update Related Fields

☐ Cascade Delete Related Records

Relationship Type: One-To-Many

OK · Cancel · Join Type.. · Create New..

Access 2016, Windows 10, Microsoft Corporation

FIGURE 2.27 Relationships Between Tables

a. Click the **Database Tools tab** and click **Relationships** in the Relationships group.

The Relationships window opens and the Show Table dialog box displays.

> **TROUBLESHOOTING:** If the Show Table dialog box does not open, click Show Table in the Relationships group on the Relationship Tools Design tab.

b. Double-click each of the three tables displayed in the Show Table dialog box to add them to the Relationships window. Click **Close** in the Show Table dialog box.

> **TROUBLESHOOTING:** If you have a duplicate table, click the title bar of the duplicated table and press Delete.

c. Click and drag the border of the Customers table field list to resize it so that all of the fields are visible. Arrange the tables as shown in Figure 2.27.

d. Drag the **BranchID field** (the primary key) in the Branch table onto the BranchID field (the foreign key) in the Accounts table. The Edit Relationships dialog box opens. Click the **Enforce Referential Integrity** and **Cascade Update Related Fields check boxes** to select them. Click **Create**.

A black line displays, joining the two tables. It has a 1 at the end near the Branch table and an infinity symbol on the end next to the Accounts table. You have established a one-to-many relationship between the Branch and Accounts tables. Each single branch is connected with many accounts.

e. Drag the **CustomerID field** (the primary key) in the Customers table onto the CustomerID field (the foreign key) in the Accounts table. The Edit Relationships dialog box opens. Click the **Enforce Referential Integrity** and **Cascade Update Related Fields check boxes** to select them. Click **Create**.

   You have established a one-to-many relationship between the Customers and Accounts tables. A customer will have only a single CustomerID number. The same customer may have many different accounts: Savings, Checking, Credit Card, and so forth.

> **TROUBLESHOOTING:** If you get an error message when you click Create, verify that the data types of the joined fields are the same. To check the data types from the Relationships window, right-click the title bar of a table and select Table Design from the shortcut menu. Modify the data type of the join fields, if necessary. Customer ID should be Number and Branch ID should be Short Text in both tables.

f. Click **Save** on the Quick Access Toolbar to save the changes to the relationships. Close the Relationships window.

STEP 6 » ENFORCE REFERENTIAL INTEGRITY

The design of the Bank database must be 100% correct; otherwise, data entry may be compromised. Even though you are confident that the table relationships are set correctly, you decide to test them by entering some invalid data. If referential integrity is enforced, the invalid data will be rejected by Access. Refer to Figure 2.28 as you complete Step 6.

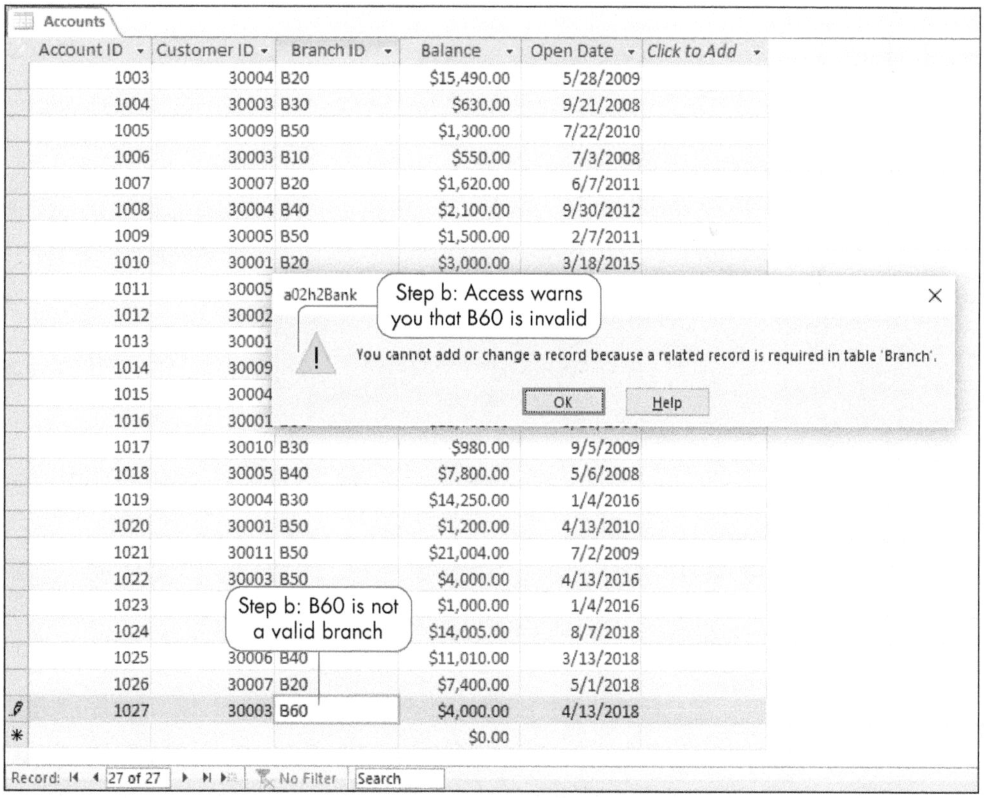

Accounts

Account ID	Customer ID	Branch ID	Balance	Open Date	Click to Add
1003	30004	B20	$15,490.00	5/28/2009	
1004	30003	B30	$630.00	9/21/2008	
1005	30009	B50	$1,300.00	7/22/2010	
1006	30003	B10	$550.00	7/3/2008	
1007	30007	B20	$1,620.00	6/7/2011	
1008	30004	B40	$2,100.00	9/30/2012	
1009	30005	B50	$1,500.00	2/7/2011	
1010	30001	B20	$3,000.00	3/18/2015	
1011	30005				
1012	30002				
1013	30001				
1014	30009				
1015	30004				
1016	30001				
1017	30010	B30	$980.00	9/5/2009	
1018	30005	B40	$7,800.00	5/6/2008	
1019	30004	B30	$14,250.00	1/4/2016	
1020	30001	B50	$1,200.00	4/13/2010	
1021	30011	B50	$21,004.00	7/2/2009	
1022	30003	B50	$4,000.00	4/13/2016	
1023			$1,000.00	1/4/2016	
1024			$14,005.00	8/7/2018	
1025	30006	B40	$11,010.00	3/13/2018	
1026	30007	B20	$7,400.00	5/1/2018	
1027	30003	B60	$4,000.00	4/13/2018	
			$0.00		

Record: 27 of 27 No Filter Search

a02h2Bank

You cannot add or change a record because a related record is required in table 'Branch'.

OK Help

Step b: Access warns you that B60 is invalid

Step b: B60 is not a valid branch

Access 2016, Windows 10, Microsoft Corporation

FIGURE 2.28 Referential Integrity Enforces Accurate Data Entry

a. Double-click the **Accounts table** to open it in Datasheet view.

b. Add a new record, pressing **Tab** after each field: Account ID: **1027**, Customer ID: **30003**, Branch: **B60**, Balance: **4000**, Open Date: **4/13/2018**. Press **Enter**.

You attempted to enter a nonexistent BranchID (B60) and were not allowed to make that error. A warning message is telling you that a related record in the Branch table is required, because the Accounts table and the Branch table are connected by a relationship with Enforce Referential Integrity checked.

c. Click **OK**. Double-click the **Branch table** in the Navigation Pane and examine the data in the BranchID field. Notice the Branch table has no B60 record. Close the Branch table.

d. Replace B60 with **B50** in the new Accounts record and press **Tab** three times. As soon as the focus moves to the next record, the pencil symbol disappears and your data are saved.

You successfully identified a BranchID that Access recognizes. Because referential integrity between the Accounts and Branch tables has been enforced, Access looks at each data entry item in a foreign key and matches it to a corresponding value in the table where it is the primary key. In Step b, you attempted to enter a nonexistent BranchID and were not allowed to make that error. In Step d, you entered a valid BranchID. Access examined the index for the BranchID in the Branch table and found a corresponding value for B50.

e. Close the Accounts table.

f. Close any open tables.

g. Keep the database open if you plan to continue with the Hands-On Exercise. If not, close the database and exit Access.

Single-Table Queries

A ***query*** enables you to ask questions about the data stored in a database and then provides the answers to the questions by creating subsets or summaries of data in a datasheet. If you wanted to see which customers currently have an account with a balance over $5,000, you could find the answer by creating an Access query.

In this section, you will use the Simple Query Wizard and Query Design view to create single-table queries that display only data that you select. Multitable queries will be covered in the next section.

Creating a Single-Table Query

Because data are stored in tables in a database, you always begin a query by determining which table (or tables) contain the data that you need. For the question about account balances over $5,000, you would use the Accounts table. You can create a single-table query in two ways—by using the Simple Query Wizard or the Query Design tool in the Queries group on the Create tab. While the Simple Query Wizard offers a step-by-step guide to creating a query, the Query Design tool allows for more flexibility and customization, and is often the preferred method for creating queries.

After you design a query, you run it to display the results in a datasheet. A query's datasheet looks like a table's datasheet, except that it is usually a subset of the fields and records found in the table on which it is based. The subset shows only the records that match the criteria that were added in the query design. The subset may contain different sorting of the records than the sorting in the underlying table. You can enter new records in a query, modify existing records, or delete records in Datasheet view. Any changes made in Datasheet view are reflected in the underlying table on which the query is based.

Create a Single-Table Select Query

Select queries are a type of query that displays only the fields and records that match criteria entered in the query design process.

To create a select query using the Query Design tool, complete the following steps:

1. Click the Create tab.
2. Click Query Design in the Queries group on the Design tab.
3. Select the table you want for your query from the Show Table dialog box.
4. Click Add to add the table to the top pane of the query design and close the Show Table dialog box.
5. Drag the fields needed from the table's field list to the query design grid (or alternatively, double-click the field names); then add criteria and sorting options.
6. Click Run in the Results group on the Design tab to show the results in Datasheet view.

Use Query Design View

Query Design view is divided into two sections: The top pane displays the tables from which the data will be retrieved, and the bottom pane (known as the query design grid) displays the fields and the criteria that you set. In the query design grid, you select only the fields that contain the data you want in the query and arrange them in the order that you want them displayed in the query results. You add criteria to further limit (or filter) the records to display only those that you require in the results. The design grid also enables you to sort the records based on one or more fields. You can create calculated fields to display data based on expressions that use the fields in the underlying table. For example, you could calculate the monthly interest earned on each bank account by multiplying the Balance by an interest rate. If a query contains more than one table, the join lines between tables display as they were created in the Relationships window.

The query design grid (the bottom pane) contains columns and rows. Each field in the query has its own column and contains multiple rows. The rows allow you to control the query results.

- The Field row displays the field name.
- The Table row displays the data source (in some cases, a field occurs in more than one table, for example, when it is a join field; therefore, it is often beneficial to display the table name in the query design grid).
- The Sort row enables you to sort in ascending or descending order (or neither).
- The Show row controls whether the field will be displayed or hidden in the query results.
- The ***Criteria row*** is used to set the rules that determine which records will be selected, such as customers with account balances greater than $5,000.

Figure 2.29 displays the query design grid with the Show Table dialog box open. The Accounts table has been added from the Show Table dialog box. Figure 2.30 shows Design view of a sample query with four fields, with a criterion set for one field and sorting set on another. The results of the query display in Datasheet view, as shown in Figure 2.31.

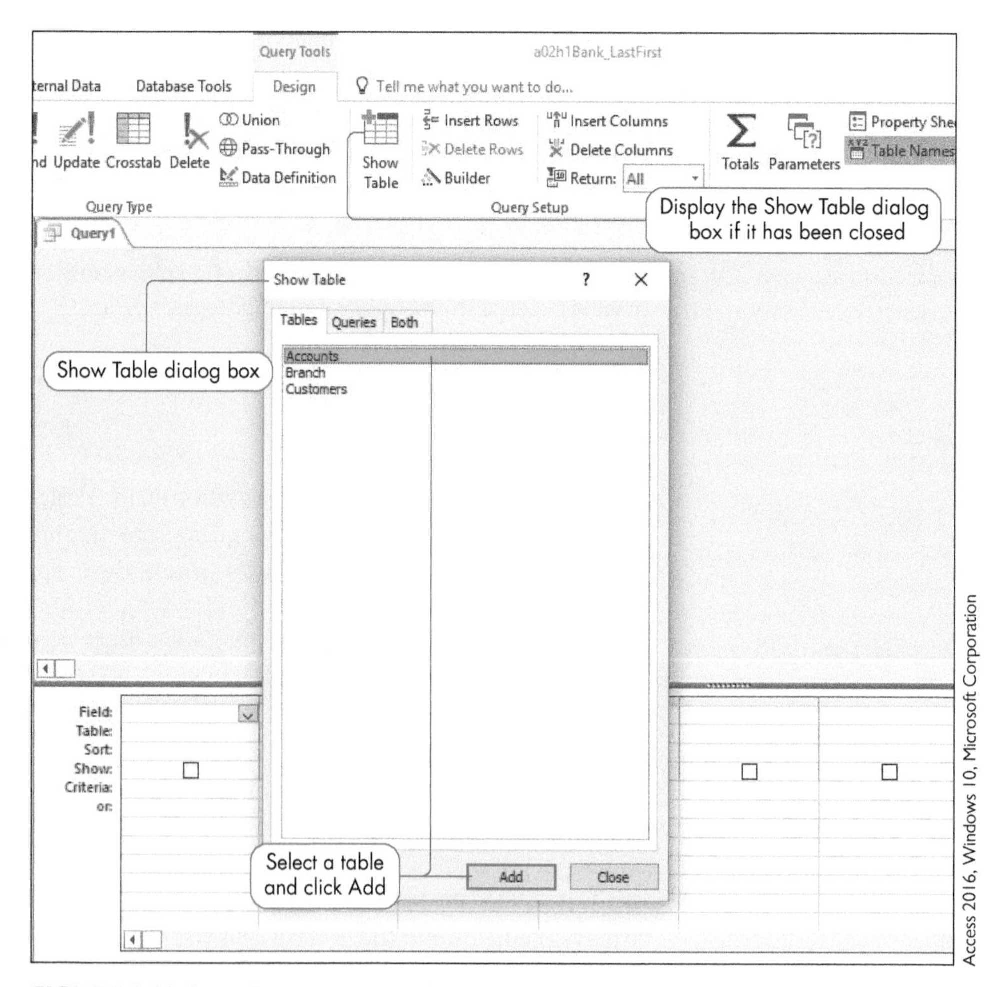

FIGURE 2.29 Query Design View with Show Table Dialog Box

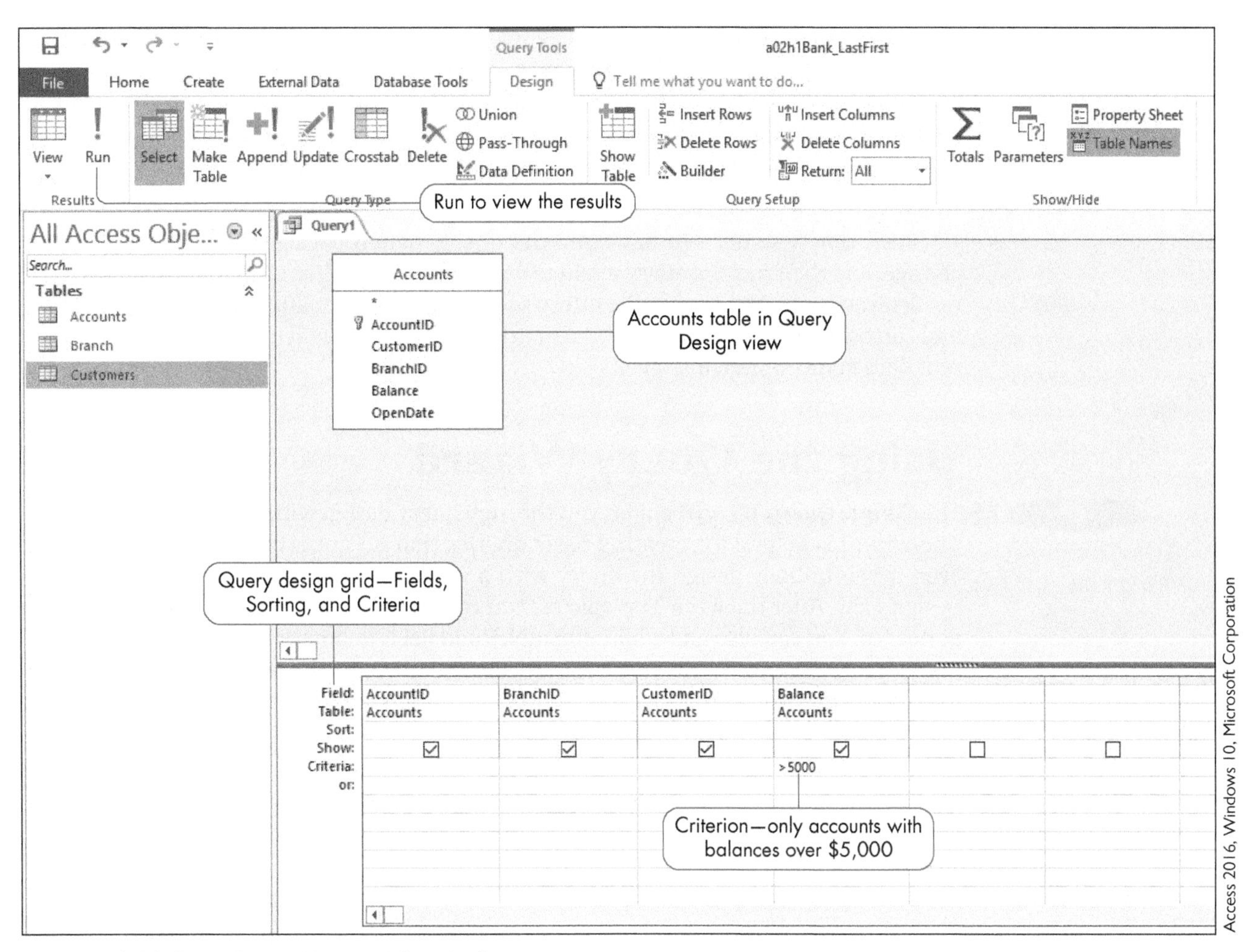

FIGURE 2.30 Query Design View with Sample Criterion

Query1

Account ID	Branch ID	Customer ID	Balance
1014	B10	30009	$16,700.00
1026	B20	30007	$7,400.00
1013	B20	30001	$10,000.00
1003	B20	30004	$15,490.00
1019	B30	30004	$14,250.00
1016	B30	30001	$18,700.00
1025	B40	30006	$11,010.00
1018	B40	30005	$7,800.00
1028	B50	30005	$8,000.00
1024	B50	30011	$14,005.00
1021	B50	30011	$21,004.00
1020	B50	30001	$12,000.00
1001	B50	30010	$5,600.00
*			$0.00

Query results in Datasheet view

Only accounts with a balance over $5,000

Record: 1 of 13 No Filter Search

Access 2016, Windows 10, Microsoft Corporation

FIGURE 2.31 Query Results in Datasheet View

TIP: EXAMINE THE RECORDS

Be sure to examine the records returned in the query results. Verify that the records in the query results match the criteria that you specified in Design view. If the results are not what you anticipated, return to Design view, and check your criteria. Unexpected results can also occur from inaccurate data, so troubleshooting your queries is a skill that you will acquire as your experience progresses.

Each time you need to fine-tune the query, switch back to Design view, make a change, and then run the query again to view the results. After you are satisfied with the results, you may want to save the query so it becomes a permanent part of the database and can be used later. Each time you run a query, the results will update based on the current data in the underlying table(s).

Using the Query Wizard

The ***Simple Query Wizard*** guides you through query design with a step-by-step process. The wizard is helpful for creating basic queries that do not require criteria. However, even if you initially design the query with a wizard, you are able to modify it later in Design view. After the wizard completes, you can switch to Design view and add criteria as needed. You can also add additional tables and fields to an existing query when conditions change. To launch the Query Wizard, click the Create tab and click Query Wizard in the Queries group (see Figure 2.32).

Access 2016, Windows 10, Microsoft Corporation

FIGURE 2.32 Launching the Query Wizard

Select Simple Query Wizard in the New Query dialog box, as shown in Figure 2.33.

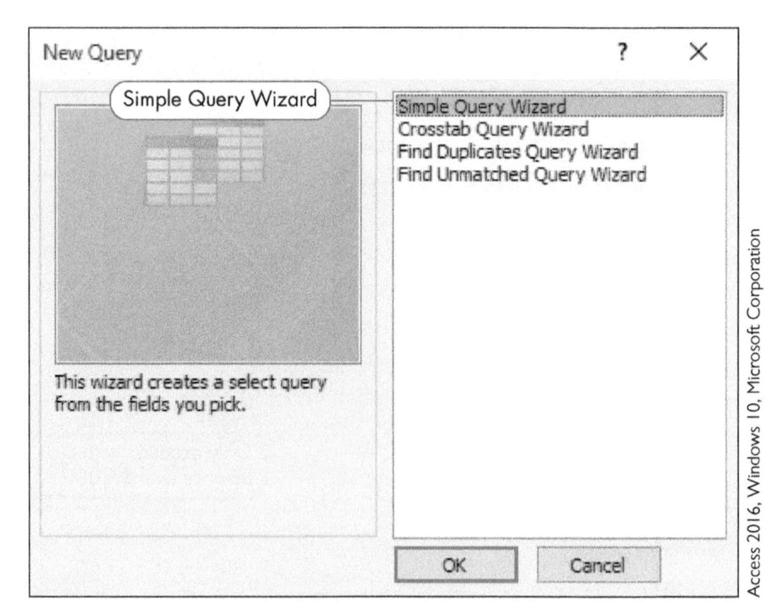

FIGURE 2.33 Simple Query Wizard

In the first step of the Simple Query Wizard dialog box, you specify the tables or queries and fields required in your query. When you select a table from the Tables/Queries arrow (queries can also be based on other queries), a list of the table's fields displays in the Available Fields list box (see Figures 2.34 and 2.35).

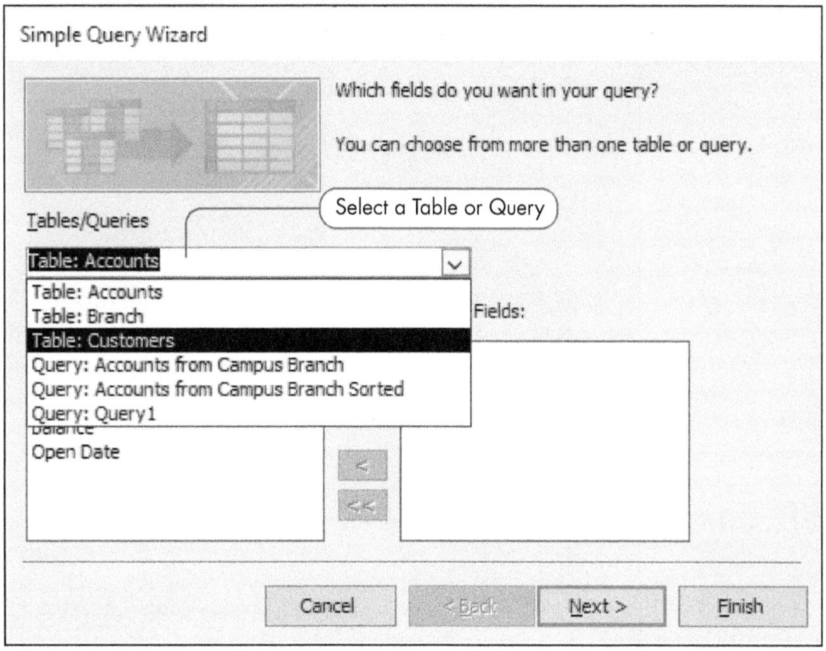

FIGURE 2.34 Specify Which Tables or Queries to Use

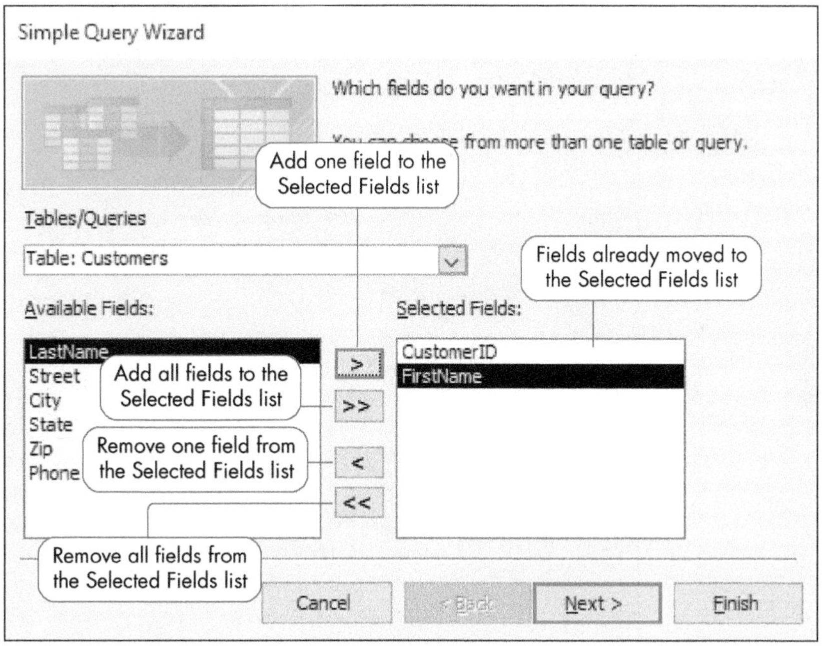

FIGURE 2.35 Specify the Fields for the Query

Select the necessary fields and add them to the Selected Fields list box using the directional arrows shown in Figure 2.35. In the next screen (shown in Figure 2.36), you choose between a detail and a summary query. The detail query shows every field of every record in the result. The summary query enables you to group data and view only summary records. For example, if you were interested in the total funds deposited at each of the bank branches, you would set the query to Summary, click Summary Options, and then click Sum on the Balance field. Access would then sum the balances of all accounts for each branch.

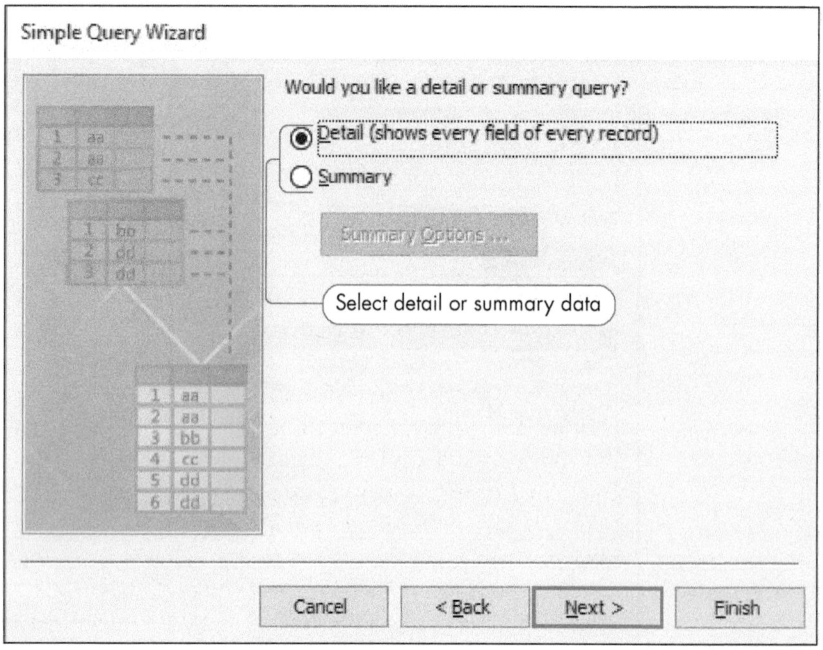

Access 2016, Windows 10, Microsoft Corporation

FIGURE 2.36 Choose Detail or Summary Data

The final dialog box of the Simple Query Wizard prompts for the name of the query. Assign descriptive names to your queries so that you can easily identify what each one does (see Figure 2.37).

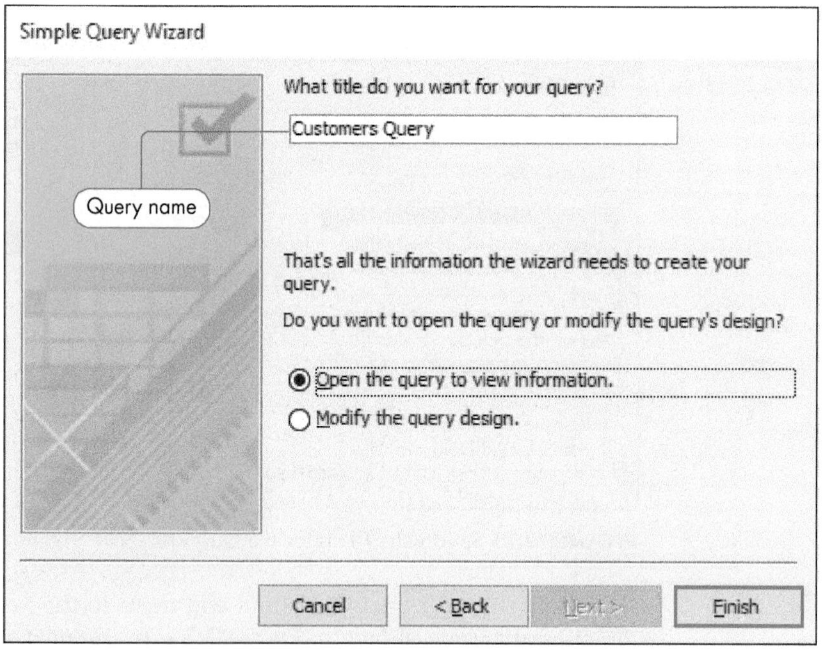

Access 2016, Windows 10, Microsoft Corporation

FIGURE 2.37 Name the Query

Specifying Query Criteria for Different Data Types

You set criteria to limit the records to display only those that you require in the query results. When specifying a criterion for a query, you may need to include a delimiter—a special character that surrounds a criterion's value. The delimiter required is determined by the field data type. Text fields require quotation marks before and after the text; for example, "Campus" could be used to display customers from the Campus branch in the Bank database. Access automatically adds the quotation marks around text, but to ensure that the correct delimiter is used, you may want to include the delimiters yourself.

When the criterion is in a date field, you enclose the criterion in pound signs, such as #10/14/2018#. Access automatically adds the pound signs around dates, but to ensure that the correct delimiter is used, you may want to include the delimiters yourself. A date value can be entered using any allowed format, such as February 2, 2018, 2/2/2018, or 2-Feb-18. Use plain digits (no delimiter) for the criteria of a numeric field, currency, or AutoNumber. You can enter numeric criteria with or without a decimal point and with or without a minus sign. Commas and dollar signs are not allowed. You enter criteria for a Yes/No field as Yes or No. See Table 2.4 for query criteria and examples.

TABLE 2.4 Query Criteria

Data Type	Criteria	Example
Text	"Harry"	For a FirstName field, displays only text that matches Harry exactly. The quotation marks can be typed, or Access will add them automatically.
Numeric	5000	For a Quantity field, displays only numbers that match 5000 exactly (do not specify commas, currency symbols, etc.).
Date	#2/2/2018#	For a ShippedDate field, shows orders shipped on February 2, 2018.
Yes/No	Yes	For a Discontinued field, returns records where the check box is selected, denoting Yes.

Use Wildcards

Wildcards are special characters that can represent one or more characters in a text value. Suppose you want to use a criterion to search for the last name of a customer, but you are not sure how to spell the name; however, you know that the name starts with the letters *Sm*. You can use a wildcard with a text value (such as Sm*) to search for the name.

You enter wildcard characters in text values in the Criteria row of a query. Therefore, if you want to search for names that start with the letters *Sm*, specify the criterion in the LastName field as *Sm**. All last names that begin with *Sm* would display in the results. Wildcard characters can be placed in the beginning, middle, or end of a text string. Table 2.5 shows more query criterion examples that use wildcards.

TABLE 2.5 Query Criteria Using Wildcards

Character	Description	Example	Result
*	Matches any number of characters in the same position as the asterisk	Sm*	Small, Smiley, Smith, Smithson
?	Matches a single character in the same position as the question mark	H?ll	Hall, Hill, Hull
[ ]	Matches any single character within the brackets	F[ae]ll	Fall and Fell, but not Fill or Full
[!]	Matches any character not in the brackets	F[!ae]ll	Fill and Full, but not Fall or Fell

Use Comparison Operators in Queries

Comparison operators, such as equal (=), not equal (<>), greater than (>), less than (<), greater than or equal to (>=), and less than or equal to (<=), can be used in query criteria. Comparison operators enable you to limit the query results to only those records that meet the criteria. For example, if you only want to see accounts that have a balance greater than $5,000, you would type >5000 in the Criteria row of the Balance field. Table 2.6 shows more comparison operator examples.

TABLE 2.6 Comparison Operators in Queries

Expression	Example
=10	Equals 10
<>10	Not equal to 10
>10	Greater than 10
>=10	Greater than or equal to 10
<10	Less than 10
<=10	Less than or equal to 10

Pearson Education, Inc.

Work with Null

Sometimes finding null values is an important part of making a decision. For example, if you need to know which orders have been completed but not shipped, you would create a query to find the orders with a null (missing) ShipDate. The term that Access uses for a blank field is ***null***. Table 2.7 provides two examples of when to use the null criterion in a query.

TABLE 2.7 Establishing Null Criteria Expressions

Expression	Description	Example
Is Null	Use to find blank fields	For a SalesRepID field in the Customers table when the customer has not been assigned to a sales representative.
Is Not Null	Used to find fields with data	For a ShipDate field; a value has been entered to indicate that the order was shipped to the customer.

Pearson Education, Inc.

Establish AND, OR, and NOT Criteria

Remember the earlier question, "Which customers currently have an account with a balance over $5,000?" This question was answered by creating a query with a single criterion. At times, questions are more focused and require queries with multiple criteria. For example, you may need to know "Which customers from the Eastern branch currently have an account with a balance over $5,000?" To answer this question, you specify two criteria in different fields using the ***AND condition***. This means that the query results will display only records that match *all* criteria. When the criteria are in the same row of the query design grid, Access interprets this as an AND condition. You can also use the AND logical operator to test two criteria in the same field, as shown in Table 2.8.

When you have multiple criteria and you need to satisfy only one, not all of the criteria, use the ***OR condition***. The query results will display records that match any of the specified criteria. You can use the OR logical operator, and type the expression into the Criteria row, separating the criteria with the OR keyword. Table 2.8 shows an example of an OR condition created using this method. You can also type the first criterion into the Criteria row and then type the next criterion by using the Or row in the same field or a different field in the design grid (see Figure 2.38).

The NOT logical operator returns all records except the specified criteria. For example, "Not Eastern" would return all accounts except those opened at the Eastern branch.

TABLE 2.8 AND, OR, and NOT Queries

Logical Operator	Example	Result
AND	>5000 AND <10000	For a Balance field, returns all accounts with a balance greater than $5,000 and less than $10,000.
OR	"Eastern" OR "Campus"	For a Location field, returns all accounts that are at the Eastern or the Campus branch.
NOT	Not "Campus"	For a Location field, returns all records except those in the Campus branch.

Field:	AccountID	CustomerID	BranchID	Balance
Table:	Accounts	Accounts	Accounts	Accounts
Sort:	Ascending			
Show:			☑	☑
Criteria:			"B50"	<5000
or:				

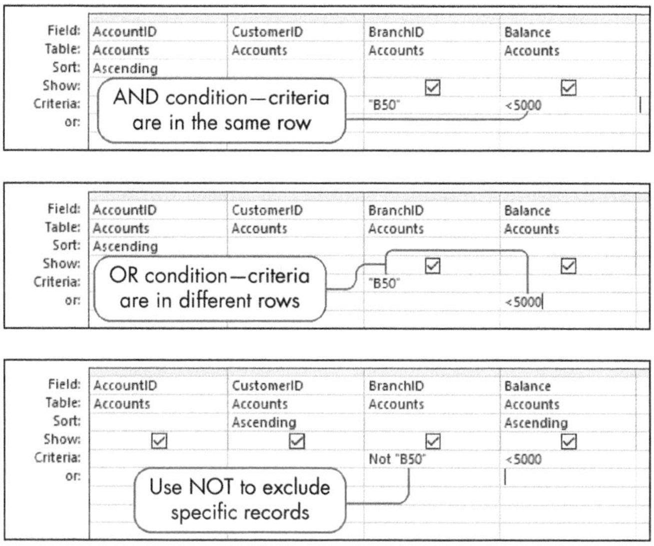

AND condition—criteria are in the same row

Field:	AccountID	CustomerID	BranchID	Balance
Table:	Accounts	Accounts	Accounts	Accounts
Sort:	Ascending			
Show:			☑	☑
Criteria:			"B50"	
or:				<5000

OR condition—criteria are in different rows

Field:	AccountID	CustomerID	BranchID	Balance
Table:	Accounts	Accounts	Accounts	Accounts
Sort:		Ascending		Ascending
Show:	☑	☑	☑	☑
Criteria:			Not "B50"	<5000
or:				

Use NOT to exclude specific records

FIGURE 2.38 Query Design Views Showing the AND, OR, and NOT Operators

TIP: FINDING VALUES IN A DATE RANGE

To find the values contained within a date range, use the greater than (>) and less than (<) operators. For example, to find the values of dates on or after January 1, 2018, and on or before December 31, 2018, use the criterion >=1/1/2018 and <=12/31/2018. You can also use the BETWEEN operator to find the same inclusive dates, for example, BETWEEN 1/1/2018 and 12/31/2018.

Understanding Query Sort Order

The query sort order determines the order of records in a query's Datasheet view. You can change the order of records by specifying the sort order in Design view. When you want to sort using more than one field, the sort order is determined from left to right. The order of columns should be considered when first creating the query. For example, a query sorted by LastName and then by FirstName must have those two fields in the correct order in the design grid. When modifying sort order, it is sometimes necessary to rearrange fields, or add and delete columns in the query design grid.

To change order, add, or delete fields in the query design grid, complete one of the following steps:

- Change the order of a field: select the column you want to move by clicking the column selector. Click again and drag the selected field to its new location.
- Insert an additional column in the design grid: select a column and click Insert Columns in the Query Setup group on the Design tab. The additional column will insert to the left of the selected column.
- Delete a column: click the column selector to select the column and click Delete Columns in the Query Setup group, or press Delete on the keyboard.

Running, Copying, and Modifying a Query

Once your query is designed and saved, you run it to view the results. After you create a query, you may want to create a duplicate copy to use as the basis for creating a similar query. Duplicating a query saves time when you need the same tables and fields but with slightly different criteria.

Run a Query

There are several ways to run a query. One method is from within Design view; click Run in the Results group on the Design tab. Another method is to locate the query in the Navigation Pane and double-click it (or select the query in the Navigation Pane and press Enter). The results will display in a datasheet as a tab in the main window.

Copy and Modify a Query

Sometimes you want a number of queries in which each query is similar to another that you have created. To avoid having to recreate each query from scratch, you can create a copy of an existing query and then modify it to accommodate the new criteria. For example, you need a list of accounts in each branch. In a case like this, you create a query for one branch and then save a copy of the query and give it a new name. Finally, you would change the criteria to specify the next branch.

To create a query based on an existing query, complete the following steps:

1. Open the query you want to copy.
2. Click the File tab and click Save As.
3. Click Save Object As in the File Types section.
4. Ensure that Save Object As is selected in the Database File Types section and click Save As.
5. Type the name you want to use for the new query in the Save As dialog box and click OK (see Figure 2.39).
6. Switch to Design view of the copied query and modify the query criteria, as necessary.
7. Save and run the modified query.

TIP: COPYING THE QUERY IN THE NAVIGATION PANE

You can also right-click the original query in the Navigation Pane and from the shortcut menu, select Copy. Right-click in the empty space of the Navigation Pane again and then select Paste. Type a name for the new query in the Paste As dialog box and click OK.

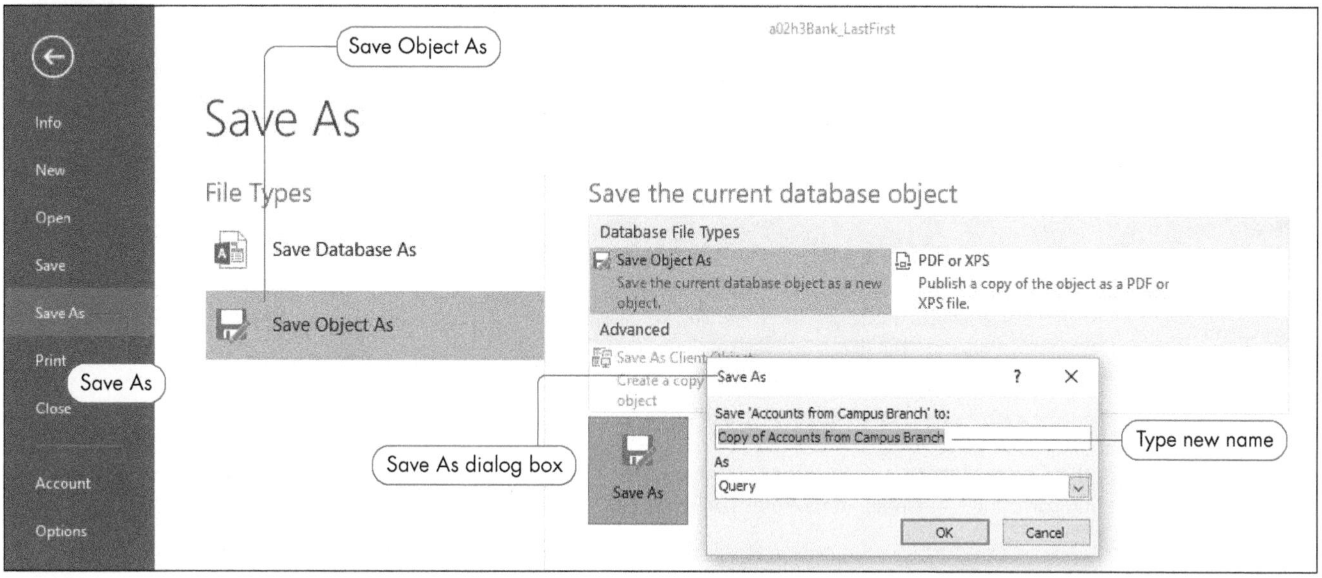

FIGURE 2.39 Using Save Object As to Save a Copy of a Query

Change Query Data

STEP 3 Be aware that query results in the datasheet display the actual records that are stored in the underlying table(s). Being able to correct an error immediately while it is displayed in the query datasheet is an advantage. You can save time by not having to close the query, open the table, find the error, fix it, and then run the query again. However, use caution when editing records in query results since you will be changing the original table data.

Quick Concepts

8. Define a single-table query. Give an example. ***p. 766***
9. Give an example of how to use the Criteria row to find certain records in a table. ***p. 768***
10. Why would you use an OR condition in a query? ***p. 774***
11. Why would you want to copy an existing query? ***p. 776***

Hands-On Exercises

Watch the Video for this Hands-On Exercise!
MyITLab®
HOE3 Training

Skills covered: Use the Query Wizard • Specify Query Criteria • Specify Query Sort Order • Change Query Data • Run, Copy, and Modify a Query

3 Single-Table Queries

The tables and table relationships have been created, and some data have been entered in the Bank database. Now, you begin the process of analyzing the bank data for the auditor. You will do so using queries. You decide to begin with the Accounts table.

STEP 1 » USE THE QUERY WIZARD

You decide to start with the Query Wizard, knowing you can always alter the design of the query later in Design view. You will show the results to the auditor using Datasheet view. Refer to Figure 2.40 as you complete Step 1.

Accounts from Campus Branch

Account ID	Customer ID	Branch ID	Balance
1001	30010	B50	$5,600.00
1002	30001	B10	$1,200.00
			$15,490.00
1004	30003	B30	$630.00
1005	30009	B50	$1,300.00
1006	30003	B10	$550.00
1007	30007	B20	$1,620.00
1008	30004	B40	$2,100.00
1009	30005	B50	$1,500.00
1010	30001	B20	$3,000.00
1011	30005	B10	$290.00
1012	30002	B30	$1,900.00
1013	30001	B20	$10,000.00
1014	30009	B10	$16,700.00
1015	30004	B30	$460.00
1016	30001	B30	$18,700.00
1017	30010	B30	$980.00
1018	30005	B40	$7,800.00
1019	30004	B30	$14,250.00
1020	30001	B50	$1,200.00
1021	30011	B50	$21,004.00
1022	30003	B50	$4,000.00
1023	30011	B50	$1,000.00
1024	30011	B50	$14,005.00
		B40	$11,010.00
1026	30007	B20	$7,400.00
1027	30003	B50	$4,000.00

Record: 1 of 27 No Filter Search

Step e: Fields added to query

Step h: 27 records displayed

Access 2016, Windows 10, Microsoft Corporation

FIGURE 2.40 Query Results Before Criteria Are Applied

a. Open *a02h2Bank_LastFirst* if you closed it at the end of Hands-On Exercise 2, and save it as **a02h3Bank_LastFirst**, changing h2 to h3.

b. Click the **Create tab** and click **Query Wizard** in the Queries group.

The New Query dialog box opens. Simple Query Wizard is selected by default.

c. Click **OK**.

d. Verify that Table: Accounts is selected in the Tables/Queries box.

e. Click **AccountID** in the Available Fields list, then click **Add One Field** [>] to move it to the Selected Fields list. Repeat the process with **CustomerID**, **BranchID**, and **Balance**.

The four fields should now display in the Selected Fields list box.

f. Click **Next**.

g. Confirm that Detail (shows every field of every record) is selected and click **Next**.

h. Name the query **Accounts from Campus Branch**. Click **Finish**.

This query name describes the data in the query results. Your query should have four fields: AccountID, CustomerID, BranchID, and Balance. The Navigation bar indicates that 27 records meet the query criteria.

STEP 2 » SPECIFY QUERY CRITERIA AND SORT ORDER

The auditor indicated that the problem seems to be confined to the Campus branch. You use this knowledge to revise the query to display only Campus accounts. Refer to Figure 2.41 as you complete Step 2.

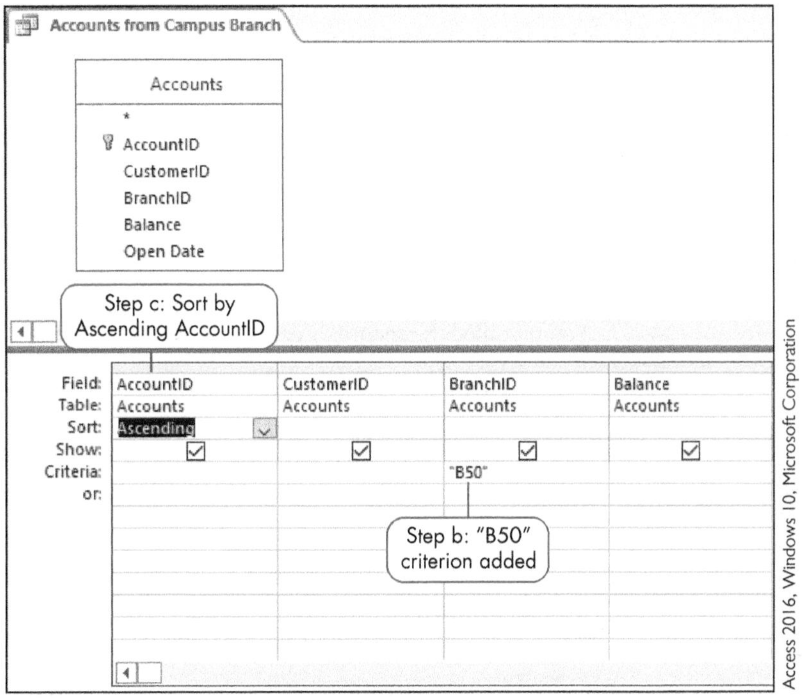

FIGURE 2.41 Enter Criteria and Add Sort Order

a. Click the **Home tab** and click **View** in the Views group.

The Accounts from Campus Branch query opens in Design view. You have created this query to view only those accounts at the Campus branch. However, other branches' accounts also display. You need to limit the query results to only the records of interest.

b. Click in the **Criteria row** (fifth row) in the BranchID column, type **B50**, and press **Enter**.

B50 is the BranchID for the Campus branch. Access queries are not case sensitive; therefore, b50 and B50 will produce the same results. Access adds quotation marks around text criteria after you press Enter, or you can type them yourself.

c. Click in the **Sort row** (third row) in the AccountID column and select **Ascending**.

d. Click **Run** in the Results group.

You should see nine records in the query results, all from Branch B50, sorted in ascending order by Account ID.

STEP 3 » CHANGE QUERY DATA AND RUN, COPY, AND MODIFY A QUERY

When the query results are on the screen, the auditor notices that some of the data are incorrect, and one of the accounts is missing. From your experience with Access, you explain to the auditor that the data can be changed directly in a query rather than switching back to the table. Refer to Figure 2.42 as you complete Step 3.

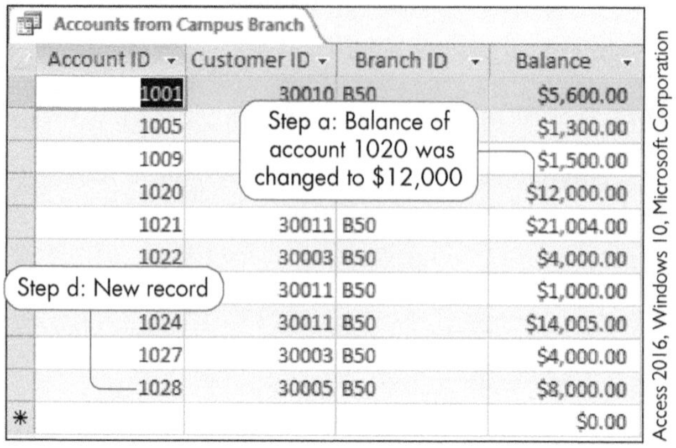

Accounts from Campus Branch

Account ID	Customer ID	Branch ID	Balance
1001	30010	B50	$5,600.00
1005			$1,300.00
1009			$1,500.00
1020			$12,000.00
1021	30011	B50	$21,004.00
1022	30003	B50	$4,000.00
	30011	B50	$1,000.00
1024	30011	B50	$14,005.00
1027	30003	B50	$4,000.00
1028	30005	B50	$8,000.00
*			$0.00

Step a: Balance of account 1020 was changed to $12,000

Step d: New record

Access 2016, Windows 10, Microsoft Corporation

FIGURE 2.42 Changes Made in the Query Datasheet

a. Click in the **Balance field** in the record for account 1020. Change $1,200 to **$12,000**. Press **Enter**. Save and close the query.

You modified the record directly in the query results.

b. Double-click the **Accounts table** in the Navigation Pane

Only one account shows a $12,000 balance. The Account ID is 1020 and the Customer ID is 30001. The change you made in the Accounts table from the Campus Branch query datasheet automatically changed the data stored in the underlying table.

c. Open the Customers table. Notice the name of the customer whose CustomerID is 30001, Allison Millward. Close the Customers table.

d. Add a new record to the Accounts table with the following data: **1028** (Account ID), **30005** (Customer ID), **B50** (Branch ID), **8000** (Balance), and **8/4/2018** (Open Date). Press **Tab**.

> **TROUBLESHOOTING:** If the Accounts table is not open, double-click Accounts in the Navigation Pane.

The new record is added to the Accounts table.

e. Double-click the **Accounts from Campus Branch query** in the Navigation Pane.

Customer 30005 now shows two accounts: one with a balance of $1,500 and one with a balance of $8,000.

f. Click the **File tab**, click **Save As**, click **Save Object As**, and then click **Save As**. Type **Accounts from Campus Branch Sorted** as the query name. Click **OK**.

g. Click **View** in the Views group to return to Design view of the copied query.

h. Click in the **Sort row** of the AccountID field and select **(not sorted)**. Click in the **Sort row** of the CustomerID field and select **Ascending**. Click in the **Sort row** of the BalanceID field and select **Ascending**.

i. Click **Run** in the Results group.

Customer 30005 now shows two accounts with the two balances sorted in ascending order. Likewise, all other customers with more than one account are listed in ascending order by balance.

j. Save the query. Close the Accounts from Campus Branch Sorted query and close the Accounts table.

k. Keep the database open if you plan to continue with the Hands-On Exercise. If not, close the database and exit Access.

Multitable Queries

Multitable queries contain two or more tables, and enable you to take advantage of the relationships that have been set in your database. When you extract information from a database with a query, often you will need to pull data from multiple tables. One table may contain the core information that you want, while another table may contain the related data that make the query provide the complete results.

For example, the sample Bank database contains three tables: Customers, Accounts, and Branch. You connected the tables through relationships in order to store data efficiently and to enforce consistent data entry between them. The Customers table provides the information for the owners of the accounts. However, the Accounts table includes the balances of each account—the key financial information. Therefore, both the Customers and Accounts tables are needed to provide the information that you want: which Customers own which Accounts.

Creating a Multitable Query

There are several ways to create multitable queries. The simplistic method is to add tables to an existing query, or to copy an existing query and then add to it. You can also create a multitable query from scratch either using the Query Wizard or the Query Design tool.

Add Additional Tables to a Query

STEP 1 » One way to create a multitable query is to add tables and fields to an existing query, for example to add branch or customer data to a query that includes account information.

To add tables to a saved query, complete the following steps:

1. Open the existing query in Design view.
2. Add additional tables to a query by dragging tables from the Navigation Pane directly into the top pane of the query design window.
3. Add fields, criteria, and sorting options in the query design grid.
4. Run and save the query.

For example, the Branch and Customers tables were added to the query, as shown in Figure 2.43. The join lines between tables indicate that relationships were previously set in the Relationships window. With the additional tables and fields available, you can now add the customer's name (from Customers) and the branch location name (from Branch) rather than using CustomerID and BranchID in your results. The datasheet will contain more readily identifiable information than ID numbers for customers and locations.

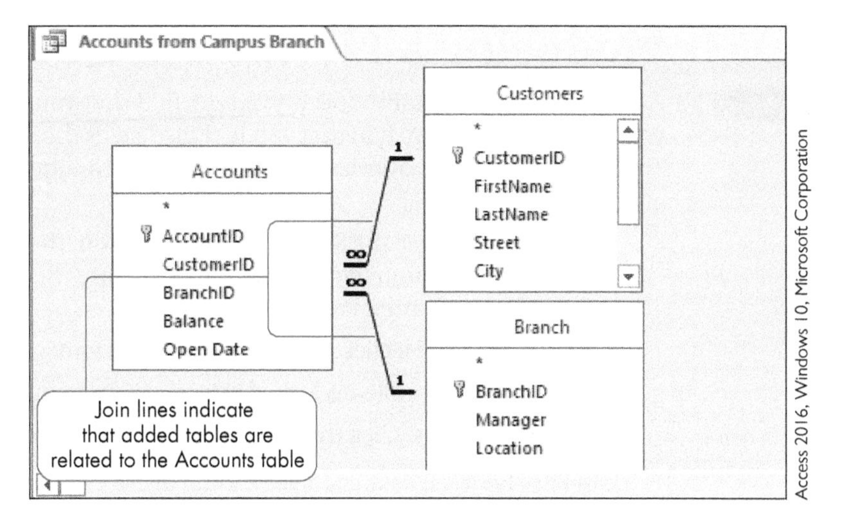

FIGURE 2.43 Two Additional Tables Added to a Query

Create a Multitable Query

STEP 2 Creating a multitable query from scratch is similar to creating a single-table query; however, choosing the right tables and managing the relationships in the query might require some additional skills. First, you should only use related tables in a multitable query. Related tables are tables that are joined in a relationship using a common field. Generally, related tables should already be joined in the Relationships window when you begin to create a multitable query. Using Figure 2.43 as a guide, creating a query with the Accounts and Branch tables would be acceptable, as would using Accounts and Customers tables, or Accounts, Branch, and Customers tables. All three scenarios include related tables. However, creating a query with only the Branch and Customers tables would not be acceptable because these tables are not directly related to one another (in other words, they do not have a common field).

To create a multitable query, complete the following steps:

1. Click the Create tab.
2. Click Query Design in the Queries group.
3. Add the tables you want in your query from the Show Table dialog box. Close the Show Table dialog box.
4. Drag the fields you want to display from the tables to the query design grid (or alternatively, double-click the field names); then add criteria and sorting options.
5. Click Run in the Results group on the Design tab to show the results in Datasheet view.

TIP: PRINT THE RELATIONSHIP REPORT TO HELP CREATE A MULTITABLE QUERY

When you create a multitable query, you only include related tables. As a guide, when the Relationships window is open, you can print the Relationship Report. Click the Database Tools tab, then click Relationship Report in the Tools group on the Relationship Tools Design tab. This report will provide a diagram that displays the tables, fields, and relationships in your database. The report is exportable to other formats such as Word if you want to share it with colleagues.

Modifying a Multitable Query

STEP 3 After creating a multitable query, you may find that you did not include all of the fields you needed, or you may find that you included fields that are unnecessary to the results. To modify multitable queries, use the same techniques you learned for single-table queries.

- To add tables, use the Show Table dialog box in the Query Setup group on the Query Tools Design tab (or drag the tables into the top pane of the query design from the Navigation Pane).
- To remove tables, click the unwanted tables and press Delete.
- To add fields, double-click the fields you want to include.
- To remove fields, click the column selector of each field and press Delete.

Join lines between related tables should display automatically in a query if the relationships were previously established, as shown in Figure 2.43.

TIP: MULTITABLE QUERIES INHERIT RELATIONSHIPS

When you add two or more related tables to a query, join lines display automatically. You can delete a join line in a query with no impact on the relationship set in the database. Deleting a join line only affects the relationship in the individual query. The next time you create a query with the same tables, the relationships will be inherited from the database. And, if you open the Relationships window, you will find the join lines intact.

Add and Delete Fields in a Multitable Query

In Figure 2.44, three tables, as well as the join lines between the tables, display in the top pane of Design view. All the fields from each of the tables are now available for use in the query design grid. Figure 2.44 shows that Location (from the Branch table) replaced BranchID and LastName (from the Customers table) replaced CustomerID to make the results more useful. BranchID was deleted from the query; therefore, the "B50" criterion was removed as well. "Campus" was added to the Location field's Criteria row in order to extract the names of the branches rather than their BranchID numbers. Because criteria values are not case sensitive, typing "campus" is the same as typing "Campus" and both will return the same results. The results of the revised query are shown in Figure 2.45.

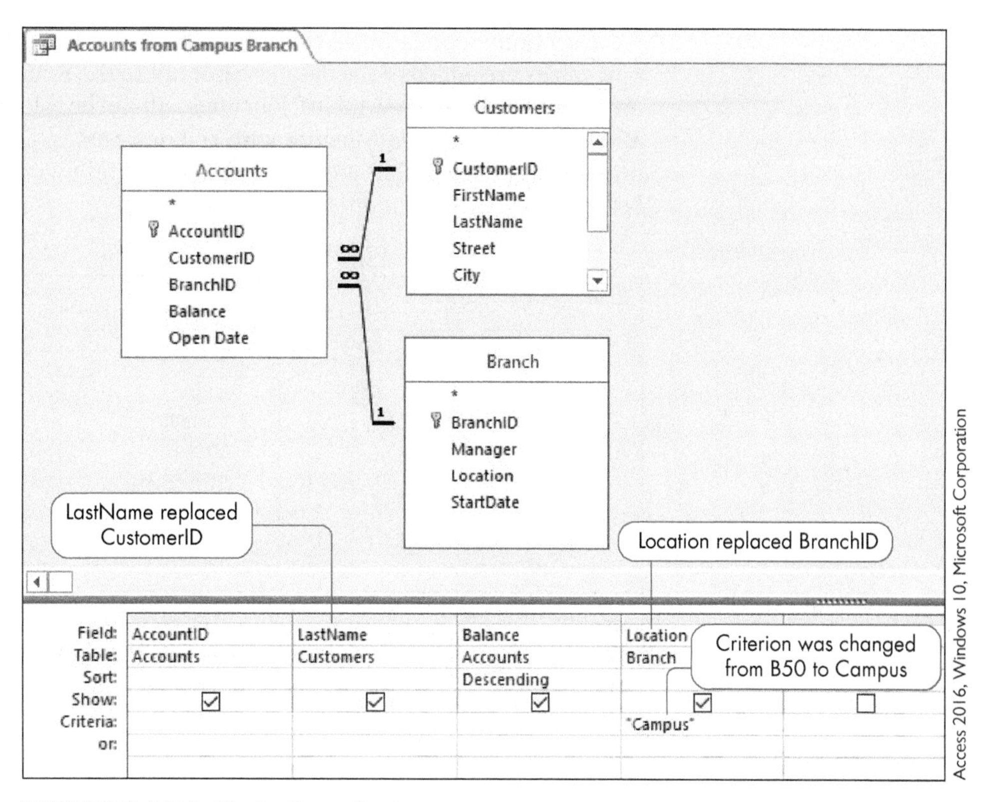

FIGURE 2.44 Modify the Query Design

Accounts from Campus Branch

Account ID	LastName	Balance	Branch Location
1021	YourName	$21,004.00	Campus
1024	YourName	$14,005.00	Campus
1020	M		Campus
1028	W		Campus
1001	Peterson	$5,600.00	Campus
1027	Hayes	$4,000.00	Campus
1022	Hayes	$4,000.00	Campus
1009	Wagner	$1,500.00	Campus
1005	Nunn	$1,300.00	Campus
1023	YourName	$1,000.00	Campus

Accounts are from the Campus branch

Access 2016, Windows 10, Microsoft Corporation

FIGURE 2.45 Datasheet View of a Multitable Query

Add Join Lines in a Multitable Query

In Figure 2.46, two tables are added to the query design, but no join line connects them. The results of the query will be unpredictable and will display more records than expected. The Customers table contains 11 records, and the Branch table contains 5 records. Because Access does not know how to interpret the unrelated tables, the results will show 55 records—every possible combination of customer and branch (11 × 5). See Figure 2.47.

To fix this problem, you can create join lines using existing tables if the tables contain a common field with the same data type. In this example, in which there is no common field, you can add an additional table that provides join lines between all three tables. You can add the Accounts table, which provides join lines between the two existing tables, Customers and Branch, and the added Accounts table. As soon as the third table is added to the query design, the join lines display automatically.

Over time, your databases may grow, and additional tables will be added. Occasionally, new tables are added to the database but not to the Relationships window. When queries are created with the new tables, join lines will not be established. When this happens, add join lines to create relationships with the new tables. Or you can create temporary join lines in the query design window. These join lines will provide a temporary relationship between tables (for that query only) and enable Access to interpret the query properly.

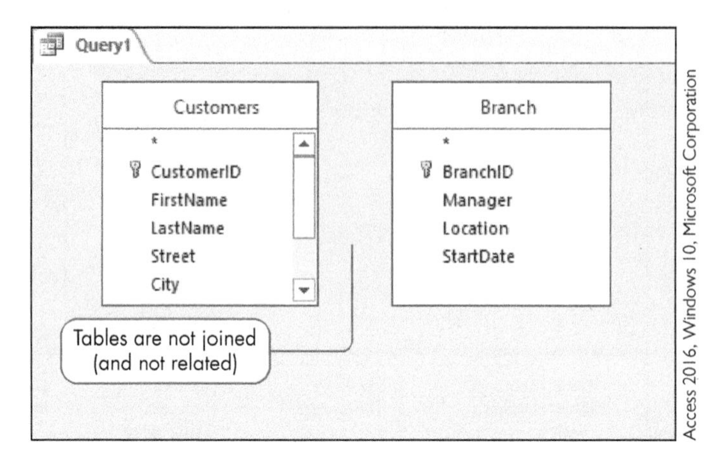

FIGURE 2.46 Query Design with Unrelated Tables

Query1

LastName	Branch ID	Branch Location	Manager's Start Date
Millward	B10	Uptown	12/3/2014
Millward	B20	Eastern	6/18/2013
Millward	B30	Western	3/13/2011
Millward	B40	Southern	9/15/2014
Millward	B50	Campus	10/11/2016
Fox	B10	Uptown	2014
Fox	B20	Eastern	013
Fox	B30	Western	011
Fox	B40	Southern	014
Fox	B50	Campus	10/11/2016
Hayes	B10	Uptown	12/3/2014
Hayes	B20	Eastern	6/18/2013
Hayes	B30	Western	3/13/2011
Hayes	B40	Southern	9/15/2014
Hayes	B50	Campus	10/11/2016
Collins	B10	Uptown	12/3/2014
Collins	B20	Eastern	6/18/2013
Collins	B30	Western	3/13/2011
Collins	B40	Southern	9/15/2014
Collins	B50	Campus	10/11/2016
Wagner	B10	Uptown	12/3/2014
Wagner	B20	Eastern	6/18/2013
Wagner	B30	Western	3/13/2011
		Southern	9/15/2014
Wagner	B50	Campus	10/11/2016
Williams	B10	Uptown	12/3/2014
Williams	B20	Eastern	6/18/2013

Record: 1 of 55 No Filter Search

Access shows one record for every Branch for each Customer

Result shows 55 records

Access 2016, Windows 10, Microsoft Corporation

FIGURE 2.47 Query Results Using Unrelated Tables

Summarize Data Using a Multitable Query

You can get valuable information from your database using a multitable query. For example, if you want to know how many accounts each customer has, you would create a new query and add both the Customers and Accounts tables to Design view. After you verify that the join lines are correct, you add the CustomerID field from the Customers table and the AccountID field from the Accounts table to the query design grid. When you initially run the query, the results show duplicates in the CustomerID column because some customers have multiple accounts.

To summarize this information (how many accounts each customer has), complete the following steps:

1. Switch to Design view and click Totals in the Show/Hide group on the Query Tools Design tab. The Total row displays. Both fields show the Group By option in the Total row. The Total row enables you to summarize records by using functions such as Sum, Average, Count, etc.
2. Click in the Total row of the AccountID field, select Count from the list of functions, and run the query again. This time the results show one row for each customer and the number of accounts for each customer.

Query1

Customer ID	CountOfAccountID
30001	5
30002	1
30003	4
30004	4
30005	4
30006	1
30007	2
30009	2
30010	2
30011	3

Access 2016, Windows 10, Microsoft Corporation

FIGURE 2.48 Datasheet Results with the Count of Accounts per Customer

Quick Concepts

12. What is the advantage of creating a multitable query? ***p. 782***
13. What is the benefit of summarizing data in a multitable query? ***p. 786***
14. What is the result of creating a query with two unrelated tables? ***p. 785***

Hands-On Exercises

Skills covered: Add Additional Tables to a Query • Create a Multitable Query • Modify a Multitable Query • Summarize Data Using a Multitable Query

4 Multitable Queries

Based on the auditor's request, you will evaluate the data further. This requires creating queries that are based on multiple tables rather than on a single table. You decide to open an existing query, add additional tables, and then save the query with a new name.

STEP 1 » ADD ADDITIONAL TABLES TO A QUERY

The previous query was based on the Accounts table, but now you need to add information to the query from the Branch and Customers tables. You will add the Branch and Customers tables to the query. Refer to Figure 2.49 as you complete Step 1.

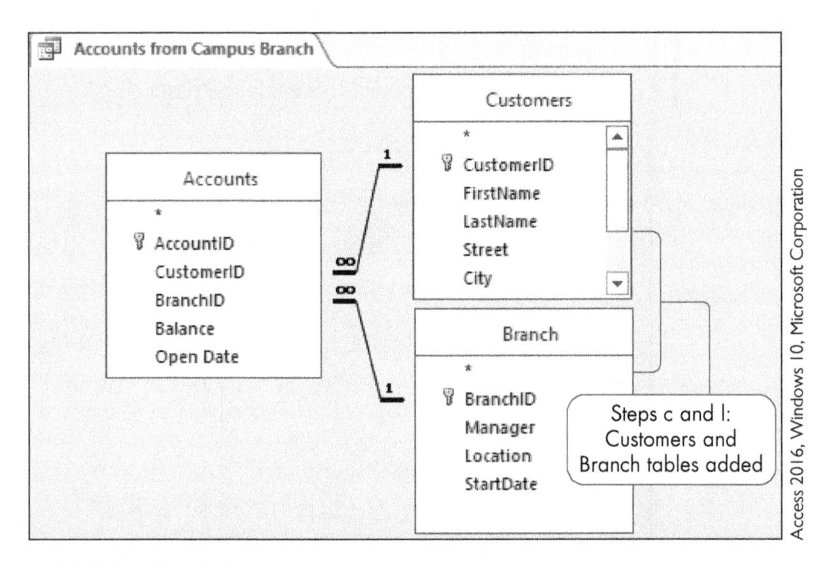

FIGURE 2.49 Add Tables to an Existing Query

a. Open *a02h3Bank_LastFirst* if you closed it at the end of Hands-On Exercise 3, and save it as **a02h4Bank_LastFirst**, changing h3 to h4.

b. Right-click the **Accounts from Campus Branch query** in the Navigation Pane and select **Design View** from the shortcut menu.

c. Drag the **Branch table** from the Navigation Pane to the top pane of the query design grid to the right of the Accounts table.

A join line connects the Branch table to the Accounts table. The tables in the query inherit the relationship created earlier in the Relationships window.

d. Drag the **Location field** from the Branch table to the first empty column in the design grid.

The Location field should be positioned to the right of the Balance field.

e. Click the **Show check box** below the BranchID field to clear the check box and hide this field from the results.

The BranchID field is no longer needed in the results because the Location field provides the branch name instead. Because you deselected the BranchID Show check box, the BranchID field will not display the next time the query is run.

f. Delete the B50 criterion in the BranchID field.

g. Type **Campus** as a criterion in the Location field and press **Enter**.

Access adds quotation marks around Campus for you because Campus is a text criterion. You are substituting the Location criterion *(Campus)* in place of the BranchID criterion (B50).

h. Click in the AccountID field **Sort row**, click the arrow, and then click **(not sorted)**. Click in the **Sort row** of the Balance field. Click the arrow and select **Descending**.

i. Click **Run** in the Results group.

The BranchID field does not display in Datasheet view because you hid the field in Step e. Only Campus accounts display in the datasheet (10 records). Next, you will add the Customers LastName field to and delete the CustomerID field from the query.

j. Save the changes to the query design.

k. Click **View** in the Views group to return to Design view. Point over the column selector at the top of the BranchID field, and when a downward arrow displays, click to select it. Press **Delete**.

The BranchID field has been removed from the grid.

l. Drag the **Customers table** from the Navigation Pane to the top pane of the query design grid and reposition the tables so that the join lines are not blocked (see Figure 2.49).

The join lines automatically connect the Customers table to the Accounts table (similar to Step c above).

m. Drag the **LastName field** in the Customers table to the second column in the design grid.

The LastName field should be positioned to the right of the AccountID field.

n. Click the **column selector** in the CustomerID field to select it. Press **Delete**.

The CustomerID field is no longer needed in the results because we added the LastName field instead.

o. Click **Run** in the Results group.

The last names of the customers now display in the results.

p. Save and close the query.

STEP 2 » CREATE A MULTITABLE QUERY

After discussing the query results with the auditor, you realize that another query is needed to show those customers with account balances of $1,000 or less. You create the query and view the results in Datasheet view. Refer to Figure 2.50 as you complete Step 2.

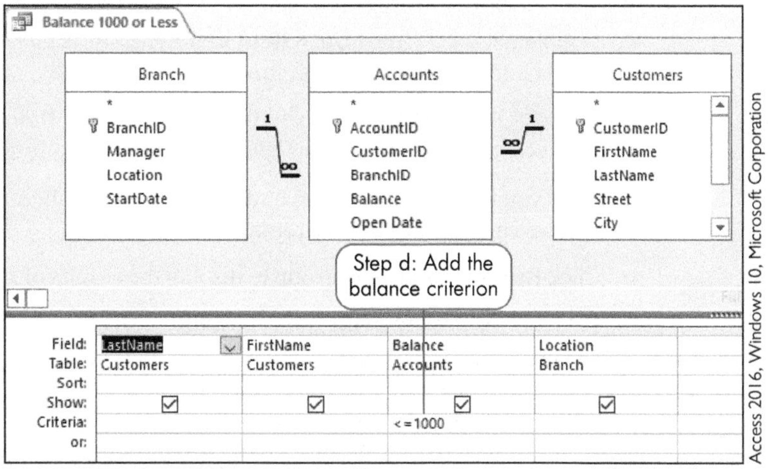

Access 2016, Windows 10, Microsoft Corporation

FIGURE 2.50 Create a Multitable Query

a. Click the **Create tab** and click **Query Design** in the Queries group.

b. Double-click the **Branch table name** in the Show Table dialog box. Double-click **Accounts** and **Customers** so that all three are added to Design view. Click **Close** in the Show Table dialog box.

Three tables are added to the query.

c. Double-click the following fields to add them to the query design grid: **LastName**, **FirstName**, **Balance**, and **Location**.

d. Type **<=1000** in the Criteria row of the Balance column.

e. Click **Run** in the Results group to see the query results.

Six records that have a balance of $1,000 or less display.

f. Click **Save** on the Quick Access Toolbar and type **Balance 1000 or Less** as the Query Name in the Save As dialog box. Click **OK**.

STEP 3 » MODIFY A MULTITABLE QUERY

The auditor requests additional changes to the Balance 1000 or Less query you just created. You will modify the criteria to display the accounts that were opened on or after January 1, 2011, with balances of $2,000 or less. Refer to Figure 2.51 as you complete Step 3.

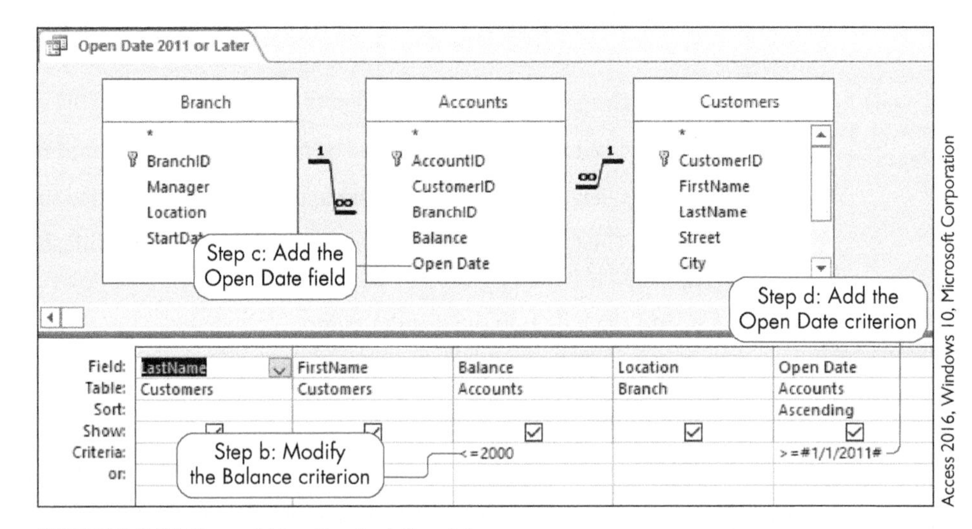

FIGURE 2.51 Query Using the And Condition

a. Click **View** in the Views group to switch the Balance 1000 or Less query to Design view.

b. Type **<=2000** in place of <=1000 in the Criteria row of the Balance field and press **Enter**.

c. Double-click the **Open Date field** in the Accounts table in the top pane of Design view to add it to the first blank column in the design grid.

d. Type **>=1/1/2011** in the Criteria row of the Open Date field and press **Enter** to extract only accounts that have been opened since January 1, 2011.

After you type the expression and then move to a different column, Access will add the # symbols around the date automatically.

e. Click **Run** in the Results group to display the results of the query.

Five records display in the query results.

f. Click the **File tab**, click **Save As**, click **Save Object As**, and then click **Save As**. Type **Open Date 2011 or Later** as the query name. Click **OK**.

g. Click **View** in the Views group to return to Design view of the copied query.

h. Click in the **Sort row** of the Open Date field and select **Ascending**.

i. Click **Run** in the Results group.

The records are sorted from the earliest open date on or after January 1, 2011, to the most recent open date.

j. Save and close the query.

STEP 4 » SUMMARIZE DATA USING A MULTITABLE QUERY

The auditor wants to know the number of accounts each customer has opened. You create a query using a Total row to obtain these data. Refer to Figure 2.52 as you complete Step 4.

Step h: Field renamed as Number of Accounts

Step i: Each row displays a count of the customer's accounts

Number of Customer Accounts

Customer ID	Number of Accounts
30001	5
30002	1
30003	4
30004	4
30005	4
30006	1
30007	2
30009	2
30010	2
30011	3

FIGURE 2.52 Number of Accounts per Customer

a. Click the **Create tab** and click **Query Design** in the Queries group.

b. Add the **Accounts table** and the **Customers table** to the top section of Design view. Click **Close** in the Show Table dialog box.

c. Double-click the **CustomerID** in the Customers table in the top section of Design view to add it to the first blank column in the design grid, and double-click the **AccountID** in the Accounts table to add it to the second column.

d. Click **Run** in the Results group.

The results show there are 28 records. Every account a customer has opened is displayed. The auditor wants only the total number of accounts a customer has, so you modify the query.

e. Click **View** in the Views group to return to Design view of the query.

f. Click **Totals** in the Show/Hide group.

Both columns show the Group By option in the Total row.

g. Click **Group By** in the Total row of the AccountID field and select **Count**.

h. Modify the AccountID field to read **Number of Accounts: AccountID**.

You typed a new field name followed by a colon that will display Number of Accounts in the datasheet when you run the query.

i. Click **Run** in the Results group. Resize the columns of the datasheet to fully display the results.

The results show one row for each customer and the number of accounts each customer has opened since the database was created.

j. Click **Save** on the Quick Access Toolbar and type **Number of Customer Accounts** as the query name. Close the query.

k. Close the database and exit Access. Based on your instructor's directions, submit a02h4Bank_LastFirst.

Chapter Objectives Review

After reading this chapter, you have accomplished the following objectives:

1. Design a table.

- Include necessary data: Consider the output requirements when creating table structure. Determine the data required to produce the expected information.
- Design for now and for the future: When designing a database, anticipate the future needs of the system and build in the flexibility to satisfy those demands.
- Store data in their smallest parts: Store data in their smallest parts for more flexibility. Storing a full name in a Name field is more limiting than storing a first name in a separate FirstName field and a last name in a separate LastName field.
- Determine primary keys: When designing your database tables, it is important to determine which field will uniquely identify each record in a table.
- Plan for common fields between tables: Tables are joined in relationships using common fields. Name the common fields with the same name and make sure they have the same data type.
- Design to accommodate calculations: Calculated fields are frequently created with numeric data. You can use date arithmetic to subtract one date from another to find the number of days, months, or years that have elapsed between them.

2. Create and modify tables and work with data.

- You can create tables in Datasheet view or Design view. Alternatively, you can import data from another database or an application such as Excel to create tables in an Access database.
- Determine data type: Data type properties determine the type of data that can be entered and the operations that can be performed on that data. Access recognizes 12 data types.
- Set a table's primary key: The primary key is the field that uniquely identifies each record in a table.
- Explore a foreign key: A foreign key is a field in one table that is also the primary key of another table.
- Work with field properties: Field properties determine how the field looks and behaves. Examples of field properties are the Field Size property and the Caption property.
- Create a new field in Design view: It may be necessary to add table fields that were not included in the original design process. While it is possible to add fields in Datasheet view, Design view offers more flexibility.
- Modify the table in Datasheet view: Datasheet view is used to add, edit, and delete records. Design view is used to create and modify the table structure by enabling you to add and edit fields and set field properties.

3. Share data.

- Import Excel data: You can import data from other applications such as an Excel spreadsheet.
- Import Access data: You can import data from another database by using the Import Wizard.
- Modify an imported table's design and add data: After importing a table, examine the design and make necessary modifications. Modifications may include changing a field name, adding new fields, or deleting unnecessary fields.

4. Establish table relationships.

- Use Show Table to add tables to the Relationships window. Drag a field name from one table to the corresponding field name in another table to join the tables.
- Enforce referential integrity: Referential integrity enforces rules in a database that are used to preserve relationships between tables when records are changed.
- Set cascade options: The Cascade Update Related Fields option ensures that when the primary key is modified in a primary table, Access will automatically update all foreign key values in a related table. The Cascade Delete Related Records option ensures that when the primary key is deleted in a primary table, Access will automatically delete all records in related tables that reference the primary key.
- Establish a one-to-many relationship: A one-to-many relationship is established when the primary key value in the primary table can match many of the foreign key values in the related table. One-to-one and many-to-many are also relationship possibilities, but one-to-many relationships are the most common.

5. Create a single-table query.

- Create a single-table select query: A single-table select query uses fields from one table to display only those records that match certain criteria.
- Use Query Design view: Use Query Design view to create and modify a query. The top portion of the view contains tables with their respective field names and displays the join lines between tables. The bottom portion, known as the query design grid, contains columns and rows that you use to control the query results.

6. Use the Query Wizard.

- The Query Wizard is an alternative method for creating queries. It enables you to select tables and fields from lists. The last step of the wizard prompts you to save the query.

7. Specify query criteria for different data types.

- Different data types require different syntax. Date fields are enclosed in pound signs (#) and text fields in quotations (" "). Numeric and currency fields require no delimiters.
- Use wildcards: Wildcards are special characters that can represent one or more characters in a text value. A question mark (?) is a wildcard that stands for a

single character in the same position as the question mark, while an asterisk (*) is a wildcard that stands for any number of characters in the same position as the asterisk.

- Use comparison operators in queries: Comparison operators such as equal (=), not equal (<>), greater than (>), less than (<), greater than or equal to (>=), and less than or equal to (<=) can be used in the criteria of a query to limit the query results to only those records that meet the criteria.
- Work with null: Access uses the term null for a blank field. Null criteria can be used to find missing information.
- Establish AND, OR, and NOT criteria: The AND, OR, and NOT conditions are used when queries require logical criteria. The AND condition returns only records that meet all criteria. The OR condition returns records meeting any of the specified criteria. The NOT logical operator returns all records except the specified criteria.

8. Understand query sort order.

- The query sort order determines the order of records in a query's Datasheet view. You can change the order of records by specifying the sort order in Design view.
- The sort order is determined from the order of the fields from left to right. Move the field columns to position them in left to right sort order.

9. Run, copy, and modify a query.

- Run a query: To obtain the results for a query, you must run the query. To run the query, click Run in the Results group in Design view. Another method is to locate the query in the Navigation Pane and double-click it. A similar method is to select the query and press Enter.
- Copy and modify a query: To save time, after specifying tables, fields, and conditions for one query, copy the query, rename it, and then modify the fields and criteria in the second query.
- Change query data: You can correct an error immediately while data is displayed in the query datasheet. Use caution when editing records in query results because you will be changing the original table data.

10. Create a multitable query.

- Add additional tables to a query: Open the Navigation Pane and drag the tables from the Navigation Pane directly into the top section of Query Design view.
- Create a multitable query: Multitable queries contain two or more tables enabling you to take advantage of the relationships that have been set in your database.

11. Modify a multitable query.

- Add and delete fields in a multitable query: Multitable queries may need to be modified. Add fields by double-clicking the field name in the table you want; remove fields by clicking the column selector and pressing Delete.
- Add join lines in a multitable query: If the tables have a common field, create join lines by dragging the field name of one common field onto the field name of the other table. Or you can add an additional table that will provide a join between all three tables.
- Summarize data using a multitable query: Use the total row options of a field such as Count to get answers.

Key Terms Matching

Match the key terms with their definitions. Write the key term letter by the appropriate numbered definition.

a. AND condition
b. AutoNumber
c. Caption property
d. Cascade Delete Related Records
e. Cascade Update Related Fields
f. Comparison Operator
g. Criteria row
h. Data redundancy
i. Data type
j. Field property
k. Foreign key
l. Multitable query
m. Null
n. One-to-many relationship
o. OR condition
p. Query
q. Referential Integrity
r. Simple Query Wizard
s. Wildcard

1. _____ Special character that can represent one or more characters in the criterion of a query. **p. 773**

2. _____ Characteristic of a field that determines how it looks and behaves. **p. 742**

3. _____ Returns only records that meet all criteria. **p. 773**

4. _____ A row in the Query Design view that determines which records will be selected. **p. 768**

5. _____ Determines the type of data that can be entered and the operations that can be performed on that data. **p. 739**

6. _____ Used to create a more understandable label than a field name label that displays in the top row in Datasheet view and in forms and reports. **p. 742**

7. _____ Enables you to ask questions about the data stored in a database and provides answers to the questions in a datasheet. **p. 767**

8. _____ The term Access uses to describe a blank field. **p. 774**

9. _____ A number that automatically increments each time a record is added. **p. 739**

10. _____ The unnecessary storing of duplicate data in two or more tables. **p. 737**

11. _____ When the primary key value in the primary table can match many of the foreign key values in the related table. **p. 756**

12. _____ A field in one table that is also the primary key of another table. **p. 741**

13. _____ An option that directs Access to automatically update all foreign key values in a related table when the primary key value is modified in a primary table. **p. 756**

14. _____ Rules in a database that are used to preserve relationships between tables when records are changed. **p. 755**

15. _____ Contains two or more tables, enabling you to take advantage of the relationships that have been set in your database. **p. 782**

16. _____ Returns records meeting any of the specified criteria. **p. 774**

17. _____ Provides a step-by-step guide to help you through the query design process. **p. 770**

18. _____ When the primary key value is deleted in a primary table, Access will automatically delete all foreign key values in a related table. **p. 756**

19. _____ Uses greater than (>), less than (<), greater than or equal to (>=), and less than or equal to (<=), etc. to limit query results that meet these criteria. **p. 772**

Multiple Choice

1. All of the following are suggested guidelines for table design *except*:

(a) Include all necessary data.
(b) Store data in its smallest parts.
(c) Avoid date arithmetic.
(d) Link tables using common fields.

2. Which of the following determines how the field names can be made more readable in table and query datasheets?

(a) Field size
(b) Data type
(c) Caption property
(d) Normalization

3. When entering, deleting, or editing input masks:

(a) The table must be in Design view.
(b) The table must be in Datasheet view.
(c) The table may be in either Datasheet or Design view.
(d) Data may only be entered in a form.

4. With respect to importing data into Access, which of the following statements is *true*?

(a) The Import Wizard works only for Excel files.
(b) The Import Wizard is found on the Create tab.
(c) You can assign a primary key while you are importing Excel data.
(d) Imported table designs cannot be modified in Access.

5. The main reason to set a field size in Access is to:

(a) Limit the length of values in a table.
(b) Make it possible to delete records.
(c) Keep your database safe from unauthorized users.
(d) Keep misspelled data from being entered into a table.

6. An illustration of a one-to-many relationship would be:

(a) An employee listed in the Employees table earns a raise so the Salaries table must be updated.
(b) A customer may have more than one account in an accounts table.
(c) Each employee in an Employees table has a matching entry in the Salaries table.
(d) An employee leaves the company so that when he is deleted from the Employees table, his salary data will be deleted from the Salaries table.

7. A query's specifications as to which tables to include must be entered on the:

(a) Table row of the query design grid.
(b) Show row of the query design grid.
(c) Sort row of the query design grid.
(d) Criteria row of the query design grid.

8. When adding date criteria to the Query Design view, the dates you enter must be delimited by:

(a) Parentheses ().
(b) Pound signs (#).
(c) Quotes (" ").
(d) At signs (@).

9. It is more efficient to make a copy of an existing query rather than to create a new query when which of the following is *true*?

(a) The existing query contains only one table.
(b) The existing query and the new query use the same tables and fields.
(c) The existing query and the new query have the exact same criteria.
(d) The original query is no longer being used.

10. Which of the following is *true* for the Query Wizard?

(a) No criteria can be added as you step through the Wizard.
(b) You can only select related tables as a source.
(c) Fields with different data types are not allowed.
(d) You are required to summarize the data.

Practice Exercises

1 Philadelphia Bookstore

Tom and Erin Mullaney own and operate a bookstore in Philadelphia, Pennsylvania. Erin asked you to help her create an Access database to store the publishers and the books that they sell. The data for the publishers and books is currently stored in Excel worksheets that you decide to import into a new database. You determine that a third table—for authors—is also required. Your task is to create and populate the three tables, set the table relationships, and enforce referential integrity. You will then create queries to extract information from the tables. Refer to Figure 2.53 as you complete this exercise.

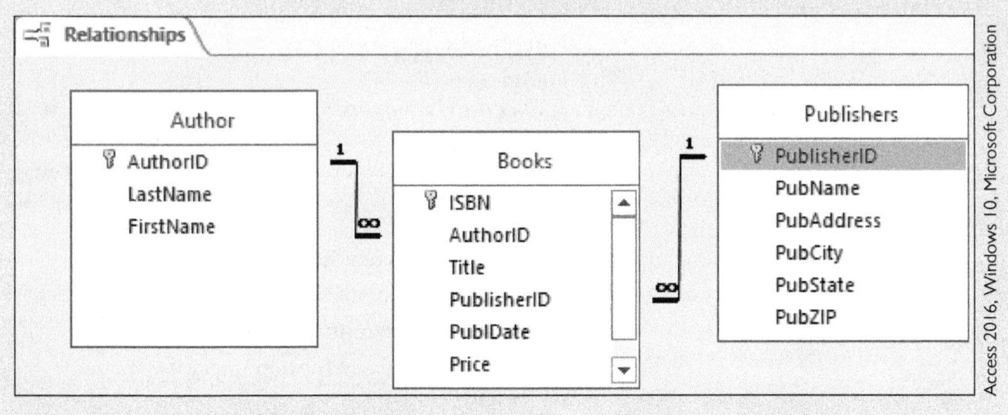

FIGURE 2.53 Books Relationships Window

a. Open Access and click **Blank desktop database**. Type **a02p1Books_LastFirst** in the **File Name box**. Click **Browse** to navigate to the location where you are saving your files in the File New Database dialog box, click **OK** to close the dialog box, and then click **Create** to create the new database.

b. Type **11** in the Click to Add column and click **Click to Add**. The field name becomes Field1, and *Click to Add* now displays as the third column. In the third column, type **Beschloss**, and then press **Tab**. Repeat the process for the fourth column; type **Michael R.** and press **Tab** two times. The insertion point returns to the first column where (New) is selected.

c. Press **Tab**. Type the rest of the data using the following table. These data will become the records of the Author table.

ID	Field1	Field2	Field3
1	11	Beschloss	Michael R.
(New)	**12**	**Turow**	**Scott**
	13	**Rice**	**Anne**
	14	**King**	**Stephen**
	15	**Connelly**	**Michael**
	16	**Rice**	**Luanne**
	17	*your last name*	*your first name*

d. Click **Save** on the Quick Access Toolbar. Type **Author** in the Save As dialog box and click **OK**.

e. Click **View** in the Views group to switch to Design view of the Author table.

f. Select **Field1**—in the second row—in the top portion of the table design and type **AuthorID** to rename the field. In the Field Properties section in the lower pane of the table design, type **Author ID** in the Caption box and verify that Long Integer displays for the Field Size property.

g. Select **Field2** and type **LastName** to rename the field. In the Field Properties section in the bottom portion of Design view, type **Author's Last Name** in the Caption box and type **20** as the field size.

h. Select **Field3** and type **FirstName** to rename the field. In the Field Properties section in the bottom portion of the table design, type **Author's First Name** as the caption and type **15** as the field size.

i. Click the **ID field row selector** (which displays the primary key) to select the row, and then click **Delete Rows** in the Tools group. Click **Yes** two times to confirm both messages.

j. Click the **AuthorID row selector**, and then click **Primary Key** in the Tools group to set the primary key.

k. Click **Save** on the Quick Access Toolbar to save the design changes. Click **Yes** to the *Some data may be lost* message. Close the table.

l. Click the **External Data tab** and click **Excel** in the Import & Link group to launch the Get External Data – Excel Spreadsheet feature. Verify that the *Import the source data into a new table in the current database* option is selected, click **Browse**, and then navigate to your student data folder. Select the *a02p1Books* workbook, click **Open**, and then click **OK**. This workbook contains two worksheets. Follow the steps below:

- Select the **Publishers worksheet** and click **Next**.
- Click the **First Row Contains Column Headings check box** to select it and click **Next**.
- Ensure that the PubID field is selected, click the **Indexed arrow**, select **Yes (No Duplicates)**, and then click **Next**.
- Click the **Choose my own primary key arrow**, ensure that PubID is selected, and then click **Next**.
- Accept the name Publishers for the table name, click **Finish**, and then click **Close** without saving the import steps.

m. Use the Import Wizard again to import the Books worksheet from the *a02p1Books* workbook into the Access database. Follow the steps below:

- Ensure that the Books worksheet is selected and click **Next**.
- Click the **First Row Contains Column Headings check box** to select it, and click **Next**.
- Click the **ISBN column**, click the down arrow, set the Indexed property box to **Yes (No Duplicates)**, and then click **Next**.
- Click the **Choose my own primary key arrow**, select **ISBN** as the primary key field, and then click **Next**.
- Accept the name Books as the table name. Click **Finish** and click **Close** without saving the import steps.

n. Right-click the **Books table** in the Navigation Pane and select **Design View**. Make the following changes:

- Click the **PubID field** and change the name to **PublisherID**.
- Set the caption property to **Publisher ID.**
- Change the PublisherID Field Size property to **2**.
- Click the **ISBN field** and change the Field Size property to **13**.
- Change the AuthorCode field name to **AuthorID**.
- Change the AuthorID Field Size property to **Long Integer**.
- Click the **ISBN field row selector** (which displays the primary key) to select the row. Click and drag to move the row up to the first position in the table design.
- Click **Save** on the Quick Access Toolbar to save the design changes to the Books table. Click **Yes** to the *Some data may be lost* warning.
- Close the table.

o. Right-click the **Publishers table** in the Navigation Pane and select **Design View**. Make the following changes:

- Click the **PubID field** and change the name to **PublisherID**.
- Change the PublisherID Field Size property to **2**.
- Change the Caption property to **Publisher's ID**.
- Change the Field Size property to **50** for the PubName and PubAddress fields.

- Change the Pub Address field name to **PubAddress** (remove the space).
- Change the PubCity Field Size property to **30**.
- Change the PubState Field Size property to **2**.
- Change the Pub ZIP field name to **PubZIP** (remove the space).
- Click **Save** on the Quick Access Toolbar to save the design changes to the Publishers table. Click **Yes** to the *Some data may be lost* warning. Close all open tables.

p. Click the **Database Tools tab** and click **Relationships** in the Relationships group. Click **Show Table**, if the Show Table dialog box does not open automatically. Follow the steps below:

- Double-click each table name in the Show Table dialog box to add it to the Relationships window and close the Show Table dialog box.
- Drag the **AuthorID field** from the Author table onto the AuthorID field in the Books table.
- Click the **Enforce Referential Integrity** and **Cascade Update Related Fields check boxes** in the Edit Relationships dialog box to select them. Click **Create** to create a one-to-many relationship between the Author and Books tables.
- Drag the **PublisherID field** from the Publishers table onto the PublisherID field in the Books table.
- Click the **Enforce Referential Integrity** and **Cascade Update Related Fields check boxes** in the Edit Relationships dialog box to select them. Click **Create** to create a one-to-many relationship between the Publishers and Books tables.
- Click **Save** on the Quick Access Toolbar to save the changes to the Relationships window, then in the Relationships group, click **Close**.

q. Click the **Create tab**, and then click **Query Wizard** in the Queries group. With Simple Query Wizard selected, click **OK**.

- Select the Publishers table, double-click to add **PubName**, **PubCity**, and **PubState** to the Selected Fields list. Click **Next**, and then click **Finish**. In Datasheet view, double-click the border to the right of each column to set the column widths to Best Fit. Click **Save** on the Quick Access Toolbar.

r. Click the **File tab**, click **Save As**, and then double-click **Save Object As**. Modify the copied query name to **New York Publishers Query**, and then click **OK**.

- Click **View** in the Views group on the Home tab to switch to Design view of the query. Click and drag the **Books table** from the Navigation Pane into the top pane of the query design window.
- Select the Books table, double-click **Title** and **PublDate** to add the fields to the query design grid.
- Click in the Criteria row of the PubState field, and type **NY**. Click the **Sort** cell of the PublDate field, click the arrow, and then click **Descending**.
- Click **Run** in the Results group (12 records display in the Datasheet sorted by PublDate in descending order). Double-click the border to the right of each column to set the column widths to Best Fit.
- Save and close the query.

s. Close the database and exit Access. Based on your instructor's directions, submit a02p1Books_LastFirst.

2 Employee Salary Analysis

The Morgan Insurance Company offers a full range of insurance services. They store all of the firm's employee data in an Access database. This file contains each employee's name and address, job performance, salary, and title, but needs to be imported into a different existing database. A database file containing two of the tables (Location and Titles) already exists; your job is to import the employee data from Access to create the third table. Once imported, you will modify field properties and set new relationships. The owner of the company, Victor Reed, is concerned that some of the Atlanta and Boston salaries may be below the guidelines published by the national office. He asks that you investigate the salaries of the two offices and create a separate query for each city. Refer to Figure 2.54 as you complete this exercise.

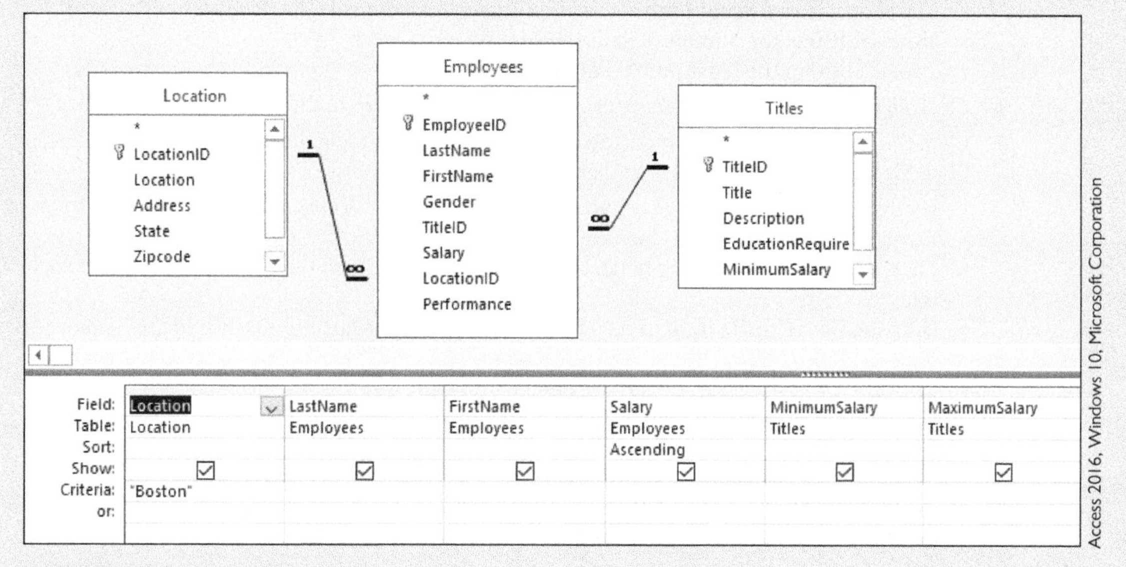

FIGURE 2.54 Boston Salaries Query Design

a. Open *a02p2Insurance* and save it as **a02p2Insurance_LastFirst**. Double-click the **Location table** and review the data to become familiar with the field names and the type of information stored in the table. Review the Titles table. Close both tables.

b. Click the **External Data tab**, click **Access** in the Import & Link group, and then complete the following steps:
   - Click **Browse** and navigate to the *a02p2Employees* database in the location of your student data files. Select the file, click **Open**.
   - Click **OK** in the Get External Data – Access Database dialog box.
   - Select the **Employees table**, and then click **OK**.
   - Click **Close** without saving the import steps.

c. Double-click the **Employees table** in the Navigation Pane, then click **View** in the Views group on the Home tab to switch to Design view of the Employees table. Make the following changes:
   - Ensure that the EmployeeID field is selected, and then click **Primary Key** in the Tools group.
   - Click the **LastName field** and change the Field Size property to **20**.
   - Change the Caption property to **Last Name**.
   - Click the **FirstName field** and change the Field Size property to **20**.
   - Change the Caption property to **First Name**.
   - Click the **LocationID field** and change the Field Size property to **3**.
   - Change the Caption property to **Location ID**.
   - Click the **TitleID field** and change the Field Size property to **3**.
   - Change the Caption property to **Title ID**.
   - Change the Salary field data type to **Currency** and change General Number in the Format property in field properties to **Currency**.
   - Save the design changes. Click **Yes** to the *Some data may be lost* warning.

d. Click **View** in the Views group to view the Employees table in Datasheet view and examine the data. Click any record in the Title ID and then click **Ascending** in the Sort & Filter group on the Home tab. Multiple employees are associated with the T01, T02, T03, and T04 titles.

e. Double-click the **Titles table** in the Navigation Pane to open it in Datasheet view. Notice that the T04 title is not in the list.

f. Add a new record in the first blank record at the bottom of the Titles table. Use the following data:

- Type **T04** in the TitleID field.
- Type **Senior Account Rep** in the Title field.
- Type **A marketing position requiring a technical background and at least three years of experience** in the Description field.
- Type **Four year degree** in the Education Requirements field.
- Type **45000** in the Minimum Salary field.
- Type **75000** in the Maximum Salary field.

g. Close all tables. Click **Yes** if you are prompted to save changes to the Employees table.

h. Click the **Database Tools tab** and click **Relationships** in the Relationships group, and then Click **Show Table**. Follow the steps below:

- Double-click each of the three table names in the Show Table dialog box to add it to the Relationships window and close the Show Table dialog box.
- Click and drag to adjust the height of the Employees table so that all fields display in each one.
- Drag the **LocationID field** in the Location table onto the LocationID field in the Employees table.
- Click the **Enforce Referential Integrity** and **Cascade Update Related Fields check boxes** in the Edit Relationships dialog box to select them. Click **Create** to create a one-to-many relationship between the Location and Employees tables.
- Drag the **TitleID field** in the Titles table onto the TitleID field in the Employees table (move the field lists by clicking and dragging their title bars as needed so that they do not overlap).
- Click the **Enforce Referential Integrity** and **Cascade Update Related Fields check boxes** in the Edit Relationships dialog box to select it. Click **Create** to create a one-to-many relationship between the Titles and Employees tables.
- Click **Save** on the Quick Access Toolbar to save the changes to the Relationships window and close the Relationships window.

i. Click the **Create tab** and click the **Query Wizard** in the Queries group. Follow the steps below:

- Select **Simple Query Wizard** and click **OK**.
- Select **Table: Employees** in the Tables/Queries box.
- Double-click **LastName** in the Available Fields list to move it to the Selected Fields list.
- Double-click **FirstName** in the Available Fields list to move it to the Selected Fields list.
- Double-click **LocationID** in the Available Fields list to move it to the Selected Fields list.
- Click **Next**.
- Type **Employees Location** as the query title and click **Finish**.
- Click **View** in the Views group on the Home tab to switch to Design view of the query. Click and drag the **Titles** table from the Navigation Pane into the top pane of the query design window.
- Double-click **Title** in the Titles table to add the field to the query design grid.
- Click the **Sort** cell of the LocationID field, click the arrow, and then click **Ascending**.
- Click **Run** in the Results group (311 records display in the Datasheet sorted by LocationID in ascending order). Double-click the border to the right of each column to set the column widths to Best Fit.
- Save and close the query.

j. Click the **Create tab** and click the **Query Wizard** in the Queries group. Follow the steps below:

- Select **Simple Query Wizard** and click **OK**.
- Select **Table: Location** in the Tables/Queries box.
- Double-click **Location** in the Available Fields list to move it to the Selected Fields list.
- Select **Table: Employees** in the Tables/Queries box.

- Double-click **LastName**, **FirstName**, and **Salary**.
- Select **Table: Titles** in the Tables/Queries box.
- Double-click **MinimumSalary** and **MaximumSalary**. Click **Next**.
- Ensure that the *Detail (shows every field of every record)* option is selected, and click **Next**.
- Type **Atlanta Salaries** as the query title and click **Finish**.

k. Click **View** in the Views group on the Home tab to switch to Design view of the Atlanta Salaries query.

- Click in the Criteria row of the Location field, and type **Atlanta**. Click the **Sort cell** of the Salary field, click the arrow, and then click **Ascending**.
- Click **Run** in the Results group. Review the data to determine if any of the Atlanta employees have a salary less than the minimum or greater than the maximum when compared to the published salary range. These salaries will be updated later.
- Save and close the query.

l. Right-click the **Atlanta Salaries query** in the Navigation Pane and from the shortcut menu, select **Copy**. Right-click a blank area in the Navigation Pane and select **Paste**. In the Paste As dialog box, type **Boston Salaries** for the query name. Click **OK**.

m. Right-click the **Boston Salaries query** in the Navigation Pane and select **Design View**. In the Criteria row of the Location field, replace Atlanta with **Boston**.

- Click **Run** in the Results group. Review the data to determine if any of the Boston employees have a salary less than the minimum or greater than the maximum when compared to the published salary range.
- Modify some data that have been incorrectly entered. In the query results, for the first employee, Frank Cusack, change the salary to **$48,700.00**; for Brian Beamer, **$45,900.00**; for Lorna Weber, **$45,700.00**; for Penny Pfleger, **$45,800.00**.
- Save and close the query.

n. Close the database and exit Access. Based on your instructor's directions, submit a02p2Insurance_LastFirst.

Mid-Level Exercises

1 My Game Collection

ANALYSIS CASE

Over the years, you have collected quite a few video games, so you have cataloged them in an Access database, in the Games table. After opening the database, you will create two more tables—one to identify the game system (System) that runs your game and the other to identify the category or genre of the game (Category). Then, you will join each table in a relationship so that you can query the database.

a. Open *a02m1Games* and save the database as **a02m1Games_LastFirst**. Open the Games table and review the fields containing the game information. Close the table.
b. Click the **Create tab** and click **Table Design** in the Tables group.
c. Type **SystemID** for the first Field Name and select **AutoNumber** as the Data Type.
d. Type **SystemName** for the second Field Name and accept **Short Text** as the Data Type.
e. Set **SystemID** as the primary key. Add the caption **System ID**.
f. Change the SystemName Field Size property to **15**. Add the caption **System Name**, making sure there is a space between System and Name. Save the table as **System**. Switch to Datasheet view.
g. Add the system names to the System table as shown below, letting Access use AutoNumber to create the SystemID values. Close the table when finished.

System ID	System Name
1	**XBOX 360**
2	**PS3**
3	**Wii**
4	**NES**
5	**PC Game**
6	**Nintendo 3DS**

h. Click the **Create tab** and click **Table Design** in the Tables group. Type **CategoryID** for the first Field Name and select **AutoNumber** as the Data Type. Set the CategoryID as the primary key.
i. Type **CategoryDescription** for the second Field Name and accept **Short Text** as the Data Type. Change the Field Size property to **25**. Add the caption **Category Description**, making sure there is a space between Category and Description. Save the table as **Category**, saving the changes to the table design. Switch to Datasheet view.
j. Add the category descriptions to the Category table as shown below, letting Access use AutoNumber to create the CategoryID values. Close the table when finished.

CategoryID	Category Description
1	**Action**
2	**Adventure**
3	**Arcade**
4	**Racing**
5	**Rhythm**
6	**Role-playing**
7	**Simulation**
8	**Sports**

k. Click the **Database Tools tab** and click **Relationships** in the Relationships group. Display all three tables in the Relationships window and close the Show Table dialog box. Create a one-to-many relationship between CategoryID in the Category table and CategoryID in the Games table. Enforce referential integrity and cascade update related fields.
l. Create a one-to-many relationship between SystemID in the System table and SystemID in the Games table. Enforce referential integrity and cascade update related fields. Close the Relationships window, saving the changes.
m. Use the Query Wizard to create a simple query using the Games table. Add the following fields in the query (in this order): GameName, Rating. Save the query as **Ratings Query**.

n. Switch to Design view. Sort the Rating field in ascending order and run the query. Close the query, saving the changes.

o. Create a multitable query in Design view using all three tables. Add the following fields (in this order): GameName, CategoryDescription, Rating, SystemName, and DateAcquired.

p. Sort the query in ascending order by GameName and run the query. Save the query as **Game List Query** and close the query.

DISCOVER

q. Copy the **Game List Query** and paste it into the Navigation Pane using the name **PS3 Games**. Modify the query in Design view by using **PS3** as the criterion for SystemName. Remove the sort by GameName and sort in ascending order by Rating. The query results should include 7 records.

r. Close the PS3 Games query, saving the changes. Assume you are going home for Thanksgiving and you want to take your **Wii** gaming system and games home with you—but you only want to take home games with a rating of **Everyone**.

s. Create a query named **Thanksgiving Games** that shows the name of the game, its rating, the category description of the game, and the system name for each. Run the query. The results of the query will tell you which games to pack. Close the query.

t. Close the database and exit Access. Based on your instructor's directions, submit a02m1Games_LastFirst.

2 The Prestige Hotel

The Prestige Hotel chain caters to upscale business travelers and provides state-of-the-art conference, meeting, and reception facilities. It prides itself on its international, four-star cuisine. Last year, it began a member reward club to help the marketing department track the purchasing patterns of its most loyal customers. All of the hotel transactions are stored in the database. Your task is to help the managers of the Prestige Hotels in Denver and Chicago identify their customers who stayed in a room last year and who had three persons in their party.

a. Open *a02m2Hotel* and save the file as **a02m2Hotel_LastFirst**. Review the data contained in the three tables. Specifically, study the tables and fields containing the data you need to analyze: dates of stays in Denver and Chicago suites, the members' names, and the numbers in the parties.

b. Import the location data from the Excel file *a02m2Location* into your database as a new table. The first row of the worksheet contains column headings. Set the LocationID Indexed property to **Yes (No Duplicates)** and set the Data Type to **Long Integer**. Select the **LocationID field** as the primary key. Name the table **Location**. Do not save the import steps.

c. Open the Relationships window and create a relationship between the Location table and the Orders table using the LocationID field. Enforce referential integrity and cascade update related fields. Create a relationship between the Orders and Members tables using the MemNumber field, ensuring that you enforce referential integrity and cascade update related fields. Create a relationship between the Orders and Service tables using the ServiceID field, ensuring that you enforce referential integrity and cascade update related fields. Save and close the Relationships window.

d. Open the Members table and use the Find command to locate Bryan Gray's name. Replace his name with your own first and last names. Locate Nicole Lee's name and replace it with your name. Close the table.

e. Create a query using the following fields: ServiceDate (Orders table), City (Location table), NoInParty (Orders table), ServiceName (Service table), FirstName (Members table), and LastName (Members table). Set the criteria to limit the output to **Denver**. Use the Between operator to show services only from **7/1/2017** to **6/30/2018**. Set the NoInParty criterion to **3**. Sort the results in ascending order by the ServiceDate.

f. Run the query and examine the number of records in the status bar at the bottom of the query. It should display 155. If your number of records is different, examine the criteria and make corrections.

g. Change the order of the query fields so that they display as FirstName, LastName, ServiceDate, City, NoInParty, and ServiceName. Save the query as **Denver Rooms 3 Guests**. Close the query.

DISCOVER

h. Copy the **Denver Rooms 3 Guests** query and paste it, renaming the new query **Chicago Rooms 3 Guests**.

i. Open the Chicago Rooms 3 Guests query in Design view and change the criterion for City to **Chicago**. Run the query and save the changes. It should display 179 results. Close the query.

DISCOVER

j. Review the criteria of the two previous queries and then create a third query named **Denver and Chicago Rooms 3 Guests**. Use the criteria from the two individual queries as a basis to create a combination AND–OR condition. The results will display guests in **Denver** or **Chicago** with **3** guests and service dates between **7/1/2013** and **6/30/2018**. The records returned in the results should equal the sum of the records in the two individual queries (334 records). Run, save, and close the query.

k. Close the database and exit Access. Based on your instructor's directions, submit a02m2Hotel_LastFirst.

3 New Castle County Technical Services

RUNNING CASE

New Castle County Technical Services (NCCTS) provides technical support for a number of companies in the greater New Castle County, Delaware area. Once you have completed the changes to the database tables and set the appropriate relationships, you will be ready to extract information by creating queries.

a. Open the database *a01m3NCCTS_LastFirst* and save it as a02m3NCCTS_LastFirst changing 01 to 02.

TROUBLESHOOTING: If you did not complete the Chapter 1 case, return to Chapter 1, complete the case to create the database, and then return to this exercise.

b. Open the Call Types table in Design view. Before you create your queries, you want to modify some of the table properties:
   - Set the caption of the HourlyRate field to **Hourly Rate**.
   - View the table in Datasheet view, and save the changes when prompted.

c. Close the table.

d. Make the following additional changes to the tables:
   - Open the Calls table in Design view. Change the data type of the CallTypeID field to **Number**.
   - Set the caption of the HoursLogged field to **Hours Logged**.
   - Set the caption of the OpenedDate field to **Opened Date** and set the format to **Short Date**.
   - Set the caption of the ClosedDate field to **Closed Date** and set the format to **Short Date**.
   - Set the caption of the CustomerSatisfaction field to **Customer Satisfaction**.
   - View the table in Datasheet view, and save the changes when prompted. You will not lose any data by making this change, so click **Yes** in the message box when prompted. Close the table.
   - Open the Customers table in Design view. Set the field size of CompanyName to **50** and the caption to **Company Name**. View the table in Datasheet view, and save the changes when prompted. You will not lose any data by making this change, so click **Yes** in the message box when prompted. Close the table.
   - Open the Reps table in Design view. Set the caption of the RepFirst field to **Rep First Name**. Set the caption of the RepLast field to **Rep Last Name**. View the table in Datasheet view, and save the changes when prompted. Close the table.

e. Open the Relationships window. Create a join line between the Call Types and Calls tables, ensuring that you enforce referential integrity and cascade update related fields. Set a relationship between Reps and Calls and between Customers and Calls using the same options. Save and close the Relationships window.

f. Create a multitable query, following the steps below:

- Add the following fields (in this order): **CallID** (from Calls), **Description** (from Call Types), **CompanyName** (from Customers), and **RepFirst** and **RepLast** (from Reps).
- Run the query, and then modify it to add **HoursLogged** (from Calls).
- Sort the query by HoursLogged in ascending order. Set the criteria of the HoursLogged field to **Is Not Null** and run the query again.
- Modify the criteria of the HoursLogged field to **>=5** and **<=10**, the description to **Disaster Recovery**, and the rep to **Barbara**.
- Save the query as **Complex Disaster Recovery Calls_Barbara**. Run and then close the query.

g. Create a copy of the **Complex Disaster Recovery Calls_Barbara** query, and modify it following the steps below:

- Save the copy of the query as **Complex Network Installation Calls_Barbara**.
- Modify the query so that the description displays Barbara's network installation calls that logged between 5 and 10 hours.
- Save, run, and then close the query.

h. Close the database and exit Access. Based on your instructor's directions, submit a02m3NCCTS_LastFirst.

Beyond the Classroom

Database Administrator Position

Create a database to keep track of candidates for open positions at Secure Systems, Inc., database management experts. Use the Internet to search for information about database management positions. One useful site is published by the federal government's Bureau of Labor Statistics. It compiles an Occupational Outlook Handbook describing various positions, the type of working environment, the education required, salary information, and the projected growth. The website is http://www.bls.gov/ooh. Research the necessary information in order to create the database using these requirements:

a. Create a new database named **a02b1Admin_LastFirst**.

b. Create three tables including the field names as follows, and in the specified orders:
- **Candidates (CandidateID, FirstName, LastName, Phone, Email).**
- **JobOpenings (JobOpeningID, JobName, RequiredSkill, HourlyPayRate, DataPosted, Supervisor).**
- **Interviews (InterviewSequenceID, CandidateID, JobOpeningID, InterviewedBy, DateOfInterview, Rank).**

c. Set the data types, field properties, and a primary key for each table.

d. Set table relationships, and be sure to enforce referential integrity between them. Cascade update related fields

e. Add 10 candidates to the Candidates table.

f. Add a **Database Administrator** job and four other sample jobs to the JobOpenings table.

g. Add eight sample interviews—four for the Database Administrator position and four others. Rank each candidate on a scale of 1 to 5 (with 5 as the highest).

h. Create a query that lists the LastName, FirstName, JobOpeningID, InterviewedBy, DateOfInterview, and Rank fields. Display only Database Administrator interviews with a ranking of 3 or lower. Sort by LastName and then by FirstName. Run and save the query as **Database Admin Low Rank**. Close the query

i. Close the database and exit Access. Based on your instructor's directions, submit a02b1Admin_LastFirst.

May Beverage Sales

A coworker explained that he was having difficulty with queries that were not returning correct results, and asked you to help diagnose the problem. Open *a02b2Traders* and save it as **a02b2Traders_LastFirst**. It contains two queries, *May 2018 Orders of Beverages and Confections* and *2018 Beverage Sales by Ship Country*. The May 2018 Orders of Beverages and Confections query is supposed to contain only information for orders shipped in May 2018. You find other shipped dates included in the results. Change the criteria to exclude the other dates. Run and save the query. Close the query.

The 2018 Beverage Sales by Ship Country query returns no results. Check the criteria in all fields and modify so that the correct results are returned. Run and save the query. Close the query.

Close the database and exit Access. Based on your instructor's directions, submit a02b2Traders_LastFirst.

Capstone Exercise

MyITLab® Grader

The Morris Arboretum in Chestnut Hill, Pennsylvania tracks donors in Excel. They also use Excel to store a list of plants in stock. As donors contribute funds to the Arboretum, they can elect to receive a plant gift from the Arboretum. These plants are both rare plants and hard-to-find old favorites, and they are part of the annual appeal and membership drive to benefit the Arboretum's programs. The organization has grown, and the files are too large and inefficient to handle in Excel. You will begin by importing the files from Excel into a new Access database. Then you will create a table to track donations, create a relationship between the two tables, and create some baseline queries.

Create a New Database

You will examine the data in the Excel worksheets to determine which fields will become the primary keys in each table and which fields will become the foreign keys.

a. Open the *a02c1Donors* Excel workbook, examine the data, and close the workbook.

b. Open the *a02c1Plants* Excel workbook, examine the data, and close the workbook.

c. Create a new, blank database named **a02c1Arbor_LastFirst**. Close the new blank table created automatically by Access without saving it.

Import Data from Excel

You will import two Excel workbooks into the database.

a. Click the **External Data tab** and click **Excel** in the Import & Link group.

b. Navigate to and select the *a02c1Donors* workbook to be imported.

c. Select the **First Row Contains Column Headings** option.

d. Set the DonorID field Indexed option to **Yes (No Duplicates)**.

e. Choose **DonorID** as the primary key when prompted and accept the table name Donors.

f. Import the *a02c1Plants* workbook, set the **ID field** as the primary key, and then change the indexing option to **Yes (No Duplicates)**.

g. Accept the table name Plants.

h. Change the ID field name in the Plants table to **PlantID**.

i. Open each table in Datasheet view to examine the data. Close the tables.

Create a New Table

You will create a new table to track the donations as they are received from the donors.

a. You will create a new table in Design view and save the table as **Donations**.

b. Add the following fields in Design view and set the properties as specified:

- Add the primary key field as **DonationID** with the **Number Data Type** and a field size of **Long Integer**.
- Add **DonorID** (a foreign key) with the **Number Data Type** and a field size of **Long Integer**.
- Add **PlantID** (a foreign key) as a **Number** and a field size of **Long Integer**.
- Add **DateOfDonation** as a **Date/Time** field.
- Add **AmountOfDonation** as a **Currency** field.

c. Switch to Datasheet view, and save the table when prompted. You will enter data into the table in a later step. Close the table.

Create Relationships

You will create the relationships between the tables using the Relationships window.

a. Open the Donors table in Design view and change the Field Size property for DonorID to **Long Integer** so it matches the Field Size property of DonorID in the Donations table. Save and close the table.

b. Open the Plants table in Design view and change the Field Size property for PlantID to **Long Integer** so it matches the Field Size property for PlantID in the Donations table. Save and close the table.

c. Identify the primary key fields in the Donors table and the Plants table and join them with their foreign key counterparts in the related Donations table. Enforce referential integrity and cascade and update related fields. Save and close the Relationships window.

Add Sample Data to the Donations Table

You will add 10 records to the Donations table.

a. Add the following records to the Donations table:

Donation ID	Donor ID	Plant ID	Date of Donation	Amount of Donation
10	8228	611	3/1/2018	$150
18	5448	190	3/1/2018	$ 55
6	4091	457	3/12/2018	$125
7	11976	205	3/14/2018	$100
1	1000	25	3/17/2018	$120
12	1444	38	3/19/2018	$ 50
2	1444	38	4/3/2018	$ 50
4	10520	49	4/12/2018	$ 60
5	3072	102	4/19/2018	$ 50
21	1204	25	4/22/2018	$120

b. Sort the Donations table by the AmountOfDonation field in descending order. Close the table.

Use the Query Wizard

You will create a query of all donations greater than $100 in the Donations table.

a. Add the DonorID and AmountOfDonation fields from Donations (in that order).

b. Save the query as **Donations Over 100**.

c. Add criteria to include only donations of more than $100.

d. Sort the query results in ascending order by AmountOfDonation.

e. Run the query.

f. Save and close the query.

Create a Query in Design View

You will create a query that identifies donors and donations.

a. Create a query that identifies the people who made a donation after April 1, 2018. This list will be given to the Arboretum staff so they can notify the donors that a plant is ready for pickup. The query should list the date of the donation, donor's full name (LastName, FirstName), phone number, the amount of the donation, and name of the plant they want (in that order). Add the tables and fields necessary to produce the query.

b. Sort the query by date of donation in descending order, then by donor last name in ascending order.

c. Run, close, and save the query as **Plant Pickup List**.

Copy and Modify a Query in Design View

You will copy a query and modify it to add and sort by a different field.

a. Copy the Plant Pickup List query and paste it using **ENewsletter** as the query name.

b. Open the ENewsletter query in Design view and delete the DateofDonation column.

c. Add the ENewsletter field to the first column of the design grid and set it to sort in ascending order, so that the query sorts first by ENewsletter and then by LastName.

d. Run, save, and close the query. Close the database and exit Access. Based on your instructor's directions, submit a02c1Arbor_LastFirst.

Access

Using Queries to Make Decisions

LEARNING OUTCOME You will create queries to perform calculations and summarize data.

OBJECTIVES & SKILLS: After you read this chapter, you will be able to:

CASE STUDY | Real Estate Investors

After completing their degrees in Business at Passaic County Community College (PCCC) and a weekend seminar in real estate investing, Donald Carter and Matthew Nevoso were ready to test their skills in the marketplace. Don and Matt had a simple strategy—buy distressed properties at a significant discount, then resell the properties for a profit. Based on their seminar, they knew to gather key information such as the asking price, the number of bedrooms, square feet, and days on the market. Because they are just starting out, they decided to consider less expensive houses.

Based on a tip from the real estate seminar, they decide to create a database using Access, using data from a variety of home listing services. They approached you to help them find houses that meet their criteria. This new database approach should hopefully help them acquire their first investment property.

Perform Calculations and Summarize Data Using Queries

CHAPTER 3

List Price Calculations | Mortgage Payments

First Name	Last Name	List Price	Square Feet	Listing	Sold	Price Per Sq Ft	Payment
Philip	DeFranco	$109,140.00	1133	10004	No	$96.33	$416.84
Chardae	Myles	$129,780.00	1132	10028	No	$114.65	$495.67
Makarem	Abdeljawad	$136,680.00	1375	10008	No	$99.40	$522.02
Meera	Shah	$138,990.00	1276	10016	No	$108.93	$530.85
StudentFirst	StudentLast	$140,693.00	1490	10069	No	$94.42	$537.35
Makarem	Abdeljawad	$140,904.00	1301	10061	No	$108.30	$538.16
Makarem	Abdeljawad	$142,380.00	1373	11028	No	$103.70	$543.80
Chardae	Myles	$163,737.00	1476	10910	No	$110.93	$625.36
Jaynish	Mody	$164,436.00	1850	10117	No	$88.88	$628.03
Jaynish	Mody	$166,320.00	1437	10082	No	$115.74	$635.23
Chardae	Myles	$166,552.00	1623	10851	No	$102.62	$636.12
Chardae	Myles	$166,800.00	1598	10014	No	$104.38	$637.06
Philip	DeFranco	$168,000.00	1680	10002	No	$100.00	$641.65
Chardae	Myles	$168,354.00	1651	10885	No	$101.97	$643.00
Philip	DeFranco	$174,230.00	1771	10104	No	$98.38	$665.44
StudentFirst	StudentLast	$174,720.00	1610	10921	No	$108.52	$667.31
Meera	Shah	$174,720.00	1694	11035	No	$103.14	$667.31
Chardae	Myles	$175,336.00	1855	10868	No	$94.52	$669.66
StudentFirst	StudentLast	$175,560.00	1562	11036	No	$112.39	$670.52
Meera	Shah	$176,176.00	1761	10025	No	$100.04	$672.87
Jaynish	Mody	$177,984.00	1707	10066	No	$104.27	$679.78
Chardae	Myles	$179,088.00	1837	10010	No	$97.49	$683.99
Chardae	Myles	$179,100.00	1946	11079	No	$92.03	$684.04
Chardae	Myles	$179,712.00	1854	10102	No	$96.93	$686.38
Chardae	Myles	$180,180.00	1896	10019	No	$95.03	$688.17
Makarem	Abdeljawad	[illegible]	[illegible]	[illegible]	[illegible]	[illegible]	[illegible]
Total		$167,100.47		32		$102.10	

Record: 1 of 32 No Filter Search

FIGURE 3.1 Real Estate Investors Property Database – Mortgage Payments Query

Results by Realtor Revised

NameOfList	AvgOfSalePrice	Number Sold	DaysOnMarket
Algernon Listings	$324,697.22	18	23.50
FastHouse	$288,314.50	6	22.33
Houses 4 Sale	$218,039.00	2	23.50
Local Listings	$341,085.67	9	23.56
Major Houses	$235,757.88	8	24.75
Trullo	$236,885.21	19	26.05
Wholesaler	$276,654.92	26	26.12
Total		88	

FIGURE 3.2 Real Estate Investors Property Database – Results by Realtor Revised Query

CASE STUDY | Real Estate Investors

Starting File	Files to be Submitted
a03h1Property	**a03h1PropertyCheck_LastFirst** **a03h3Property_LastFirst**

Calculations and Expressions

There are going to be times, when manipulating data in an Access database, that you will want to perform calculations. A field storing the number of hours worked multiplied by a field storing the hourly pay rate will calculate the gross pay, for example. Unfortunately, calculations may not always be that easy. If you have received a paycheck, you realize your gross pay is not the same as the amount as your paycheck. Your net pay will be lower, due to common deductions such as Social Security, Medicare, federal and state income taxes, unemployment insurance, and union dues. Some deductions may be a flat rate, and others may be calculated based on the paycheck amount, so even what appears to be a simple calculation can be complex.

At first glance, you may not see an obvious location for you to enter a calculation in Access. However, Access includes many built-in calculations and functions. Calculations appear commonly in queries, but can also be added to tables, forms, and reports.

In this section, you will learn how to create a calculated field in a query. You will also format the calculations to enhance readability.

Creating a Query with a Calculated Field

Rather than performing a calculation outside of the database and then inputting the result into your database, you should instead store the components of the calculation in the database. Calculating values rather than inputting values will reduce errors and inconsistencies. If your database stored the hours worked and paycheck amount, both fields would have to be updated if there was a change in the hours the employee worked. However, if you store only the hours worked and calculate the paycheck amount, you do not have to worry about updating multiple fields. The next time the paycheck is calculated, the results will be updated and corrected.

As another example, a table might contain the times when employees clock in and out of work. You could create a calculation in a query to determine how many hours each employee worked by subtracting the ClockIn field from the ClockOut field. A combination of elements that produce a value is known as an ***expression***. A ***calculated field*** is a field that displays the result of an expression rather than data stored in a field.

You may find one or more of the following elements in a calculated field:

- Arithmetic operator (for example, *, /, +, or −)
- ***Constant***, a value that does not change (such as −20 or 3.14)
- Function (built-in calculations like Pmt)
- Identifier (the names of fields, controls, or properties)

Understand the Order of Operations

The ***order of operations*** determines the sequence by which operations are calculated in a mathematical expression. Evaluate expressions in parentheses first, then exponents, then multiplication and division, and, finally, addition and subtraction. You may remember PEMDAS (or the mnemonic device "Please Excuse My Dear Aunt Sally") from a math class. Table 3.1 shows some examples of the order of operations. Access uses the following symbols:

- Parentheses ( )
- Exponentiation ^
- Multiplication *
- Division /
- Addition +
- Subtraction −

TABLE 3.1 Examples of Order of Operations

Expression	Order to Perform Calculations	Output
=2+3*3	Multiply first and then add.	11
=(2+3)*3	Add the values inside the parentheses first and then multiply.	15
=2+2^3	Evaluate the exponent first, 2^3=2*2*2 (or 8). Then add.	10
=10/2+3	Divide first and then add.	8
=10/(2+3)	Add first to simplify the parenthetical expression and then divide.	2
=10*2–3*2	Multiply first and then subtract.	14

Build Expressions

STEP 1 As mentioned earlier, expressions can contain a number of different elements. Expressions can be typed manually or inserted using Access tools.

The challenging part is typically creating the expression. Consider the following scenario. Your company plans on allowing customers to pay off their balance in 12 monthly payments. The balance is stored in your Access database in a field named Balance. To divide this into equal payments, you would type Balance/12 in the Field row of a blank column. For example, if the Balance field was $1,200, you divide by 12. You are left with a monthly payment of $100. See Figure 3.3 for an example of the Balance field added to a query.

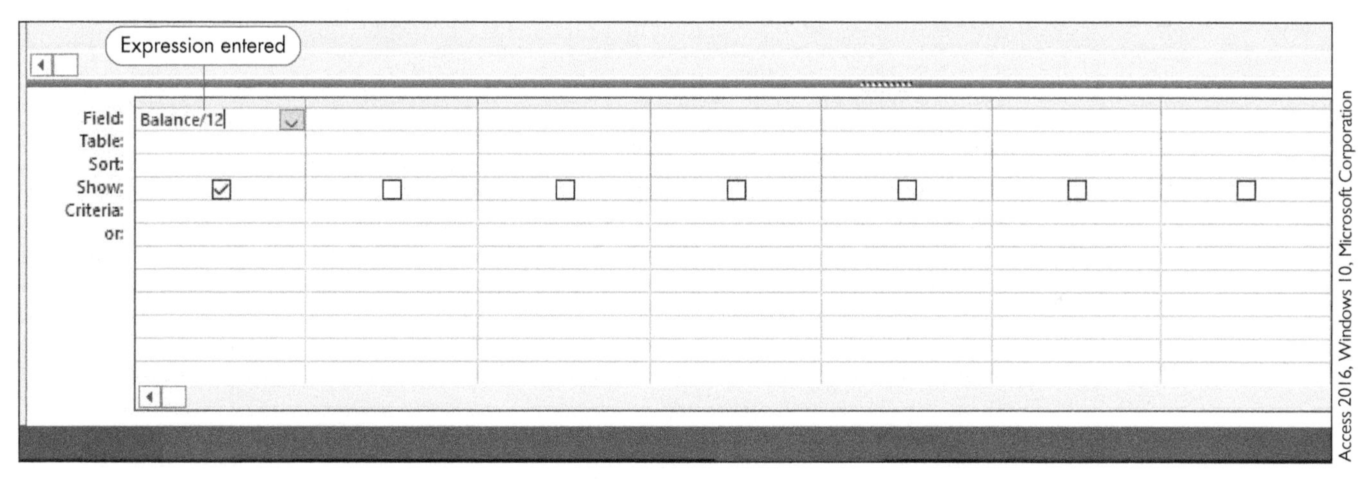

FIGURE 3.3 Balance Field in a Query

However, many companies will apply some sort of surcharge or add interest when customers pay balances off in installments. From your perspective as someone creating a query, this makes the calculation more complex. Your company may decide to add a surcharge of 20% (or, .20) of the balance. In this case, you will need to include a multiplication step in the above calculation. You will multiply the results by 1.20. Why multiply by 1.20 rather than .20? If you multiplied by .20 and divided by 12, you would only see the surcharge amount and not the total amount due for each payment. If the Balance field was $1,200, the monthly payment needs to be more than the $100 in the previous example.

If you multiply $1,200 by .20, you get a result of $20. The $20 does not represent the amount due, it represents the surcharge. Therefore, multiplying by 1.20 will give you the balance plus the surcharge. Dividing that by 12 gives you a monthly payment of $120. Note that there are multiple ways to implement this calculation, so this is not the only solution.

To create a calculated field within a query, complete the following steps:

1. Open the query in Design view.
2. Click the Field row (top row) of a blank column. Recall that the Field row is found in the bottom pane of the design.
3. Type the desired expression. See Figure 3.4 for an example of a query with an expression.
4. Click Run in the Results group to display the results in Datasheet view.

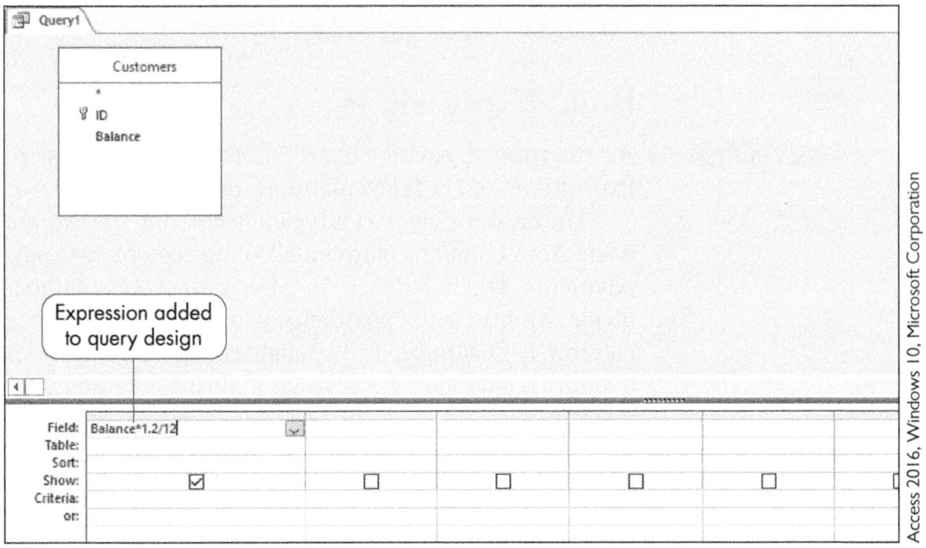

FIGURE 3.4 Sample Expression in a Query

When you type the preceding expression into the Field row and click another field, Access adds a few things to the expression. As shown in Figure 3.5, Access adds brackets [ ] around Balance, which Access uses to indicate a field name. In addition, you see that Access has added Expr1: to the start of the expression. This is how Access assigns a column heading to this field.

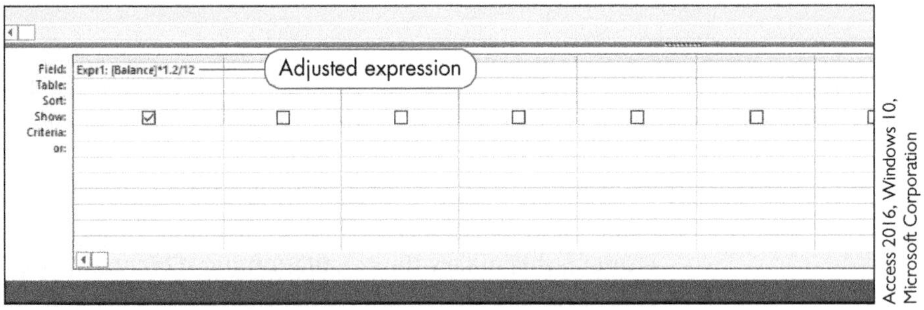

FIGURE 3.5 Modified Expression

If you were to run the query, the column heading would be *Expr1*. If you wanted to name this column MonthlySurcharge, you would start the expression with the name, followed by a colon, followed by the expression (or, if Expr1: already appears, replace Expr1 with the name and leave the colon in place). The column is renamed MonthlySurcharge in Figure 3.6.

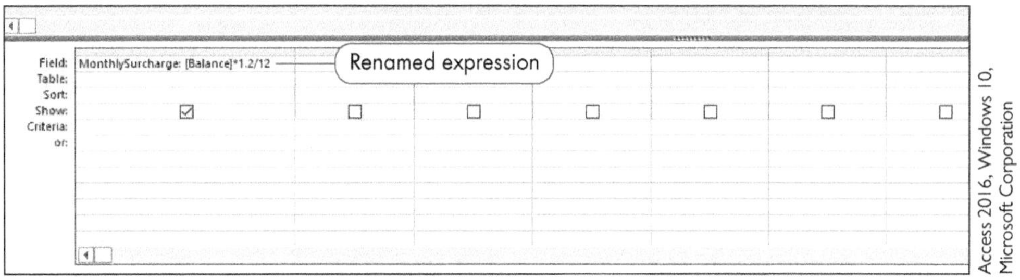

Field: MonthlySurcharge: [Balance]*1.2/12
Renamed expression
Access 2016, Windows 10, Microsoft Corporation

FIGURE 3.6 Expression Renamed

The query results, as shown in Figure 3.7, display a decimal number in the MonthlySurcharge column. Notice that the results are not easy to read and should be formatted.

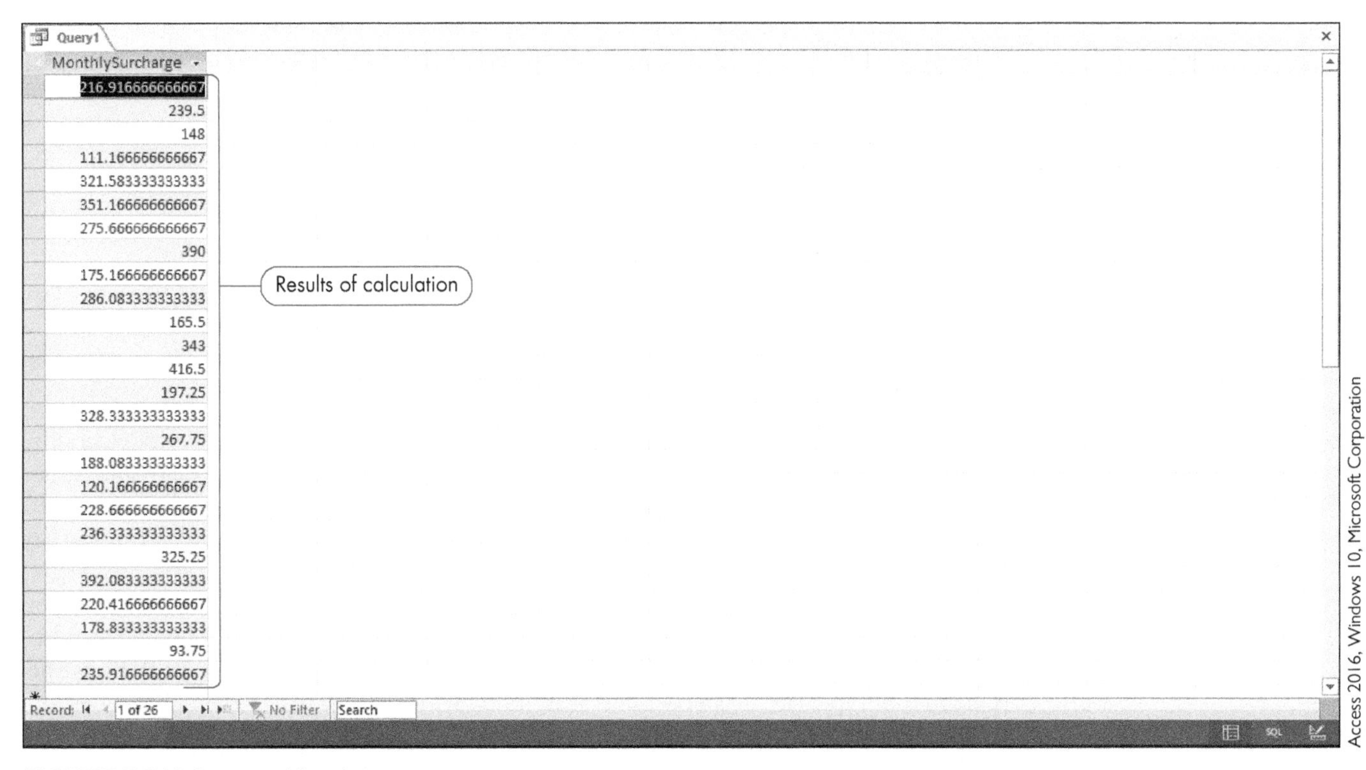

FIGURE 3.7 Unformatted Results

> **TIP: USE ZOOM TO VIEW LONG EXPRESSIONS**
> To see the entire calculated field expression in Design view, right-click the Field row and select Zoom. A new window (the Zoom window) will open to enable you to easily see and edit the entire contents of the cell, as shown in Figure 3.8. Once you are done modifying a field, click Close in the top-right corner of the Zoom window.

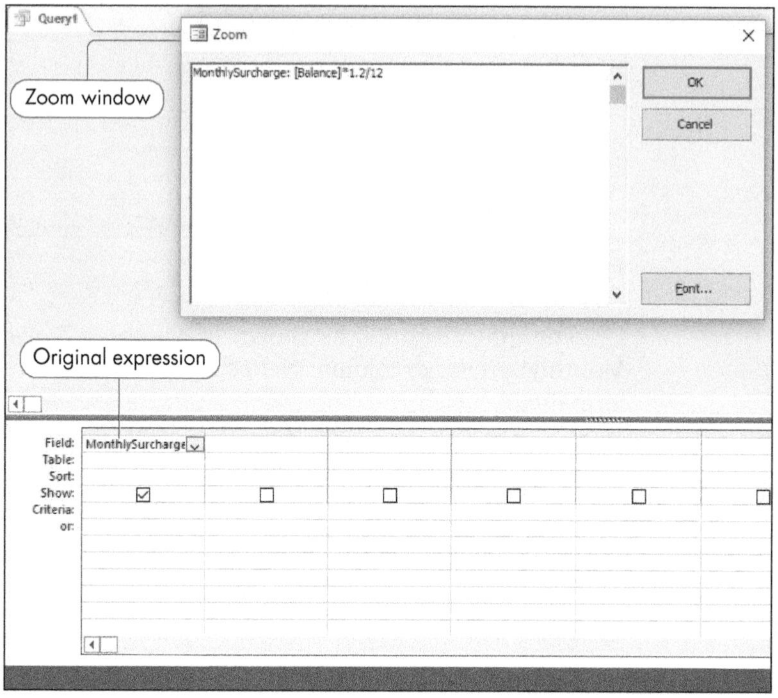

Access 2016, Windows 10, Microsoft Corporation

FIGURE 3.8 Zoom Window

Formatting Calculated Results

When using calculated fields in queries, you may want to format the results. Spending a few moments formatting your output will make your query results more readable. For example, if you are calculating a net pay, you likely do not care about anything after two decimal places. It makes more sense to say you are making $980.15 a week than to say you are making $980.14983432743.

To format a field in a query, use the ***Property Sheet***. The Property Sheet enables you to change the way a field appears. For example, a numeric field has settings such as number format and number of decimal places, while other data types will have settings specific to that type. The Property Sheet is in many ways similar to the Field Properties in a table.

To format a field, complete the following steps:

1. Open the query in Design view.
2. Click the Field row of the field you want to format.
3. Click Property Sheet in the Show/Hide group on the Design tab.
4. Click the appropriate option and choose the setting desired. You can change the format by clicking the Format property arrow and selecting your desired format (such as Currency for numeric fields). For numeric fields, the Decimal Places property will allow you to choose the number of decimal places that display. To change the caption (which appears as the name of the column), click the text box next to the Caption property and type your desired column heading. Figure 3.9 shows the Property Sheet options related to a numeric field.
5. Close the Property Sheet, if desired, by clicking Close as shown in Figure 3.9. After using the Property Sheet, it will be displayed in the future when the query is opened in Design view, unless you close it. However, as most of your users will not be viewing the query in Design view, it should not matter either way if the Property Sheet is closed or not.

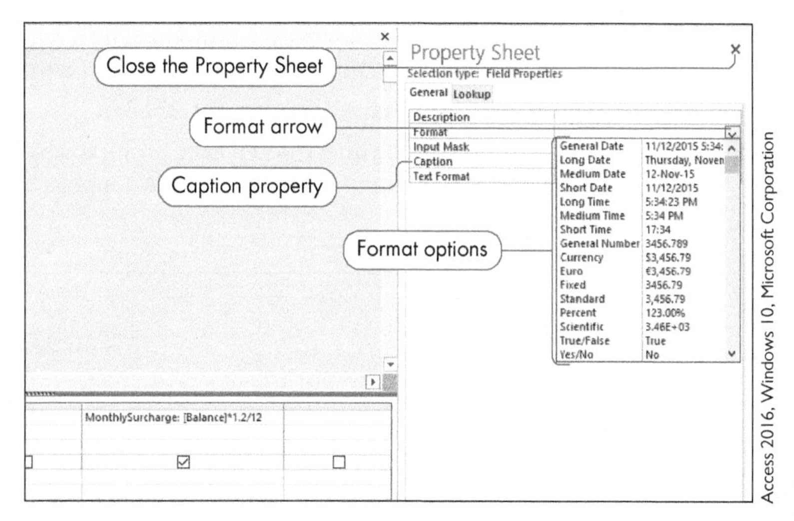

FIGURE 3.9 Property Sheet Options

Recovering from Common Errors

When creating calculated fields, there are a number of common errors that can occur. Learning how to recognize errors and recover from issues is important. Some common types of errors are shown below:

- Forgetting the colon between the column title and the formula

  A correct formula would look like this:

  MonthlySurcharge: [Balance]*1.2/12

  If you forget the colon, the formula looks like this instead:

  MonthlySurcharge [Balance]*1.2/12

  and you will get an invalid syntax error, indicating something is wrong with the way the formula is written, as shown in Figure 3.10.

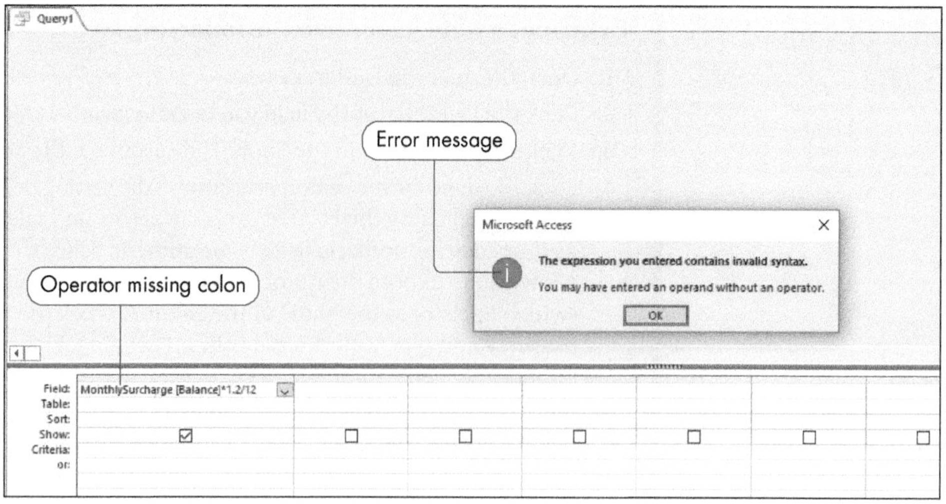

FIGURE 3.10 Syntax Error Warning

- Spelling a field name incorrectly

  If a field's name is Balance and you mistype it, you will get an error when you run the query. You may end up with a formula that looks like this:

  MonthlySurcharge: [Baalnce]*1.2/12

  When you run the query, you will be prompted by Access to give a value for Baalnce, as shown in Figure 3.11. This happens because Access does not know what Baalnce is.

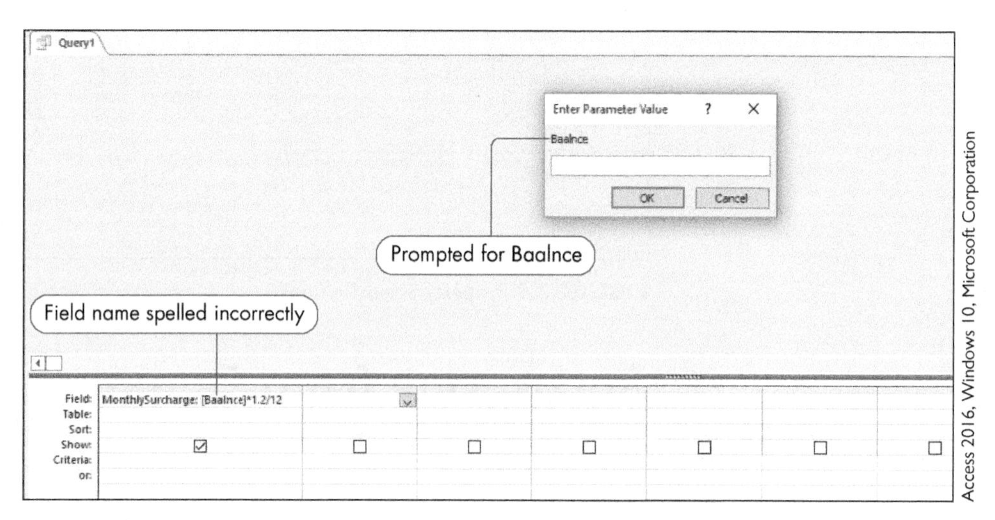

FIGURE 3.11 Result of Spelling Error in Field Name

- Forgetting the order of operations

  If you do not check your formulas, you may get bad values. For example, the following would not produce the expected output:

  NewMonthlyBalance: [Balance] + 100/12

  If you want addition to be done before division, you must remember the parentheses:

  NewMonthlyBalance: ([Balance] + 100)/12

Verifying Calculated Results

After your query runs, look at the field values in Datasheet view and look at the calculated values. You may find that the results do not make sense. In a real-world scenario, you will not be given step-by-step directions, and instead will apply critical thinking skills to your work. Access will calculate exactly what you tell it to calculate, even if you make logical errors in the calculation.

When you run a query, you need to analyze the results and ask yourself if the results make sense. Assume you are calculating a car payment for a $10,000 car, with monthly payments for 5 years. If your formula is incorrect, you may end up with a monthly payment result like $1,000. If you look at your results, you should say to yourself, "Does it make sense for me to pay $1,000 every month for five years to finance a $10,000 car?"

You can verify results with a calculator or by copying and pasting data into Excel. Recreate the calculations in Excel and compare the answers to the query results in Access. The Access calculated field, the calculator, and the Excel calculations should all return identical results.

Quick Concepts

1. What are the four types of elements that can appear as part of an expression in Access? ***p. 812***
2. Briefly describe the order of operations. Give an example of how the order of operations makes a difference in a calculation. ***p. 812***
3. How does Access respond when you spell a field name incorrectly in a query? ***p. 818***
4. How can the Property Sheet make query results more readable? ***p. 817***

Hands-On Exercises

Watch the Video
for this Hands-On
Exercise!
MyITLab®
HOE1 Training

Skills covered: Build Expressions • Format Fields • Recognize and Correct Common Errors • Evaluate Results

1 Calculations and Expressions

Using the data from the homes for sale lists that Don and Matt acquired, you are able to help them target properties that meet their criteria. As you examine the data, you discover other ways to analyze the properties. You create several queries and present your results to the two investors for their comments.

STEP 1 ›› BUILD EXPRESSIONS

You begin your analysis by creating a query using the Properties and Agents tables from the Property database. The Properties table contains all the properties the investors will evaluate; the Agents table contains a list of real estate agents who represent the properties' sellers. In this exercise, you will add requested fields and only show properties that have not been sold. You will then build an expression to calculate the price per square foot for each property. Refer to Figure 3.12 as you complete Step 1.

Price Per Square Foot

First Name	Last Name	List Price	Square Feet	Sold	PricePerSqFt
Philip	DeFranco	$109,140.00	1133	No	96.3283318623124
Chardae	Myles	$129,780.00	1132	No	114.646643109541
Makarem	Abdeljawad	$136,680.00	1375	No	99.4036363636364
Meera	Shah	$138,990.00	1276	No	108.926332288401
StudentFirst	StudentLast	$140,693.00	1490	No	94.4248322147651
Makarem	Abdeljawad	$140,904.00	1301	No	108.304381245196
Makarem	Abdeljawad	$142,380.00	1373	No	103.699927166788
Chardae	Myles	$163,737.00	1476	No	110.932926829268
Jaynish	Mody	$164,436.00	1850	No	88.8843243243243
Jaynish	Mody	$166,320.00	1437	No	115.741127348643
Chardae	Myles	$166,552.00	1623	No	102.619839802834
Chardae	Myles	$166,800.00	1598	No	104.380475594493
Philip	DeFranco	$168,000.00	1680	No	100
Chardae	Myles	$168,354.00	1651	No	101.970926711084
Philip	DeFranco	$174,230.00	1771	No	98.3794466403162
Meera	Shah	$174,720.00	1694	No	103.140495867769
StudentFirst	StudentLast	$174,720.00	1610	No	108.521739130435
Chardae	Myles	$175,336.00	1855	No	94.5207547169811
StudentFirst	StudentLast	$175,560.00	1562	No	112.394366197183
Meera	Shah	$176,176.00	1761	No	100.04315729699
Jaynish	Mody	$177,984.00	1707	No	104.267135325132
Chardae	Myles	$179,088.00	1837	No	97.4893848666304
Chardae	Myles	$179,100.00	1946	No	92.0349434737924
Chardae	Myles	$179,712.00	1854	No	96.9320388349515
Chardae	Myles	$180,180.00	1896	No	95.0316455696203
Makarem	Abdeljawad	$180,810.00	1667	No	108.464307138572

Record: 1 of 215 No Filter Search

Step 1: Column heading matches field name

Step 1: Calculated field results

Step j: 215 results

Access 2016, Windows 10, Microsoft Corporation

FIGURE 3.12 Modified Expression

a. Open *a03h1Property*. Save the database as **a03h1Property_LastFirst**.

> **TROUBLESHOOTING:** Throughout the remainder of this chapter and textbook, click Enable Content whenever you are working with student files.

> **TROUBLESHOOTING:** If you make any major mistakes in this exercise, you can close the file, open *a03h1Property* again, and then start this exercise over.

b. Open the Agents table and replace the name *Dilson Herrera* with your name. Close the table.

c. Click the **Create tab** and click **Query Design** in the Queries group to create a new query.

The Show Table dialog box opens so you can specify the table(s) and/or queries to include in the query design.

d. Select the **Agents table** and click **Add**. Select the **Properties table** and click **Add**. Click **Close** to close the Show Table dialog box.

e. Double-click the **FirstName** and **LastName fields** in the Agents table to add them to the query.

f. Double-click the **ListPrice**, **SqFeet**, and **Sold fields** in the Properties table to add them to the query.

g. Click **Run** in the Results group to display the results in Datasheet view.

A total of 303 properties appear in the results.

h. Switch to Design view. Type **No** in the Criteria row of the Sold field.

i. Click the **Sort row** in the ListPrice field. Click the **arrow** and select **Ascending**.

j. Click **Run** to see the results.

The 215 unsold properties appear in the datasheet, with the least expensive houses displayed first.

k. Click **Save** on the Quick Access Toolbar and type **Price Per Square Foot** as the Query Name in the Save As dialog box. Click **OK**.

l. Switch to Design view. Click the **Field row** of the first blank column of the query design grid. Right-click and select **Zoom** to show the Zoom window. Type **PricePerSqFt: ListPrice/SqFeet** and click **OK**.

Access inserts square brackets around the fields for you. The new field divides the values in the ListPrice field by the values in the SqFeet field.

m. Click **Run** in the Results group to view the results. Adjust column widths as necessary.

The new calculated field, PricePerSqFt, is displayed. Compare your results to those shown in Figure 3.12.

TROUBLESHOOTING: If you see pound signs (#####) in an Access column, double-click the vertical line between column headings to increase the width.

TROUBLESHOOTING: If, when you run the query, you are prompted for a value, cancel and return to Design view. Ensure that you have entered the formula from Step l in the first row of a blank column, not the criteria line.

n. Save the changes to the query and close the query.

STEP 2 » FORMAT FIELDS

Don and Matt would like the field formatted with two decimal places. You will change the format to Currency and add a caption to the calculated field. Refer to Figure 3.13 as you complete Step 2.

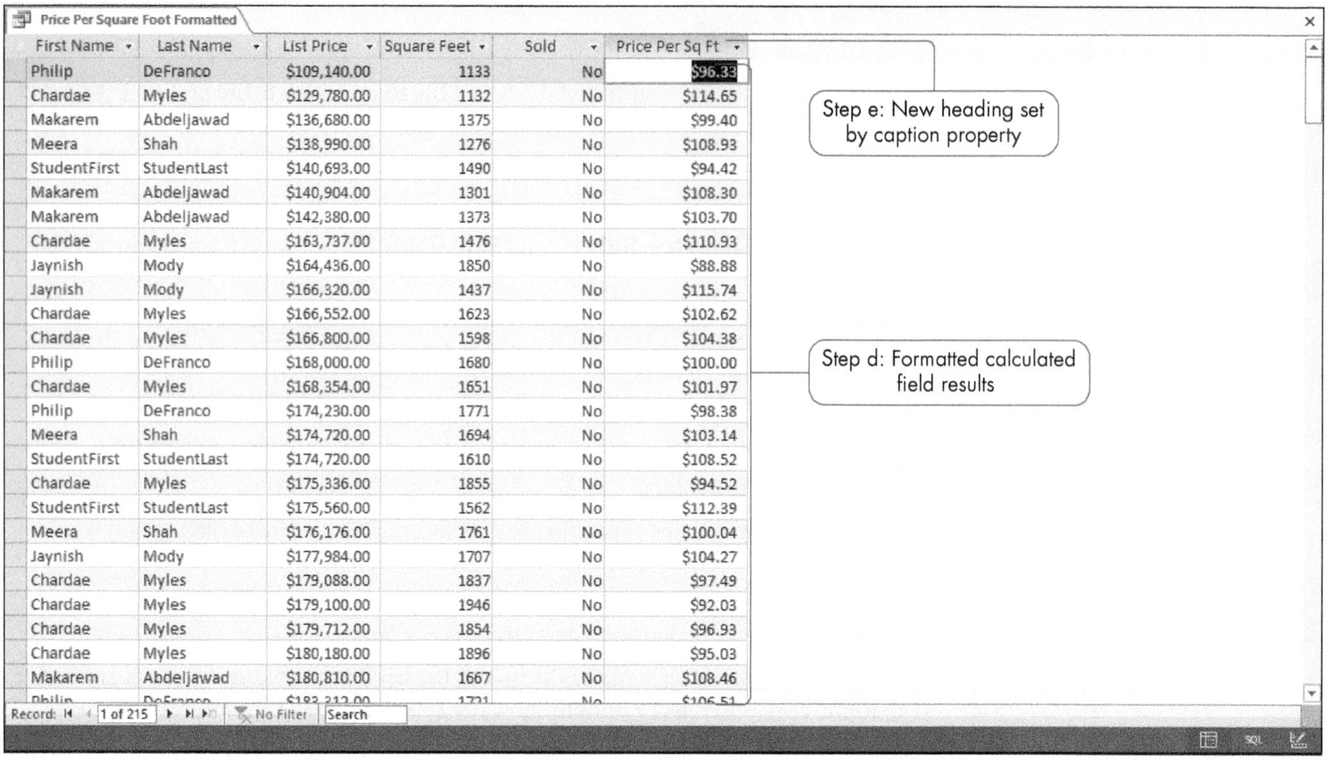

Price Per Square Foot Formatted

First Name	Last Name	List Price	Square Feet	Sold	Price Per Sq Ft
Philip	DeFranco	$109,140.00	1133	No	$96.33
Chardae	Myles	$129,780.00	1132	No	$114.65
Makarem	Abdeljawad	$136,680.00	1375	No	$99.40
Meera	Shah	$138,990.00	1276	No	$108.93
StudentFirst	StudentLast	$140,693.00	1490	No	$94.42
Makarem	Abdeljawad	$140,904.00	1301	No	$108.30
Makarem	Abdeljawad	$142,380.00	1373	No	$103.70
Chardae	Myles	$163,737.00	1476	No	$110.93
Jaynish	Mody	$164,436.00	1850	No	$88.88
Jaynish	Mody	$166,320.00	1437	No	$115.74
Chardae	Myles	$166,552.00	1623	No	$102.62
Chardae	Myles	$166,800.00	1598	No	$104.38
Philip	DeFranco	$168,000.00	1680	No	$100.00
Chardae	Myles	$168,354.00	1651	No	$101.97
Philip	DeFranco	$174,230.00	1771	No	$98.38
Meera	Shah	$174,720.00	1694	No	$103.14
StudentFirst	StudentLast	$174,720.00	1610	No	$108.52
Chardae	Myles	$175,336.00	1855	No	$94.52
StudentFirst	StudentLast	$175,560.00	1562	No	$112.39
Meera	Shah	$176,176.00	1761	No	$100.04
Jaynish	Mody	$177,984.00	1707	No	$104.27
Chardae	Myles	$179,088.00	1837	No	$97.49
Chardae	Myles	$179,100.00	1946	No	$92.03
Chardae	Myles	$179,712.00	1854	No	$96.93
Chardae	Myles	$180,180.00	1896	No	$95.03
Makarem	Abdeljawad	$180,810.00	1667	No	$108.46

Record: 1 of 215 No Filter Search

Step e: New heading set by caption property

Step d: Formatted calculated field results

Access 2016, Windows 10, Microsoft Corporation

FIGURE 3.13 Modified Expression

a. Right-click the **Price Per Square Foot query** in the Navigation Pane and click **Copy**. Right-click in the Navigation Pane again and click **Paste**. Type **Price Per Square Foot Formatted** in the Paste As dialog box and click **OK**.

b. Open the Price Per Square Foot Formatted query in Design view.

c. Click the **PricePerSqFt calculated field cell**. Click **Property Sheet** in the Show/Hide group on the Design tab.

The Property Sheet displays.

d. Click the **Format property**. Click the **Format property arrow** and select **Currency**.

e. Click the **Caption property** and type **Price Per Sq Ft**. Press **Enter**. Close the Property Sheet.

f. Click **Run** to view your changes.

The calculated field values are formatted as Currency, and the column heading displays Price Per Sq Ft instead of PricePerSqFt.

g. Compare your result to Figure 3.13. Save the changes to the query.

STEP 3 » RECOGNIZE AND CORRECT COMMON ERRORS

A few errors arise as you test the new calculated fields. You check the spelling of the field names in the calculated fields because that is a common mistake. Refer to Figure 3.14 as you complete Step 3.

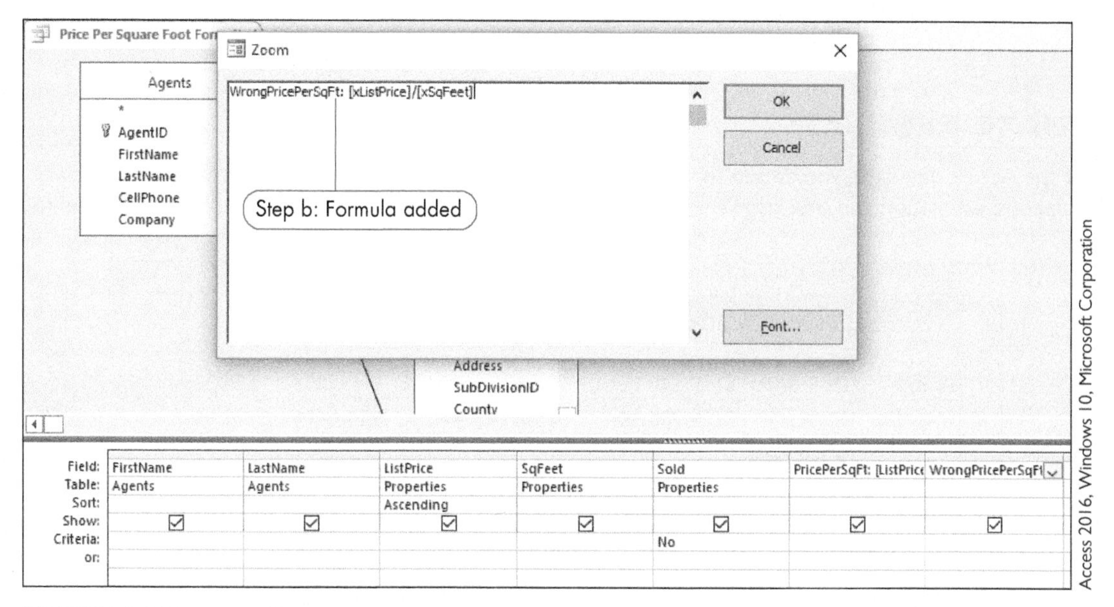

FIGURE 3.14 Incorrect Expression

a. Switch to Design view of the Price Per Square Foot Formatted query. Scroll to the first blank column of the query design grid and click the Field row.

b. Right-click and select **Zoom** to display the Zoom window. Type **WrongPricePerSqFt: xListPrice/xSqFeet**. Your formula should match Figure 3.14. Click OK in the Zoom window.

Be sure that you added the extra *x*'s to the field names. You are intentionally misspelling the field names to see how Access will respond.

c. Click **Property Sheet** in the Show/Hide group of the Design tab. Click the **Format property**. From the menu, select **Currency**. Click the **Caption box** and type **Wrong Price Per Sq Ft**. Close the Property Sheet.

d. Click **Run** in the Results group.

You should see the Enter Parameter Value dialog box. Access does not recognize xListPrice in the tables defined for this query in the first record. When Access does not recognize a field name, it will ask you to supply a value.

e. Type **100000** in the first parameter box. Press **Enter** or click **OK**.

Another Enter Parameter Value dialog box displays, asking that you supply a value for xSqFeet. Again, this error occurs because the tables defined for this query do not contain an xSqFeet field.

f. Type **1000** in the second parameter box and press **Enter**.

The query has the necessary information to run and returns the results in Datasheet view.

g. Examine the results of the calculation for Wrong Price Per Sq Ft.

All of the records show 100 because you entered the values 100000 and 1000, respectively, into the parameter boxes. The two values are treated as constants and give the same results for all records.

h. Return to Design view. Display the Zoom window. Correct the errors in the WrongPricePerSqFt field by changing the formula to **WrongPricePerSqFt: [ListPrice]/[SqFeet]**. Click **OK**.

i. Run and save the query. Close the query.

The calculated values in the last two columns should be the same.

STEP 4 » EVALUATE RESULTS

Because you are in charge of the Access database, you decide to verify your data prior to showing it to the investors. You use two methods to check your calculations: estimation and checking your results using Excel. Refer to Figure 3.15 as you complete Step 4.

	A	B	C	D	E	F	G	H
1	First Name	Last Name	List Price	quare Fee	Sold	ricePerSqFt		
2	Philip	DeFranco	$109,140.00	1133	FALSE	96.32833	$96.33	
3	Chardae	Myles	$129,780.00	1132	FALSE	114.6466	$114.65	
4	Makarem	Abdeljaw ad	$136,680.00	1375	FALSE	99.40364	$99.40	
5	Meera	Shah	$138,990.00	1276	FALSE	108.9263	$108.93	
6	StudentF irst	StudentL ast	$140,693.00	1490	FALSE	94.42483	$94.42	
7	Makarem	Abdeljaw ad	$140,904.00	1301	FALSE	108.3044	$108.30	
8	Makarem	Abdeljaw ad	$142,380.00	1373	FALSE	103.6999	$103.70	
9	Chardae	Myles	$163,737.00	1476	FALSE	110.9329	$110.93	
10	Jaynish	Mody	$164,436.00	1850	FALSE	88.88432	$88.88	
11	Jaynish	Mody	$166,320.00	1437	FALSE	115.7411	$115.74	
12								
13								
14								
15								
16								
17								
18								
19								
20								

Sheet1

Ready

Step e: Formula results in Excel

Access 2016, Windows 10, Microsoft Corporation

FIGURE 3.15 Calculation Copied to Excel

a. Open the Price Per Square Foot query in Datasheet view. Examine the PricePerSqFt field.

One of the ways to verify the accuracy of the calculated data is to ask yourself if the numbers make sense.

b. Locate the 13th record with Philip DeFranco as the listing agent, an asking price of $168,000, and square footage of 1680. The result ($100.00) makes sense, since 168,000/1680 = 100.

> **TROUBLESHOOTING:** If the 13th record is not the one listed above, ensure that you have sorted the query by the List Price in ascending order, as specified in Step 1i.

c. Open a new, blank workbook in Excel and then switch to Access. Select the first 10 records. Click **Copy** in the Clipboard group on the Home tab.

You will verify the calculation in the first 10 records by pasting the results in Excel.

d. Switch to Excel and click the **Paste** button in the Clipboard group on the Home tab.

The field names display in the first row, and the 10 records display in the next 10 rows. The fields are located in columns A–F. The calculated field results are pasted in column F as values rather than as a formula.

> **TROUBLESHOOTING:** If you see pound signs (#####) in an Excel column, double-click the vertical line between column headings to increase the width.

e. Click **cell G2**. Type **=C2/D2** and press **Enter**. Click **cell G2**, and click **Copy** in the Clipboard group. Select the **range G3:G11** and click **Paste** in the Clipboard group. Compare your results to Figure 3.15.

The formula divides the list price by the square feet. Compare the results in columns F and G. The numbers should be the same, except for the number of decimal places.

f. Save the Excel workbook as **a03h1PropertyCheck_LastFirst**. Close the file, and exit Excel. You will submit this file to your instructor at the end of the last Hands-On Exercise.

g. Keep the database open if you plan to continue with the next Hands-On Exercise. If not, close the database and exit Access.

The Expression Builder and Functions

In the last Hands-On Exercise, you calculated the price per square foot for real estate properties to help evaluate properties on the investment list. You were able to type the expression manually.

When you encounter more complex expressions, the ***Expression Builder*** tool can help you create more complicated expressions. The Expression Builder's size enables you to easily see complex formulas and functions in their entirety. In addition, it provides easy access to objects, operators, and functions.

In this section, you will learn how to create expressions with the Expression Builder. You also will learn how to use built-in functions.

Creating Expressions Using the Expression Builder

STEP 1 »» The Expression Builder helps you create expressions by supplying you with access to fields, operators, and functions. When you use the Expression Builder to help create expressions, you can eliminate spelling errors in field names. Another advantage is that when you insert a function, placeholders tell you which values belong where. Experienced users may have functions memorized, but new users have the Expression Builder to provide support.

Once you open the Expression Builder, the Expression Builder dialog box displays. The top portion is an empty rectangular box known as the expression box. The left column of the Expression Builder dialog box contains Expression Elements (see Figure 3.16), which include the built-in functions, objects from the current database (including tables), and common expressions.

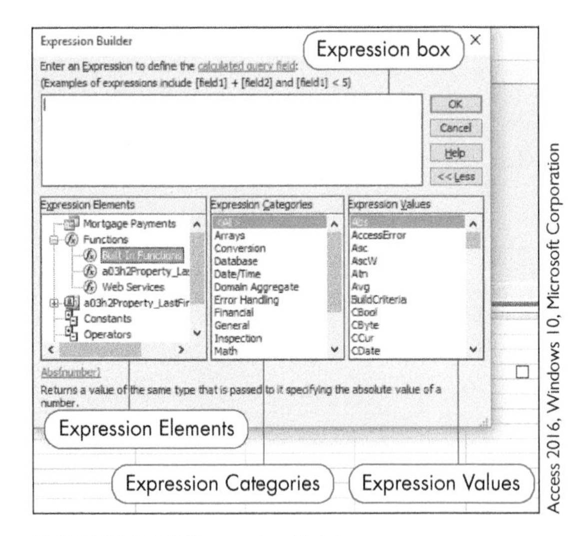

FIGURE 3.16 Expression Builder

The middle column displays the Expression Categories based on the item selected in the Expression Elements box (see Figure 3.16 above). For example, when the Built-In Functions item is selected in the Expression Elements box, the available built-in function categories, such as the Math category, are displayed in the Expression Categories box.

The right column displays the Expression Values, if any, for the categories that you selected in the Expression Categories box (see Figure 3.16 above). For example, if you click Built-In Functions in the Expression Elements box and click Date/Time in the Expression Categories box, the Expression Values box lists all of the built-in functions in the Date/Time category.

You can create an expression by manually typing text in the expression box or by double-clicking the elements from the bottom section in the Expression Builder dialog box.

To create an expression with the Expression Builder, complete the following steps:

1. Open a query in Design view (or create a new query).
2. Click the Field row of a blank column.
3. Click Builder in the Query Setup group of the Design tab to launch the Expression Builder.
4. Type the calculated field name and type a colon if you want to name the column. Although this is not required, as mentioned earlier in this chapter, this will change the title of the column in Datasheet view.
5. Type the name of a field (surrounded in [ ] brackets). Alternately, you can click the source table or query listed in the Expression Elements section and double-click the field you want. Using the second method will insert a field in a format resembling [Properties]![Beds] as shown in Figure 3.17. In this example, the table name Properties appears in brackets, followed by an exclamation point, followed by the field name Beds in brackets. As long as you do not have multiple fields with the same name, you can safely delete the table name and exclamation point (leaving you with [Beds] in this example). If you want to use operators (such as +) you can type those manually.
6. Repeat the previous step for each field you want to add to the calculation, remembering to take the order of operations into account. See Figure 3.17 as an example formula created in the Expression Builder.
7. Click OK to close the Expression Builder window.
8. Click Run in the Results group to view the results in Datasheet view.

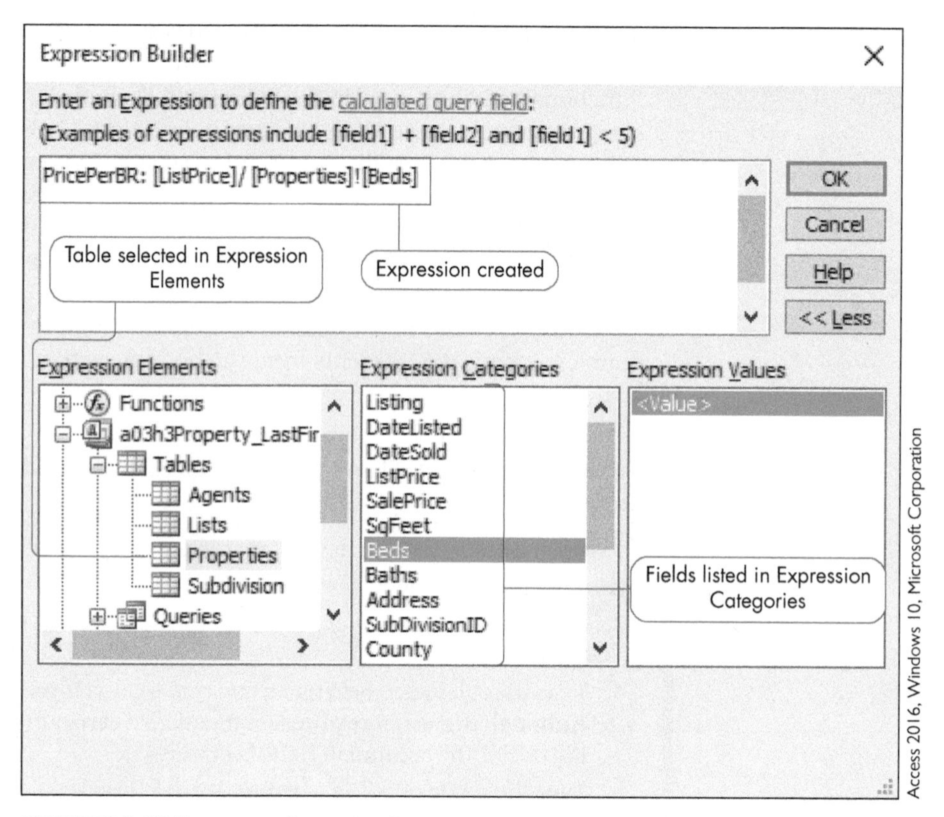

Access 2016, Windows 10, Microsoft Corporation

FIGURE 3.17 Expression Created in Expression Builder

Using Built-In Functions

A ***function*** is a predefined computation that performs a complex calculation. There are around 150 functions built into Access. If you are familiar with Excel, many of these will be familiar to you. Functions produce results based on inputs. Each input (such as a field name or a number) used to produce output for a function is known as an ***argument***. Some functions have optional arguments, which are not required but may be necessary for your task.

Many of the tasks that are built-in would otherwise be difficult to perform. Figuring out the payment of a loan or determining the year portion of a date without functions would not be easy.

Once you identify what functionality is required, you can check the Built-In Functions in the Expression Builder to see if the function exists, or use search engines or Access Help. If the function exists, add the function to the expression box and replace «placeholder text» with the argument values. See Figure 3.18 for an example function inserted using the Expression Builder.

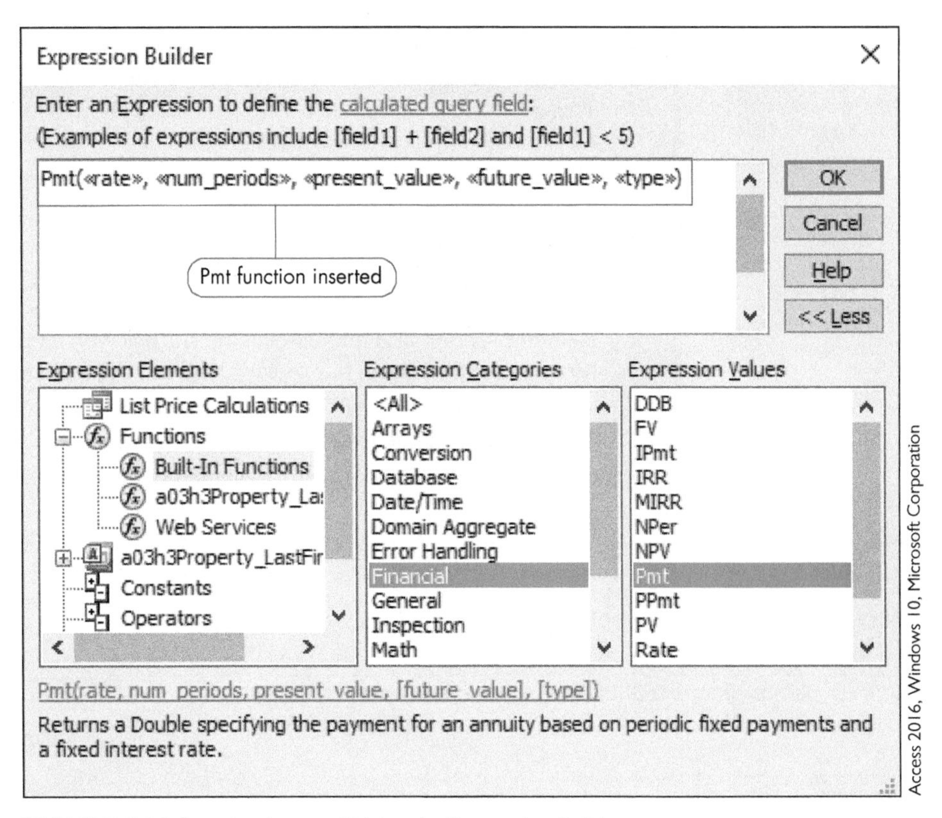

FIGURE 3.18 Function Inserted Using the Expression Builder

Functions work the same in Access, Excel, and programming languages (such as C#, Java, or Python). This chapter will demonstrate one function.

To create an expression containing a function with the Expression Builder, complete the following steps:

1. Open a query in Design view (or create a new query).
2. Click the Field row of a blank column.
3. Click Builder in the Query Setup group of the Design tab to launch the Expression Builder.
4. Type the calculated field name and type a colon if you want to name the column. Although this is not required, as mentioned earlier in this chapter, this will change the title of the column in Datasheet view.
5. Double-click Functions in the Expression Elements section of the window (see Figure 3.19). Click Built-In Functions. The list of available functions will appear in the Expression Categories box.
6. Locate and click the function category in the Expression Categories section, as shown in Figure 3.19. If you are unsure of the category, you can use Help or search through the category labeled <All>.

7. Double-click the function name in the Expression Values section to add it. Most functions include one or more placeholder text fields, text surrounded by «» symbols. These provide you guidance as to what data should be entered in each location. Notice an example of placeholder text in Figure 3.19.
8. Click a placeholder text element to select it, unless your function does not have placeholder text.
9. Type the number, field name, or calculation you want to replace the placeholder (for example, in Figure 3.19, the first placeholder text was replaced by .05/12). Note that you can also add a field by clicking the desired table or query listed in the Expression Elements section and double-clicking the field you want. In Figure 3.19, notice that [Properties]![ListPrice] has replaced the third placeholder. As discussed earlier, the table name and exclamation point can often be removed safely.
10. Click OK to close the Expression Builder window.
11. Click Run in the Results group to view the results in Datasheet view.

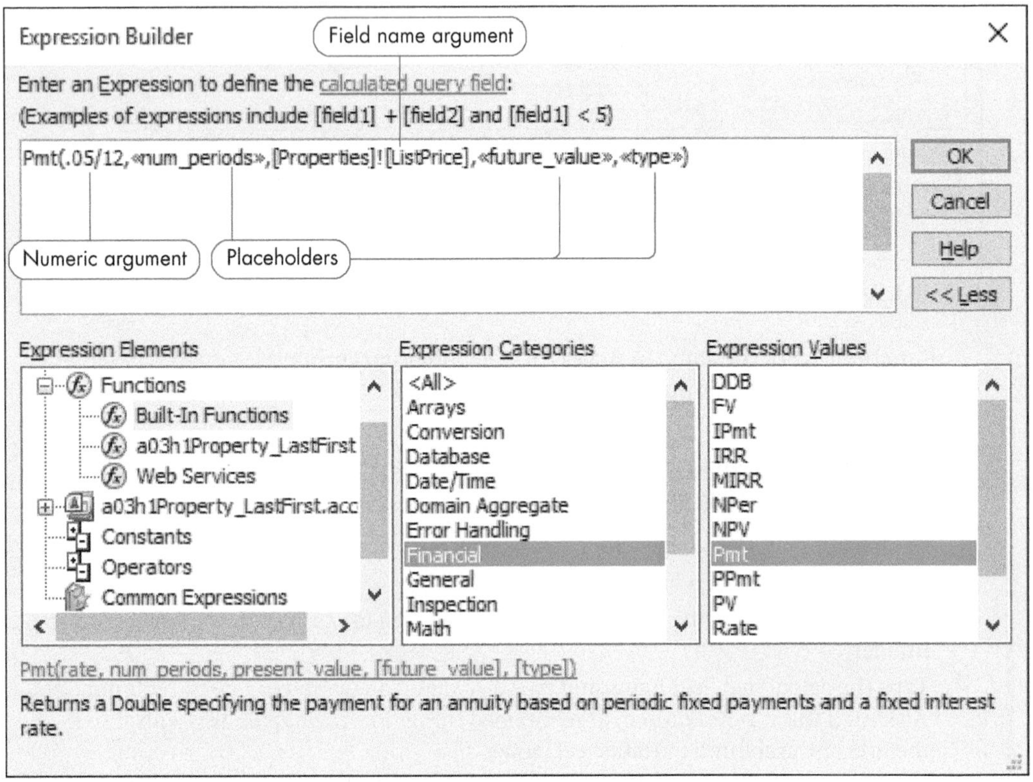

Expression Builder
Field name argument
Enter an Expression to define the calculated query field:
(Examples of expressions include [field1] + [field2] and [field1] < 5)
Pmt(.05/12,«num_periods»,[Properties]![ListPrice],«future_value»,«type»)
Numeric argument
Placeholders
OK
Cancel
Help
<< Less
Expression Elements
Functions
Built-In Functions
a03h1Property_LastFirst
Web Services
a03h1Property_LastFirst.acc
Constants
Operators
Common Expressions
Expression Categories
<All>
Arrays
Conversion
Database
Date/Time
Domain Aggregate
Error Handling
Financial
General
Inspection
Math
Expression Values
DDB
FV
IPmt
IRR
MIRR
NPer
NPV
Pmt
PPmt
PV
Rate
Pmt(rate, num_periods, present_value, [future_value], [type])
Returns a Double specifying the payment for an annuity based on periodic fixed payments and a fixed interest rate.

Access 2016, Windows 10, Microsoft Corporation

FIGURE 3.19 Expression with Some Arguments Filled In

Calculate a Loan Payment with the Pmt Function

STEP 2 The ***Pmt function*** calculates the loan payment given the rate, number of periods (also known as term), and the present value of the loan (the principal). If necessary, two other arguments (future value and type) can be used, but they are not necessary for many calculations. The Pmt function uses the following syntax:

```
Pmt(rate, num_periods, present_value, future_value, type)
```

After inserting the function using the Expression Builder, you will supply at least the rate, num_periods, and present_value arguments. The arguments are as follows:

- **rate:** Interest rates are usually stated as yearly rates, so the rate must be converted to the rate per period. If a loan is paid monthly, divide the yearly rate by 12. Typically this is entered as a decimal followed by the division (for example, .05/12). It is also acceptable to enter this as a percentage (5%/12).

- **num_periods:** Multiply the number of years of the loan by the number of payments per year. The total number of payments for a monthly payment would be calculated as the number of years multiplied by 12.
- **present_value:** The amount of the loan.
- **future_value** and **type:** The last two arguments—future value and type—are both optional, so they are usually left blank or filled in with zero.

The following example shows how to use the Pmt function to calculate the payment for a loan with a 5% interest rate, paid 12 times a year. This loan will be paid for four years and has a present value of $12,500. Figure 3.20 shows how it appears in the Expression Builder.

Expression Builder

Enter an Expression to define the calculated query field:
(Examples of expressions include [field1] + [field2] and [field1] < 5)

Pmt(.05/12, 4*12, 12500, 0, 0)

Optional arguments set to zero
Interest rate per period
Number of periods
Present value of loan

OK
Cancel
Help
<< Less

Expression Elements: Web Services, a03h3Property_LastFir, Tables, Agents, Lists, Properties, Subdivision, Queries

Expression Categories: Listing, DateListed, DateSold, ListPrice, SalePrice, SqFeet, Beds, Baths, Address, SubDivisionID, County

Expression Values: <Value>

Access 2016, Windows 10, Microsoft Corporation

FIGURE 3.20 Pmt Function with Arguments Filled In

The Pmt function will return a negative value, as a loan payment is considered a debit. In this case, it returns −287.87. If you would like to display this as a positive number, place a negative sign in front of the loan amount.

Pmt(.05/12, 4*12, −12500, 0, 0)

By default, the column heading will display Expr1 for any calculated field, as shown in the first Hands-On Exercise. To change this, you can replace Expr1 with the desired column heading, followed by a colon (:), to the left of the calculation.

MonthlyPmt: Pmt(.05/12, 4*12, −12500, 0, 0)

Quick Concepts

5. List two benefits of using the Expression Builder to create expressions. ***p. 826***
6. What is an example argument in the Pmt function? What does this argument do? ***p. 830***
7. Given the following function: Pmt(.05/12, 5*12, 50000, 0, 0), how many years is the loan for and how much is the initial amount of the loan? ***p. 831***

Hands-On Exercises

Watch the Video for this Hands-On Exercise!
MyITLab®
HOE2 Training

Skills covered: Use the Expression Builder • Calculate a Loan Payment with the Pmt Function

2 The Expression Builder and Functions

When Don and Matt ask you to calculate the price per bedroom and the price per room for each property, you use the Expression Builder to make the task easier. You also create an additional calculated field showing the estimated mortgage for each property.

STEP 1 » USE THE EXPRESSION BUILDER

You will create a copy of the Price Per Square Foot Formatted query from the previous Hands-On Exercise and paste it using a new name. You will add a few more calculated fields to the new query. You will create one calculation to determine the price per bedroom for each house. You will create a second field to calculate the price per room. For this calculation, you will assume that each property has a kitchen, a living room, a dining room, and the listed bedrooms and bathrooms. The calculations you will create are shown in Figure 3.21. Your expected output is shown in Figure 3.22.

Field:	FirstName	LastName	ListPrice	SqFeet	Sold	PricePerBR: [ListPrice]/[Beds]	PricePerRoom: [ListPrice]/([Beds]+[Baths]+3)
Table:	Agents	Agents	Properties	Properties	Properties		
Sort:			Ascending				
Show:	☑	☑	☑	☑	☑	☑	☑
Criteria:					No		
or:							

Step i: PricePerBR calculation

Step s: PricePerRoom calculation

Access 2016, Windows 10, Microsoft Corporation

FIGURE 3.21 Expanded Calculations

Mortgage Payments | List Price Calculations

First Name	Last Name	List Price	Square Feet	Sold	Price Per Bedroom	Price Per Room
Philip	DeFranco	$109,140.00	1133	No	$54,570.00	$18,190.00
Chardae	Myles	$129,780.00	1132	No	$64,890.00	$21,630.00
Makarem	Abdeljawad	$136,680.00	1375	No	$68,340.00	$22,780.00
Meera	Shah	$138,990.00	1276	No	$69,495.00	$23,165.00
StudentFirst	StudentLast	$140,693.00	1490	No	$70,346.50	$23,448.83
Makarem	Abdeljawad	$140,904.00	1301	No	$70,452.00	$23,484.00
Makarem	Abdeljawad	$142,380.00	1373	No	$71,190.00	$20,340.00
Chardae	Myles	$163,737.00	1476	No	$81,868.50	$27,289.50
Jaynish	Mody	$164,436.00	1850	No	$82,218.00	$23,490.86
Jaynish	Mody	$166,320.00	1437	No	$83,160.00	$27,720.00
Chardae	Myles	$166,552.00	1623	No	$83,276.00	$23,793.14
Chardae	Myles	$166,800.00	1598	No	$83,400.00	$27,800.00
Philip	DeFranco	$168,000.00	1680	No	$84,000.00	$25,846.15
Chardae	Myles	$168,354.00	1651	No	$84,177.00	$28,059.00
Philip	DeFranco	$174,230.00	1771	No	$87,115.00	$29,038.33
Meera	Shah	$174,720.00	1694	No	$87,360.00	$29,120.00
StudentFirst	StudentLast	$174,720.00	1610	No	$87,360.00	$26,880.00
Chardae	Myles	$175,336.00	1855	No	$87,668.00	$29,222.67
StudentFirst	StudentLast	$175,560.00	1562	No	$87,780.00	$29,260.00
Meera	Shah	$176,176.00	1761	No	$88,088.00	$25,168.00
Jaynish	Mody	$177,984.00	1707	No	$88,992.00	$27,382.15
Chardae	Myles	$179,088.00	1837	No	$89,544.00	$29,848.00
Chardae	Myles	$179,100.00	1946	No	$89,550.00	$25,585.71
Chardae	Myles	$179,712.00	1854	No	$89,856.00	$27,648.00
Chardae	Myles	$180,180.00	1896	No	$90,090.00	$30,030.00
Makarem	Abdeljawad	$180,810.00	1667	No	$90,405.00	$30,135.00

Record: 2 of 215 | No Filter | Search

Step k: Caption set for first calculation

Step t: Caption set for second calculation

Access 2016, Windows 10, Microsoft Corporation

FIGURE 3.22 Payment Calculation

a. Open *a03h1Property_LastFirst* if you closed it at the end of Hands-On Exercise 1, and save it as **a03h2Property_LastFirst**, changing h1 to h2.

b. Create a copy of the Price Per Square Foot Formatted query with the name **List Price Calculations**.

c. Open the List Price Calculations query in Design view. Click the **WrongPricePerSqFt field**. Click **Delete Columns** in the Query Setup group on the Design tab.

d. Click the **Field row** in the PricePerSqFt column and click **Builder** in the Query Setup group.

The Expression Builder dialog box opens, displaying the current formula.

e. Double-click the **PricePerSqFt field name** and type **PricePerBR**.

f. Double-click the **[SqFeet] field** in the expression and press **Delete**.

g. Click the **plus sign** ⊞ next to the a03h2Property_LastFirst database in the Expression Elements box to expand the list. Click the **plus sign** next to Tables and select the **Properties table**.

The fields from the Properties table are now listed in the middle column (Expression Categories).

h. Double-click the **Beds field** to add it to the expression box.

The expression now reads PricePerBR: [ListPrice]/[Properties]![Beds].

i. Highlight the **[Properties]! prefix** in front of *Beds* and press **Delete**.

The expression now reads PricePerBR: [ListPrice]/[Beds]. As the Beds field name is unique within our query, the table name is not necessary. Removing this makes the query easier to read. If a field named Beds appeared in more than one table in our query, removing the table name would cause problems.

j. Click **OK** and click **Run** to view the query results.

Notice that the column heading still reads Price Per Sq Ft. Also notice that the column's contents are formatted as Currency. These settings were copied when the query was copied.

k. Switch to Design view and ensure that the PricePerBR field is selected. Click **Property Sheet** in the Show/Hide group and change the **Caption** to **Price Per Bedroom**. Close the Property Sheet. Run the query and examine the changes.

The PricePerBR column now has an appropriate caption.

l. Switch to Design view. Select the entire **PricePerBR expression**, right-click the selected expression, and then select **Copy**. Right-click the **Field row** of the next blank column and select **Paste**.

You will edit the copied expression so that it reflects the price per room, assuming that the kitchen, living room, dining room, and the bedrooms and bathrooms will make up the number of rooms.

m. Click **Builder** in the Query Setup group.

n. Change the PricePerBR field name to **PricePerRoom**.

o. Add **an opening parenthesis** before the [Beds] portion of the formula. Type a **plus sign** after [Beds].

As you want the addition to be done first, enclose the addition in parentheses. The expression box should read PricePerRoom: [ListPrice]/([Beds]+

p. Click the **plus sign** next to the a03h2Property_LastFirst database in the Expression Elements box to expand the list. Click the **plus sign** next to Tables and select the **Properties table**.

The fields from the Properties table are now listed in the Expression Categories box.

q. Double-click the **Baths field** to add it to the expression box.

r. Type another plus sign after [Baths] and type **3** followed by a right parenthesis. In other words, you will type **+3)** in the expression box.

s. Delete the [Properties]! portion of the expression and click **OK** to close the Expression Builder.

The expression now reads PricePerRoom: [ListPrice]/([Beds]+[Baths]+3). Your final formula is the list price divided by the total number of rooms. The total number of rooms is the number of bedrooms (in the Beds field), plus the number of bathrooms (found in the Baths field), plus 3 (a constant representing the kitchen, living room, and dining room).

t. Click **Property Sheet** in the Show/Hide group. Type **Price Per Room** in the Caption box. Click the Format box, click the drop-down menu, and select **Currency**. Close the Property Sheet.

Compare your formulas to Figure 3.21. This figure has expanded the column widths for readability.

u. Run the query. Adjust column widths as necessary. Compare your results to Figure 3.22.

v. Save and close the query.

STEP 2 » CALCULATE A LOAN PAYMENT WITH THE PMT FUNCTION

Don and Matt feel like they are close to making an offer on a house. They would like to restrict the query to houses that cost $190,000 or less. They would also like to calculate the estimated mortgage payment for each house. You create this calculation using the Pmt function. You make the following assumptions: 80% of the sale price to be financed, a 30-year term, monthly payments, and a fixed 4.0% annual interest rate. Refer to Figures 3.23 and 3.24 as you complete Step 2.

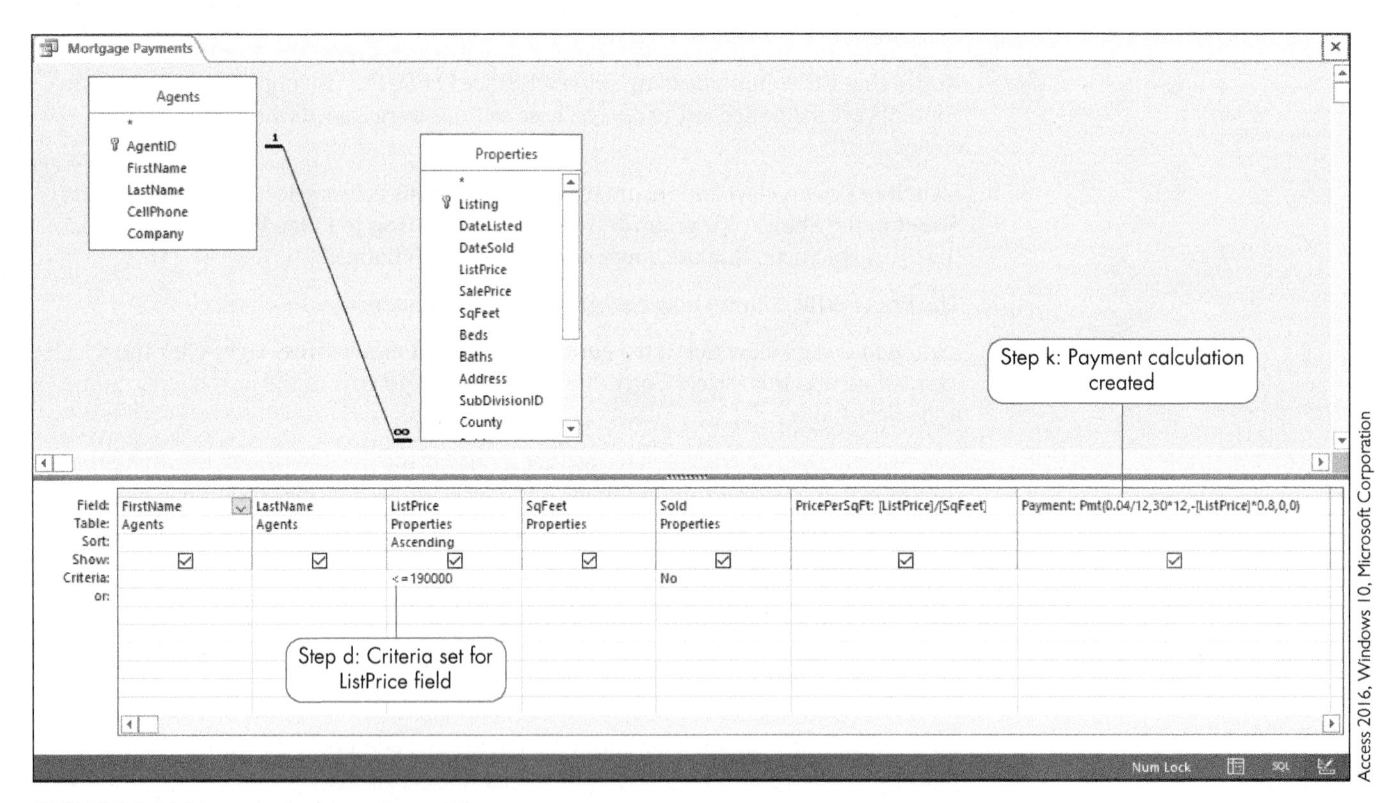

FIGURE 3.23 Mortgage Payments Design View

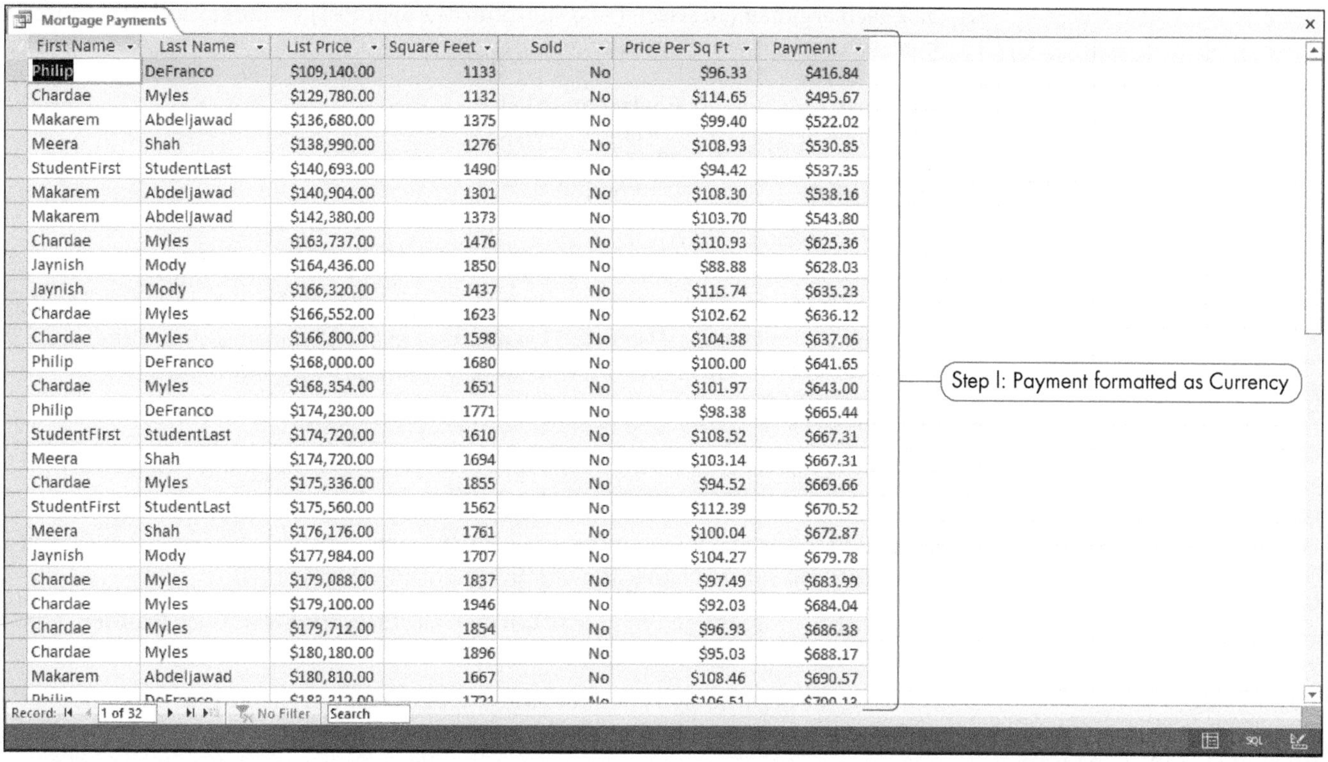

Mortgage Payments

First Name	Last Name	List Price	Square Feet	Sold	Price Per Sq Ft	Payment
Philip	DeFranco	$109,140.00	1133	No	$96.33	$416.84
Chardae	Myles	$129,780.00	1132	No	$114.65	$495.67
Makarem	Abdeljawad	$136,680.00	1375	No	$99.40	$522.02
Meera	Shah	$138,990.00	1276	No	$108.93	$530.85
StudentFirst	StudentLast	$140,693.00	1490	No	$94.42	$537.35
Makarem	Abdeljawad	$140,904.00	1301	No	$108.30	$538.16
Makarem	Abdeljawad	$142,380.00	1373	No	$103.70	$543.80
Chardae	Myles	$163,737.00	1476	No	$110.93	$625.36
Jaynish	Mody	$164,436.00	1850	No	$88.88	$628.03
Jaynish	Mody	$166,320.00	1437	No	$115.74	$635.23
Chardae	Myles	$166,552.00	1623	No	$102.62	$636.12
Chardae	Myles	$166,800.00	1598	No	$104.38	$637.06
Philip	DeFranco	$168,000.00	1680	No	$100.00	$641.65
Chardae	Myles	$168,354.00	1651	No	$101.97	$643.00
Philip	DeFranco	$174,230.00	1771	No	$98.38	$665.44
StudentFirst	StudentLast	$174,720.00	1610	No	$108.52	$667.31
Meera	Shah	$174,720.00	1694	No	$103.14	$667.31
Chardae	Myles	$175,336.00	1855	No	$94.52	$669.66
StudentFirst	StudentLast	$175,560.00	1562	No	$112.39	$670.52
Meera	Shah	$176,176.00	1761	No	$100.04	$672.87
Jaynish	Mody	$177,984.00	1707	No	$104.27	$679.78
Chardae	Myles	$179,088.00	1837	No	$97.49	$683.99
Chardae	Myles	$179,100.00	1946	No	$92.03	$684.04
Chardae	Myles	$179,712.00	1854	No	$96.93	$686.38
Chardae	Myles	$180,180.00	1896	No	$95.03	$688.17
Makarem	Abdeljawad	$180,810.00	1667	No	$108.46	$690.57
Philip	DeFranco	$182,212.00	1721	No	$106.51	$700.12

Record: 1 of 32 No Filter Search

Step I: Payment formatted as Currency

Access 2016, Windows 10, Microsoft Corporation

FIGURE 3.24 Mortgage Payments Results

a. Create a copy of the Price Per Square Foot Formatted query named **Mortgage Payments**.

b. Right-click **Mortgage Payments** and select **Design View**.

c. Delete the WrongPricePerSqFt field.

> **TROUBLESHOOTING:** If you do not see the WrongPricePerSqFt field, ensure that you copied the correct query.

d. Type **<=190000** in the Criteria row of the ListPrice column. Press **Enter**.

The query, when it is run, will show only the houses that cost $190,000 or less.

e. Click the **Field row** of the first blank column. Click **Builder** in the Query Setup group to open the Expression Builder dialog box.

f. Double-click **Functions** in the Expression Elements box and select **Built-In Functions**.

g. Select **Financial** in the Expression Categories box.

h. Double-click **Pmt** in the Expression Values box.

The expression box displays:

Pmt(«rate», «num_periods», «present_value», «future_value», «type»)

i. Position the insertion point before the Pmt function. Type **Payment:** to the left of the Pmt function, with a space after the colon. The expression box now displays:

Payment: Pmt(«rate», «num_periods», «present_value», «future_value», «type»)

j. Click each argument to select it and substitute the appropriate information. Make sure there is a comma between each argument.

Argument	Replacement Value
«rate»	.04/12
«num_periods»	30*12
«present_value»	[ListPrice]*.8
«future_value»	0
«type»	0

Note that the loan is a 30-year loan with 12 payments per year, hence the calculation for the number of payments. Also note, Don and Matt plan on financing 80% of the cost, putting 20% down. Therefore, you will multiply the list price by .8 (80%).

k. Click **OK**. Examine Figure 3.23 to make sure that you have entered the correct arguments.

l. Open the Property Sheet for the Payment field and change the format to **Currency**. Close the Property Sheet. Run the query.

Notice that the payment amounts are negative numbers (displayed in parentheses). You will edit the formula to change the negative payment values to positive.

m. Right-click the **Mortgage Payments tab** and select **Design View**. Click **Builder**. Add a **minus sign (−)** to the left of [ListPrice] and click **OK**.

By adding the negative sign in front of the ListPrice field, you ensure that the value is displayed as a positive number. The expression now reads:

Payment: Pmt(.04/12,30*12, −[ListPrice]*.8,0,0)

n. Run the query and examine the results. Adjust column widths as necessary.

The query displays a column containing the calculated monthly mortgage payment, formatted as currency, as shown in Figure 3.24.

o. Save and close the query. Keep the database open if you plan to continue with the next Hands-On Exercise. If not, close the database and exit Access.

Aggregate Functions

An ***aggregate function*** performs a calculation on an entire column of data and returns a single value. One example of an aggregate function is Sum.

Access refers to aggregate functions as Totals. Totals can be added to Datasheet view of a query, or they can be added to a query's Design view. Based on the data type, different aggregate functions will be available. Numeric fields are eligible for all of the functions, whereas Short Text fields are not. A list of common aggregate functions is shown in Table 3.2.

In the Property database, the average home price per county could be presented in a query or a report. This would give prospective buyers a good idea of home prices in their target counties. Almost every company or organization that uses a database will require some type of aggregate data.

TABLE 3.2 Common Aggregate Functions

Function	Description
Avg (Average)	Calculates the average value for a column.
Count	Counts the number of values in a column.
Max (Maximum)	Returns the item with the highest value.
Min (Minimum)	Returns the item with the lowest value.
Sum	Totals the items in a column.

In this section, you will learn how to create and work with aggregate functions. Specifically, you will learn how to use the Total row and create a totals query.

Adding Aggregate Functions to Datasheets

Aggregate data helps users evaluate the values in a single record to the aggregate of all the records. If you are considering buying a property in Story County, Iowa, for $150,000, and the average price of a property in that county is $450,000, you know you are getting a good deal (or buying a bad property).

Access provides two methods of adding aggregate functions—a ***Total row***, which displays the results of the aggregate function as the last row in Datasheet view of a table or query, and a totals query created in Query Design view. The totals query will be defined shortly.

The Total row method is quick and easy and has the advantage of showing the totals while still showing the individual records. Adding a Total row to a query or table can be accomplished by most users, even those who are not familiar with designing a query. Figure 3.25 shows the Total row added to Datasheet view of a query. In this image, the average of the List Price is displayed. The available aggregate functions are shown in the Price Per Sq Ft column. You can choose any of the aggregate functions that apply to numeric fields.

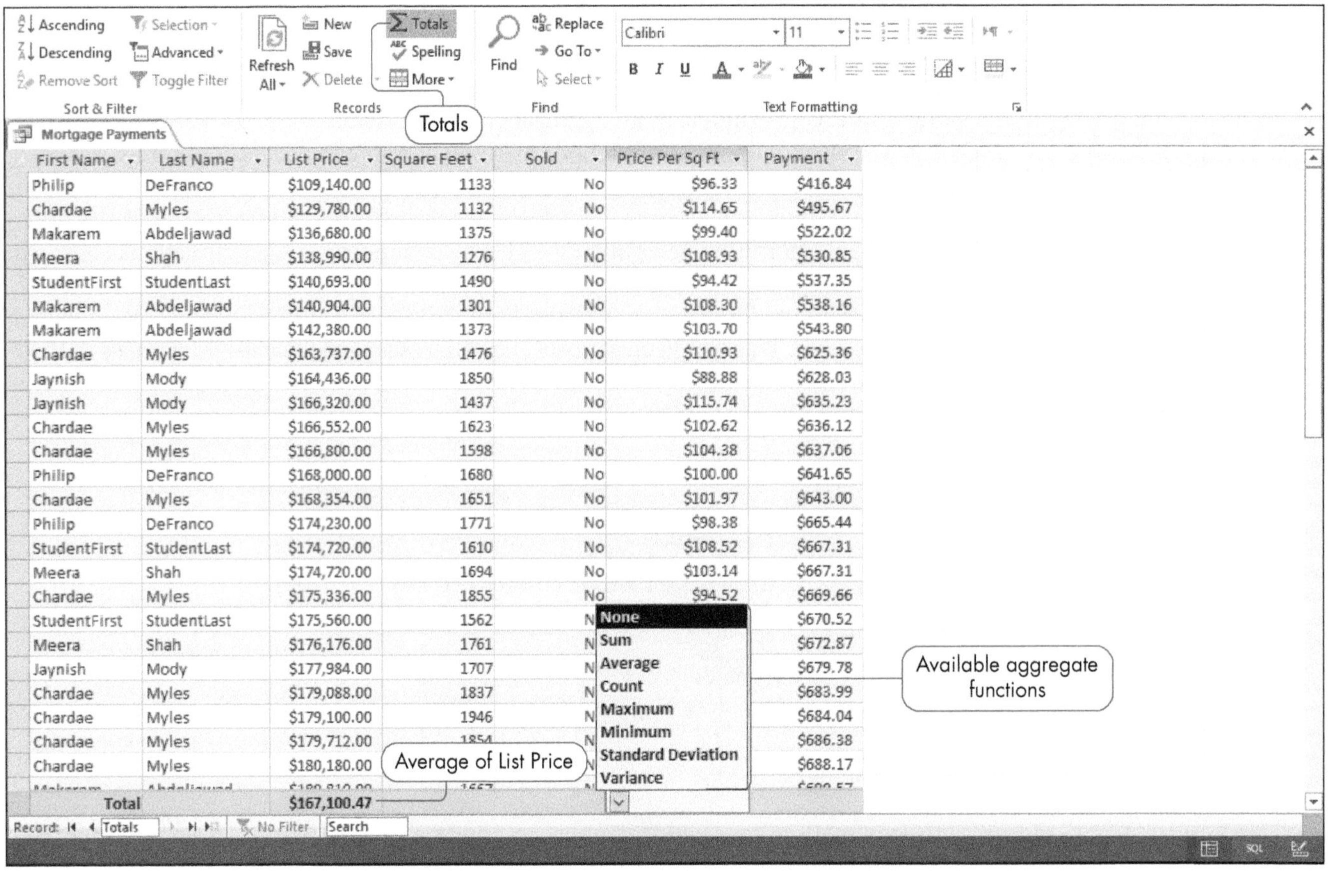

First Name	Last Name	List Price	Square Feet	Sold	Price Per Sq Ft	Payment
Philip	DeFranco	$109,140.00	1133	No	$96.33	$416.84
Chardae	Myles	$129,780.00	1132	No	$114.65	$495.67
Makarem	Abdeljawad	$136,680.00	1375	No	$99.40	$522.02
Meera	Shah	$138,990.00	1276	No	$108.93	$530.85
StudentFirst	StudentLast	$140,693.00	1490	No	$94.42	$537.35
Makarem	Abdeljawad	$140,904.00	1301	No	$108.30	$538.16
Makarem	Abdeljawad	$142,380.00	1373	No	$103.70	$543.80
Chardae	Myles	$163,737.00	1476	No	$110.93	$625.36
Jaynish	Mody	$164,436.00	1850	No	$88.88	$628.03
Jaynish	Mody	$166,320.00	1437	No	$115.74	$635.23
Chardae	Myles	$166,552.00	1623	No	$102.62	$636.12
Chardae	Myles	$166,800.00	1598	No	$104.38	$637.06
Philip	DeFranco	$168,000.00	1680	No	$100.00	$641.65
Chardae	Myles	$168,354.00	1651	No	$101.97	$643.00
Philip	DeFranco	$174,230.00	1771	No	$98.38	$665.44
StudentFirst	StudentLast	$174,720.00	1610	No	$108.52	$667.31
Meera	Shah	$174,720.00	1694	No	$103.14	$667.31
Chardae	Myles	$175,336.00	1855	No	$94.52	$669.66
StudentFirst	StudentLast	$175,560.00	1562	N	None	$670.52
Meera	Shah	$176,176.00	1761	N	Sum	$672.87
Jaynish	Mody	$177,984.00	1707	N	Average	$679.78
Chardae	Myles	$179,088.00	1837	N	Count	$683.99
Chardae	Myles	$179,100.00	1946	N	Maximum	$684.04
Chardae	Myles	$179,712.00		N	Minimum	$686.38
Chardae	Myles	$180,180.00		N	Standard Deviation	$688.17
					Variance	
Total		$167,100.47				

Totals

Average of List Price

Available aggregate functions

Access 2016, Windows 10, Microsoft Corporation

FIGURE 3.25 Total Row in Datasheet View

To add a Total row to the Datasheet view of a query or table, complete the following steps:

1. View the query or table in Datasheet view.
2. Click Totals in the Records group on the Home tab. The Total row is added at the bottom of the datasheet, below the new record row.
3. Select one of the aggregate functions (such as Average, Count, or Sum) in the new Total row by clicking in the cell and clicking the arrow.

Creating Queries with Aggregate Functions

The total row, though useful, is limited. Many times, you may require in-depth statistics. Instead of wanting to see the average sale price for houses, you may want to see the average sale price by city. Instead of seeing the average price for every item your store sells, you may want to see the average price for each category. Using the total row in the previous example, this is not feasible. Another limitation of using the total row is that you might want to see the average sale price, minimum sale price, and maximum sale price. Using the previous method, this is difficult to do.

Another way to display aggregate functions requires changes to the query design. A ***totals query*** contains an additional row in the query design grid and is used to display aggregate data when the query is run. This provides two distinct advantages over the total row. The first allows you to show only the results of the aggregate functions (and not the detail), and the second enables you to see statistics by category.

Create a Totals Query

Instead of showing detail, the overall statistics for the entire table or query may be displayed using a totals query. For example, if you want to see the number of listings, average value, and the average size in square feet for all properties in your table, you can use a totals query to get that data and not see details. Instead of having hundreds of rows of data with a summary row at the bottom (which could be missed), a totals query can display only the aggregate function results. Figure 3.26 shows a totals query in Design view, and Figure 3.27 shows the results.

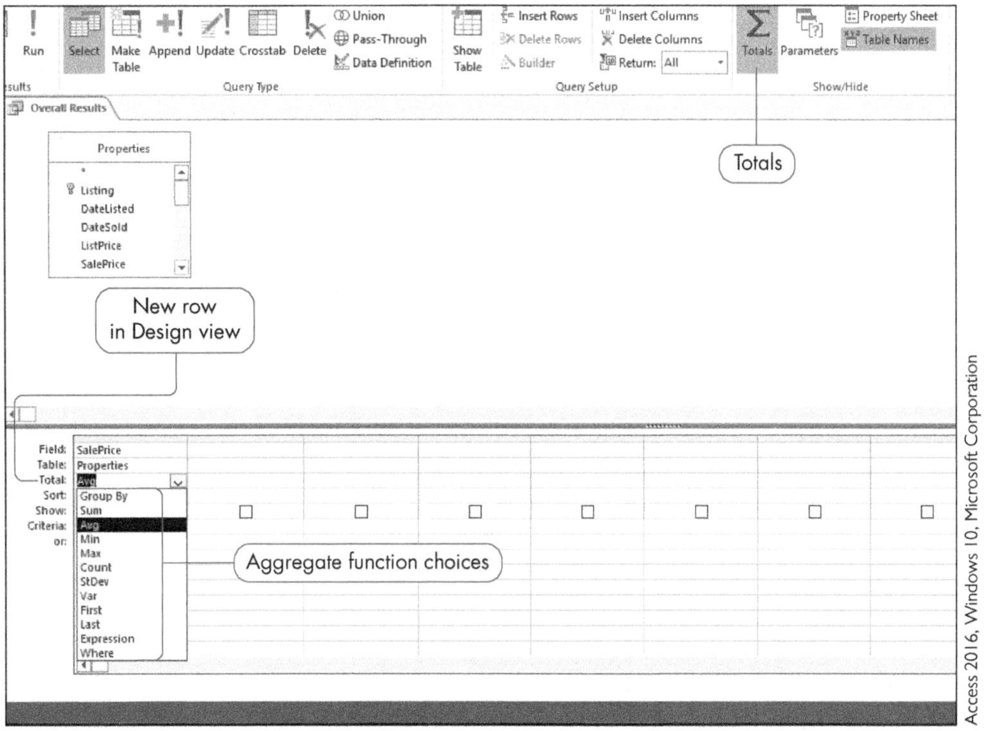

FIGURE 3.26 Totals Query Design View

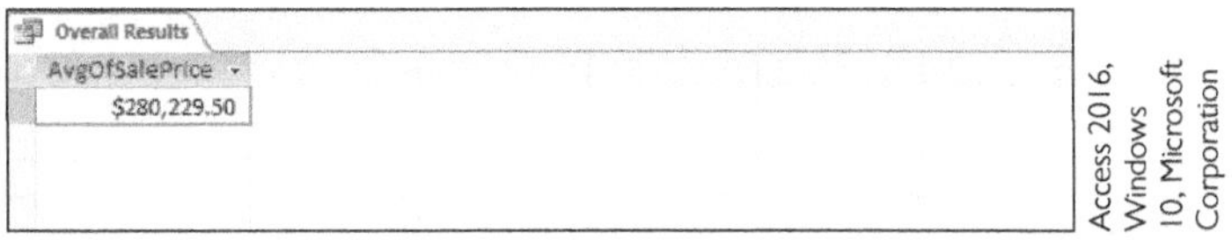

FIGURE 3.27 Totals Query Results

To create a totals query, complete the following steps:

1. Create a query in Design view and add the fields for which you want to get statistics.
2. Click Totals in the Show/Hide group on the Design tab. A new Total row displays in the query design grid between the Table and Sort rows. Notice that it defaults to Group By.
3. Click Group By and select the aggregate function you want applied for each field.
4. Display the Property Sheet (as done earlier in this chapter) and adjust settings to meet your requirements.
5. Click Run in the Results group to see the results.

> **TIP: SEE THE RESULTS OF MULTIPLE AGGREGATE FUNCTIONS FOR THE SAME FIELD**
>
> If you want to see the results of multiple aggregate functions for a single field, you can add the same field multiple times to a query. Display the Total row and select a different aggregate function for each column. When you run the query, you will see the results of each aggregate function in each column. For example, if you wanted to see the average, count, and sum of a field, you would add it three times to the query design, display the Total row, select the appropriate aggregate function for each column, and run the query.

Add Grouping to a Totals Query

Grouping a query allows you to summarize your data by the values of a field. For example, instead of seeing overall averages, you may want to see the results for each county. In this case, add County as a grouping level to see statistics by County.

To group an existing totals query, complete the following steps:

1. Add the field you want to group by to the query in Design view. For readability, the field should appear as the first field in the query.
2. Verify that the Total row displays Group By for the added field (see Figure 3.28), and run the query.

If you want to see the results by county, add the County field to the query and leave the Total row with the default of Group By. You may want to move this column to the beginning, as it will make your query easier to read.

Figure 3.28 shows Design view of a totals query with five columns, one of which is the grouping field. Figure 3.29 shows the results of this query. Notice that the resulting query shows one row for each county.

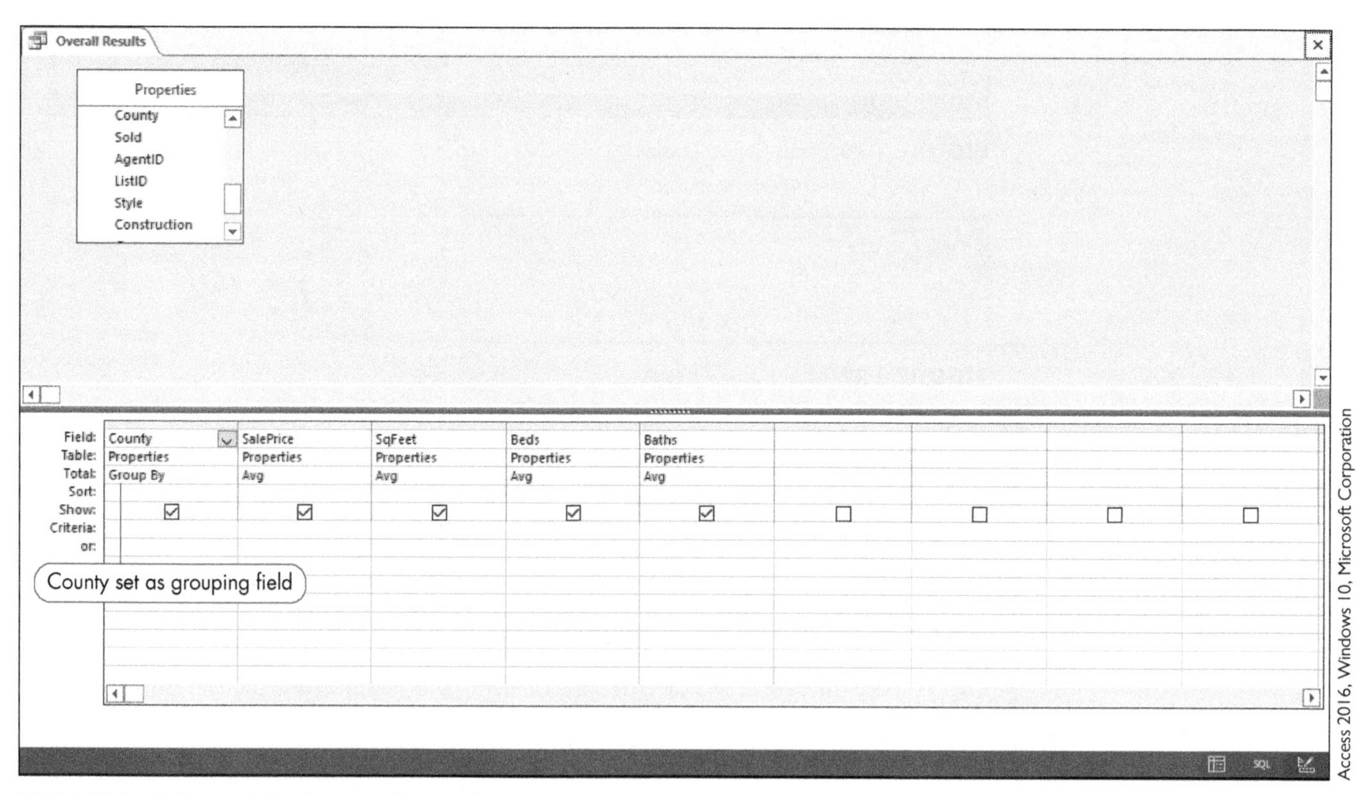

FIGURE 3.28 Grouped Totals Query Design View

Overall Results

County	AvgOfSalePrice	AvgOfSqFeet	AvgOfBeds	AvgOfBaths
Bergen	$220,431.12	2218.08163265306	3.12244897959184	1.63265306122449
Essex	$284,091.38	2844.50574712644	3.90804597701149	1.86206896551724
Hudson	$243,285.50	2645.23529411765	3.41176470588235	1.64705882352941
Mercer	$341,085.67	3242.675	4.45	2
Morris	$322,404.05	3105.6875	4.140625	1.890625
Passaic	[illegible]	2049.03846153846	2.80769230769231	1.75
Sussex	[illegible]	2968	4.5	2.1

Results shown for each county

Access 2016, Windows 10, Microsoft Corporation

FIGURE 3.29 Grouped Totals Query Results

Add Conditions to a Totals Query

Totals queries can provide even better information if you add criteria. For example, if you wanted to see the number of houses, average price, and average square feet for only the sold properties, grouped by county, you can add the Sold field to the query. Set the criteria to Yes to indicate that the Sold field is yes.

To add conditions to an existing totals query, complete the following steps:

1. Double-click the field you want to limit by to add it to the design grid. The location of this field is not important, as it will not be displayed.
2. Select Where from the menu in the Total row.
3. Enter the condition.
4. Run the query.

Figure 3.30 shows a query with a condition added, and Figure 3.31 shows the results. Compare this to Figure 3.29 to see the change in results.

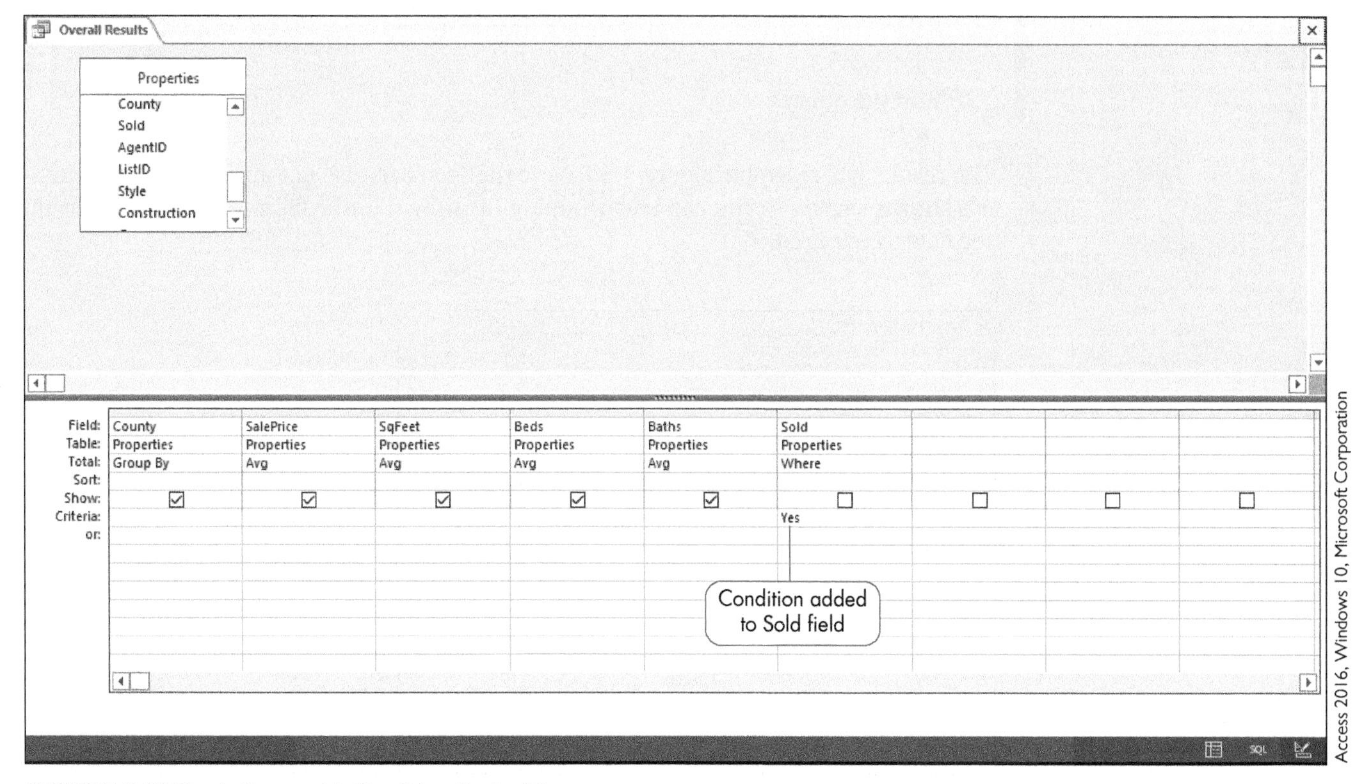

FIGURE 3.30 Totals Query with Condition Design View

Overall Results

County	AvgOfSalePrice	AvgOfSqFeet	AvgOfBeds	AvgOfBaths
Bergen	$220,431.12	2223.11764705882	3.29411764705882	1.73529411764706
Essex	$284,091.38	2829.53846153846	3.96153846153846	1.94230769230769
Hudson	$243,285.50	2432.25	3	1.75
Mercer	$341,085.67	3440.55555555556	4.55555555555556	2
Morris	$322,404.05	3233.42857142857	4.33333333333333	1.9047619047619
Passaic	$219,325.20	2171.4	2.8	1.8
Sussex	$269,411.17	2610	3.83333333333333	2

Access 2016, Windows 10, Microsoft Corporation

FIGURE 3.31 Totals Query with Condition Results

> **TIP: MULTIPLE GROUPING LEVELS**
> At times, you may want to add multiple grouping fields. For example, instead of grouping by state, you might want to group by city. However, if you group by city, customers with the same city name in different states would be grouped together. For example, all 50 states have a location named Greenville. If you grouped by city, all customers with a city of Greenville, regardless of state, would appear as a group. This is probably not your intention. Instead, you probably would want to see results by city and state, and thus would want to add both fields to a query and select Group By.

Add a Calculated Field to a Totals Query

STEP 3 Calculated fields can also have aggregate functions applied to them. For example, you may want to calculate mortgage payments, and see the average of your calculation.

To apply an aggregate function to a totals query, complete the following steps:

1. Create the calculation you want to summarize, using any of the methods discussed earlier this chapter.
2. Select the appropriate aggregate function from the menu in the Total row (see Figure 3.32).
3. Run the query.

The results will resemble Figure 3.33. Note that you can also use any of the other methods shown earlier, so you can add grouping (as shown in the figures below) and format the field as required.

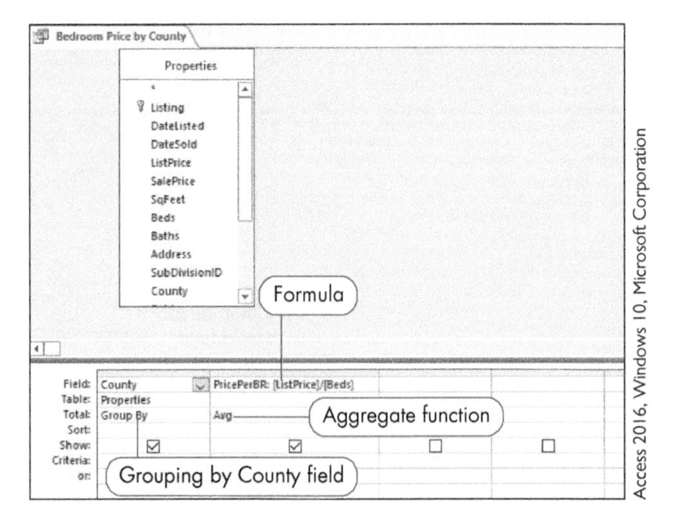

FIGURE 3.32 Adding Calculated Field to Totals Query

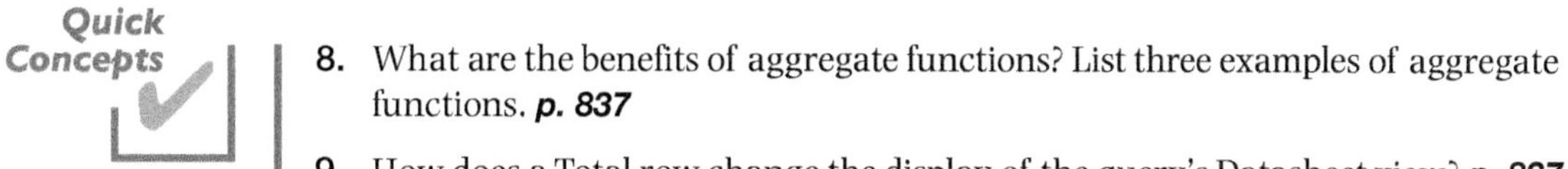

FIGURE 3.33 Calculated Field Results

Quick Concepts

8. What are the benefits of aggregate functions? List three examples of aggregate functions. ***p. 837***
9. How does a Total row change the display of the query's Datasheet view? ***p. 837***
10. What is a totals query? ***p. 838***
11. What would it mean if a query is "grouped by" state? ***p. 840***

Hands-On Exercises

Watch the Video for this Hands-On Exercise!

MyITLab®
HOE3 Training

Skills covered: Display a Total Row for a Query • Create a Totals Query • Add Grouping to a Totals Query • Add Conditions to a Totals Query • Add a Calculated Field to a Totals Query

3 Aggregate Functions

The investors decide it would be helpful to analyze the property lists they purchased. Some of the lists do not have homes that match their target criteria. The investors will either purchase new lists or alter their criteria. You create several totals queries to evaluate the property lists.

STEP 1 » DISPLAY A TOTAL ROW FOR A QUERY

You begin your property list analysis by creating a total row in Datasheet view of the Mortgage Payments query. This will give you a variety of aggregate information for important columns. Refer to Figure 3.34 as you complete Step 1.

Mortgage Payments

First Name	Last Name	List Price	Square Feet	Listing	Sold	Price Per Sq Ft	Payment
Philip	DeFranco	$109,140.00	1133	10004	No	$96.33	$416.84
Chardae	Myles	$129,780.00	1132	10028	No	$114.65	$495.67
Makarem	Abdeljawad	$136,680.00	1375	10008	No	$99.40	$522.02
Meera	Shah	$138,990.00	1276	10016	No	$108.93	$530.85
StudentFirst	StudentLast	$140,693.00	1490	10069	No	$94.42	$537.35
Makarem	Abdeljawad	$140,904.00	1301	10061	No	$108.30	$538.16
Makarem	Abdeljawad	$142,380.00	1373	11028	No	$103.70	$543.80
Chardae	Myles	$163,737.00	1476	10910	No	$110.93	$625.36
Jaynish	Mody	$164,436.00	1850	10117	No	$88.88	$628.03
Jaynish	Mody	$166,320.00	1437	10082	No	$115.74	$635.23
Chardae	Myles	$166,552.00	1623	10851	No	$102.62	$636.12
Chardae	Myles	$166,800.00	1598	10014	No	$104.38	$637.06
Philip	DeFranco	$168,000.00	1680	10002	No	$100.00	$641.65
Chardae	Myles	$168,354.00	1651	10885	No	$101.97	$643.00
Philip	DeFranco	$174,230.00	1771	10104	No	$98.38	$665.44
StudentFirst	StudentLast	$174,720.00	1610	10921	No	$108.52	$667.31
Meera	Shah	$174,720.00	1694	11035	No	$103.14	$667.31
Chardae	Myles	$175,336.00	1855	10868	No	$94.52	$669.66
StudentFirst	StudentLast	$175,560.00	1562	11036	No	$112.39	$670.52
Meera	Shah	$176,176.00	1761	10025	No	$100.04	$672.87
Jaynish	Mody	$177,984.00	1707	10066	No	$104.27	$679.78
Chardae	Myles	$179,088.00	1837	10010	No	$97.49	$683.99
Chardae	Myles	$179,100.00	1946	11079	No	$92.03	$684.04
Chardae	Myles	$179,712.00	1854	10102	No	$96.93	$686.38
Chardae	Myles	$180,180.00	1896	10019	No	$95.03	$688.17
Total		$167,100.47		32		$102.10	

Record: 1 of 32 No Filter Search

Step f: Average Price Per Sq Ft

Step f: Count of Listing

Step e: Average List Price

FIGURE 3.34 Totals Added to Datasheet View

a. Open *a03h2Property_LastFirst* if you closed it at the end of Hands-On Exercise 2 and save it as **a03h3Property_LastFirst**, changing h2 to h3.

b. Open the **Mortgage Payments query** in Design view. Drag the **Listing field** from the Properties table to the fifth column.

The Listing field is now in the fifth column, between the SqFeet and Sold fields. The other columns shift to the right.

> **TROUBLESHOOTING:** If you drag the Listing field to the wrong position, you can drag it again to the correct location.

c. Switch to Datasheet view. Click **Totals** in the Records group on the Home tab.

d. Click the **cell** that intersects the Total row and the List Price column.

e. Click the **arrow** and select **Average** to display the average value of all the properties that have not sold. Adjust column widths as necessary to ensure that all values are displayed.

   The average list price of all properties is $167,100.47.

f. Click the **arrow** in the Total row in the Listing column and select **Count** from the list.

   The count of properties in this datasheet is 32.

g. Click the **arrow** in the Total row in the Price Per Sq Ft column and select **Average** from the list.

   The average price per square foot is $102.10.

h. Compare your results to Figure 3.34. Save and close the query.

STEP 2 » CREATE A TOTALS QUERY AND ADD GROUPING AND CONDITIONS

You create a totals query to help Don and Matt evaluate the properties in groups. Refer to Figure 3.35 and Figure 3.36 as you complete Step 2.

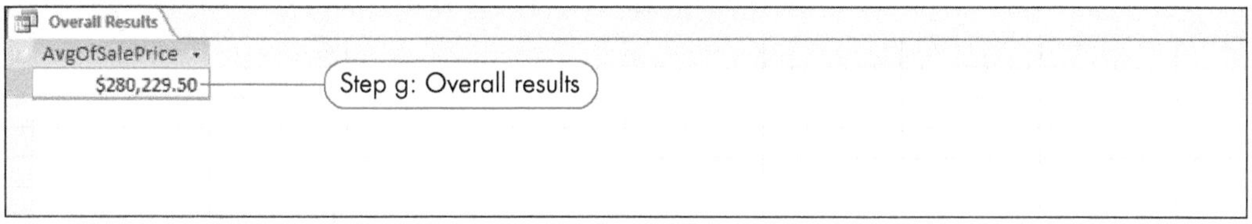

Overall Results

AvgOfSalePrice
$280,229.50

Step g: Overall results

Access 2016, Windows 10, Microsoft Corporation

FIGURE 3.35 Overall Results Query Output

Results by Realtor

NameOfList	AvgOfSalePrice	Number Sold
Algernon Listings	$324,697.22	18
FastHouse	$288,314.50	6
Houses 4 Sale	$218,039.00	2
Local Listings	$341,085.67	9
Major Houses	$235,757.88	8
Trullo	$236,885.21	19
Wholesaler	$276,654.92	26

Step q: Caption changed

Step m: Average sale price displayed

Access 2016, Windows 10, Microsoft Corporation

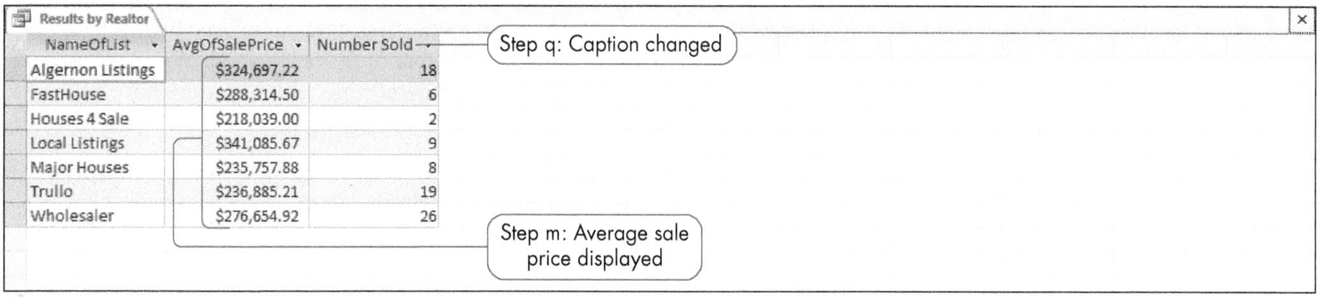

FIGURE 3.36 Results by Realtor Query Output

a. Click **Query Design** in the Queries group of the Create tab.

   You create a new query in Query Design; the Show Table dialog box opens.

b. Click the **Properties table** in the Show Table dialog box and click **Add**. Close the Show Table dialog box.

c. Double-click the **SalePrice** and **Sold** fields to add them to the query.

d. Click **Totals** in the Show/Hide group of the Design tab to show the Total row.

   A new row labeled Totals displays in the query design grid, between the Table and Sort rows. Each field has Group By listed in the new row by default.

e. Click the **Group By arrow** in the SalePrice column Total row and select **Avg**.

f. Click the **Group By arrow** in the Sold column Total row and select **Where**. Type **Yes** in the Criteria row.

This criterion will limit the results to sold houses only.

g. Click the **SalePrice field** and click **Property Sheet** in the Show/Hide group. Change the SalePrice format to **Currency**. Close the Property Sheet. Run the query and adjust the column width if necessary. Compare your results to Figure 3.35.

The results show an overall average of $280,229.50 for the sold properties in the database.

h. Click **Save** on the Quick Access Toolbar and type **Overall Results** in the Save As dialog box. Click **OK**. Close the query.

i. Click **Query Design** in the Query group of the Create tab to create a new query.

j. Add the Properties table and the Lists table from the Show Table dialog box. Close the Show Table dialog box.

k. Add the NameOfList field from the Lists table and the SalePrice, Listing, and Sold fields from the Properties table to the query.

l. Click **Totals** in the Show/Hide group to show the Total row.

A new row labeled Total appears between the Table and Sort rows.

m. Change the Total row for SalePrice to **Avg**.

n. Change the Total row for Listing to **Count**.

o. Change the Total row for Sold to **Where**. Type **Yes** in the Criteria row.

This criterion will limit the results to sold houses only.

p. Click the **SalePrice field** and click **Property Sheet** in the Show/Hide group. Change the SalePrice format to **Currency**.

q. Click the **Listing field** and change the caption to **Number Sold**. Close the Property Sheet. Run the query and widen the columns as shown in Figure 3.36.

Notice that Houses 4 Sale has the lowest average sale price. As Don and Matt are hoping to focus on inexpensive properties, they can focus on properties offered by this source. Notice also that the query results show the number of properties sold in each source, in addition to the average sale price. This will help determine which sources have been more effective.

r. Click **Save** on the Quick Access Toolbar and type **Results By Realtor** in the Save As dialog box. Click **OK**. Keep the query open for the next step.

STEP 3 » ADD A CALCULATED FIELD TO A TOTALS QUERY

The previous query shows the average value of the properties by realtor. However, Don and Matt learned at the seminar they attended that the longer a property has been on the market, the better your chances of negotiating a better price. You will revise the query to show, on average, how long each realtor takes to sell a house. Refer to Figure 3.37 as you complete Step 3.

Results by Realtor Revised

NameOfList	AvgOfSalePrice	Number Sold	DaysOnMarket
Algernon Listings	$324,697.22	18	23.50
FastHouse	$288,314.50	6	22.33
Houses 4 Sale	$218,039.00	2	23.50
Local Listings	$341,085.67	9	23.56
Major Houses	$235,757.88	8	24.75
Trullo	$236,885.21	19	26.05
Wholesaler	$276,654.92	26	26.12
Total		88	

Step e: Average days a property has been on the market displayed

FIGURE 3.37 Results by Realtor Revised Query Output

a. Click the **File tab**, select **Save As**, and click **Save Object As**. Click **Save As** and type **Results By Realtor Revised**. Click **OK**.

b. Click **Totals** in the Records group of the Home tab. Click in the Total row for the **NumberSold** column, click the arrow and select **Sum**.

   The total number of houses sold (88) now displays at the bottom of the Number Sold column.

c. Switch to Design view. In the field row of the first blank column, type **DaysOnMarket: [DateSold]-[DateListed]** to create a new calculated field. Change the Total row from Group By to **Avg**.

   The DaysOnMarket field will show the average number of days on the market for each sold listing.

d. Display the Property Sheet for the DaysOnMarket field and change the Format property to **Fixed**. Close the Property Sheet.

e. Run the query and examine the DaysOnMarket field. Adjust column widths as necessary. Compare your results to Figure 3.37.

   Houses 4 Sale listings have an average of 23.50 days on the market. Since this is in-line with their competitors, it lets you know they are neither fast nor slow with sales.

f. Save and close the query.

g. Close the database and exit Access. Based on your instructor's directions, submit the following files:

   a03h1PropertyCheck_LastFirst
   a03h3Property_LastFirst

Chapter Objectives Review

After reading this chapter, you have accomplished the following objectives:

1. Create a query with a calculated field.

- Expressions can contain a combination of arithmetic operators, constants, functions, and identifiers.
- Understand the order of operations: Calculated fields follow the same order of operations as mathematical equations—parentheses, then exponentiation, then multiplication and division, and finally addition and subtraction.
- Build expressions: Expressions must be written in a certain way. Rules govern the way you give instructions to Access.

2. Format calculated results.

- Calculated results may not have the format you want; change the properties of a calculated field using the Property Sheet.

3. Recover from common errors.

- Common errors include forgetting the colon in the appropriate location, spelling errors, and misuse of the order of operations.

4. Verify calculated results.

- Always check the results of your equation; Access will check for errors in the way something is written, but not logic errors.

5. Create expressions using the Expression Builder.

- The Expression Builder will help you create complex expressions by enabling you to choose fields and built-in functions easily.
- Click the Builder icon to open the tool.

6. Use built-in functions.

- Access includes 150 built-in functions, or predefined computations that perform complex calculations.
- Some functions require arguments, which are inputs (often fields or constants) given to a function.
- Calculate a loan payment with the Pmt function: The Pmt function accepts the rate, number of payments, and loan amount and calculates a loan payment. Two other arguments, future value and type, are typically left as zero.

7. Add aggregate functions to datasheets.

- Aggregate functions, including functions such as Sum, Avg, and Count, perform calculations on an entire column of data and return a single value.
- The total row displays at the bottom of a query or table; it can perform any aggregate function on each column.

8. Create queries with aggregate functions.

- Create a totals query: Create a query as usual and click the Totals button in Design view.
- Add grouping to a totals query: Grouping enables you to summarize your data by the values of a field. For example, instead of showing overall averages, add County as a grouping field and see averages for each county.
- Add conditions to a totals query: Similar to other queries, conditions can be added to totals queries, such as only showing listings with the Sold field equal to No.
- Add a calculated field to a totals query: You can apply an aggregate function to the results of a calculation; for example, subtract one date from another, and calculate the overall average of the difference between those dates.

Key Terms Matching

Match the key terms with their definitions. Write the key term letter by the appropriate numbered definition.

- **a.** Aggregate function
- **b.** Argument
- **c.** Calculated field
- **d.** Constant
- **e.** Expression
- **f.** Expression Builder
- **g.** Function
- **h.** Grouping
- **i.** Order of operations
- **j.** Pmt function
- **k.** Property Sheet
- **l.** Total row
- **m.** Totals query

1. _______ A combination of elements that produce a value. **p. 812**

2. _______ A field that displays the result of an expression rather than data stored in a field. **p. 812**

3. _______ A predefined computation that performs a complex calculation. **p. 828**

4. _______ A value that does not change. **p. 812**

5. _______ A method of summarizing data by the values of a field. **p. 840**

6. _______ An Access tool that helps you create more complicated expressions. **p. 826**

7. _______ Calculates the loan payment given the rate, number of periods (also known as term), and the present value of the loan (the principal). **p. 830**

8. _______ A way to display aggregate data when a query is run. **p. 837**

9. _______ The sequence by which operations are performed in a mathematical expression. **p. 812**

10. _______ A method to display aggregate function results as the last row in Datasheet view of a table or query. **p. 838**

11. _______ The location where you change settings such as number format and number of decimal places. **p. 817**

12. _______ The input used to produce output for a function. **p. 828**

13. _______ A calculation performed on an entire column of data that returns a single value. Includes functions such as Sum, Avg, and Count. **p. 837**

Multiple Choice

1. Which of the following *cannot* be used in a calculated field?
   (a) The number 12
   (b) An asterisk (*)
   (c) [HoursWorked] (a field in the current database)
   (d) All of these can be used in a calculated field

2. When creating a calculation, which of the following would be identified as an error by Access?
   (a) A field name spelled wrong in a calculation.
   (b) An incorrect formula (for example, adding two numbers instead of subtracting).
   (c) An order of operations error (for example, [HourlyPay] + 2 * [HoursWorked]).
   (d) A missing colon in the expression (for example: TotalHours [OTHours]+[RegHours]).

3. What is the result of the following expression?
   2 * 5 + 8 - 6 / 2
   (a) 6
   (b) 15
   (c) 20
   (d) 23

4. Which of the following *cannot* be adjusted in the Property Sheet?
   (a) Caption
   (b) Mathematical expression
   (c) Number format (for example, displaying numbers as Currency)
   (d) Number of decimal places

5. Which of the following could *not* be done using an aggregate function?
   (a) Averaging a series of numbers
   (b) Calculating the payment amount of a loan
   (c) Counting the number of values that exist
   (d) Finding the smallest value

6. Which of the following can be added to a totals query?
   (a) Conditions
   (b) Grouping fields
   (c) Aggregate functions
   (d) All of the above can be added to a totals query.

7. Which statement about a totals query is true?
   (a) A totals query is created in Datasheet view.
   (b) A totals query may contain several grouping fields but only one aggregate field.
   (c) A totals query is limited to only two fields, one grouping field and one aggregate field.
   (d) A totals query may contain several grouping fields and several aggregate fields.

8. Which of the following statements is true?
   (a) A total order cost is an example of a common field to group by.
   (b) A last name is an example of a common field to group by.
   (c) For best results, add as many "group by" fields as possible.
   (d) None of the above statements is true.

9. If you want to calculate aggregate statistics about graduation rates for students in a college database, which of the following would provide the *least* useful information if you were to group by it?
   (a) Gender
   (b) High School
   (c) Race
   (d) Social Security Number

10. Which of the following about the Total row in Query design is *false*?
   (a) The Total row enables you to apply aggregate functions to the fields.
   (b) The Total row is hidden by default in all new queries.
   (c) The Total row is located between the Table and Sort rows.
   (d) The Total row applies only to non-numeric fields.

Practice Exercises

1 Conforto Insurance

The Conforto Insurance Agency is a mid-sized company with offices located across the country. Each employee receives an annual performance review. The review determines employee eligibility for salary increases and the annual performance bonus. The employee data is stored in an Access database, which is used to monitor and maintain employee records. Your task is to calculate the salary increase for each employee; you will also calculate the average salary for each position. Refer to Figure 3.38 as you complete this exercise.

Average Salary By Position

TitleName	AvgOfSalary
Account Rep	$44,412.89
Manager	$88,895.00
SeniorRep	$58,119.23
Trainee	$23,269.53

Access 2016, Windows 10, Microsoft Corporation

FIGURE 3.38 Average Salary by Position Results

a. Open *a03p1Insurance*. Save the database as **a03p1Insurance_LastFirst**.

b. Click the **Create tab** and click **Query Design** in the Queries group to create a new query. Select the **Employees table** and click **Add**. Select the **Titles table** and click **Add**. Click **Close** to close the Show Table dialog box.

c. Double-click the **LastName**, **FirstName**, **Performance**, and **Salary** fields from the Employees table to add them to the query. Double-click the **Increase** field from the Titles table to add it to the query.

d. Click the Field row of the first blank column in the query design grid and type **NewSalary: [Salary]+[Salary]*[Increase]** to create a calculated field that adds the existing salary to the increase.

e. Click **Run** in the Results group to run the query.

f. Switch to Design view. Ensure the NewSalary calculated field is selected. Click **Property Sheet** in the Show/Hide group to display the Property Sheet. Click the **Format property** in the Property Sheet. Click the **Format property arrow** and select **Currency**. Type **New Salary** in the Caption box.

g. Click **Run** in the Results group to view the results. Adjust column widths as necessary. Save the query as **Updated Salaries**. Close the query.

h. Click the **Create tab** and click **Query Design** in the Queries group to create a new query. Select the **Employees table** and click **Add**. Select the **Titles table** and click **Add**. Click **Close** to close the Show Table dialog box.

i. Double-click the **TitleName field** from the Titles table. Double-click the **Salary field** from the Employees table.

j. Click **Totals** in the Show/Hide group to display the Total row. Change the Total row for Salary to **Avg**. Leave the TitleName field set to Group By.

k. Click the **Salary field**. Click the **Format property** in the Property Sheet. Click the **Format property arrow** and select **Currency**.

l. Click **Run** in the Results group to view the results. Adjust column widths as necessary. Save the query as **Average Salary By Position** and compare your results to Figure 3.38. Close the query.

m. Close the database and exit Access. Based on your instructor's directions, submit a03p1Insurance_LastFirst.

2 South Bend Yachts

South Bend Luxury Motor Yachts, a local boat seller, hired a new Chief Financial Officer (CFO). The new CFO, Rosta Marinova, asked the financing department to provide her with some summaries. She would like to determine how much financing the company is currently offering, offer financing with interest to customers, and see aggregate purchase statistics for local cities. Refer to Figure 3.39 as you complete this exercise.

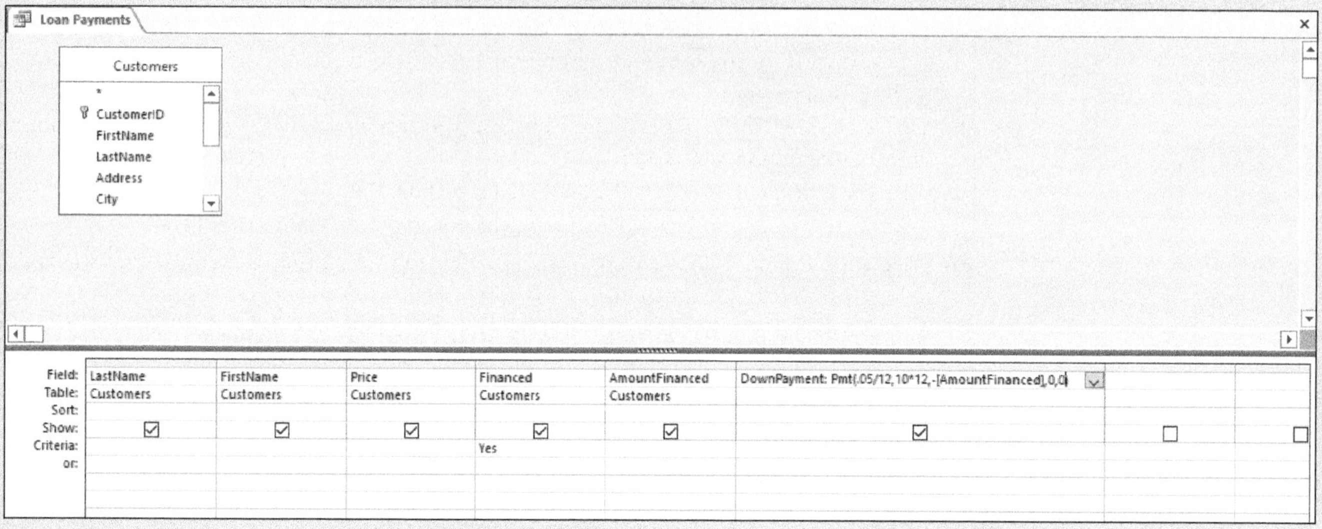

Access 2016, Windows 10, Microsoft Corporation

FIGURE 3.39 Loan Payments Design

a. Open *a03p2Boats* and save the database as **a03p2Boats_LastFirst**.

b. Click the **Create tab** and click **Query Design** in the Queries group to create a new query. Select the **Customers table** and click **Add**. Click **Close** to close the Show Table dialog box.

c. Double-click the **LastName**, **FirstName**, **Price**, **Financed**, and **AmountFinanced** fields.

d. Click the **Field row** of the first blank column and type **DownPayment: [Price]-[AmountFinanced]**.

e. Click **Run** in the Results group to run the query. Examine the results. Adjust column widths as necessary.

f. Click **Save** on the Quick Access Toolbar and type **Down Payment Amounts** as the Query Name in the Save As dialog box. Click **OK**.

g. Switch to Design view. Click the **Criteria row** for the Financed field and type **Yes**.

This will limit the results to financed boats. Boats that were not financed were paid for in full when purchased.

h. Click the **checkbox** on the Show row of the Financed field so it does not display when the query is run.

i. Sort the query by DownPayment in descending order by clicking the **Sort row** for the DownPayment field and selecting **Descending**.

j. Click **Property Sheet** in the Show/Hide group. In the Caption box, type **Down Payment**.

k. Click **Run** in the Results group to view the results. Adjust column widths as necessary. Notice that the column heading for the DownPayment field appears with a space in the name.

l. Save and close the query.

m. Click the **Create tab** and click **Query Design** in the Queries group to create a new query. Select the **Customers table** and click **Add**. Click **Close** to close the Show Table dialog box.

n. Double-click the fields **LastName**, **FirstName**, **Price**, **Financed**, and **AmountFinanced** to add them to the query.

o. Click the Field row of the first blank column. Click **Builder** in the Query Setup group to open the Expression Builder. Double-click **Functions**, and select **Built-In Functions**. Select **Financial**, and double-click **Pmt** in the Expression Values box.

p. Position the insertion point before the Pmt function. Type **DownPayment:** to the left of the function (including the colon).

q. Click each argument to select it, and substitute the appropriate information below. Once you have entered the information, click **OK**.

- **.05/12** for rate (5% interest, paid monthly).
- **10*12** for num_periods (10 year loan, 12 payments per year).
- Use **[AmountFinanced]** for the present_value.
- Use **0** in place of future_value and type.

r. Click **Property Sheet** in the Show/Hide group. In the Caption box, type **Monthly Payment**. Select **Currency** as the format.

s. Click the **Criteria row** for the Financed field and type **Yes**.

t. Click **Run** in the Results group to examine the results.

u. Click **Totals** in the Show/Hide group on the Design tab. Click Group By in the Monthly Payment column, click the drop-down menu, and select **Avg**.

v. Switch to Design view. Add a **minus sign** in front of [AmountFinanced] in the DownPayment calculation to display the results as positive numbers. Compare your design to Figure 3.39.

w. Click **Run** in the Results group to examine the results. Adjust column widths as necessary. Save the query as **Loan Payments** and close the query.

x. Close the database and exit Access. Based on your instructor's directions, submit a03p2Boats_LastFirst.

Mid-Level Exercises

1 Small Business Loans

You are the manager of a regional business loan department for the U.S. Small Business Administration office. You have decided to evaluate whether Access could be used in place of the Excel worksheet you are currently using. You will create a blank desktop database, add a table, add some sample customers, and import some recent data from an Excel spreadsheet. You will calculate the payments for the loans that are currently on the books by creating a query using the Pmt function. You will also summarize loans by the type of loan (M = Mortgage, C = Car, and O = Other).

a. Open Access and create a new blank desktop database named **a03m1Loans_LastFirst**.

b. Switch to Design view. Type **Customers** in the **Save As dialog box** and click **OK**.

c. Change the first Field Name to **CustomerID** and accept AutoNumber as the Data Type. Type **Company** in the second row and press **Tab**. Accept Short Text as the Data Type. Type **FirstName** in the third row and press **Tab**. Accept Short Text as the Data Type.

d. Type the remainder of the fields, selecting Short Text for the data type:

LastName	**Short Text**
City	**Short Text**
State	**Short Text**
Zip	**Short Text**

e. Verify that the first field is set as the primary key.

f. Switch to Datasheet view. Click **Yes** to save the table. Add the records as shown in the following table. Note that Access will assign an ID. Once you have typed the records, close the Customers table.

Company	FirstName	LastName	City	State	Zip
Jones and Co	**Robert**	**Paterson**	**Greensboro**	**NC**	**27401**
Elements, Inc.	**Merve**	**Kana**	**Paterson**	**NJ**	**07505**
Godshall Meats, LLC	**Francisco**	**De La Cruz**	**Beverly Hills**	**CA**	**90210**

DISCOVER

g. Click the **External Data tab** and click **Excel** in the Import & Link group. Click **Browse** to locate the *a03m1Loans* spreadsheet. Select the workbook and click **Open** at the bottom of the dialog box.

h. Ensure that *Import the source data into a new table in the current database.* is selected and click **OK**. Click **Next** three times, accepting the defaults, until you are asked to add a primary key. Click the *Choose my own Primary Key* option, and ensure **LoanID** is selected. Click **Next** once more and click **Finish**, accepting Loans as the table name. Click **Close** in the Get External Data dialog box.

i. Open the Loans table in Design view. Select the **InterestRate field** and change the format to **Percent**. Change the field size for the CustomerID field to **Long Integer**. Save and close the table, selecting **Yes** when prompted that some data may be lost.

j. Click the **Database Tools tab** and click **Relationships** in the Relationships group. Add both tables to the Relationships window and close the Show Table dialog box.

k. Drag the **CustomerID field** from the Customers table and drop it onto the **CustomerID field** in the Loans table. Check the **Enforce Referential Integrity** checkbox in the Edit Relationships dialog box and click **Create**. Save and close the Relationships window.

l. Create a query in Design view using the two tables. Add the **Company** field from the Customers table and the **LoanID**, **Amount**, **InterestRate**, **Term**, and **LoanClass fields** from the Loans table. Sort the query by LoanID in ascending order. Save the query as **Loan Payments**.

★ m. Add a calculated field named **Payment** in the first blank column to calculate the loan payment for each loan, using the Expression Builder. Use the Pmt function. Insert the appropriate field names in place of the placeholder arguments. Assume that the loans have monthly payments (12 payments per year). Ensure that the payment displays as a positive number. Run the query.

The first loan should have a value of 243.154499654298 (the extra decimal places will be removed shortly).

TROUBLESHOOTING: If you cannot see the fields from your current query, ensure that you have saved the query. Try closing and reopening the query.

n. Switch to Design view and change the format for the Payment field to **Currency**. Run the query again to verify your change.

o. Click **Totals** in the Records group on the Home tab. Change the value for the Total row for the Amount column to **Sum** and the values for the InterestRate and Term to **Average**. Adjust column widths as necessary. Save and close the query.

p. Create a copy of Loan Payments. Save the new query as **Loan Payments Summary**.

q. Open the Loan Payments Summary query in Design view and rearrange the columns as follows: LoanClass, LoanID, Amount, and InterestRate. Delete columns Company, Term, and Payment. Click **Totals** in the Show/Hide group. Change the Total row for LoanID field to **Count**, for the Amount field to **Sum**, and for the InterestRate field to Avg. Run the query.

r. Switch to Design view and display the Property Sheet. For the LoanID field, change the caption to **Loans**. For the Amount field, change the caption to **Total Amount** and change the format to **Currency**. For the InterestRate field, change the caption to **Avg Interest Rate** and change the format to **Percent**. Run the query. Adjust column widths as necessary. Save and close the query.

s. Close the database and exit Access. Based on your instructor's directions, submit a03m1Loans_LastFirst.

2 Investment Properties

You are in charge of Dysan Investment's database, which contains all of the information on the properties your firm has listed and sold. Your task is to determine the length of time each property was on the market before it sold. You also have been tasked with calculating the sales commission from each property sold. Two agents will receive commission on each transaction: the listing agent and the selling agent. You also will summarize the sales data by employee and calculate the average number of days each employee's sales were on the market prior to selling and the total commission earned by the employees.

a. Open *a03m2Homes*. Save the database as **a03m2Homes_LastFirst**.

b. Create a new query, add the Agents, Properties, and SubDivision tables, and then add the following fields: from the Agents table, add the LastName field; from the Properties table, the DateListed, DateSold, SalePrice, SellingAgent, and ListingAgent fields; and from the SubDivision table, the Subdivision field.

c. Add criteria to the table to ensure that the DateSold field is not empty (in other words, properties that have not been sold). You will need to use a function named IsNull to accomplish this. Format the SalePrice field as **Currency**. Save the query as **Sales Report**.

d. Create a calculated field using the Expression Builder named **DaysOnMarket** by subtracting DateListed from DateSold. This will calculate the number of days each sold property was on the market when it sold. Add a caption of **Days on Market**.

e. Calculate the commissions for the selling and listing agents using two calculated fields. The listing commission rate is 3.5% of the sale price, and the selling commission rate is 2.5% of the sale price. You can type these in directly or use the Expression Builder. Name the newly created fields **ListComm** and **SellComm**. Add captions of **Listing Commission** and **Selling Commission** and format the fields as **Currency**.

f. Run the query. Adjust column widths as necessary. Display the Total row. Calculate the average number of days on the market and the sum for the SalePrice and the two commission fields. Adjust column widths so all values are visible, and save and close the query.

g. Create a copy of the Sales Report query named **Sales Summary by Last Name**. Remove the DateListed, SellingAgent, ListingAgent, and Subdivision fields.

h. Display the Total row. Group by LastName and change the DateSold field Total row to **Where**, so the condition carries over. Show the sum of SalePrice, the average of DaysOnMarket, and the sum for both ListComm and SellComm. Change the caption for the SalePrice field to **Total Sales** and format the DaysOnMarket field as **Fixed**. Run the query. Adjust column widths as necessary.

i. Adjust the Total row in Datasheet view so it shows the sum of TotalSales. Adjust column widths as necessary. Save and close the query.

DISCOVER

j. Create a copy of the Sales Summary by Last Name query named **Sales Summary by Subdivision** and open the query in Design view. Remove the LastName field. Add the Subdivision field to the query and ensure the Total row is set to Group By. Sort the query results on the DaysOnMarket field in Ascending order. Limit the results to only return the top five values (hint: look in the Query Setup group of the Design tab).

k. Run the query and ensure only the top 5 values display. Save and close the query.

l. Close the database and exit Access. Based on your instructor's directions, submit a03m2Homes_LastFirst.

3 New Castle County Technical Services

RUNNING CASE

New Castle County Technical Services (NCCTS) provides technical support for a number of local companies. Part of their customer service evaluation involves logging how calls are closed and a quick, one-question survey given to customers at the end of a call, asking them to rate their experience from 1 (poor) to 5 (excellent). To evaluate the effectiveness of their operation, they asked you to create some queries to help evaluate the performance of the company.

a. Open the database you finished last chapter *a02m3NCCTS_LastFirst* and save the database as **a03m3NCCTS_LastFirst**.

TROUBLESHOOTING: If you did not complete the Chapter 2 case, return to Chapter 2, complete the case to create the database, and then return to this exercise.

b. Create a new query in Design view. Select the rep first and last names from the Reps table, and the CallID and CustomerSatisfaction fields from the Calls table.

c. Group by the RepFirst and RepLast fields. Display the count of the CallID field and average for the CustomerSatisfaction field.

d. Change the caption for the CallID field to **Num Calls**.

e. Format the CustomerSatisfaction average in Standard format and change the caption to **Avg Rating**.

f. Add a new calculated field named **AvgResponse**. Subtract the OpenedDate from the ClosedDate. Format the field as **Fixed**. Display the average for this field.

g. Run the query. Adjust column widths to ensure all data is displayed. Save the query as **Tech Ratings** and close the query.

h. Create a new query in Design view. Select the Description field from the Call Types table, and the CallID and CustomerSatisfaction field from the Calls table.

i. Group by the Description field. Display the count of the CallID field and average for the CustomerSatisfaction field.

j. Change the caption for the CallID field to **Num Calls**.

k. Format the CustomerSatisfaction average in Standard format and change the caption to **Avg Rating**.

l. Run the query. Adjust column widths as necessary. Save the query as **Call Type Effectiveness** and close the query.

m. Create a new query in Design view. Select the CompanyName field from the Customers table, and the CallID and CustomerSatisfaction field from the Calls table.

n. Group by the CompanyName field. Display the count of the CallID field and average for the CustomerSatisfaction field.

o. Format the CustomerSatisfaction average in Standard format and change the caption to **Avg Rating**.

p. Change the caption for the CallID field to **Num Calls**.

q. Run the query. Display the Total row. Show the sum of the Num Calls column. Adjust column widths as necessary.

r. Save the query as **Customer Happiness** and close the query.

s. Close the database and exit Access. Based on your instructor's directions, submit a03m3NCCTS_LastFirst.

Beyond the Classroom

Denton Credit Union

GENERAL CASE

Open *a03b1Denton*, which contains data from a local credit union. Save the database as **a03b1Denton_LastFirst**. Replace Your Name in the Branch table with your first and last name.

Create a query to calculate how long each manager has worked for the credit union: Display the manager and start date, and create a calculated field named **YearsWithCompany** to determine the number of years each manager has been in his or her position. Hint: Find a built-in Date/Time function to use the current date, subtract the start date, and divide the result by 365.25 (Note: the .25 at the end accounts for leap years). Display the calculated field in Fixed format, and add a caption to the field to display Years With Company as the column heading. Adjust column widths in Datasheet view as necessary. Save the query as Longevity.

Create a totals query to summarize each customer's account balances. List the customer's last name and first name from the Customer table, and the sum of all account balances (found in the Account table), grouping by both the last and first name. Format the total of the balances as Currency and add a caption of **Total Balance**. Display the sum of the total balances in Datasheet view ($141,074), adjust column widths as necessary, and save the query as **Customer Balances**.

Create a totals query to show each city (found in the Customer table) and total account balances for each city. For example, the total amount for customers in Denton is $61,510. Format the sum of the Balance field as currency with a caption of **Total Balance**. Adjust column widths as necessary in Datasheet view. Save the query as **Balances by City**.

Close the database and exit Access. Based on your instructor's directions, submit a03b1Denton_LastFirst.

Too Many Digits

This chapter introduced you to calculated fields. Open the database *a03b2Interest* and save the database as **a03b2Interest_LastFirst**. Open the Monthly Interest Payments query in Datasheet view. Notice the multiple digits to the right of the decimal in the MonthlyInterest column; there should only be two digits. Search the Internet or Access Help to find a function that will resolve this rounding problem. You only want to display two digits to the right of the decimal. Display the Total row in Datasheet view and display the total of the MonthlyInterest field. Adjust column widths as necessary. Save and close the query. Close the database and exit Access. Based on your instructor's directions, submit a03b2Interest_LastFirst.

Capstone Exercise

MyITLab® Grader

Northwind Traders, an international gourmet food distributor, hired a new CEO. She asked for your assistance in providing summaries of data that took place before she started with the company. To help her with her strategic planning, you will create queries to perform data analysis. Based on your meeting, you plan on creating four queries. One query will find orders with major delays. Another query will summarize the cost impact of customer discounts. A third query will be used to help evaluate financing. The final query will calculate the total sales by country.

Database File Setup

You will open the Northwind Traders food database, use Save As to make a copy of the database, and then use the new database to complete this capstone exercise. You will add yourself to the employee database.

a. Locate and open *a03c1Food* and save the database as **a03c1Food_LastFirst**.

b. Open the Employees table. Add yourself as an employee. Fill in all information, with the hire date as the current date. Set your Title to **Technical Aide**, extension to **1144**, and the Reports To field to **Buchanan, Steven**. Leave the Photo and Notes fields blank.

c. Close the Employees table.

Shipping Efficiency Query

You will create a query to calculate the number of days between the date an order was placed and the date the order was shipped for each order. The result of your work will be a list of orders that took more than 30 days to ship. The salespeople will be required to review the records and report the source of the delay for each order. The CEO feels there may be issues with one of the shipping companies, and would like data to back that up.

a. Create a query using Query Design. From the Customers table, include the fields CompanyName, ContactName, ContactTitle, and Phone. From the Orders table, include the fields OrderID, OrderDate, and ShippedDate.

b. Run the query and examine the records. Save the query as **Shipping Efficiency**.

c. Add a calculated field named **DaysToShip** to calculate the number of days taken to fill each order. (Hint: The expression will include the OrderDate and the ShippedDate; the results will not contain negative numbers.)

d. Run the query and examine the results. Does the data in the DaysToShip field look accurate? Save the query.

e. Add criteria to limit the query results to include only orders that took more than 30 days to ship.

f. Add the Quantity field from the Order Details table and the ProductName field from the Products table to the query. Sort the query by ascending OrderID. When the sales reps contact these customers, these two fields will provide useful information about the orders.

g. Add the caption **Days to Ship** to the DaysToShip field. Switch to Datasheet view to view the results. Adjust column widths as necessary.

h. Save and close the query.

Order Summary Query

The CEO is considering the financial impact of discounts. She asked for a query showing the employee name, number of orders they have taken, and the total discount amount they have given customers. She hopes to see if there is a correlation between the discount offered and the number of sales.

a. Create a query using Query Design and add the Orders, Order Details, Products, and Customers tables. Add the fields OrderID and OrderDate from the Orders table. Set both fields' Total row to **Group By**.

b. Add a calculated field in the third column. Name the field **ExtendedAmount**. This field should multiply the quantity ordered (from the Order Details table) by the unit price for that item (from the Products table). This will calculate the total amount for each order. Format the calculated field as **Currency** and change the caption to **Total Dollars**. Change the Total row to **Sum**.

c. Add a calculated field in the fourth column. Name the field **DiscountAmount**. The field should multiply the quantity ordered, the unit price for that item, and the discount field (from the Customers table). This will calculate the total discount for each order. Format the calculated field as **Currency** and add a caption of **Discount Amt**. Change the Total row to **Sum**.

d. Run the query. Examine the results. Most customers should have a discount of 10% of the total dollars, but some customers will have no discount. Save the query as **Order Summary**. Return to Design view.

e. Add criteria to the OrderDate field so only orders made between 1/1/2016 and 12/31/2016 are displayed. Change the Total row to **Where**. This expression will display only orders that were placed in 2016.

f. Run the query and view the results. Adjust column widths as necessary. Save and close the query.

Order Financing Query

The CEO would like the salespeople to discuss financing with customers. In order to do so, she would like you to create a query showing the impact on price for prior orders. This way, the reps can give customers a comparison with an order they have already placed. For the moment, she is considering a 5% interest rate, paid over 12 months. She would like you to leave the results as negative numbers.

a. Create a copy of the Order Summary query named **Order Financing**.

b. Open the Order Financing query in Design view and remove the DiscountAmount field.

c. Add a new field using the Expression Builder named **SamplePayment**. Insert the Pmt function with the following parameters:

- Use **.05/12** for the rate argument (5% interest, paid monthly).
- Use the number **12** for the num_periods argument (12 months).
- Use the calculated field **[ExtendedAmount]** for the present_value.
- Use the value **0** for both future_value and type.

d. Change the Total row to **Expression** for the SamplePayment field.

e. Change the Format for the SamplePayment field to **Currency**.

f. Run the query and examine the results. Adjust column widths as necessary. The results appear as negative numbers, as requested. Save and close the query.

Order Summary by Country Query

The company is planning on opening up some shipping centers internationally. The previous CEO had been considering Brazil, Denmark, and Germany as potential shipping center locations, but he was working from older data. You will provide a list of total shipment value by country for the year before the current CEO started to best inform her decision making.

a. Create a copy of the Order Summary query named **Order Summary by Country**.

b. Open the query in Design view. Replace the OrderID field with the Country field from the Customers table.

c. Run the query and examine the summary records; there should be 21 countries listed.

d. Switch to Design view and change the sort order so that the country with the highest ExtendedAmount is first and the country with the lowest ExtendedAmount is last.

e. Run the query and verify the results. Note the ExtendedAmount field has a caption of Total Dollars, so this is the field the query will be sorted by.

f. Save and close the query.

g. Close the database and exit Access. Based on your instructor's directions, submit a03c1Food_LastFirst.

Access

Creating and Using Professional Forms and Reports

LEARNING OUTCOMES

- You will develop and modify forms to input and manage data.
- You will create and modify reports to display and present information.

OBJECTIVES & SKILLS: After you read this chapter, you will be able to:

CASE STUDY | Coffee Shop Starts New Business

Coffee shop owner Ryung Park decided to use her knowledge of the coffee and retail industry to sell her specialty products to businesses around the country. She created an Access database to help track her customer, product, and order information.

Ryung created a database with tables to store data for customers, products, sales reps, and orders. She is currently using these tables to enter data and retrieve information. Ryung realizes that forms have an advantage over tables because they can be designed to display one record at a time—this can reduce potential data-entry errors. Ryung would like to create several reports so she can stay on top of her business by reviewing them each week. You have been hired to help Ryung create the new forms and reports that she needs.

Moving Beyond Tables and Queries

Sales Reps1

Sales Reps

Sales Rep ID	S0001	Gender	M
Last Name	Garcia	Birth Date	1/1/1968
First Name	Rodrigo	Hire Date	1/1/2007
Address	476 Frosty Drive	Highest Degree	Master's Degree
City	Webber	Current Salary	$50,000
State	KS	Previous Salary	
Zip Code	66970-	Date of Last Raise	
Home Phone	(555) 555-1222	SalesRepPhoto	
Cell Phone	(555) 555-5556		
Social Security Number	111-11-1111		

Customer ID	Customer Name	Contact	E-mail Address	HomePage	Address1
C0001	McAfee, Rand, & Karahalis	Paula Fields		www.mrk.org	5000 Jefferson La
C0003	Advantage Sales	Tracy Beck	service@advantagesales.com		4215 South 81 St
C0006	Lugo Computer Sales	StudentFirst Studer	service@lugocomputer.net		6000 Tigertail Av

Record: 1 of 3 No Filter Search

Products Report

Products Report Monday, October 26, 2015 9:35:21 PM

Brand	Product ID	Product Name	Description	Cost	OnHand	Markup Percent
Discount						
	P0012	Sugar Substitute	500/Case, 1-Serving Bags	$21.85	10	50.00%
	P0005	Coffee - Decaf	24/Case, Pre-Ground 1.75 Oz Bags	$23.00	10	50.00%
	P0008	Creamers - Assorted Flavors	400/Case, 8 50-count Boxes	$23.00	10	100.00%
	P0016	Stirrers - Wood	1000/Box	$1.44	10	100.00%
	P0015	Stirrers - Plastic	1000/Box	$1.72	10	75.00%
	P0001	Coffee - Colombian Supreme	24/Case, Pre-Ground 1.75 Oz Bags	$18.40	10	50.00%
House						
	P0003	Coffee - Mild Blend	24/Case, Pre-Ground 1.75 Oz Bags	$23.00	10	50.00%
	P0004	Coffee - Assorted Flavors	18/Case. Pre-Ground 1.75 Oz Bags	$26.45	10	50.00%
	P0006	Tea Bags - Regular	75/Box, Individual Tea Bags	$5.75	10	75.00%
	P0007	Tea Bags - Decaf	75/Box, Individual Tea Bags	$8.05	10	75.00%
	P0010	Sugar Packets	2000/Case	$20.70	10	100.00%
	P0011	Ceramic Mug	SD Company Logo	$5.75	10	100.00%
	P0014	Napkins	3000/Case, White	$23.00	10	100.00%
	P0025	Milk - 1 pint	Delivered Daily	$1.15	10	100.00%

FIGURE 4.1 Coffee Shop Starts New Business Database

CASE STUDY | Coffee Shop Starts New Business

Starting File	Files to be Submitted
a04h1Coffee	**a04h2Coffee_LastFirst** **a04h2Products_LastFirst**

Form Basics

Most Access database applications use forms rather than tables for data entry and for finding information. A ***form*** is a database object used to add data to or edit data in a table. Three main reasons exist for using forms rather than tables for adding, updating, and deleting data:

- You are less likely to edit the wrong record by mistake.
- You can create a form that shows data from more than one table simultaneously.
- You can create Access forms to resemble the paper (or other types of) forms that users employ in their data entry processes.

When you are adding or editing data using a table with many records, you may navigate to the wrong record accidentally. A form is less likely to allow this type of error because most forms restrict entry to one record at a time.

Many forms require two tables as their record sources. For example, you may want to view a customer's details (name, address, email, phone, etc.) as well as all of the orders he or she has placed at the same time. This would require using data from both the Customers and the Orders tables in one form. Such a form enables a user to view two record sources at the same time and make changes—additions, edits, or deletions—to one or both sources of data. When a change is made in the form, the data in the underlying table (or tables) are affected. A form is really a mirror image of the data in the tables and simply presents a user-friendly interface for users of the database.

Access forms can be designed to emulate the paper documents already used by an organization. When paper forms are currently used to collect data, it is a good idea to design the electronic forms to resemble the paper forms. This will make the data entry process more efficient and ease the transition from paper form to electronic form

In this section, you will learn the basics of form design. You will discover multiple methods to create and modify Access forms.

Creating Forms Using Form Tools

Access provides a variety of options for creating forms. You will eventually develop a preference for one or two types of form layouts, but keep in mind that you have a good variety of options, if needed. You will want your forms to balance ease of use with the power to be effective.

Access provides 14 different tools for creating forms. You can find these options in the Forms group on the Create tab. The Forms group contains four of the most common form tools (Form, Form Design, Blank Form, and Form Wizard), a list of Navigation forms, and More Forms. The Navigation list provides six templates to create a user interface for a database; the More Forms list provides four additional form tools (Multiple Items, Datasheet, Split Form, and Modal Dialog). Select a table or query in the Navigation Pane, click one of the tools, and Access will create a form based on the selected table or query. The most common of these tools, the ***Form tool***, is used to create data entry forms for customers, employees, products, and other types of tables. You can also find Application Parts, which are predefined building blocks that you can use to build database objects, in the Templates group on the Create tab.

A list of the Form tools available in Access is found in Table 4.1. Several of the tools will be covered in this chapter. Some tools will not be covered in detail, because they are not commonly used or because they are beyond the scope of this chapter (e.g., Form Design, Blank Form, Navigation forms, and Modal Dialog Form). Use Microsoft Access Help to find more information about Form tools not covered in this chapter.

TABLE 4.1 Form Tools in Access	
Form Tool	**Use**
Form	Creates a form with a stacked layout that displays all of the fields in the record source.
Form Design	Creates a new blank form in Design view.
Blank Form	Creates a new blank form in Layout view.
Form Wizard	Creates a custom form based on your answers to a series of step-by-step questions.
Navigation	Creates user-interface forms that can also be used on the Internet. Six different Navigation form layouts are available from the list.
Split Form	Creates a two-part form with a stacked layout in one section and a tabular layout in the other.
Multiple Items	Creates a tabular layout form that includes all of the fields from the record source.
Datasheet	Creates a form that resembles the datasheet of a table or query.
Modal Dialog	Creates a custom dialog box that requires user input that is needed for a database object.

TIP: USABILITY TESTING

After a database object (such as a form) is finalized, it should be tested by both the database designer and the end users. The designer should be certain that the form meets any requirements the users have given him or her. The designer should also browse through the records to make sure the values in all records (and not just the first record) display correctly. After testing is completed by both designer and end users, the form should be modified and tested again before it is deployed with the database.

Ideally, a form should simplify data entry. Creating a form is a collaborative process between the database designer and the end users. This process continues throughout the life of the form, because the data needs of an organization may change over time. Forms designed long ago to collect data for a new customer account may not include an email or a website field; both the customer table and its associated form would have to be modified to include these fields. The designer needs to strike a balance between collecting the data required for use by the database and cluttering the form with extraneous fields. The database users generally offer good opinions about which fields should be on a form and how the form should behave. If you listen to their suggestions, your forms will function more effectively, the users' work will be easier, and the data will contain fewer data-entry errors.

After discussing the form with the users, it will help you to create the form in Access if you sketch the form first. After sketching the form, you will have a better idea of which form tool to use to create the form. After the form is created, use the sketch to determine which fields are required and what the order of the fields should be.

Identify a Record Source

Before you create a form, you must identify the record source. A ***record source*** (or data source) is the table or query that supplies the records for a form or report. Use a table if you want to include all the records from a single table. Create a query as the record source first if you need to filter the records in the source table, combine records from two or more related tables, or if you do not want to display all fields from the table(s) on your form. For example, if a sales rep wants to create a form that displays customers from a single state only—where his customers reside—he or she should base the form on a query.

Use the Form Tool

As noted earlier, the Form tool is the most common tool for creating forms. A usable form can be created with a single click.

To use the Form tool, complete the following steps:

1. Select a table or query in the Navigation Pane.
2. Click Form in the Forms group on the Create tab.

Based on the table or query selected, Access automatically creates a new form. You may need to modify the form slightly, but you can create a stacked layout form with just one click. A ***stacked layout*** displays fields in a vertical column for one record at a time, as shown in Figure 4.2. The other type of layout you can use is a ***tabular layout***, which displays data horizontally across the page.

Products

Products

Product ID	P0001
Product Name	Coffee - Colombian Supreme
Description	24/Case, Pre-Ground 1.75 Oz Bags
Cost	$18.40
Markup Percent	50.00%
Refrigeration Needed	☐
Brand	Discount
Year Introduced	2018

Access 2016, Windows 10, Microsoft Corporation

FIGURE 4.2 Form with a Stacked Layout

Understand Controls

Controls are the text boxes, buttons, labels, and other tools you use to add, edit, and display the data in a form or report. Notice in Figure 4.3 that each field has a label on the left and a text box on the right, both of which are referred to as controls. The form controls that display values are generally text box controls, and the boxes describing those values are label controls. In Figure 4.3, Product ID, Product Name, Description, etc. are label controls. The boxes containing the values for each field (P0001, Coffee–Colombian Supreme, etc.) are text box controls.

A ***layout control*** provides guides to help keep controls aligned horizontally and vertically and give your form a neat appearance, as shown in Figure 4.3.

There may be times when you will select controls in order to format, delete, or move them during your design process. To select an individual control, click the text box or the label as needed.

To select multiple controls to work with them simultaneously, complete one of the following steps:

- Click the first control, press and hold Ctrl, and then click the additional controls you want to include in the selection.
- Press Ctrl+A to select all of the controls on a form at one time.

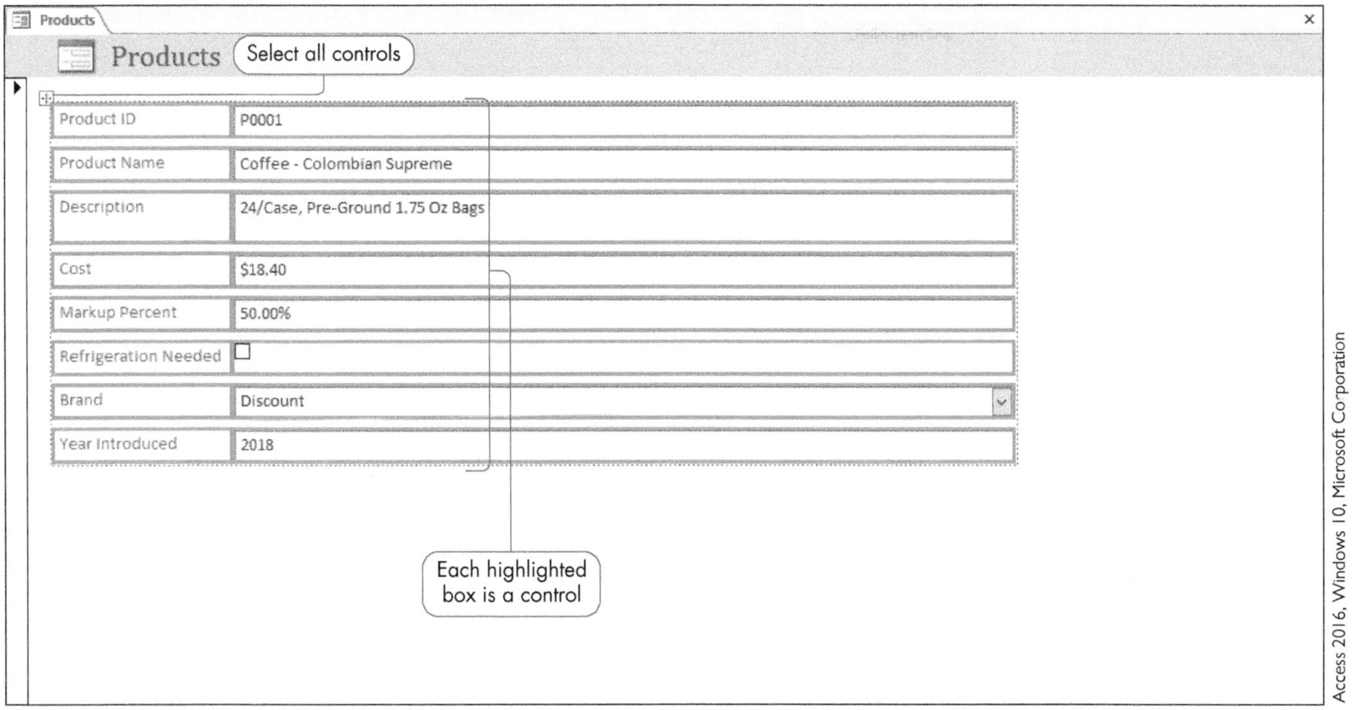

Access 2016, Windows 10, Microsoft Corporation

FIGURE 4.3 Form with Label and Text Box Controls

Work with Form Views

There are three different views of a form available. The first, ***Form view***, is the user interface primarily used for data entry and modification. You cannot make changes to the form layout or design in Form view. Figure 4.4 shows a form in Form view. Notice that forms can be designed to include time-saving features such as drop-down lists and check boxes.

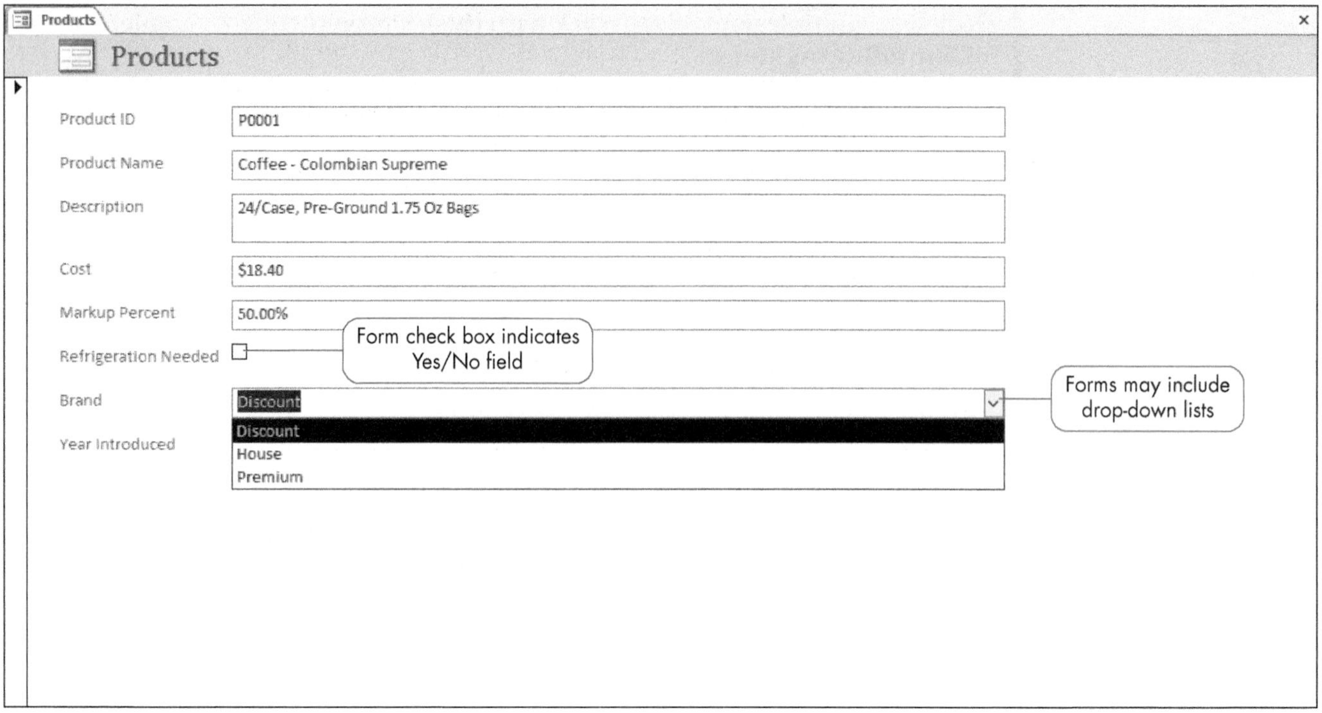

Products

Products

Product ID P0001

Product Name Coffee - Colombian Supreme

Description 24/Case, Pre-Ground 1.75 Oz Bags

Cost $18.40

Markup Percent 50.00%

Refrigeration Needed

Form check box indicates Yes/No field

Brand Discount

Forms may include drop-down lists

Year Introduced

Discount

House

Premium

Access 2016, Windows 10, Microsoft Corporation

FIGURE 4.4 Form in Form View

The second view, ***Layout view***, enables you to make changes to the layout while simultaneously viewing the data in the form. Layout view is useful for testing the functionality of the form and adjusting the sizes of controls (text boxes and labels) as needed while viewing the data. When you create a form using the Form tool, Access opens the form in Layout view, ready for this type of customization, as shown in Figure 4.5.

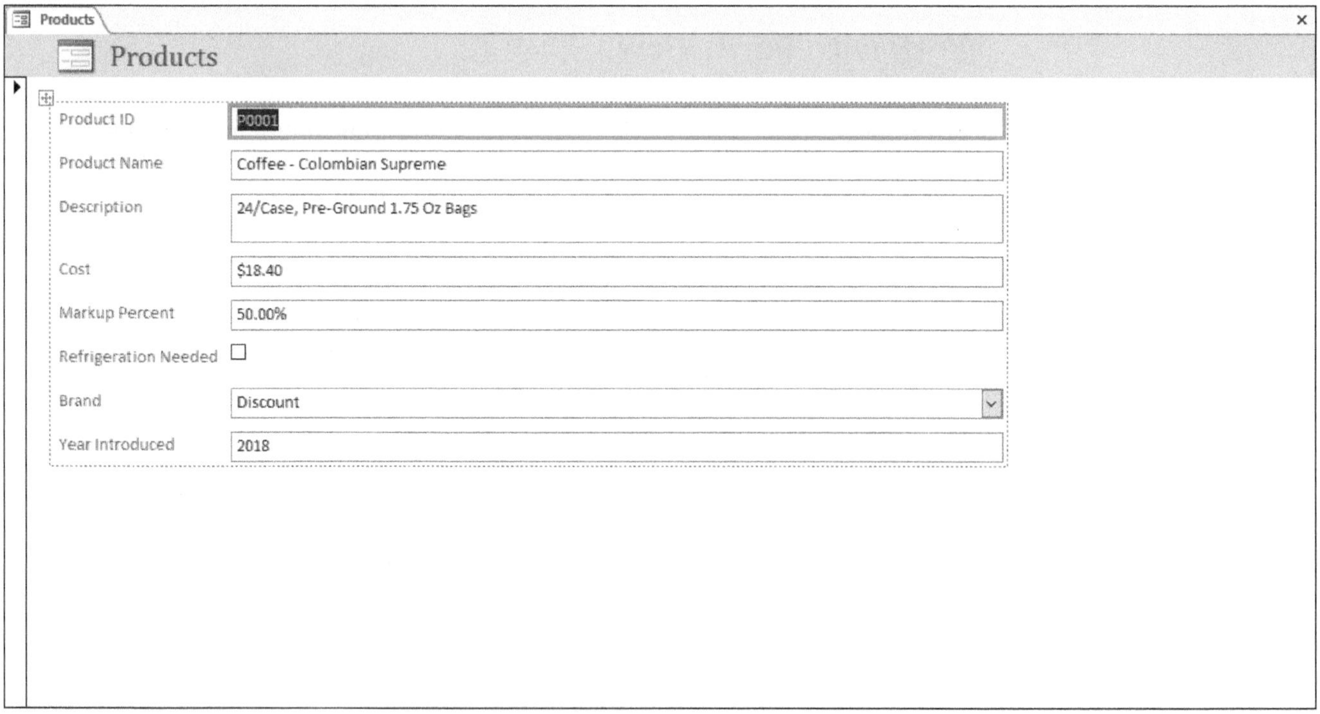

Products

Products

Product ID P0001

Product Name Coffee - Colombian Supreme

Description 24/Case, Pre-Ground 1.75 Oz Bags

Cost $18.40

Markup Percent 50.00%

Refrigeration Needed

Brand Discount

Year Introduced 2018

Access 2016, Windows 10, Microsoft Corporation

FIGURE 4.5 Form in Layout View

The third view, ***Design view***, enables you to change advanced design settings that are not available in Layout view, such as removing a layout control, and gives you even more control over form design. Many forms can be made by toggling back and forth between Layout view for modifications and Form view for usability testing; however, Design view offers possibilities for more advanced adjustments. Figure 4.6 shows a form in Design view. Form views will be described in more detail later in this chapter.

To switch between the Form views, with the form open, click the View arrow in the Views group on the Home tab, and then select Form View, Layout View, or Design View. Alternatively, click the View buttons on the status bar at the bottom of the Access window, or right-click the form's window tab and select an option from the shortcut menu.

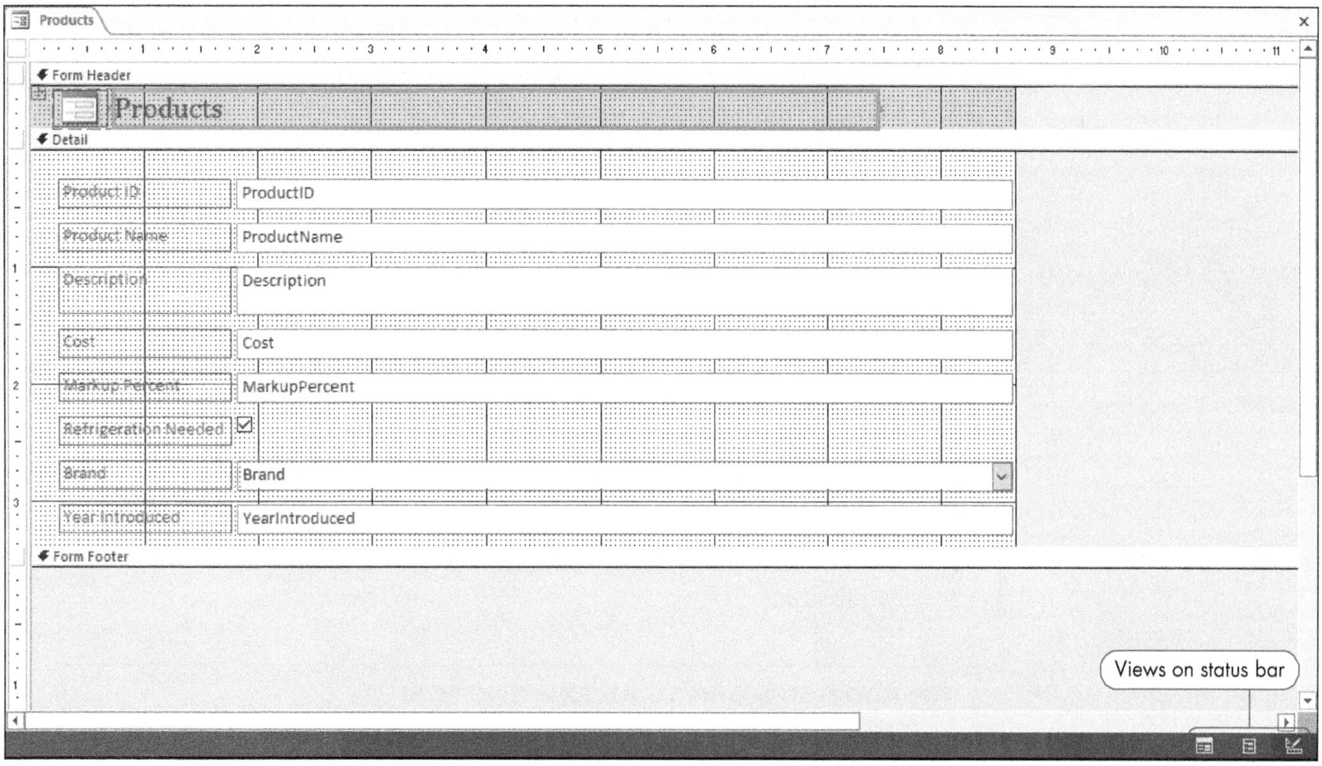

Access 2016, Windows 10, Microsoft Corporation

FIGURE 4.6 Form in Design View

Work with a Subform

When you use the Form tool to create a form, Access analyzes the table relationships in the database. If the table that the main form is based upon is related to another table, Access automatically adds a subform to the main form. The subform displays records in the related table, generally laid out in a datasheet format. For example, assume you have sales representatives stored in a Sales Reps table and related customer information stored in a Customers table. In this example, if you create a new form based on the Sales Reps table using the Form tool, Access will add a Customers subform to the bottom of the main form, displaying all customers assigned to each sales representative (see Figure 4.7). At times, you may want the subform as part of your form; at other times, you may want to remove it if it is not relevant to the requirements of the form design.

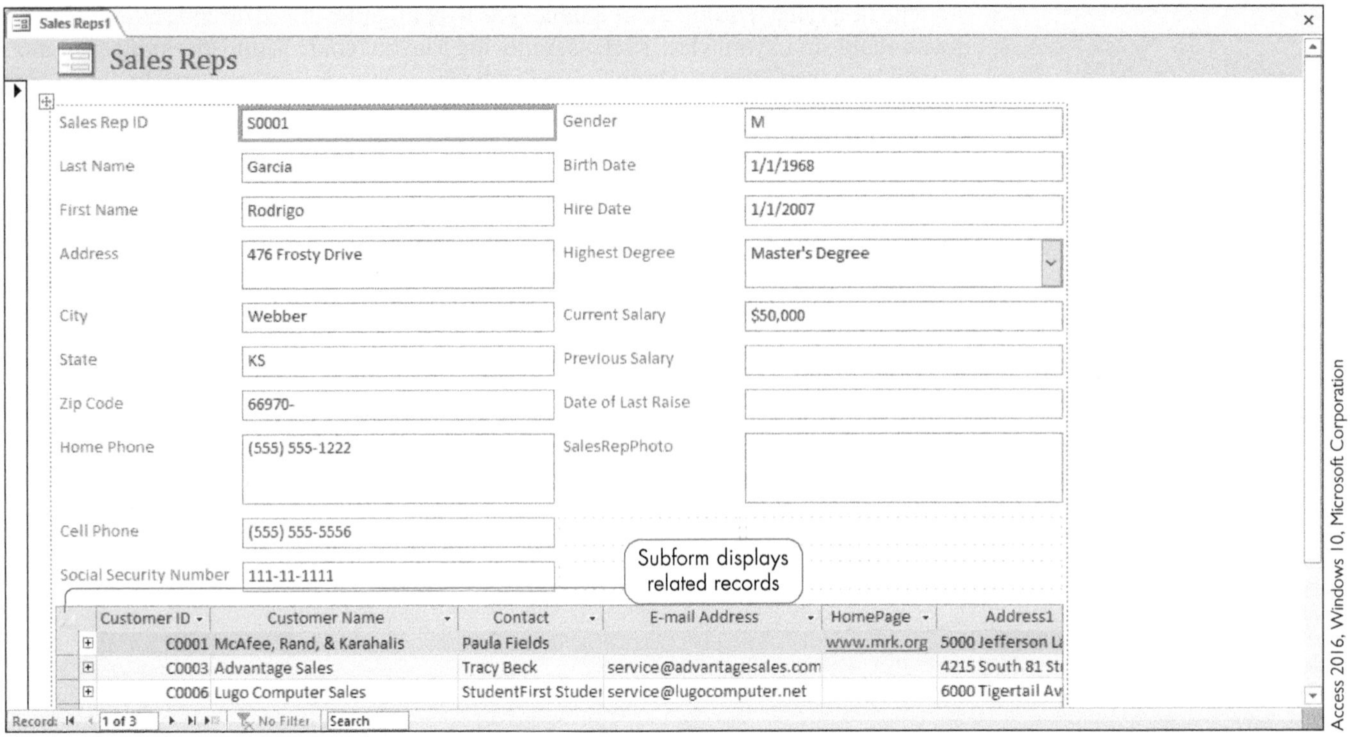

FIGURE 4.7 Sales Reps Form with Related Customers Subform

Access 2016, Windows 10, Microsoft Corporation

To remove a subform from a form, complete the following steps:

1. Click the View arrow in the Views group on the Home tab, and select Design View.
2. Click anywhere in the subform control and press Delete.
3. Save the form.

TIP: ADD A SUBFORM TO AN EXISTING FORM

It is possible to add a subform to an existing form by using the SubForm Wizard. In Design view of the form, in the Controls group, click the Subform/Subreport tool, and then click in the form where you want the subform to display. The wizard will prompt you for the record source and through the steps for creating the subform.

Create a Split Form

A ***split form*** combines two views of the same record source—by default; the top section is displayed in a stacked layout (Form view) and the bottom section is displayed in a tabular layout (Datasheet view). If you select a record in the top section of the form, the same record will be selected in the bottom section of the form and vice versa. For example, if you create a split form based on an Orders table, you can select an Order in the bottom (datasheet) section and then enter or edit the order's information in the top (Form view) section (see Figure 4.8). This gives you the option to navigate between orders more quickly in the bottom section, and then when you locate the one you need, you can move to the top section to work with the record in Form view; however, you can add, edit, or delete records in either section. The splitter bar divides the form into two halves. You can adjust the splitter bar up or down (unless this option is disabled).

To create a split form, complete the following steps:

1. Select a table or query in the Navigation Pane.
2. Click More Forms, and click Split Form in the Forms group on the Create tab.

Access 2016, Windows 10, Microsoft Corporation

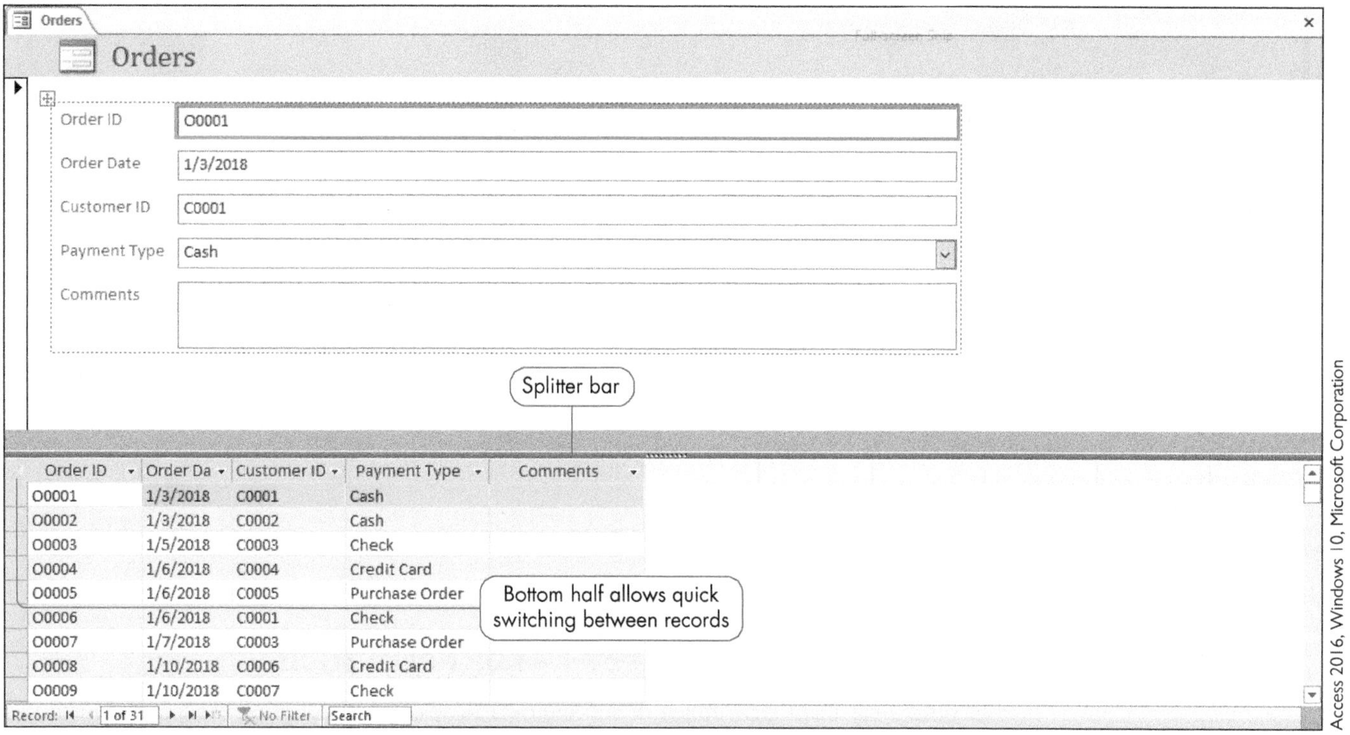

FIGURE 4.8 Split Form

Create a Multiple Items Form

A ***multiple items form*** displays multiple records in a tabular layout similar to a table's Datasheet view. However, a multiple items form provides you with more customization options than a datasheet, such as the ability to add graphical elements, buttons, and other controls. Figure 4.9 shows a multiple items form created from the Sales Rep table.

To create a multiple items form, complete the following steps:

1. Select a table or query in the Navigation Pane.
2. Click More Forms, and click Multiple Items in the Forms group on the Create tab.

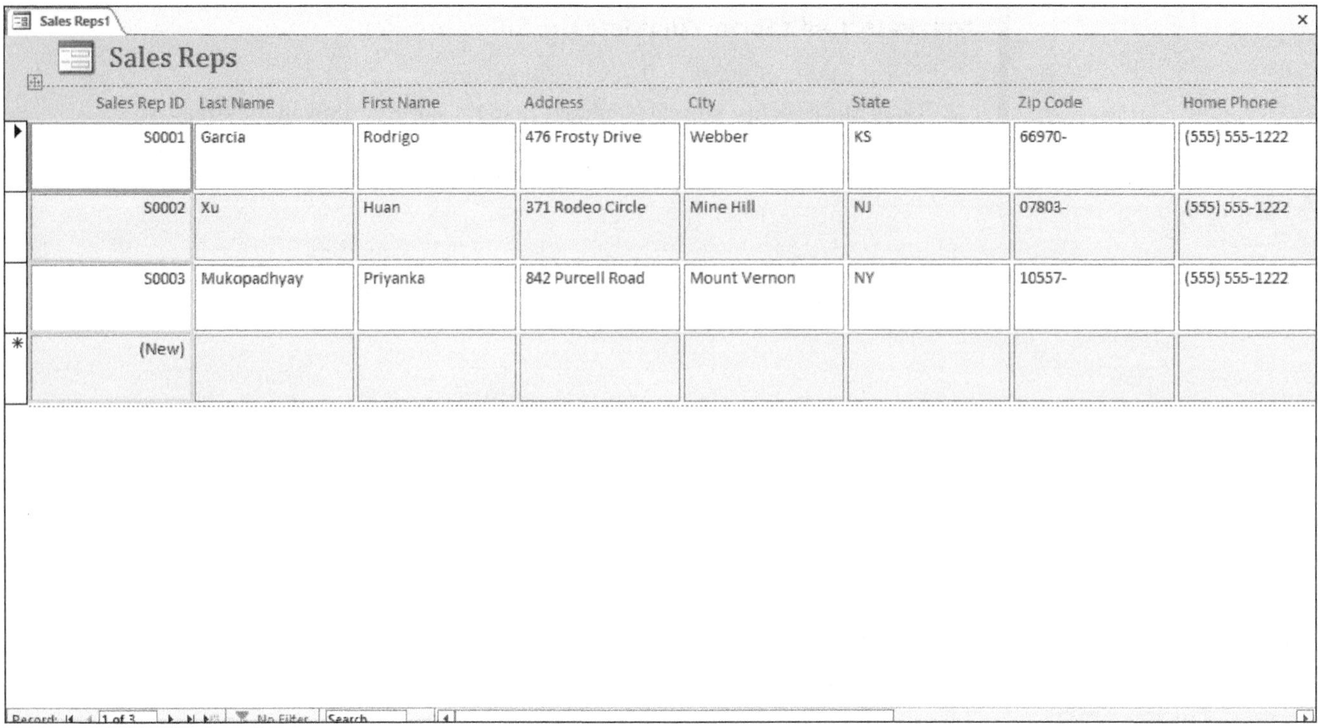

Sales Reps1

Sales Reps

Sales Rep ID	Last Name	First Name	Address	City	State	Zip Code	Home Phone
S0001	Garcia	Rodrigo	476 Frosty Drive	Webber	KS	66970-	(555) 555-1222
S0002	Xu	Huan	371 Rodeo Circle	Mine Hill	NJ	07803-	(555) 555-1222
S0003	Mukopadhyay	Priyanka	842 Purcell Road	Mount Vernon	NY	10557-	(555) 555-1222
(New)							

Record: 1 of 3 No Filter Search

FIGURE 4.9 Multiple Items Form

Create Forms Using the Other Form Tools

A datasheet form is a replica of a table or query's Datasheet view except that it allows form properties to be set to control the behavior of the form. For example, you can create a datasheet form to display data in a table-like format but change the form's property so as not to allow a record to be deleted. This protects the data from accidental deletions while still providing users with the familiar Datasheet view.

TIP: FORM PROPERTIES

A form's Property Sheet enables you to control the behavior and formatting of controls in your forms. To access the Property Sheet, from Layout view or Design view, click Property Sheet in the Tools group on the Design tab. At the top of the Property Sheet, use the list arrow to select a control; you will see multiple tabs containing many individual attributes of the selected control that you can change. For example, the Format tab contains options for changing the styling of a control.

The Form Design tool and the Blank Form tools can be used to create forms manually from scratch in Design view or Layout view, respectively. Use these form types if you want to have complete control over your form's design. In either case, after opening a completely blank form, click Add Existing Fields in the Tools group on the Design tab, and then add the necessary fields by dragging and dropping them onto the blank form from the Field List pane.

The Navigation commands in the Forms group enable you to create user interfaces that have the look and feel of Web-based forms and enable users to open and close the objects of a database. For example, you can create a form that enables users to click buttons for the various forms, reports, and other objects that you want them to view in the database. This is an excellent way to simplify the database navigation for data-entry personnel who may not be that familiar with navigating in Access. These forms are also useful for setting up an Access database on the Internet.

The Modal Dialog Form tool can be used to create a dialog box. This feature is useful when you need to gather information from the user or provide information to the user, such as a message. Dialog boxes are common in all Microsoft Office applications.

TIP: PRINT WITH CAUTION!

You can print a form by clicking the Print option on the File tab. However, printing from a form should be handled with caution. Forms are not generally designed for printing, so you may end up with hundreds of pages of printouts. A form with a stacked layout and 1,000 records could print thousands of pages unless you select the Selected Record(s) option in the Print dialog box. The Selected Record(s) option, as shown in Figure 4.10, will only print the current record (or selected records).

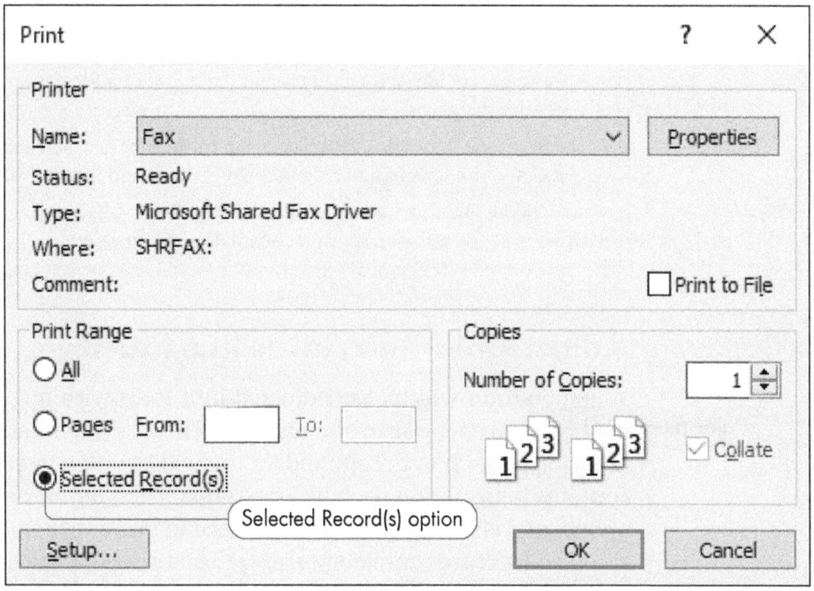

FIGURE 4.10 Print Selected Records Using a Form

Modifying Forms

As previously mentioned, Access provides different views for a form; most forms display Layout, Form, and Design views. As you work with the form tools to create and modify forms, you will need to switch between the three form views in Access. Much of your design work can be done in Layout view; sometimes, you will need to switch to Design view to use a more advanced feature, such as changing the order of the fields as you press Tab to move from one to the next, or to use an option that is otherwise unavailable. Users of the form will typically only work in Form view; there is little reason for a user to switch to Layout or Design view, and these views can be disabled by the database designer to protect the integrity of the form. Modifications to the form should ideally be done only by a designated designer.

Use Form View to Edit Data

STEP 2 Use Form view to add, edit, and delete data in a form; the layout and design of the form cannot be changed in this view. The Navigation bar at the bottom of the form provides buttons to move between records, and you can click the New (blank) record button to add a new record. You can move from one field to another field by pressing the Tab key or clicking the desired field with your mouse.

Use Layout View to Modify Form Design

Use Layout view to alter the form design while viewing the data. The data is not editable in this view. You use Layout view to add or delete fields in a form, change the order of fields, modify field or form properties (such as which views are available), change the control widths, and enhance a form by adding a theme or styling. Reviewing the data in

Layout view makes it easier to size controls, and to ensure that all data is visible in Form view. It is good practice to toggle back and forth between Layout view and Form view when making changes to the form's design.

> **TIP: USE THE FORM LAYOUT TOOLS TABS**
> Forms have a number of options that you can use in your design process. In Layout view, you have access to three contextual tabs on the Ribbon that provide a number of tools for modifying forms as follows:
>
> - Design tab: Use this tab to make changes to the design of the form, such as applying themes, inserting headers and footers, and additional controls.
> - Arrange tab: Use this tab to change the layout of a form, to move fields up or down, or to control margins.
> - Format tab: Use this tab to work with fonts, font size, and colors, to add or remove bolding, italics, or underlining, adjust text alignment, or add a background image.
>
> Similarly, in Design view, the Form Design Tools tabs are available (Design, Arrange, and Format) with many of the same options you will find in Layout view.

Adjust Column Widths in a Form

When column widths are adjusted in a form with a stacked layout, all field sizes will increase and decrease in size together. Therefore, it is best to make sure that the columns are wide enough to accommodate the widest value in each field. For example, if a form contains information such as a customer's first name, last name, address, city, state, ZIP, phone, and email address, you will need to make sure the longest address and the longest email address are completely visible (because those fields are likely to contain the longest data values).

To increase or decrease column widths in a form with a stacked layout, complete the following steps:

1. Display the form in (Stacked) Layout view, and click the text box control of the first field to select it.
2. Point to the right border of the control until the pointer turns into a double-headed arrow. Drag the right edge of the control to the left or right until you arrive at the desired width.

You will notice that all field sizes change as you change the width of the first field. All fields that are included in the layout will have a standard width. If you want to resize one specific field, you will remove that field from the layout control. Select the field and the label to be removed, right-click, and then from the shortcut menu, click Layout, and select Remove Layout. If you remove a field from the layout control, it stays on the form but can be moved and resized more freely.

Add and Delete Form Fields

There will be instances when you will want to add or delete form fields. At times, new fields may be added to tables and then need to be incorporated into forms. At other times, you may decide that while a field is present in a table, it is not necessary to display it to users in a form.

To add a field to a form, complete the following steps:

1. Display the form in (Stacked) Layout view, and click Add Existing Fields in the Tools group on the Design tab.
   A Field List pane displays at the right of the form. For a single-table form, you will see a list of fields from the table (record source). For a multiple-table form, click the plus sign (+) to the left of the appropriate table to expand it, and locate the desired field(s).
2. Click and drag the desired field to the precise location on the form, using the shaded line as a guide for positioning the new field. Alternatively, you can double-click a field to add it to the form; the field will be added below the selected field. The other fields will automatically adjust to make room for the new field, as shown in Figure 4.11.

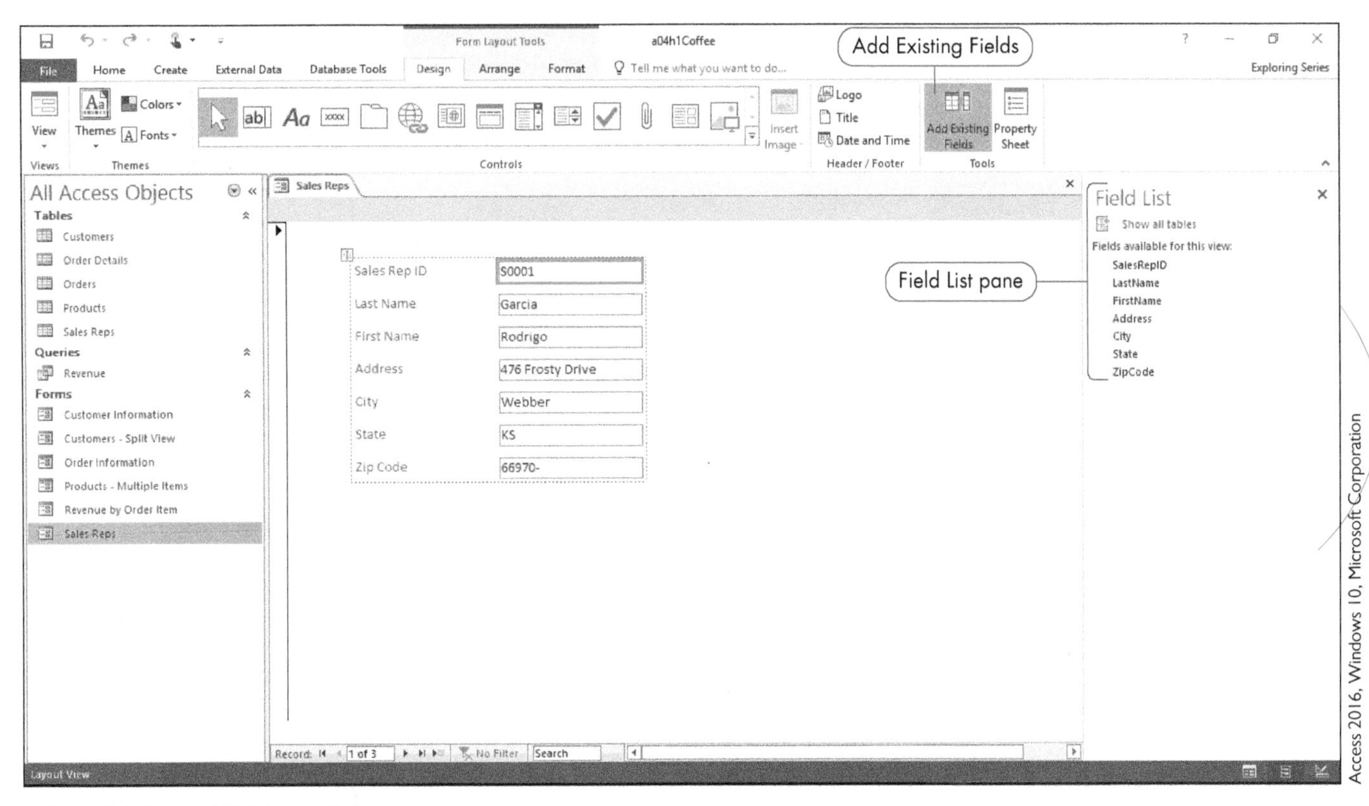

FIGURE 4.11 Add Fields to a Form

To delete a field from a form, complete the following steps:

1. Display the form in (Stacked) Layout view, and click the text box control of the field to be deleted (note the shaded border around the control).
2. Click Select Row in the Rows & Columns group on the Arrange tab in order to select the text box and its associated label. Alternatively, click the text box control, press and hold Ctrl, and then click the associated label control to select them both.
3. Press Delete.

The other fields will automatically adjust to close the gap around the deleted field.

Add a Theme to a Form

You can apply a theme to a form in order to give the form a more professional appearance. A ***theme*** is a defined set of colors, fonts, and graphics that can be applied to forms (or reports). In Layout or Design view, click Themes in the Themes group on the Design tab, point to a theme to see its name in the ScreenTip and a Live Preview of the theme in the form, and then click to select it. By default, the theme will be applied to all objects in your database.

Right-click a theme in the gallery to apply it to the current form only or to all the forms in your database that share a common theme. You can create customized themes and save them on your system so that they can be used again. Apply your custom settings, and then click the Save Current Theme command, as shown in Figure 4.12.

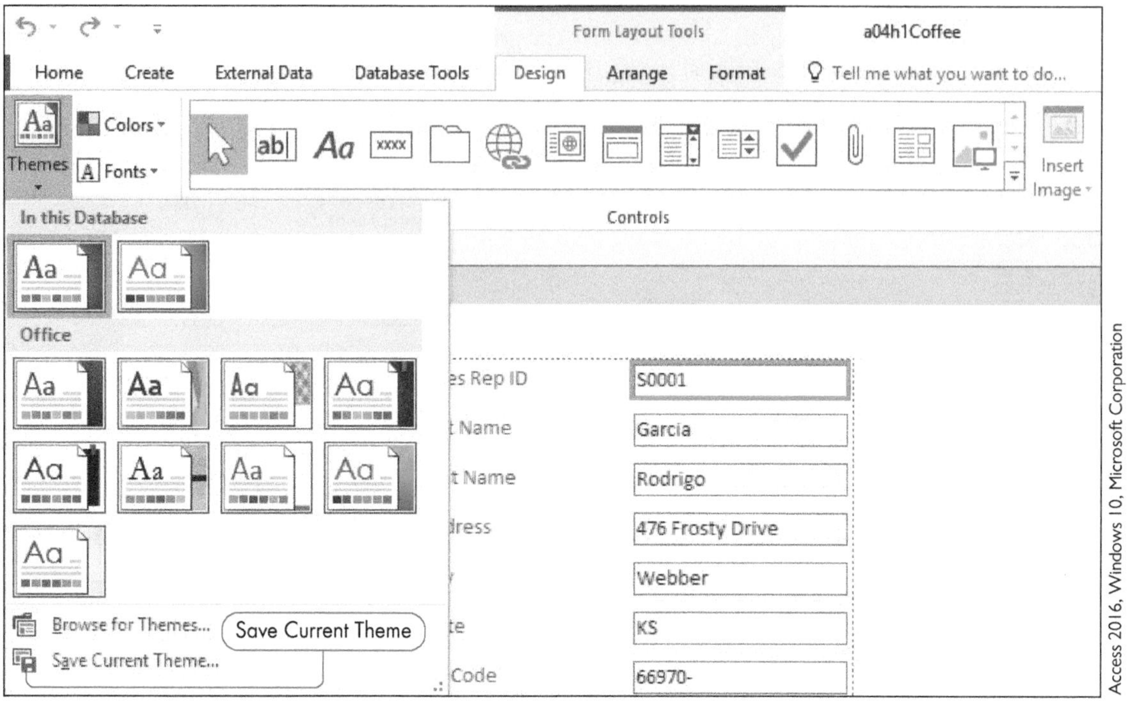

Access 2016, Windows 10, Microsoft Corporation

FIGURE 4.12 Add a Theme to a Form

Modify Form Controls

When you view a form in Layout view, the Form Layout Tools tab displays the Design, Arrange, and Format tabs. The Format tab contains a series of commands that enable you to change the font, display, and alignment of the controls on a form. At times, you may want to change the formatting of one or more controls. For example, if you have a form that shows the information about the sale of vehicles, you might want to emphasize the net profit of each transaction by changing the font or background color of the control.

From the Form Layout Tools Format tab, you can change a number of control attributes. Table 4.2 illustrates some of commands you would likely use.

TABLE 4.2 Common Formats for Form Controls

Font size	Click the Font Size arrow in the Font group.
Font emphasis	Click Bold, Italic, or Underline in the Font group.
Alignment	Click Align Left, Center, or Align Right in the Font group.
Background color	Click the Background Color arrow in the Font group.
Font color	Click the Font Color arrow in the Font group.
Number format	Use the tools in the Number group to select number formats such as Currency, Percent, Comma formatting, or to increase or decrease decimal places.

Pearson Education, Inc.

> **TIP: STYLING A FORM**
>
> Modifying the font sizes, changing the font colors, and adding background colors to controls can enhance a form and make it more user-friendly. Select familiar fonts, such as Arial or Calibri, for both the form label and text box controls. Apply bold to the labels in order to help the user distinguish labels from the text boxes. Consider right-aligning the labels and left-aligning the text box controls to reduce distance between the labels and fields, as illustrated in Figure 4.13. You may also want to separate the primary key field from the rest of the form by providing a sufficient visual boundary. One note of caution: using too many fonts, font sizes, colors, and other effects can detract from your design.

Products

Background color and size changed for primary key

Product ID P0001

Product Name Coffee - Colombian Supreme

Description 24/Case, Pre-Ground 1.75 Oz Bags

Cost $18.40 Markup Percent 50.00% Refrigeration Needed

Brand Discount Year Introduced 2018

Bright color draws attention to a field

Color changes to borders adds contrasts

Record: 1 of 25 No Filter Search

FIGURE 4.13 A Well-Designed Form with Styling

Working with a Form Layout

When you use one of the form tools to create a new form, Access adds a layout control to help align the fields. The layout control helps keep controls aligned in order to give your form a neat appearance. The layout control provides structure for the fields, but is somewhat restrictive. If you want to have more control over the location of your fields, you can remove the layout control and position the controls manually on the form.

To remove a control from a layout and reposition it, complete the following steps:

1. Select the field and the label to be removed, right-click, and from the shortcut menu, point to Layout and then select Remove Layout.
2. Drag and drop the control(s) as desired to a different location on the form.

Modify a Form Layout

You can use the tools on the Arrange tab to change the layout of a form, to move fields up and down, and to control margins. The Arrange tab displays in both Layout view and Design view.

The Table group of the Arrange tab contains commands that enable you to add gridlines to a form's layout, change the layout from stacked to tabular (and vice versa), or remove the layout (the Remove Layout command is available only in Design view).

To apply or change the layout of a form, complete the following steps:

1. Open the form in Layout or Design view.
2. Select multiple controls by clicking the first control, pressing and holding Ctrl, and then clicking the additional controls you want to include in the layout. To select all of the controls on a form, press Ctrl+A. If the controls already have a layout applied, click any control that is part of the layout, and click Select Layout in the Rows & Columns group on the Arrange tab.
3. Click Tabular or Stacked in the Table group on the Arrange tab.

To remove a form layout control, complete the following steps:

1. Switch to Design view (the Remove Layout option on the Ribbon is only available in Design view), and click any one of the controls that is currently part of the layout.
2. Click Select Layout in the Rows & Columns group on the Arrange tab.
3. Click Remove Layout in the Table group.
4. Switch to Layout view. Drag and drop the control(s) as desired to a different location on the form.

The Rows & Columns group also contains commands that enable you to insert rows and columns in a form's layout. In a form with a stacked layout, you may want to separate some controls from the rest of the fields, or create some empty space so that fields can be added or repositioned. For example, you can select a control (or multiple controls) and click Insert Below. This will create an empty row (or space) below the selected controls. This group also contains the Select Layout, Select Column, and Select Row commands, which you can use to select the entire layout, or a single column or row in a layout. In Figure 4.14, three empty rows have been inserted above the Cost field.

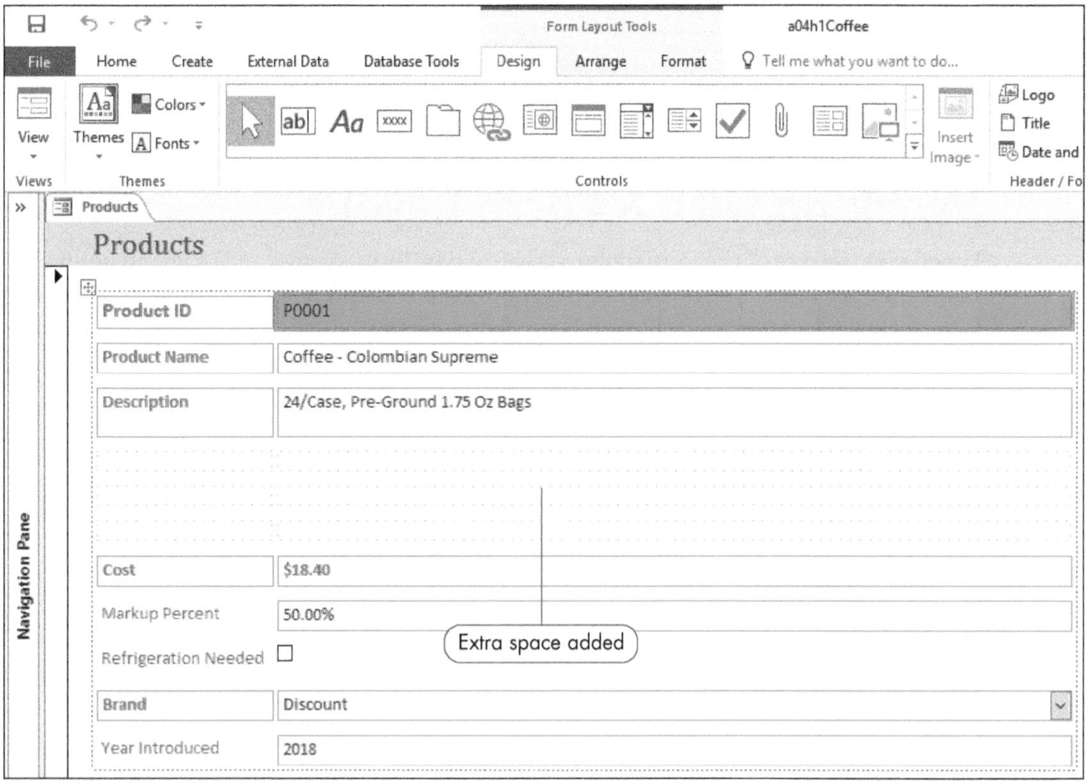

Access 2016, Windows 10, Microsoft Corporation

FIGURE 4.14 Rows Inserted in a Form Layout

TIP: APPLY A BACKGROUND IMAGE TO A FORM

To apply a background image to a form, open the form in Layout or Design view, and then click Background Image in the Background group on the Format tab. Next, click Browse to locate the image you want to apply to the form. Once the image has been applied to the form, you can change the properties of the image so that the image displays correctly. You can use the same tecÚique to add a background image to a report.

Sorting Records in a Form

When a form is created using a Form tool, the sort order of the records in the form is initially dependent on the sort order of the record source—the underlying table or query. Tables are usually sorted by the primary key, whereas queries are generally sorted in a variety of ways. No matter how the records are initially sorted, you can modify the sort order in a form. Adding and removing sorts are shown in Figure 4.15.

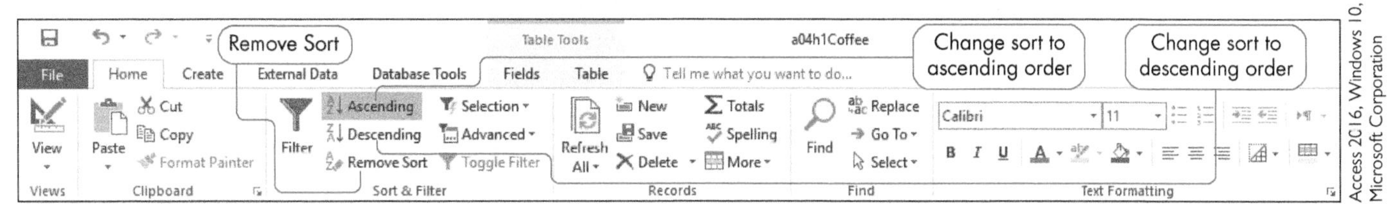

FIGURE 4.15 Adding and Removing Sort Order

Sort by a Single Field

You can easily sort on a single field, in ascending or descending order. The sort order in a form can be different from the sort order of an underlying table or query.

To sort by a single field, complete the following steps:

1. Open the form in Form view, and select the field by which you want to sort.
2. Click Ascending or Descending in the Sort & Filter group on the Home tab.

If you want to sort on multiple fields, you can create a query with a more advanced sort order, and then base the form on the query. Open the query in Design view, add the sort settings you want, save the query, and then use the query as the record source of the form. To remove the sort order in a form, open the form in Form view, then click Remove Sort in the Sort & Filter group on the Home tab.

Quick Concepts

1. How does a form simplify data entry (when compared to entering data into a table)? *p. 864*
2. What is the record source of a form? *p. 865*
3. What is the advantage of creating a form with a subform? *p. 869*
4. Why is using a layout control to keep your form fields in a neat arrangement sometimes a disadvantage? *p. 866*

Hands-On Exercises

Watch the Video for this Hands-On Exercise!

MyITLab®
HOE1 Training

Skills covered: Create a Form Using the Form Tool • Create a Split Form • Create a Multiple Items Form • Edit Data in Form View • Delete a Field • Add a Field • Format Controls • Add a Theme • Modify a Form Layout • Sort Records in a Form

1 Form Basics

After talking with Ryung about her data-entry needs, you decide to create several sample forms using different formats. You will show each form to Ryung to get feedback and see if she has any preferences.

STEP 1 » CREATE FORMS USING FORM TOOLS

You will create a number of forms using different layouts. Refer to Figure 4.16 as you complete Step 1.

Customer Information
Step e: Title changed
Customer Information

Customer ID	C0001
Customer Name	McAfee, Rand, & Karahalis
Contact	Paula Fields
E-mail Address	
HomePage	www.mrk.org
Address1	5000 Jefferson Lane
Address2	Suite 2000
City	Flatgap
State	KY
Zip Code	41219-
Phone	(555) 375-6442
Fax	(555) 375-6443
Service Start Date	1/3/2012
Credit Rating	B
Sales Rep ID	S001

Step c: Controls resized
Step b: Orders subform present

Order ID	Order Da	Payment Type	Comments
O0001	1/3/2018	Cash	
O0006	1/6/2018	Check	

Record: 1 of 14 No Filter Search

FIGURE 4.16 Customer Information Form

a. Open *a04h1Coffee* and save it as **a04h1Coffee_LastFirst.**

> **TROUBLESHOOTING:** Throughout the remainder of this chapter and textbook, click Enable Content whenever you are working with the student data files.

> **TROUBLESHOOTING:** If you make any major mistakes in this exercise, you can close the file, open *a04h1Coffee* again, and then start this exercise over.

b. Click the **Customers table** in the Navigation Pane to select the table but not to open it. Click the **Create tab**, and then click **Form** in the Forms group.

Access creates a new form with two record sources—Customers (with stacked layout, on top) and Orders (with datasheet layout, below). Access detected a one-to-many relationship between the Customers and Orders tables, and so it created a main form with its associated subform below it. The form opens in Layout view.

c. Ensure that the top text box containing *C0001* is selected. The text box is outlined with a shaded border. Move the pointer to the right edge of the shaded border until the pointer changes to a double-headed arrow. Drag the right edge to the left until the text box is approximately half of its original size.

All of the text boxes and the subform at the bottom adjust in size when you adjust the top text box. This is a characteristic of Layout view—enabling you to modify all controls at once.

> **TROUBLESHOOTING:** You may need to maximize the Access window or close the Navigation Pane if the right edge of the text box is not visible.

d. Ensure that the labels to the left of the text boxes display without being cut off. If they are cut off, adjust the size of the labels as you did in Step c.

e. Click **Save** on the Quick Access Toolbar, and then type **Customer Information** as the form name in the **Save As dialog box**. Click **OK**.

f. Click the **Customers title** at the top of the form to select it, click the title again, and then change the title to **Customer Information**. Press **Enter** to accept the change. Your form should now look like Figure 4.16. Save and close the form.

> **TROUBLESHOOTING:** If you make a mistake that you cannot easily recover from, consider deleting the form and creating it again. With the form closed, right-click the form name in the Navigation Pane, and from the shortcut menu, select Delete.

g. Verify that the Customers table is selected in the Navigation Pane. Click the **Create tab**, click **More Forms** in the Forms group, and then select **Split Form**.

Access creates a new form with a split view, one view in stacked layout and one view laid out like a datasheet.

h. Scroll down and click anywhere in the *Coulter Office Supplies* customer record in the bottom pane (datasheet) of the form (record 14).

The top pane shows all the information for this customer in a stacked layout view.

i. Click the **Customers title** at the top of the form to select it, click **Customers** again, and then change the title to **Customers - Split View**. Press **Enter** to accept the change.

j. Click **Save** on the Quick Access Toolbar and type **Customers - Split View** in the Form Name box Click **OK**. Close the form.

k. Click the **Products table** in the Navigation Pane. Click the **Create tab**, click **More Forms** in the Forms group, and then select **Multiple Items**.

Access creates a new multiple-item form based on the Products table. The form resembles a table's Datasheet view.

l. Click the **Products title** at the top of the form to select it, click **Products** again, and then change the title to **Products - Multiple Items**. Press **Enter** to accept the change.

m. Save the form as **Products - Multiple Items** and close the form.

n. Click the **Orders table** in the Navigation Pane. Click **Form** in the Forms group on the Create tab.

A form with a subform showing each line of the order is created.

o. Click the **Home tab**. Click the **View arrow** in the Views group, and select **Design View**. Click anywhere inside the subform and press **Delete**.

The subform is removed.

p. Switch to Form view to observe the change. Save the form as **Order Information**. Close all open objects.

STEP 2 » USE FORM VIEW TO EDIT DATA

Now that you have created several forms, you will show Ryung how to test the forms for usability Refer to Figure 4.17 as you complete Step 2.

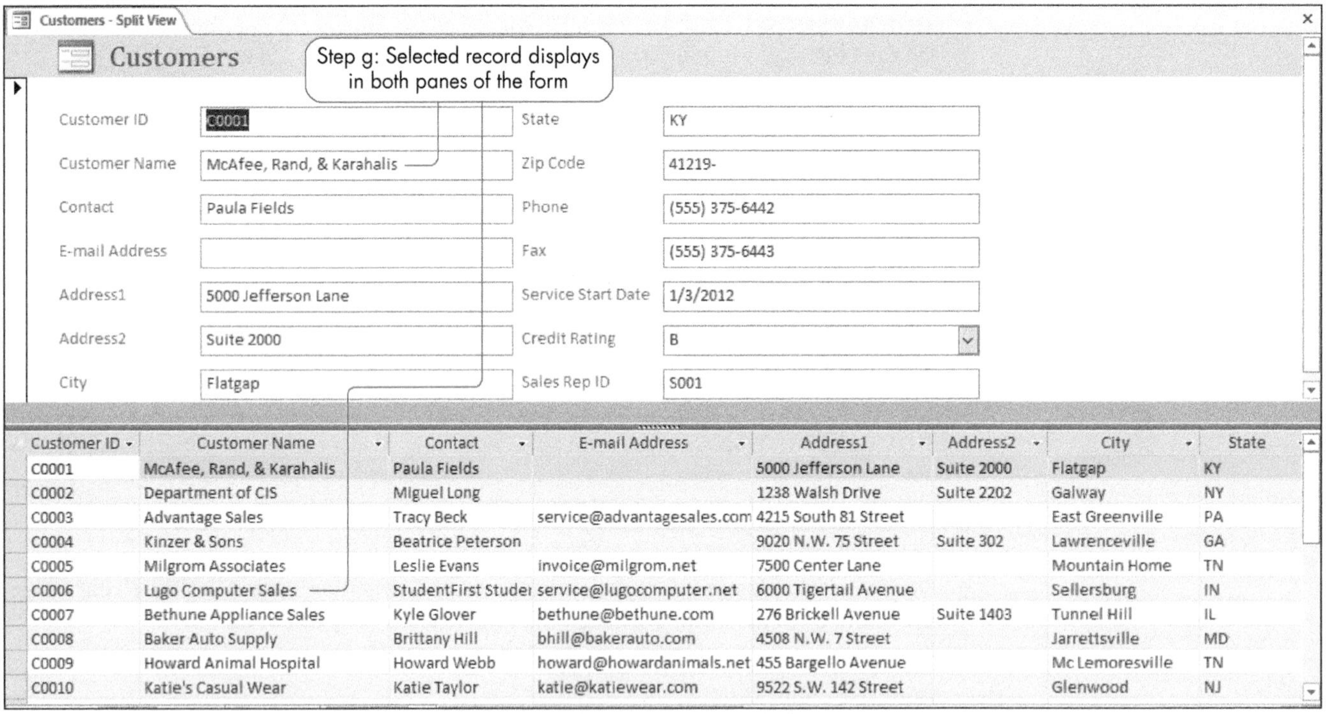

Customer ID	Customer Name	Contact	E-mail Address	Address1	Address2	City	State
C0001	McAfee, Rand, & Karahalis	Paula Fields		5000 Jefferson Lane	Suite 2000	Flatgap	KY
C0002	Department of CIS	Miguel Long		1238 Walsh Drive	Suite 2202	Galway	NY
C0003	Advantage Sales	Tracy Beck	service@advantagesales.com	4215 South 81 Street		East Greenville	PA
C0004	Kinzer & Sons	Beatrice Peterson		9020 N.W. 75 Street	Suite 302	Lawrenceville	GA
C0005	Milgrom Associates	Leslie Evans	invoice@milgrom.net	7500 Center Lane		Mountain Home	TN
C0006	Lugo Computer Sales	StudentFirst Studer	service@lugocomputer.net	6000 Tigertail Avenue		Sellersburg	IN
C0007	Bethune Appliance Sales	Kyle Glover	bethune@bethune.com	276 Brickell Avenue	Suite 1403	Tunnel Hill	IL
C0008	Baker Auto Supply	Brittany Hill	bhill@bakerauto.com	4508 N.W. 7 Street		Jarrettsville	MD
C0009	Howard Animal Hospital	Howard Webb	howard@howardanimals.net	455 Bargello Avenue		Mc Lemoresville	TN
C0010	Katie's Casual Wear	Katie Taylor	katie@katiewear.com	9522 S.W. 142 Street		Glenwood	NJ

FIGURE 4.17

a. Right-click the **Customer Information form** in the Navigation Pane, and from the shortcut menu, select **Open**. Advance to the sixth customer, *Lugo Computer Sales*, using **Next record** on the Navigation bar at the bottom of the form.

> **TROUBLESHOOTING:** Two Navigation bars exist, the inside one for the subform and the bottom-most one for the main form. Make sure you use the bottom-most one that displays the record count of 14.

b. Double-click the **Customers table** in the Navigation Pane.

Two tabs now display in the main window. You will compare the table data and the form data while you make changes to both.

c. Verify that the sixth record of the Customers table is *Lugo Computer Sales*, which corresponds to the sixth record in the Customer Information form. Click the tabs to switch between the table and the form.

d. Click the **Customer Information tab** and replace *Adam Sanchez*, the contact for Lugo Computer Sales, with your name. Advance to the next record to save the changes. Click the **Customers tab** to see that the contact name changed in the table as well.

Changes to the Contact field and the other fields in the Customer Information form automatically change the data in the underlying table. Likewise, if you change data in the table, it will update automatically in the form.

TROUBLESHOOTING: If the change from *Adam Sanchez* to your name does not display in the Customers table, check the Customer Information form to see if the pencil displays in the left margin of the record. If it does, save the record by advancing to the next customer in the form and recheck to see if the name has changed in the underlying table.

e. Close the Customer Information form and the Customers table.

f. Open the Customers – Split View form. In the bottom pane of the split form, click **Lugo Computer Sales**, the sixth record. Notice that the top pane now displays the information for Lugo Computer Sales in a stacked layout. Notice also that there is an error in the email address—*service* is misspelled. In the top pane of the form, change the email address to **service@lugocomputer.net**.

g. Click another record in the bottom pane and then click back on **Lugo Computer Sales**, as shown in Figure 4.17.

The pencil disappears from the record selector box and the changes are saved to the table.

STEP 3 » USE LAYOUT VIEW TO MODIFY A FORM DESIGN

You will make some changes to the layouts based on feedback Ryung gave you after seeing the forms in action. You will also add a missing field to the main table and then add it to the form. Refer to Figure 4.18 as you complete Step 3.

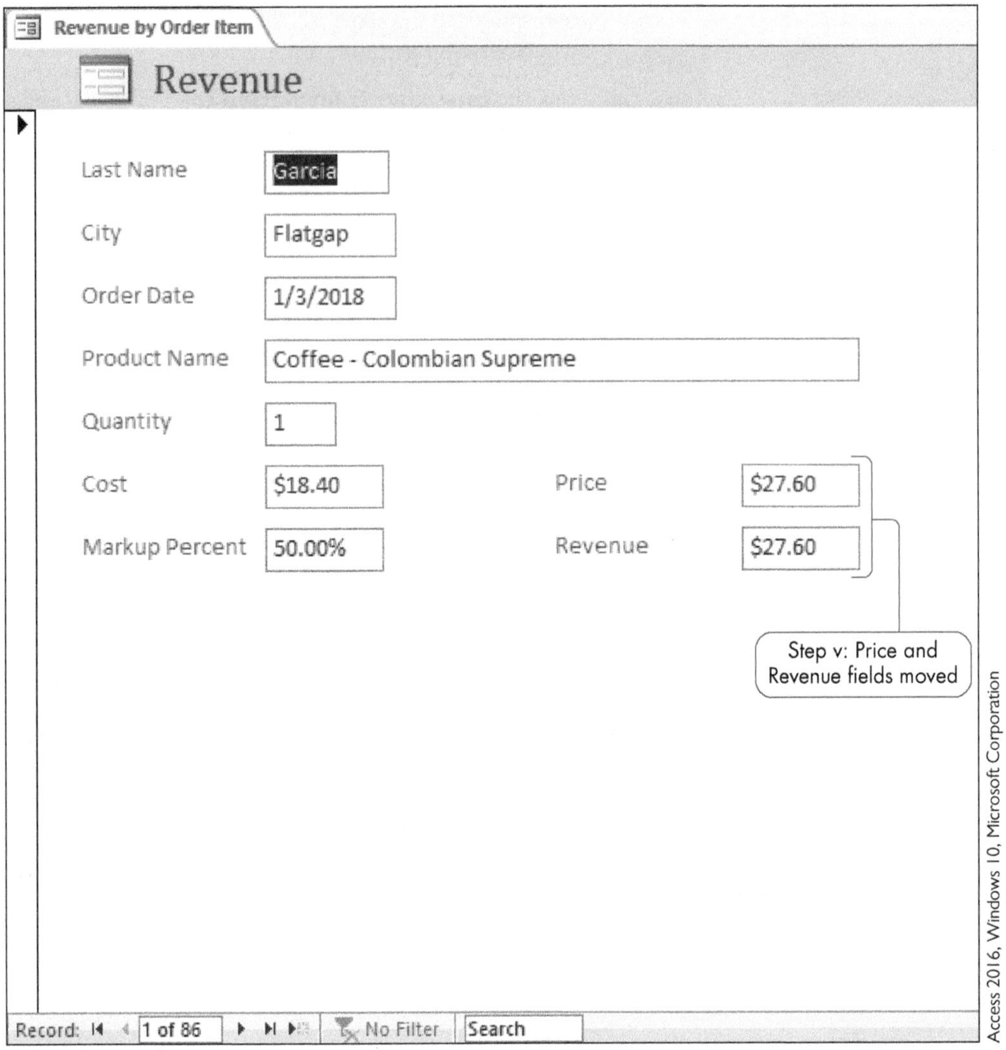

Step v: Price and Revenue fields moved

FIGURE 4.18 Completed Revenue by Order Item Form

a. Switch to Layout view with the Customers – Split View form open. Point to the **splitter bar**, the border between the top and bottom pane of the window. When the pointer shape changes to a double-headed arrow, drag the **splitter bar** until it almost touches the Sales Rep ID field. Save and close the form.

b. Open the Products – Multiple Items form in Layout view. Point to the bottom edge of **Product ID P0001** until the pointer shape changes to a double-headed arrow. Drag the bottom edge up to reduce the height of the rows so they are as tall as they need to be to accommodate the information.

   Changing the height of one row affects the height of all the rows in the form.

c. Click anywhere in the **Cost column** and click **Select Column** in the Rows & Columns group on the Arrange tab. Press **Delete** to remove the column (alternatively, right-click in the column, and from the shortcut menu, select **Delete Column)**. Delete the **MarkupPercent** column.

d. Click the **Refrigeration Needed label** to select it. Change the label to the abbreviation **Refrig?** Resize the column so it is wide enough to display the label text. Save and close the form.

e. Open the Customer Information form in Layout view.

f. Click the **Design tab**. Click **Themes** in the Themes group. Right-click the **Slice theme** and select **Apply Theme to This Object Only**.

The fonts and color scheme that are built into the theme are applied.

> **TROUBLESHOOTING:** You can determine which theme is named Slice by pointing to a theme in the gallery and waiting for a ScreenTip to display. The Office theme is displayed first and the others are displayed in alphabetical order after it.

g. Click the **Format tab**. Click **Shape Fill** in the Control Formatting group. Select **Light Turquoise, Background 2** under Theme Colors.

The background color of the CustomerID field changes to light turquoise. The theme colors in the palette are those built into the Slice theme.

> **TROUBLESHOOTING:** If you do not see Light Turquoise, Background 2 in the theme colors, ensure that you have selected the Slice theme.

> **TROUBLESHOOTING:** If the entire form background changes to turquoise, click Undo and ensure that only the Customer ID text box containing *C0001* is selected.

h. Select the **Customer Name field** (which should be *McAfee, Rand, & Karahalis*). Change the font size to **16**.

The customer name appears in a larger font, setting it apart from the other fields.

i. Save and close the form.

j. Right-click the **Customers table** in the Navigation Pane, and select **Design View**.

You will add the HomePage hyperlink field to the Customers table.

k. Click the **Address1 field** and click **Insert Rows** in the Tools group on the Design tab.

A new row is inserted above the Address1 field.

l. Type **HomePage** in the blank **Field Name box** and select **Hyperlink** as the Data Type.

m. Save and close the Customers table.

n. Right-click the **Customer Information form** in the Navigation Pane, and select **Layout View**.

You will add the HomePage field to the Customer Information form.

o. Click **Add Existing Fields** in the Tools group on the Design tab to display the Field List pane.

p. Click the **HomePage field**. Drag the field from the Field List pane to the form, below the E-mail Address field, until a shaded line displays between *E-mail Address* and *Address1* and then drop it. Close the Field List pane.

Access displays a shaded line to help you place the field in the correct location.

> **TROUBLESHOOTING:** If the placement of the field is incorrect, you can click Undo and try again. Alternatively, select the label and text box controls and use the Move Up or Move Down commands in the Arrange group.

q. Switch to Form view. Press **Tab** until you reach the HomePage field, type **www.mrk.org**, and then press **Tab**.

Because HomePage is a hyperlink field, Access formats it automatically in the form.

Save and close the form.

r. Click the **Revenue query** in the Navigation Pane. Click **Form** in the Forms group on the Create tab to create a new form based on this query.

The Revenue query is the record source for the form.

s. Switch to Design view. Click the first label, **Last Name**, press and hold **Ctrl**, and then click each of the other controls (alternatively, press Ctrl+A).

You have selected all label and text box field controls (from *Last Name* down to *Revenue*).

t. Click **Remove Layout** in the Table group on the Arrange tab. Switch back to Layout view.

TROUBLESHOOTING: Recall that the Remove Layout option only displays on the Ribbon in Design view, so if you do not see the button, ensure that you are in Design view.

u. Resize the controls individually so they are approximately the same sizes as shown in Figure 4.18.

v. Click the **Price control**. Press and hold **Ctrl** and click the **Revenue control**, the **Price label**, and the **Revenue label**. Drag the fields to the locations shown in Figure 4.18. Switch to Form view.

w. Save the form as **Revenue by Order Item**. Close the form.

STEP 4 » USE A LAYOUT CONTROL AND SORT RECORDS IN A FORM

Ryung has an old Sales Reps form that she hopes you can make easier to read but keep in the vertical format. She tested the Customer Information form and likes the way it is working; however, she asks you to change the sort order to make it easier to find customers alphabetically by their names Refer to Figure 4.19 as you complete Step 4.

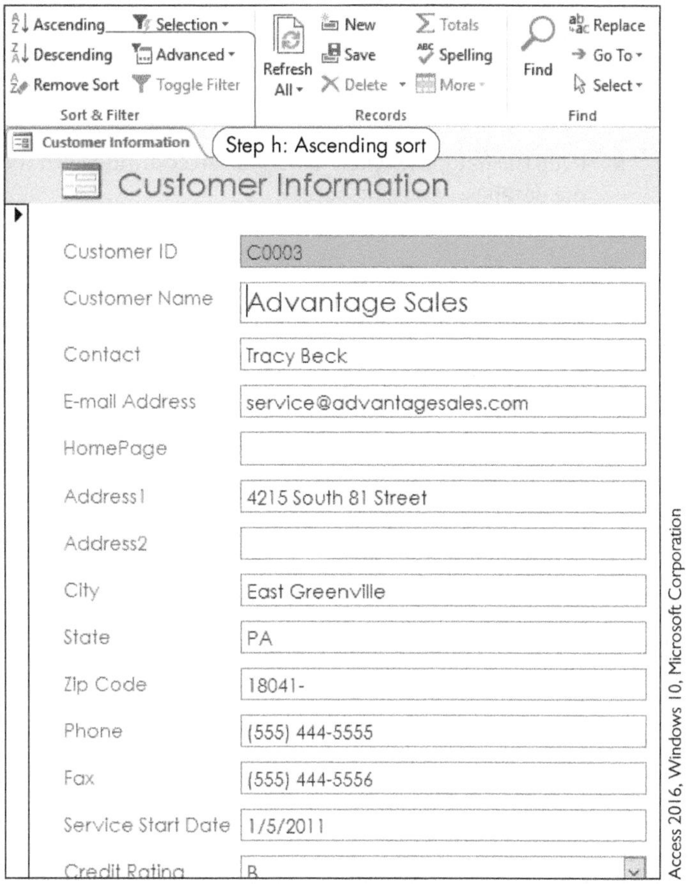

Access 2016, Windows 10, Microsoft Corporation

FIGURE 4.19

a. Open the Sales Reps form in Layout view. Notice that the form is not attractively laid out.

b. Click **Select All** in the Selection group on the Format tab.

All 14 controls are selected in the form.

c. Click **Tabular** in the Table group on the Arrange tab.

The controls are lined up horizontally across the top of the form.

d. Click **Stacked** in the Table group on the Arrange tab. Switch to Form view.

The controls are lined up vertically and the form is much easier to read.

e. Save and close the form.

f. Open the Customer Information form in Form view. Click **Next record** in the Navigation bar at the bottom several times to advance through the records.

Note that the customers are in Customer ID order.

g. Click **First record** in the Navigation bar to return to customer *McAfee, Rand, & Karahalis.*

h. Click in the **Customer Name text box**, and click **Ascending** in the Sort & Filter group on the Home tab.

Advantage Sales displays (Customer ID C0003), as it is the first customer name in alphabetical order, as shown in Figure 4.19.

i. Click **Next record** in the Navigation bar at the bottom of the form to advance through the records.

The records are now in Customer Name order.

j. Save and close the Customer Information form.

k. Keep the database open if you plan to continue with the Hands-On Exercise. If not, close the database, and exit Access.

Report Basics

By now, you know how to plan a database, create tables, establish relationships between tables, enter data into tables, and extract data using queries. In the previous section of this chapter, you learned how to create and modify several types of data-entry forms. In this section, you will learn how to create professional reports using the report-generating tools in Access.

A ***report*** is a document that displays information from a database in a format that outputs meaningful information to its readers. Access reports can be printed, viewed onscreen, or even saved as files, such as Word documents. You cannot use reports to change data in your database; a report is designed for output of information only based on data from tables or queries in your database (record sources).

The following are all examples of reports that might be created in Access:

- A telephone directory sorted by last name
- A customer report grouped by orders pending for each customer
- An employee list grouped by department
- A monthly statement from a bank
- A bill or invoice
- A set of mailing labels

Reports are used to help the reader understand and analyze information. For example, in a report you can group the customers together for each sales rep and highlight the customers who have not placed an order in six months. This is an example of using a list of customers from the Customers table together with other data in the database as an effective business analysis tool. To increase business, the sales reps could contact their customers who have not ordered in the past six months and review the findings with the sales manager. A sales report could then be run each month to see if the strategy has helped to produce any new business.

In this section, you will create reports in Access by first identifying a record source, then designing the report, and finally choosing a Report tool. You will learn how to modify a report by adding and deleting fields, resizing columns, and adding a theme. You will also learn about the report sections, the report views, and controls on reports.

Creating Reports Using Report Tools

Access provides five different report tools for creating reports. The report tools are located on the Create tab in the Reports group, as shown in Figure 4.20. The most common of the tools, the Report tool, is used to instantly create a tabular report based on a selected table or query. The Report Design tool is used to create a new blank report in Design view. This tool is used by advanced users who want to create a report from scratch with no help from Access. The Blank Report tool is used to create a new report in Layout view by inserting fields and controls manually to design the report. The Report Wizard tool will prompt you through a series of step-by-step screens and help you create a report based on your selections. The Labels tool is used to create printable labels using one of the preformatted templates provided by Access. Table 4.3 provides a summary of the five report tools and their usages. Once you create a report using one of the report tools, you can perform modifications in either Layout view or Design view.

FIGURE 4.20 Reports Group on the Create Tab

TABLE 4.3 Report Tools and Their Usages

Report Tool	Usage
Report	Create a tabular report showing all of the fields in the record source.
Report Design	Create a new blank report in Design view. Add fields and controls manually.
Blank Report	Create a new blank report in Layout view. Drag and drop to add fields and controls manually.
Report Wizard	Answer a series of step-by-step questions and Access will design a custom report for you.
Labels	Select a preformatted label template and create printable labels.

Before you create a report in Access, you should consider the following questions:

- What is the purpose of the report?
- Who will use the report?
- Which tables, queries, and fields are needed for the report?
- How will the report be distributed? Will users view the report directly from the Access database, or will they receive it through email, fax, or the Internet?
- Will the results be converted to Word, Excel, HTML, or another format?

In the Forms section of this chapter, you learned that it is helpful to talk to users and design a form before you launch Access. The same applies to creating an Access report. Users can give you solid input, and creating a design will help you determine which report tool to use to create the report.

The first step in planning your report is to identify the record source. You may use one or more tables, queries, or a combination of tables and queries as the report's record source. Sometimes, a single table contains all of the records you need for the report. Other times, you will incorporate several tables. When data from multiple related tables are needed to create a report, you can first create a single query (with criteria, if necessary) and then base the report on that query. Multiple tables used in a query must be related, as indicated with join lines.

Reports can contain text and numeric data as well as formatting, calculated fields, graphics, and so forth. For example, you can add a company logo to the report header. Be sure that you have appropriate permission to use any company logo, graphic, or photo in your reports in order to avoid inappropriate or illegal use of an asset.

Use the Report Tool

The easiest way to create a report is with the Report tool. The ***Report tool*** is used to create a tabular report based on the selected table or query.

To create a report using the Report tool, complete the following steps:

1. Select a table or query in the Navigation Pane.
2. Click Report in the Reports group on the Create tab.

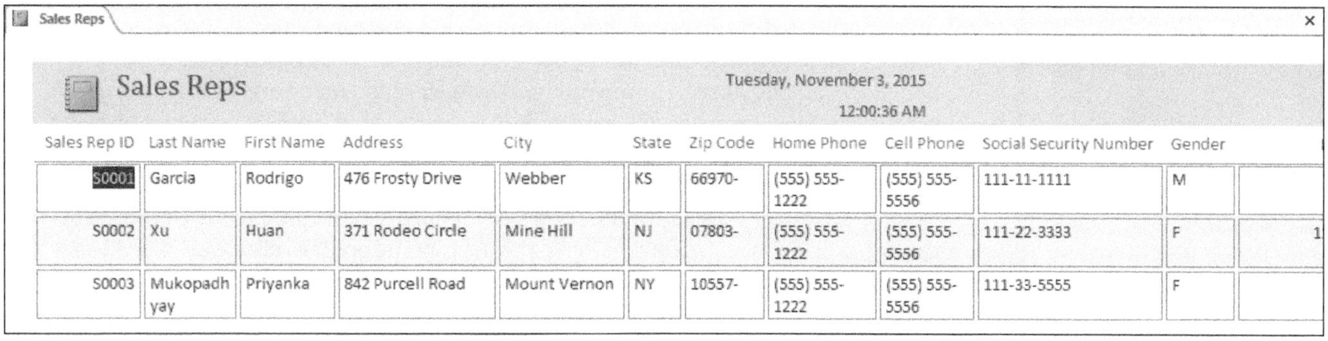

Sales Reps

Sales Reps

Tuesday, November 3, 2015
12:00:36 AM

Sales Rep ID	Last Name	First Name	Address	City	State	Zip Code	Home Phone	Cell Phone	Social Security Number	Gender	
S0001	Garcia	Rodrigo	476 Frosty Drive	Webber	KS	66970-	(555) 555-1222	(555) 555-5556	111-11-1111	M	
S0002	Xu	Huan	371 Rodeo Circle	Mine Hill	NJ	07803-	(555) 555-1222	(555) 555-5556	111-22-3333	F	1
S0003	Mukopadhyay	Priyanka	842 Purcell Road	Mount Vernon	NY	10557-	(555) 555-1222	(555) 555-5556	111-33-5555	F	

FIGURE 4.21 Tabular Report Created with the Report Tool

Access creates a tabular layout report instantly. Notice that this type of report displays data horizontally in columns across the page, as shown in Figure 4.21.

If you prefer, you can display a report using a stacked layout, which displays fields in a vertical column. This type of report is less common, as it would result in longer printouts. The number of pages depends on the number of records in the record source.

Use the Report Wizard

The ***Report Wizard*** prompts you for input in a series of steps to generate a customized report. The wizard enables you to make certain customizations quickly and easily without having to be an expert in report design.

To create a report using the Report Wizard, complete the following steps:

1. Select the report's record source (table or query) in the Navigation Pane, and click Report Wizard in the Reports group on the Create tab. The wizard opens with the selected table or query (the record source) displayed in the first dialog box. Although you chose the record source before you started, the first dialog box enables you to select fields from the selected source or additional tables or queries.
2. Click the Tables/Queries list arrow to display a list of available tables or queries, if you want to choose a different record source. Select the fields you want to include in the report. You can select an available field and then click > to add a single field to the Selected Fields list, >> to select all fields, < to remove a field, << and to remove all fields from the report. See Figure 4.22. Set the desired fields and click Next.

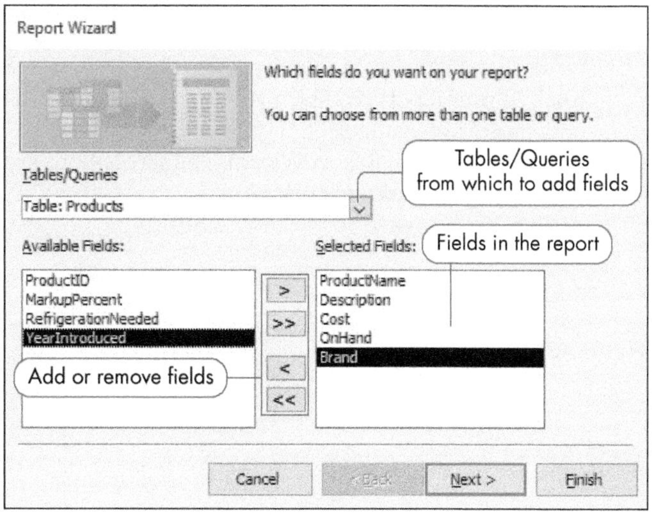

Report Wizard

Which fields do you want on your report?

You can choose from more than one table or query.

Tables/Queries

Table: Products

Tables/Queries from which to add fields

Available Fields:

ProductID
MarkupPercent
RefrigerationNeeded
YearIntroduced

Selected Fields:

Fields in the report

ProductName
Description
Cost
OnHand
Brand

Add or remove fields

Cancel | < Back | Next > | Finish

FIGURE 4.22 Selecting Fields in the Report Wizard

3. Apply the desired grouping in the next dialog box, shown in Figure 4.23. Grouping enables you to organize and summarize your data in a report, based on values in a field. For example, you can group products by their brand name and average the cost of products in each group. To group records in a report, select the field you want to group by and click Add One Field [>] to add the new group. If you need a second or third grouping level, add those field names in order. The order in which you select the groups dictates the order of display in the report. In Figure 4.23, the products are grouped by the Brand field. Once you have selected the appropriate options, click Next. For a basic report, you would not select any grouping fields, and instead just click Next.

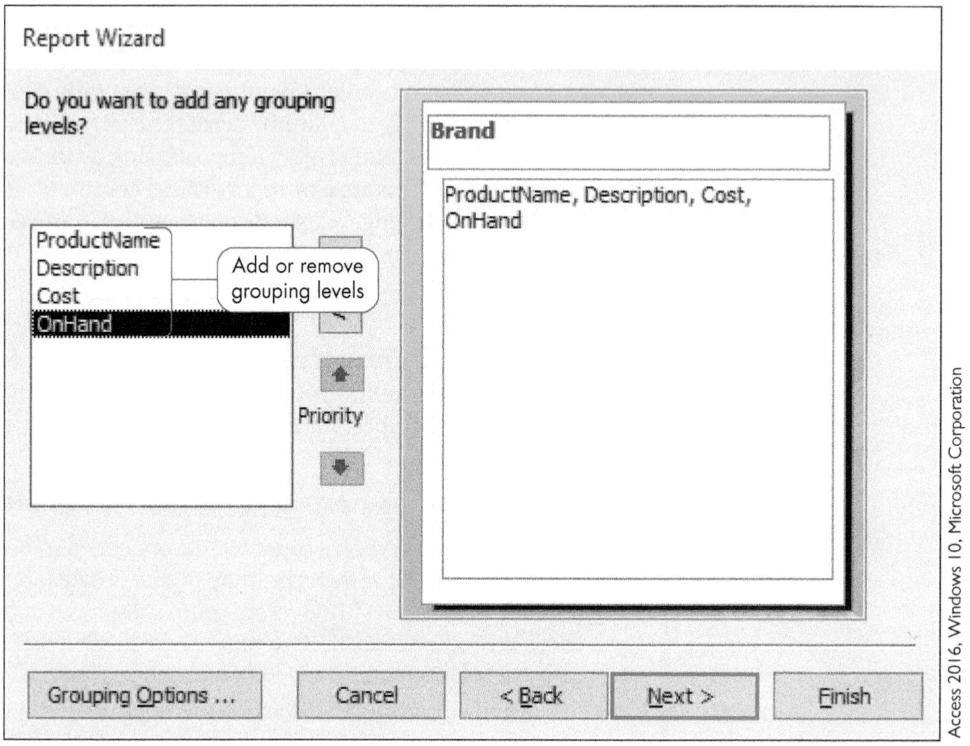

Report Wizard

Do you want to add any grouping levels?

ProductName
Description
Cost
OnHand

Add or remove grouping levels

Priority

Brand

ProductName, Description, Cost, OnHand

Grouping Options ... | Cancel | < Back | Next > | Finish

Access 2016, Windows 10, Microsoft Corporation

FIGURE 4.23 Grouping Options in the Report Wizard

4. Apply the desired sorting and summary options in the next dialog box. Figure 4.24 displays the sort options for a grouped report. You can click Summary Options if you want to add aggregate functions (e.g., sum, average, minimum, and maximum) and to specify whether you want to see detailed records on the report or only the aggregate results (see Figure 4.25). You can also choose to calculate values as percentages of totals in your report results. If no grouping is specified in your report, the summary options are not available. In Figure 4.25, no summary options are selected. Click OK to return to the Report Wizard. The sort options are the same as before. Set the appropriate options and click Next.

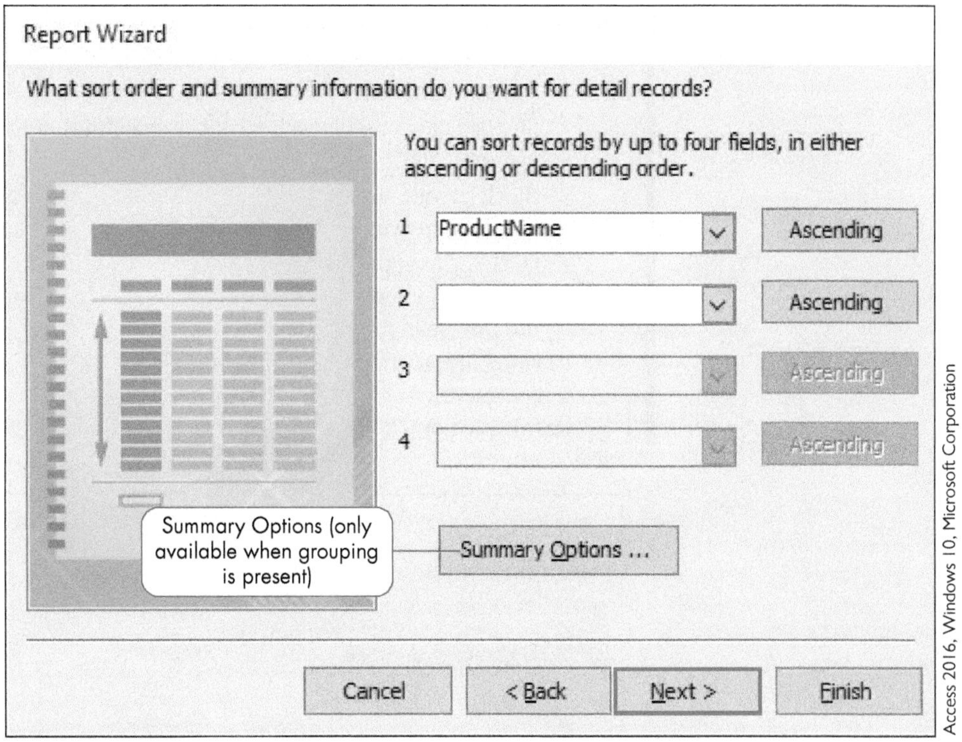

FIGURE 4.24 Sort and Summarize Grouped Data in the Report Wizard

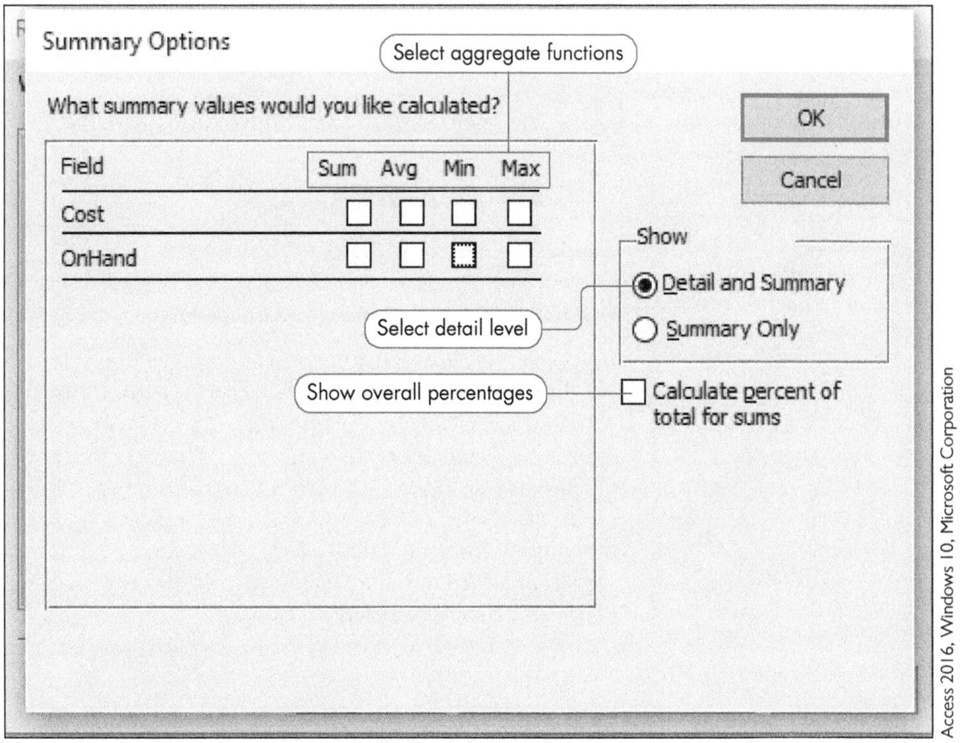

FIGURE 4.25 Summary Options Dialog Box

5. Select the layout in the next dialog box, shown in Figure 4.26, to determine the report's appearance. In a grouped report, you will be prompted to select the layout from three options:
    - Stepped Layout will display column headings at the top of the page and keep the grouping field(s) in their own row.
    - Block Layout will include the grouping field(s) in line with the data, saving some space when printing. It has one set of column headings at the top of each page.
    - Outline Layout will display the grouping field(s) on their own separate rows and has column headings inside each group. This leads to a longer report when printing but may help make the report easier to read.

    Clicking any of these layouts will give you a general preview in the preview area. In a report without grouping, the layouts are Columnar, Tabular, and Justified. You can determine how the data fits on a page by selecting Portrait or Landscape. Click Next.

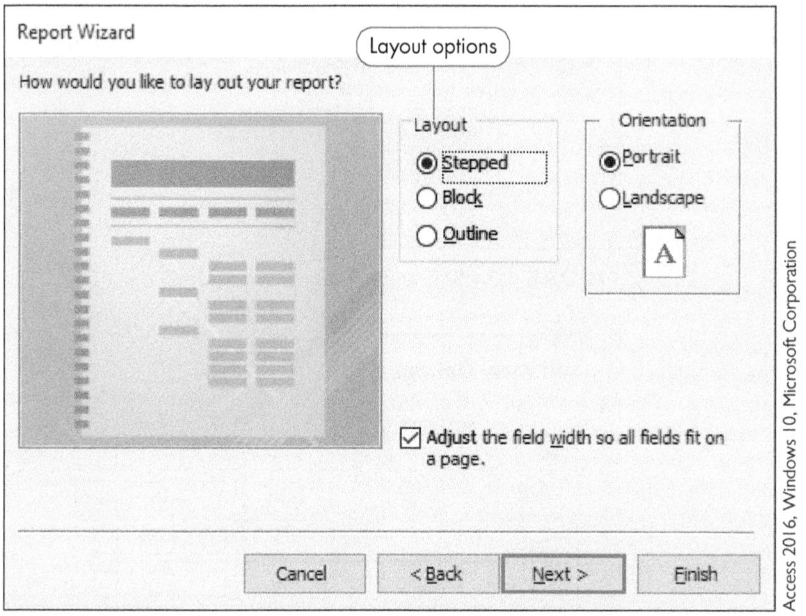

FIGURE 4.26 Layout Options for Grouped Data in the Report Wizard

6. Enter a report name and click Finish. Your grouped report will resemble Figure 4.27.

Products

Products

Grouping field displays as its own column

Brand	Product Name	Description	Cost	ınd
Discount				
	Coffee - Colombian Supren	24/Case, Pre-Ground 1.75 Oz Bags	$18.40	10
	Coffee - Decaf	24/Case, Pre-Ground 1.75 Oz Bags	$23.00	10
	Creamers - Assorted Flavor	400/Case, 8 50-count Boxes	$23.00	10
	Stirrers - Plastic	1000/Box	$1.72	10
	Stirrers - Wood	1000/Box	$1.44	10
	Sugar Substitute	500/Case, 1-Serving Bags	$21.85	10
House				
	Ceramic Mug	SD Company Logo	$5.75	10
	Coffee - Assorted Flavors	18/Case. Pre-Ground 1.75 Oz Bags	$26.45	10
	Coffee - Mild Blend	24/Case, Pre-Ground 1.75 Oz Bags	$23.00	10
	Coffee Filters	500/Case, Fits 10-12 Cup Coffee Maker	$3.45	10
	Milk - 1 pint	Delivered Daily	$1.15	10
	Milk - 1 quart	Delivered Daily	$2.30	10
	Napkins	3000/Case, White	$23.00	10
	Popcorn - Buttered	36/Case, 3.75 Oz Microwave Bags	$10.92	10
	Popcorn - Plain	36/Case, 3.75 Oz Microwave Bags	$9.78	10

Access 2016, Windows 10, Microsoft Corporation

FIGURE 4.27 Grouped Report

Use the Label Wizard

The ***Label Wizard*** enables you to easily create mailing labels, name tags, and other specialized tags. A mailing label report is a specialized report that you can create and print with name-brand labels, such as Avery and many others. If you purchase a store brand label from an office supply store, it will generally state the comparable manufacturer and product number; the wizard provides a long list of both manufacturers and label sizes.

To use the Label Wizard, complete the following steps:

1. Select the table or query that you will use as the record source for the report.
2. Click Labels in the Reports group on the Create tab.
3. Select the manufacturer, product number, unit of measure, label type, and then click Next.
4. Select the font and color options, and then click Next.
5. Add the fields to the prototype label, as shown in Figure 4.28. You add the fields exactly as you would like them to display, including adding commas, spacing, and pressing Enter to move to the next line, where applicable.

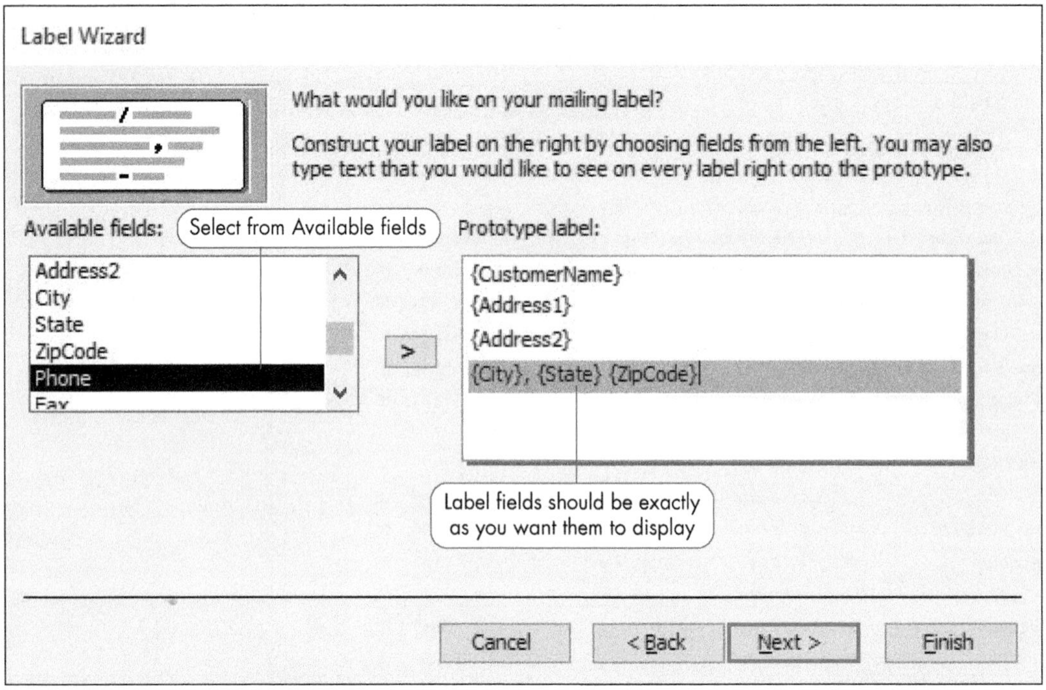

Label Wizard

What would you like on your mailing label?

Construct your label on the right by choosing fields from the left. You may also type text that you would like to see on every label right onto the prototype.

Available fields: (Select from Available fields) Prototype label:

Address2
City
State
ZipCode
Phone
Fax

{CustomerName}
{Address1}
{Address2}
{City}, {State} {ZipCode}

Label fields should be exactly as you want them to display

Cancel | < Back | Next > | Finish

Access 2016, Windows 10, Microsoft Corporation

FIGURE 4.28 Create a Customers Prototype Label

6. Add sort fields; for example, you may want to sort by state or zip code, and then click Next.
7. Name the report and then click Finish to generate your label report. The results using the Customers table are shown in Figure 4.29.

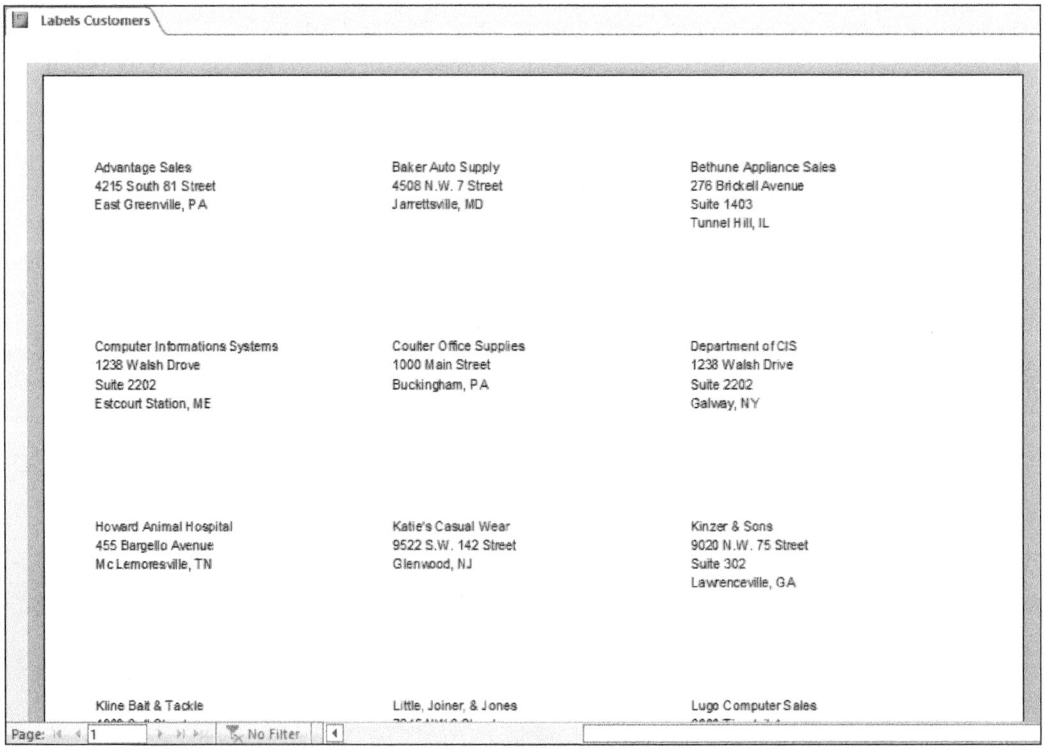

Labels Customers

Advantage Sales
4215 South 81 Street
East Greenville, PA

Baker Auto Supply
4508 N.W. 7 Street
Jarrettsville, MD

Bethune Appliance Sales
276 Brickell Avenue
Suite 1403
Tunnel Hill, IL

Computer Informations Systems
1238 Walsh Drove
Suite 2202
Estcourt Station, ME

Coulter Office Supplies
1000 Main Street
Buckingham, PA

Department of CIS
1238 Walsh Drive
Suite 2202
Galway, NY

Howard Animal Hospital
455 Bargello Avenue
McLemoresville, TN

Katie's Casual Wear
9522 S.W. 142 Street
Glenwood, NJ

Kinzer & Sons
9020 N.W. 75 Street
Suite 302
Lawrenceville, GA

Kline Bait & Tackle

Little, Joiner, & Jones

Lugo Computer Sales

Page: 1 No Filter

Access 2016, Windows 10, Microsoft Corporation

FIGURE 4.29 Customer Mailing Labels Created by Label Wizard

Using Report Views

As you work with the report tools to create and modify reports, you might need to switch between the four report views in Access—Report, Layout, Design, and Print Preview. Report view and Print Preview are generally used only for viewing or printing the report. To make modifications to a report, use Layout view and Design view. Most of the design work can be done in Layout view, but sometimes Design view is necessary to apply a more advanced feature, such as setting the tab order of the controls. To switch between the four views, click the View arrow in the Views group, and then select the desired view (alternatively, right-click the report tab, and from the shortcut menu, select the desired view).

View a Report in Report View

Report view enables you to view a report onscreen in a continuous page layout. However, because the data cannot be changed in Report view, it is simply a way of viewing the information without having to worry about accidentally moving a control. You can also use Report view to filter data, if necessary.

Print or Save a Report in Print Preview

STEP 2 »» ***Print Preview*** enables you to see exactly what the report will look like when it is printed. You cannot modify the design of the report or the data in Print Preview. By default, Print Preview will display all the pages in the report. Figure 4.29 displays the mailing labels report in Print Preview.

From Print Preview, you have the option to export and save the report to a different file type, such as Word. This is a useful option if you plan to share a report electronically but do not want to distribute the entire database. In the Data group, on the Print Preview tab, you will find a number of eligible file types, as shown in Figure 4.30. Select the option in the Data group, and then follow the onscreen prompts to export your report. Commonly used formats include Excel, Word, and Portable Document Format (PDF).

Portable Document Format (PDF) is a file type that was created for exchanging documents independently of software applications and operating system environments. In other words, you can email a report in PDF format to users running various operating systems, and they can open it even if they do not have Microsoft Access installed. PDF files open in Adobe Reader, a free downloadable program; recent versions of Windows have a built-in Reader program that displays PDF files as well.

Because databases contain a great deal of information, Access reports can become very long, requiring many pages to print. At times, reports can be formatted incorrectly, or blank pages might print in between each page of information. Be sure to troubleshoot your reports before sending them to the printer, or to recipients via email.

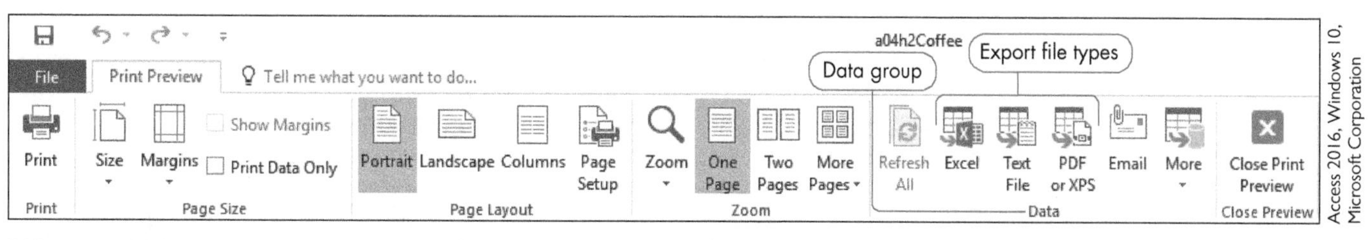

FIGURE 4.30 Data Group on Print Preview Tab

Alter a Report in Layout View

Use Layout view to alter the report design while still viewing the data. You should use Layout view to add or delete fields in the report, modify field properties, change the column widths, group, sort, and summarize data. The Page Setup tab presents options for setting the page size, orientation, and margins. Although you will be able to view your modifications along with the data in Layout view, you will still need to check the report in Print Preview to evaluate all the changes before printing it.

Modifying a Report

After you create a report by using one of the report tools, you may want to modify it. Some of the common changes you make in reports are adding and deleting controls, changing the arrangement, widths, and formatting of controls, and modifying the title. From either Layout or Design view, there are four tabs available for report modification:

- Design: Use this tab to make changes to the design of the report, such as adding fields, grouping and sorting records, changing themes, and inserting additional controls.
- Arrange: Use this tab to change the layout of a report, to move fields up and down, and to control margins and spacing.
- Format: Use this tab to work with fonts, font size, and colors, add or remove bolding, italics, or underlining, adjust text alignment, or add a background image or color.
- Page Setup: Use this tab to change paper size, margins, or page orientation, or to format reports into multiple columns.

Modify the Layout of a Report

STEP 3 The Arrange tab displays in both Layout view and Design view. Some key commands on the Arrange tab from Layout view are highlighted in Figure 4.31.

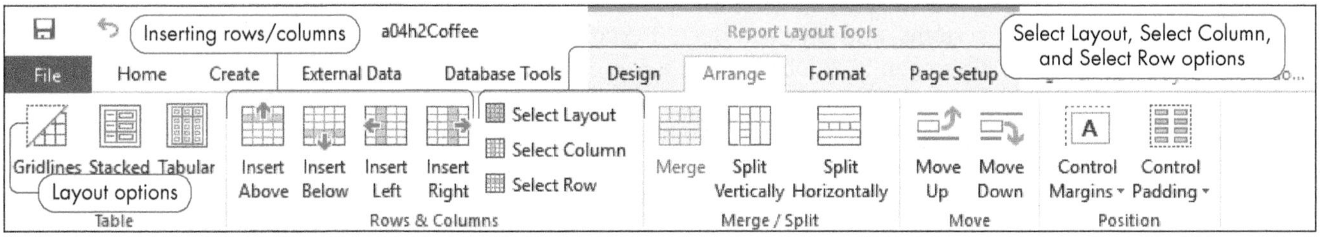

Inserting rows/columns

Select Layout, Select Column, and Select Row options

Layout options

Access 2016, Windows 10, Microsoft Corporation

FIGURE 4.31 Report Layout Tools Arrange Tab

The Table group contains commands that enable you to add gridlines to a report's layout, and to change a report's layout from stacked to tabular (and vice versa). The Remove Layout command is available in Design view only. For example, if a report was created with a tabular layout, you could change it to a stacked layout.

To change a report's layout from tabular to stacked, complete the following steps:

1. Open the report in Layout view and click the Arrange tab.
2. Click any text box in the Detail section of the report.
3. Click Select Layout in the Rows & Columns group.
4. Click Stacked in the Table group.

The Rows & Columns group contains commands that enable you to insert rows and columns inside a report's layout. In a report with a stacked layout, you may want to separate some controls from the rest of the fields, or create some empty space so that fields can be added or repositioned. For example, you can select a control (or multiple controls) and click Insert Below. This will create an empty row (or space) below the selected controls. This group also contains the Select Layout, Select Column, and Select Row commands, which you can use to select the entire layout, or a single column or row in a layout.

The Merge/Split group contains commands that enable you to merge and split the controls on a report. There are times when you might want to deviate from the basic row and column formats that the report tools create. For example, you can make a label such as *Product Name* display in two controls (Product and Name), with one positioned below the other, rather than in one single control.

The Move group contains commands to move a field up or down in a stacked layout. Moving controls up or down in a report may cause unexpected results; you can always click Undo if you need to reverse your changes.

The Position group contains commands to control the margins and the padding (the spacing between controls) in a report. The preset margin settings are convenient to use; ensure that if you change the margins, you preview the report to view the result.

Modify Report Controls

The Format tab contains a series of commands that enable you to change the font, display, and alignment of the controls on a report, as shown in Figure 4.32. The formatting tools in Access are similar to those in other Microsoft Office applications.

To format report controls, complete the following steps:

1. Open the report in Layout view (or Design view), then select the control(s) you want to format.
2. Click the Format tab, and click the formatting tools as desired.

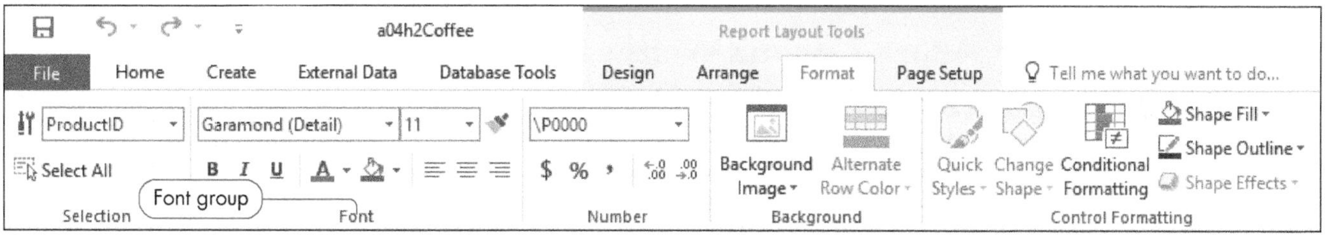

FIGURE 4.32 Report Layout Tools Format Tab

Access 2016, Windows 10, Microsoft Corporation

TIP: INSERT A LOGO IN A REPORT

To insert a logo in a report, open the report in Layout (or Design) view, and then click Logo in the Header / Footer group on the Design tab. In the Insert Picture dialog box, locate the image, click the file, and then click Open. The picture will display in the Report Header section; use the Property Sheet to modify the size and other attributes, if necessary.

Add a Field to a Report

At times, new fields may be added to tables and then need to be incorporated into reports. Alternatively, you might be creating a customized report and want to add fields individually. Adding a field to a report with a stacked or tabular layout is similar to adding a field to a form.

To add a field to a report, complete the following steps:

1. Open the report in Layout view, then click Add Existing Fields in the Tools group on the Design tab.

   The Field List pane displays at the right of the report. For a single-table report, you will be presented with a list of fields from the table (record source). For a multiple-table report, click the + (plus sign) to the left of the appropriate table to expand it, and locate the desired field(s).
2. Click and drag the desired field to the precise location on the report, using the shaded line as a guide for positioning the new field. Alternatively, you can double-click a field to add it to the report; the field will be added below the selected field. The other fields will automatically adjust to make room for the new field.

Delete a Field from a Report

You may decide that even though a field was available in a table or in a query that was used as the record source, it is not necessary to display it to users in a report. Not all fields in a database are necessarily relevant to reports that you create.

To delete a field from the Detail section of a report, complete the following steps:

1. Open the report in Layout view, and click the text box control of the field to be deleted (note the shaded border around the control).
2. Click Select Row in the Rows & Columns group on the Arrange tab in order to select the text box and its associated label. Alternatively, click the text box control, press and hold Ctrl, and then click the associated label control to select them both.
3. Press Delete.

The other fields will automatically adjust to close the gap around the deleted field.

Adjust Column Widths in a Report

You can adjust the width of each column in a tabular report individually so that each column is wide enough to accommodate the widest value in the field. For example, if a report contains first name, last name, address and city, and email address, you will need to make sure the longest value in each field is completely visible. Scroll through the records to ensure that all values can be viewed by report users.

To modify column widths in a tabular report, complete the following steps:

1. Open the report in Layout view, and click the text box control of the field you want to resize.
2. Point to the right border of the control until the pointer turns into a double-headed arrow. Drag the right edge of the control to the left or right until you arrive at the desired width.

Change Margins and Orientation

At times, you will want to print a report in Landscape orientation as opposed to Portrait; that decision will depend upon how many columns you want to display across the page, the widths of the fields, and other formatting considerations. The Page Setup tab presents options similar to those you may have used in Word. In the Page Size group, you can change the margins, and in the Page Layout group, you can work with Page Setup options, including setting the orientation of your report, as shown in Figure 4.33.

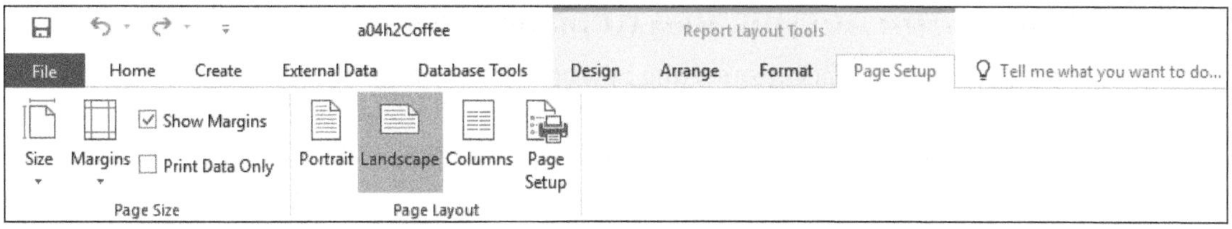

Access 2016, Windows 10, Microsoft Corporation

FIGURE 4.33 Report Layout Tools Page Setup Tab

Add a Theme to the Report

You can enhance the report's appearance by applying one of the built-in Access themes.

To apply a theme, complete the following steps:

1. Open the report in Layout or Design view, and select Themes in the Themes group on the Design tab.
2. Point to a theme to see its name in the ScreenTip and a Live Preview of the theme in the report, and click to select it. By default, the theme will be applied to all objects in your database. Right-click a theme in the gallery to apply it to the current report only, or to all the reports in your database that share a common theme.

Work with a Report Layout Control

When you use one of the report tools to create a new report, Access will add a layout control to help align the fields. Layout controls in reports work similarly to layout controls in forms. The layout control provides guides to help keep controls aligned horizontally and vertically, and give your report a neat appearance. If you want to have more control over the location of your fields, you can remove the layout control and position the controls manually on the report.

To remove the layout control from a report, complete the following steps:

1. Open the report in Design view (the option is not available on the Ribbon in Layout view), and click anywhere in the layout control you want to remove.
2. Click Select Layout in the Rows & Columns group on the Arrange tab.
3. Click Remove Layout in the Table group. All of the controls are still available in the report, but can now be managed individually.

You can add a layout control to a report by first selecting all the controls you want to include in the layout. To select multiple controls, click the first control, press and hold Ctrl, and then click the additional controls you want to include. To select all of the controls on a form, press Ctrl+A. Click Tabular or Stacked in the Table group.

Sorting Records in a Report

When a report is created using the Report tool, the sort order of the records in the report is initially dependent on the sort order of the record source—similar to the way records are sorted in a form. The primary key of the record source usually controls the sort order. However, a report has an additional feature for sorting. While in Layout view or Design view, click Group & Sort in the Grouping & Totals group on the Design tab. The Group, Sort, and Total pane displays at the bottom of the report. This pane enables you to group records together and to override the sort order in the report's record source. Note that if you do not use the Report Wizard, this is generally how you would add grouping and totals to a report.

Change the Sorting in a Report

Sorting is important because sorting by a primary key may not be intuitive. For example, sorting by a field like LastName might be a better choice as opposed to CustomerID, so users can locate the records in alphabetical order by LastName.

To change the sorting in a report, complete the following steps:

1. Open the report in Layout or Design view, and click Group & Sort in the Grouping & Totals group on the Design tab.
2. Click *Add a sort* and select the field by which you want to sort. The default sort order is ascending.
3. Add another sort by clicking *Add a sort* again. For example, you could sort first by Brand and then by ProductName, as shown in Figure 4.34.

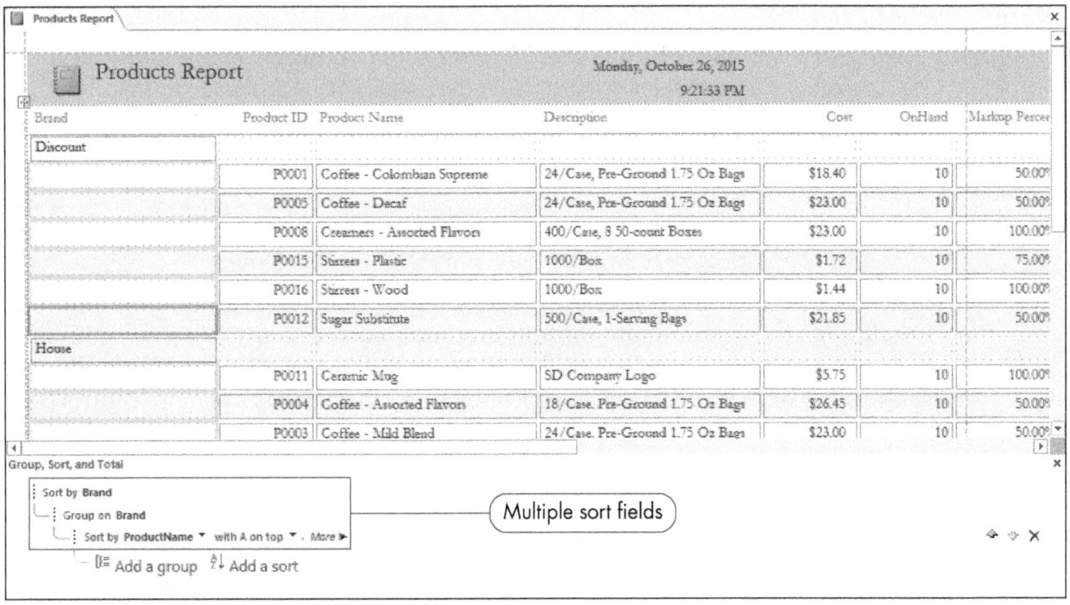

Products Report

Products Report — Monday, October 26, 2015 9:21:33 PM

Brand	Product ID	Product Name	Description	Cost	OnHand	Markup Percer
Discount						
	P0001	Coffee - Colombian Supreme	24/Case, Pre-Ground 1.75 Oz Bags	$18.40	10	50.00
	P0005	Coffee - Decaf	24/Case, Pre-Ground 1.75 Oz Bags	$23.00	10	50.00
	P0008	Creamers - Assorted Flavors	400/Case, 8 50-count Boxes	$23.00	10	100.00
	P0015	Stirrers - Plastic	1000/Box	$1.72	10	75.00
	P0016	Stirrers - Wood	1000/Box	$1.44	10	100.00
	P0012	Sugar Substitute	500/Case, 1-Serving Bags	$21.85	10	50.00
House						
	P0011	Ceramic Mug	SD Company Logo	$5.75	10	100.00
	P0004	Coffee - Assorted Flavors	18/Case. Pre-Ground 1.75 Oz Bags	$26.45	10	50.00
	P0003	Coffee - Mild Blend	24/Case. Pre-Ground 1.75 Oz Bags	$23.00	10	50.00

Group, Sort, and Total

Sort by Brand
Group on Brand
Sort by ProductName with A on top , More
Add a group Add a sort

Multiple sort fields

Access 2016, Windows 10, Microsoft Corporation

FIGURE 4.34 Report in Layout View with Two Sort Fields

Quick Concepts

5. What is the difference between Report view and Layout view? ***p. 897***
6. What is the benefit of saving a report as another type of file? ***p. 897***
7. Why is it important to view your reports in Print Preview? ***p. 897***
8. Why would you decide to remove a report layout control when modifying a report? ***p. 901***
9. Why is sorting the records in a report important? ***p. 901***

Hands-On Exercises

Watch the Video for this Hands-On Exercise!

MyITLab®
HOE2 Training

Skills covered: Use the Report Tool • Use the Report Wizard • Use Print Preview • Publish to PDF • Add a Field • Remove a Field • Change Orientation • Apply a Theme • Sort Records in a Report

2 Report Basics

You create a products report using the Access Report tool to help Ryung stay on top of the key information for her business. You will modify the column widths so that they all fit across one page. You will also use the Report Wizard to create additional reports that Ryung requires.

STEP 1 » CREATING REPORTS USING REPORT TOOLS

You use the Report tool to create an Access report to help Ryung manage her product information. This report is especially useful for determining which products she needs to order to fill upcoming orders. You also use the Report Wizard to determine sales by city. Refer to Figure 4.35 as you complete Step 1.

Sales By City

Sales By City

Step j: Grouped by City field

City	Order Date	Price	Revenue	Product Name
Birmingham				
	1/21/2018	$32.78	$32.78	Styrofoam Cups - 12 ounce
Summary for 'City' = Birmingham (1 detail record)				
Avg		32.775		
Buckingham				
	1/23/2018	$46.00	$46.00	Creamers - Assorted Flavors
	1/23/2018	$41.40	$41.40	Sugar Packets
	1/23/2018	$32.78	$32.78	Styrofoam Cups - 12 ounce
	1/26/2018	$21.84	$43.68	Popcorn - Buttered
	1/26/2018	$10.06	$20.13	Tea Bags - Regular
	1/26/2018	$4.60	$4.60	Milk - 1 quart
Summary for 'City' = Buckingham (6 detail records)				
Avg		26.113		
East Greenville				
	1/5/2018	$46.00	$92.00	Creamers - Assorted Flavors
	1/5/2018	$32.78	$32.78	Sugar Substitute
	1/5/2018	$52.90	$105.80	Coffee - Hazelnut

Step l: Average summary added

Access 2016, Windows 10, Microsoft Corporation

FIGURE 4.35 Sales by City Report

a. Open *a04h1Coffee_LastFirst* if you closed it at the end of Hands-On Exercise 1 and save it as **a04h2Coffee_LastFirst**, changing h1 to h2.

b. Select the **Products table** in the Navigation Pane. Click the **Create tab** and click **Report** in the Reports group.

Access creates a new tabular layout report based on the Products table. The report opens in Layout view ready for editing.

c. Click the **Products title** at the top of the report to select it, click again on **Products**, and then change the title to **Products Report**. Press **Enter** to accept the change.

d. Right-click the **Products report tab** and select **Print Preview**.

The report is too wide for the page; you will close Print Preview and change the orientation to Landscape.

e. Click **Close Print Preview** in the Close Preview group to return to Layout view.

f. Click the **Page Setup tab** and click **Landscape** in the Page Layout group.

The report changes to Landscape orientation. Most of the columns now fit across one page. You will make further revisions to the report later so that it fits on one page.

g. Save the report as **Products Report**. Close the report.

h. Select the **Revenue query** in the Navigation Pane. Click the **Create tab** and click **Report Wizard** in the Reports group.

The Report Wizard launches.

i. Click the **City field** and click **Add One Field** [>] to add the City field to the report. Repeat the same process for the **OrderDate**, **Price**, **Revenue**, and **ProductName fields**. Click **Next**.

j. Ensure that **City** is selected, click **Add One Field** [>] to add grouping by city. Click **Next**.

k. Click the **arrow** in the first sort box, and select **OrderDate**. Accept the default sort order as Ascending. Click **Summary Options**.

l. Click the **Avg check box** in the Price row to summarize the Price field. Click **OK**.

m. Click **Next**. Click **Next** again to accept the default layout.

n. Type **Sales by City** for the title of the report. Click **Finish**.

The report is displayed in Print Preview mode.

o. Click **Close Print Preview**.

p. Save and close the report.

STEP 2 » USING REPORT VIEWS

The Products Report you created looks good, according to Ryung. However, she does not have Access installed on her home computer, and would like to have a copy of the report saved in PDF format so she can review it outside of the office. You will save a copy of the report for her Refer to Figure 4.36 as you complete Step 2.

Step a: Report in PDF format

Products Report — Sunday, November 4, 2015 9:24:45 PM

Product ID	Product Name	Description	Cost	Markup Percent	Refrigeration Needed	Brand
P0001	Coffee - Colombian Supreme	24/Case, Pre-Ground 1.75 Oz Bags	$18.40	50.00%	☐	Discount
P0002	Coffee - Hazelnut	24/Case, Pre-Ground 1.75 Oz Bags	$26.45	100.00%	☐	Premium
P0003	Coffee - Mild Blend	24/Case, Pre-Ground 1.75 Oz Bags	$23.00	50.00%	☐	House
P0004	Coffee - Assorted Flavors	18/Case. Pre-Ground 1.75 Oz Bags	$26.45	50.00%	☐	House
P0005	Coffee - Decaf	24/Case, Pre-Ground 1.75 Oz Bags	$23.00	50.00%	☐	Discount
P0006	Tea Bags - Regular	75/Box, Individual Tea Bags	$5.75	75.00%	☐	House
P0007	Tea Bags - Decaf	75/Box, Individual Tea Bags	$8.05	75.00%	☐	House
P0008	Creamers - Assorted Flavors	400/Case, 8 50-count Boxes	$23.00	100.00%	☐	Discount
P0009	Creamers - Liquid	200/Case, Individual Creamers	$17.25	100.00%	☑	Premium
P0010	Sugar Packets	2000/Case	$20.70	100.00%	☐	House
P0011	Ceramic Mug	SD Company Logo	$5.75	100.00%	☐	House
P0012	Sugar Substitute	500/Case, 1-Serving Bags	$21.85	50.00%	☐	Discount
P0013	Coffee Filters	500/Case, Fits 10-12 Cup Coffee Maker	$3.45	50.00%	☐	House
P0014	Napkins	3000/Case, White	$23.00	100.00%	☐	House
P0015	Stirrers - Plastic	1000/Box	$1.72	75.00%	☐	Discount
P0016	Stirrers - Wood	1000/Box	$1.44	100.00%	☐	Discount
P0017	Spoons	500/Box, White Plastic	$17.25	100.00%	☐	House
P0018	Popcorn - Plain	36/Case, 3.75 Oz Microwave Bags	$9.78	100.00%	☐	House
P0019	Popcorn - Buttered	36/Case, 3.75 Oz Microwave Bags	$10.92	100.00%	☐	House
P0020	Soup - Chicken	50 Envelopes	$11.50	100.00%	☐	Premium
P0021	Soup - Variety Pak	50 Envelopes	$13.80	100.00%	☐	Premium
P0022	Styrofoam Cups - 10 ounce	1000/Case	$19.55	50.00%	☐	House

FIGURE 4.36 Products Report Saved in PDF Format

a. Open the Products Report and on the **File** tab, click **Print**, and select **Print Preview**. Click **PDF or XPS** in the Data group on the Print Preview tab. Navigate to where you are saving your files, type the file name **a04h2Products_LastFirst**, ensure that *Open file after publishing* is selected, and then click **Publish**.

Windows will open the report in your system's default PDF viewer, which may be Adobe Reader or the Windows Reader app. Close the reader window. You will submit this file to your instructor at the end of the last hands-on exercise.

b. Ensure that you return to the Access window, and in the Export – PDF dialog box, click **Close** when prompted to save the export steps.

c. Click **Close Print Preview** and close the report.

STEP 3 » MODIFYING A REPORT

Ryung realized the Products table is missing a field that she requires for her reports. She would like you to add the field to the table and update the report to include the new field. She would also like to make sure the report fits nicely across one landscape page. She also asked you to show her some sample color schemes Refer to Figure 4.37 as you complete Step 3.

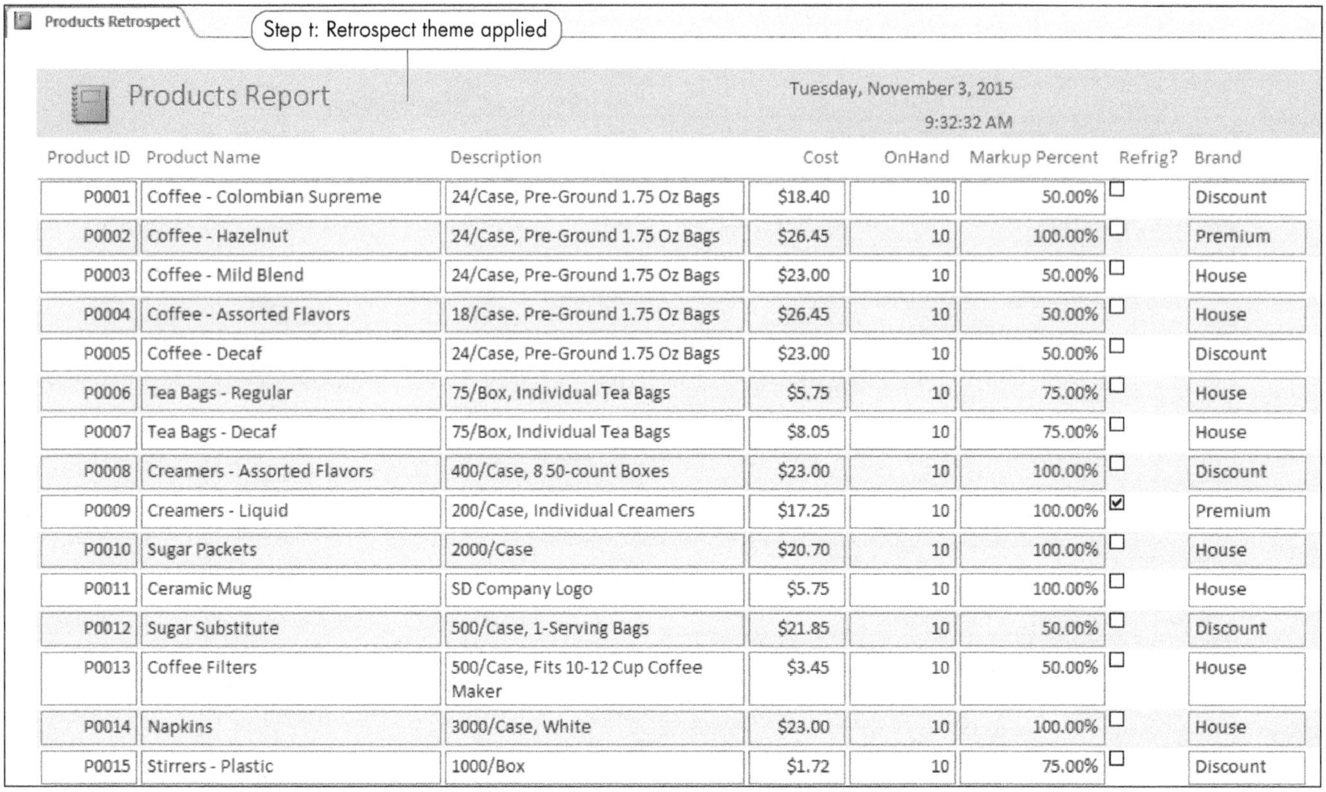

Products Retrospect

Step t: Retrospect theme applied

Products Report

Tuesday, November 3, 2015
9:32:32 AM

Product ID	Product Name	Description	Cost	OnHand	Markup Percent	Refrig?	Brand
P0001	Coffee - Colombian Supreme	24/Case, Pre-Ground 1.75 Oz Bags	$18.40	10	50.00%	☐	Discount
P0002	Coffee - Hazelnut	24/Case, Pre-Ground 1.75 Oz Bags	$26.45	10	100.00%	☐	Premium
P0003	Coffee - Mild Blend	24/Case, Pre-Ground 1.75 Oz Bags	$23.00	10	50.00%	☐	House
P0004	Coffee - Assorted Flavors	18/Case. Pre-Ground 1.75 Oz Bags	$26.45	10	50.00%	☐	House
P0005	Coffee - Decaf	24/Case, Pre-Ground 1.75 Oz Bags	$23.00	10	50.00%	☐	Discount
P0006	Tea Bags - Regular	75/Box, Individual Tea Bags	$5.75	10	75.00%	☐	House
P0007	Tea Bags - Decaf	75/Box, Individual Tea Bags	$8.05	10	75.00%	☐	House
P0008	Creamers - Assorted Flavors	400/Case, 8 50-count Boxes	$23.00	10	100.00%	☐	Discount
P0009	Creamers - Liquid	200/Case, Individual Creamers	$17.25	10	100.00%	☑	Premium
P0010	Sugar Packets	2000/Case	$20.70	10	100.00%	☐	House
P0011	Ceramic Mug	SD Company Logo	$5.75	10	100.00%	☐	House
P0012	Sugar Substitute	500/Case, 1-Serving Bags	$21.85	10	50.00%	☐	Discount
P0013	Coffee Filters	500/Case, Fits 10-12 Cup Coffee Maker	$3.45	10	50.00%	☐	House
P0014	Napkins	3000/Case, White	$23.00	10	100.00%	☐	House
P0015	Stirrers - Plastic	1000/Box	$1.72	10	75.00%	☐	Discount

FIGURE 4.37 Products Retrospect Report

a. Right-click the **Products table** and select **Design View.**

You need to add the OnHand field to the Products table.

b. Click in the **MarkupPercent field**, and then click **Insert Rows** in the Tools group on the Design tab.

A new blank row displays above the MarkupPercent field.

c. Type **OnHand** in the Field Name box and select **Number** as the Data Type.

d. Save the table. Click **View** in the Views group to switch to Datasheet view.

The new OnHand column contains no data. Next, you will add some sample data to the new field for testing purposes only.

e. Type the number **10** for each item's OnHand value.

f. Close the Products table.

g. Right-click **Products Report** in the Navigation Pane, and select **Layout View**.

h. Click **Add Existing Fields** in the Tools group on the Design tab to open the Field List pane.

i. Drag the **OnHand field** from the Field List pane between the Cost and MarkupPercent fields. Close the Field List pane.

Because of the tabular layout control, Access adjusts all the columns to make room for the new OnHand field.

j. Display the report in Print Preview.

The report is still too wide for a single page.

k. Click **Close Print Preview**. Ensure that you are in Layout view.

l. Scroll to and then click anywhere in the **Year Introduced column**. Click the **Arrange tab** and click **Select Column** in the Rows & Columns group. Press **Delete** to remove the column.

The Year Introduced column is removed from the report.

m. Scroll to and then click the **ProductID column heading** and drag the right border to the left until the Product ID heading still fits, but any extra white space is removed.

n. Scroll to and then click the **Refrigeration Needed column heading** and rename the column **Refrig?**. Adjust the width of the *Refrig?* column heading so that any extra white space is removed.

o. Click **Themes** in the Themes group on the Design tab.

The available predefined themes display.

p. Right-click the **Organic theme** and select **Apply Theme to This Object Only**. Display the report in Print Preview.

Access reformats the report using the Organic theme. The report is still too wide for a single page. You will make further adjustments in the next steps.

q. Click **Close Print Preview** and save the report. Click the **File tab**, select **Save As**, select **Save Object As**, and then click **Save As**. Type **Products Organic** as the report name and click **OK**.

You saved the report with one theme. Now, you will apply a second theme to the report and save it with a different name.

r. Ensure that the report is in Layout view. You notice that the Brand column is extending over the dashed page break to its right and needs to be resized to fit on the page. Drag the right border of the Brand column to the left so that it fits inside the page break. Scroll down the report to ensure that all of the values in the column are visible. Narrow columns as required to ensure that all columns are fitting inside the dashed page break. Save the report.

s. Click **Themes** in the Themes group to apply a different theme. Right-click the **Retrospect theme** and select **Apply Theme to This Object Only**. Display the report in Print Preview.

If you do not apply the theme to this object only, all database objects will adopt the Retrospect theme.

t. Click **Close Print Preview**. Click the **File tab**, select **Save As**, select **Save Object As**, and then click **Save As**. Type **Products Retrospect** as the report name and click **OK**. Close the report.

You will be able to show Ryung two product reports with different themes applied.

STEP 4 ›› SORTING RECORDS IN A REPORT

Ryung would like the Products Report records to be sorted and grouped by Brand. You will change the sort order, group the records, and preview the report to see the results Refer to Figure 4.38 as you complete Step 4.

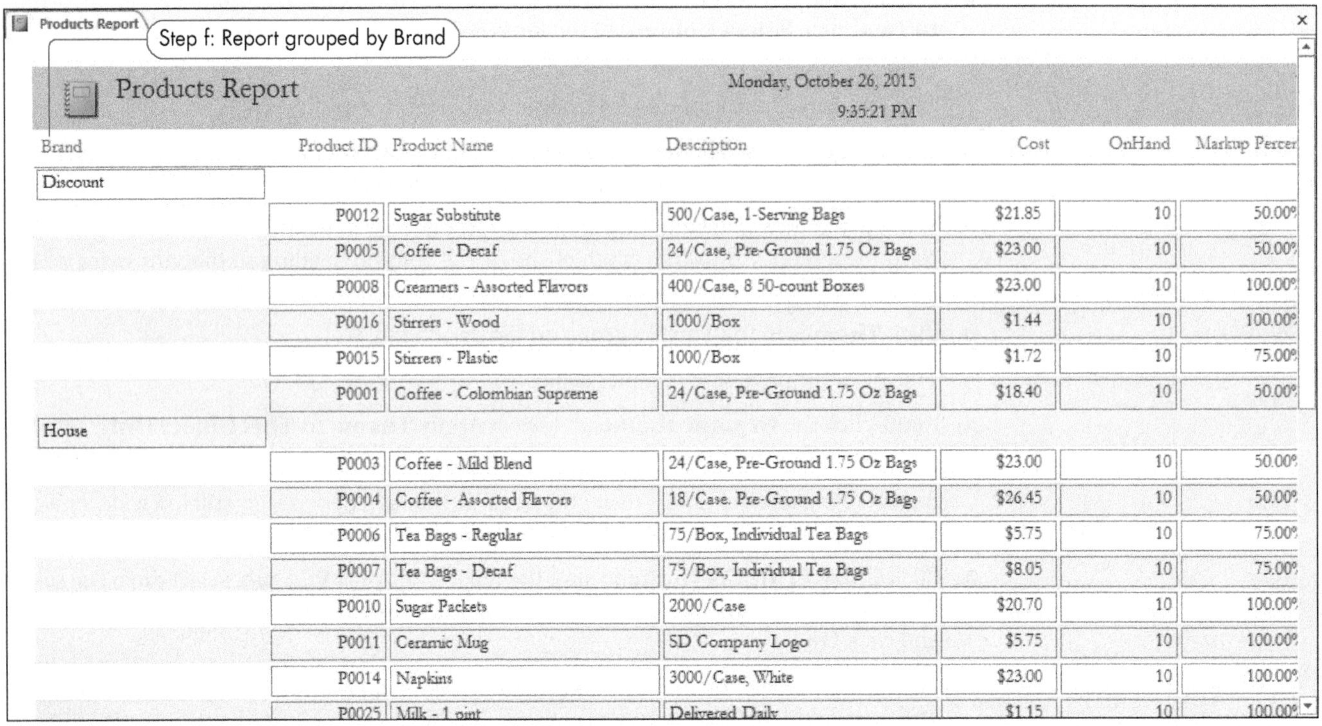

Products Report

Step f: Report grouped by Brand

Products Report — Monday, October 26, 2015 9:35:21 PM

Brand	Product ID	Product Name	Description	Cost	OnHand	Markup Percer
Discount						
	P0012	Sugar Substitute	500/Case, 1-Serving Bags	$21.85	10	50.00%
	P0005	Coffee - Decaf	24/Case, Pre-Ground 1.75 Oz Bags	$23.00	10	50.00%
	P0008	Creamers - Assorted Flavors	400/Case, 8 50-count Boxes	$23.00	10	100.00%
	P0016	Stirrers - Wood	1000/Box	$1.44	10	100.00%
	P0015	Stirrers - Plastic	1000/Box	$1.72	10	75.00%
	P0001	Coffee - Colombian Supreme	24/Case, Pre-Ground 1.75 Oz Bags	$18.40	10	50.00%
House						
	P0003	Coffee - Mild Blend	24/Case, Pre-Ground 1.75 Oz Bags	$23.00	10	50.00%
	P0004	Coffee - Assorted Flavors	18/Case. Pre-Ground 1.75 Oz Bags	$26.45	10	50.00%
	P0006	Tea Bags - Regular	75/Box, Individual Tea Bags	$5.75	10	75.00%
	P0007	Tea Bags - Decaf	75/Box, Individual Tea Bags	$8.05	10	75.00%
	P0010	Sugar Packets	2000/Case	$20.70	10	100.00%
	P0011	Ceramic Mug	SD Company Logo	$5.75	10	100.00%
	P0014	Napkins	3000/Case, White	$23.00	10	100.00%
	P0025	Milk - 1 pint	Delivered Daily	$1.15	10	100.00%

Access 2016, Windows 10, Microsoft Corporation

FIGURE 4.38 Products Report Grouped by Brand

a. Open **Products Report** in Layout view.

b. Click **Group & Sort** in the Grouping & Totals group on the Design tab.

The *Add a group* and *Add a sort* options display at the bottom of the report.

> **TROUBLESHOOTING:** If the options do not display, the Group, Sort, and Total pane may have been open. If the pane is closed after selecting the command, try clicking Group & Sort again.

c. Click **Add a sort**.

A new Sort bar displays at the bottom of the report.

d. Select **Brand** from the list.

The report is now sorted by Brand in ascending order (with Discount at the top).

e. Click **Add a group**.

f. Select **Brand** from the list.

The report is now grouped by Brand.

g. View the report in Report view. Save and close the report.

h. Close the database and exit Access. Based on your instructor's directions, submit the following:

a04h2Coffee_LastFirst

a04h2Products_LastFirst

Chapter Objectives Review

After reading this chapter, you have accomplished the following objectives:

1. Create forms using form tools.

- Identify a record source: A record source is the table or query that supplies the records for the form.
- Use the Form tool: The Form tool creates a basic form that opens in Layout view.
- Understand controls: Controls are the text boxes, buttons, labels, and other tools you use to add, edit, and display data in a form or report.
- Work with form views: Form view is a simplified interface used for data entry, but it allows no design changes. Layout view enables users to make changes to the layout while viewing the data in the form. Design view enables you to change advanced design settings that are not available in Layout view.
- Work with a subform: A subform displays data from a related table for each record in the main table.
- Create a split form: A split form combines two views of the same record source—one section is displayed in a stacked layout and the other section is displayed in a tabular layout.
- Create a multiple items form: This form displays multiple records in a tabular layout similar to a table's Datasheet view, with more customization options.
- Create forms using the other form tools: A datasheet form is a replica of a table or query's Datasheet view except that it still retains form properties. The Form Design tool and the Blank Form tools can be used to create a form manually. The Navigation option in the Forms group enables you to create user interface forms that have the look and feel of Web-based forms and enable users to open and close the objects of a database. The Modal Dialog Form tool can be used to create a dialog box.

2. Modify forms.

- Use Form view to edit data: Most users will work in Form view. This enables changes to data but not to design elements.
- Use Layout view to modify form design: Layout view enables you to change the design of a form while viewing data.
- Adjust column widths in a form: Column widths often need to be adjusted. Size the columns to accommodate the widest entry in a field.
- Add and delete form fields: Fields can be added to an existing form using the Field List. Fields can be removed by selecting the text box and the label controls and pressing Delete.
- Add a theme to a form: Themes can be applied to a single form or to all objects in the database.
- Modify form controls: The Format tab enables changes to the font, including bold, italic, underlining, font size, font color, font background, and alignment.

3. Work with a form layout.

- Modify a form layout: The Arrange tab displays in both Layout view and Design view, and enables you to change form layout, field order, and spacing options.

4. Sort records in form.

- Sort by a single field: Forms can be sorted by a single field in either ascending or descending order.

5. Create reports using report tools.

- Use the Report tool: Access has five report tools. The Report tool instantly creates a tabular report based on a table or query. The Report Design tool creates a new blank report in Design view. The Blank Report tool creates a new blank report so that you can insert controls and design the report manually in Layout view. The Report Wizard tool steps you through the process to create a report. The Labels tool creates a page of mailing labels using a template.
- Use the Report Wizard to create a report: The Report Wizard will guide you step by step through creating a report, prompting you for input and generating output. The wizard enables you to group records of a common type and summarize data in your reports.
- Use the Label Wizard: The Label Wizard can produce printable labels. Access includes predefined standard formats for common labels.

6. Use report views.

- View a report in Report view: Report view is ideal for viewing data onscreen. Neither data nor the design can be changed in this view.
- Print or save a report in Print Preview: Print Preview shows how the report will display when printed. It also enables you to save the report as a file in a number of formats, such as Word and PDF.
- Alter a report in Layout view: Layout view enables you to change the design of a report while viewing data.

7. Modify a report.

- Modify the layout of a report: The Arrange tab displays in both Layout view and Design view. The tools on the Arrange tab enable you to work with the layout of a report to give it a more uniform appearance.
- Modify report controls: The Format tab enables changes to the font, including bold, italic, underlining, font size, font color, font background, and alignment.
- Add a field to a report: Fields can be added to an existing report using the Field List.
- Delete a field from a report: Fields can be deleted either in Layout or Design view.
- Adjust column widths in a report: Column widths often need to be adjusted. Be sure to make the column wide enough to display the widest value in a field.

- Change margins and orientation: You can display the report in portrait or landscape mode and increase or decrease margin sizes.
- Add a theme to the report: Themes can be applied to a single report or to all objects in the database.
- Work with a Report Layout control: The Layout control keeps the fields neatly spaced, making it harder to move fields independently but keeping a standard format.

8. Sort records in a report.

- Change the sorting in a report: You can sort report records by a single or multiple fields.

Key Terms Matching

Match the key terms with their definitions. Write the key term letter by the appropriate numbered definition.

- **a.** Control
- **b.** Design view
- **c.** Form
- **d.** Form tool
- **e.** Form view
- **f.** Label Wizard
- **g.** Layout control
- **h.** Layout view
- **i.** Multiple Items form
- **j.** Portable Document Format (PDF)
- **k.** Print Preview
- **l.** Record source
- **m.** Report
- **n.** Report tool
- **o.** Report view
- **p.** Report Wizard
- **q.** Split form
- **r.** Stacked layout
- **s.** Tabular layout
- **t.** Theme

1. ______ A database object that is used to add data into or edit data in a table. **p. 864**

2. ______ Used to create data entry forms for customers, employees, products, and other tables. **p. 864**

3. ______ The table or query that supplies the records for a form or report. **p. 865**

4. ______ Displays fields in a vertical column. **p. 866**

5. ______ Displays fields horizontally. **p. 866**

6. ______ A text box, button, label, or other tool you use to add, edit, and display the data in a form or report. **p. 866**

7. ______ Provides guides to help keep controls aligned horizontally and vertically and give your form a uniform appearance. **p. 866**

8. ______ A simplified user interface primarily used for data entry; does not allow you to make changes to the layout. **p. 867**

9. ______ Enables users to make changes to a layout while viewing the data in the form or report. **p. 868**

10. ______ Enables you to change advanced design settings you cannot see in Layout view, such as removing a layout control. **p. 869**

11. ______ Combines two views of the same record source—one section is displayed in a stacked layout and the other section is displayed in a tabular layout. **p. 870**

12. ______ Displays multiple records in a tabular layout similar to a table's Datasheet view, with more customization options. **p. 871**

13. ______ A defined set of colors, fonts, and graphics that can be applied to a form or report. **p. 875**

14. ______ A database document that outputs meaningful information to its readers. **p. 889**

15. ______ Used to instantly create a tabular report based on the table or query currently selected. **p. 890**

16. ______ Prompts you for input and then uses your answers to generate a customized report. **p. 891**

17. ______ Enables you to easily create mailing labels, name tags, and other specialized tags. **p. 895**

18. ______ Enables you to determine what a printed report will look like in a continuous page layout. **p. 897**

19. ______ Enables you to see exactly what the report will look like when it is printed. **p. 897**

20. ______ A file type that was created for exchanging documents independent of software applications and operating system environment. **p. 897**

Multiple Choice

1. A report can be made from one or more tables or a query. The object(s) that a report is based on is known as the:
   (a) Control.
   (b) Record Source.
   (c) Theme.
   (d) Tabular Layout.

2. Which of the following statements is *false*?
   (a) Both forms and reports can use tabular and stacked layouts.
   (b) A stacked layout displays data in a vertical column.
   (c) A tabular layout displays data horizontally.
   (d) Stacked layouts are more common for reports because they use less paper when printed.

3. In order to summarize data in a report and override the sort order of the record source you would use:
   (a) A text box.
   (b) A button on a report.
   (c) The Group, Sort, and Total Pane.
   (d) A label on a report.

4. The simplest view you can use to modify control widths in a form is:
   (a) Layout view.
   (b) Form view.
   (c) Design view.
   (d) Print Preview.

5. Which of the following views provides you with the most flexibility in modifying forms and reports?
   (a) Design view
   (b) Layout view
   (c) Form view/Report view
   (d) Print Preview

6. Which of the following statements about reports is *false*?
   (a) Reports can be saved to a file (such as a Word document) on your computer.
   (b) Reports are primarily used to modify data.
   (c) Reports can produce output in a number of ways, including mailing labels.
   (d) Reports can be created simply by using the Report tool.

7. Use the ____________ to see exactly what the printed report will look like before printing.
   (a) Report tool
   (b) Report Wizard
   (c) Report view
   (d) Print Preview

8. If you need to send a report to a user who does not have Microsoft Office available, which of the following file formats would be the best choice to ensure it can be opened?
   (a) Word
   (b) Excel
   (c) Reader
   (d) Portable Document Format (PDF)

9. Which of the following statements is *false*?
   (a) Reports are generally used for printing, emailing, or viewing data on the screen.
   (b) Layouts for forms and reports are the predefined sets of colors, fonts, and graphics.
   (c) Forms are often used for inputting data.
   (d) Forms and reports both include controls, such as text boxes, that can be resized.

10. Which of the following statements is *true*?
    (a) You can group records to show a list of properties by state.
    (b) You can sort records in reports but not in forms.
    (c) A sort can only be set on one field at a time.
    (d) You can either group or sort records (but not both).

Practice Exercises

1 Financial Management Prospects

You are working as a customer service representative for a financial management firm. Your task is to contact a list of prospective customers and introduce yourself and the services of your company. You will create a form to view, add, and update data for one customer at a time. After creating the form, you will customize it and add sorting. You will also create a report to display all of the information on one screen, for viewing purposes. Refer to Figure 4.39 as you complete this exercise.

Leads Report

Leads — Monday, October 26, 2015 9:40:18 PM

State	First	Last	Zip	Phone	Email	Birth	NetWorth
AR							
	Akira	Hayashi	71638	998-628-2984	AkiHayashi11452@live.com	10/3/1970	$74,000.00
	Yon	Seo	72578	424-632-3415	YoSeo18257@comcast.net	6/11/1956	$70,000.00
AZ							
	Majida	Hayek	86405	555-543-3972	MHayek20676@live.com	11/16/1971	$106,000.00
	Jiao	Hu	85279	958-317-4881	JiaHu17572@mail.com	5/4/1968	$58,000.00
	Betty	Thomas	85346	424-860-7223	BetThomas14786@hotmail.com	1/22/1962	$156,000.00
CA							
	Ashwin	Jayaraman	95653	224-746-3969	AsJayaraman15071@gmail.com	12/28/1950	$55,000.00
	Kenji	Matsumoto	93458	958-230-7462	KenMatsumoto10685@zohomail.com	10/17/1946	$212,000.00
CT							
	Dario	Gonzalez	06029	830-448-4777	DaGonzalez17243@aol.com	5/22/1962	$169,000.00
DC							
	Hiroshi	Kobayashi	20393	351-251-8794	HiKobayashi12104@yahoo.com	7/1/1951	$190,000.00
FL							

Access 2016, Windows 10, Microsoft Corporation

FIGURE 4.39 Grouped and Sorted Leads Report

a. Open *a04p1Prospects*. Save the database as **a04p1Prospects_LastFirst**.

b. Click the **Leads table** in the Navigation Pane. Click the **Create tab,** and click **Form** in the Forms group.

A new form based on the Leads table opens in Layout view.

c. Select the **ID text box** of record 1 and drag the right border to the left to resize the column to approximately half of its original width.

The other text boxes will resize as well.

d. Change the title of the form to **New Leads**.

e. Click **Themes** in the Themes group of the Design tab. Apply the **Integral theme** to this form only.

f. Change the font size of the NetWorth text box control to **14** and change the Background Color to **Turquoise, Accent 3**.

g. Click **Select Row** in the Rows & Columns group on the Arrange tab. Click **Move Up** in the Move group until NetWorth displays above First.

> **TROUBLESHOOTING:** If the text box and the label do not move together, click Undo, ensure that both controls are selected, and then follow the instructions in Step g.

h. Save the form as **Leads Form**. Switch to Form view.

i. Navigate to Record 63. Enter your first and last names in the appropriate fields. Leave the Email field blank.

j. Click in the **Last field** and then click **Ascending** in the Sort & Filter group of the Home tab.
   Farrah Aaron should be the first record displayed unless your last name appears before hers alphabetically.
k. Save and close the form.
l. Click the **Leads table** in the Navigation Pane. Click the **Create tab**, click **More Forms** in the Forms group, and then select **Split Form**.
m. Modify the form title to read **Leads-Split Form**. Save the form as **Leads-Split Form** and close the form.
n. Click the **Leads table**. Click **Report** in the Reports group on the Create tab.
   A new report is created based on the Leads table.
o. Make the fields as narrow as possible to remove extra white space. Change the report's orientation to **Landscape**.
p. Delete the **ID**, **Address**, and **City** columns from the report.
q. Ensure that **Group & Sort** is selected in the Grouping & Totals group on the Design tab. Group the records by **State** and sort them by **LastName** in ascending order. Close the Group, Sort, and Total pane.
r. Save the report as **Leads Report**. Close the report.
s. Close the database and exit Access. Based on your instructor's directions, submit a04p1Prospects_LastFirst.

2 Salary Analysis

The Human Resources department of the Comfort Insurance Agency has initiated its annual employee performance reviews. You will create a form for them to perform data entry using the Form tool and a multiple items form. You will create a report to display locations, and a report displaying employee salary increases by location. Additionally, you will save the salary increases report as a PDF file. Refer to Figure 4.40 as you complete this exercise.

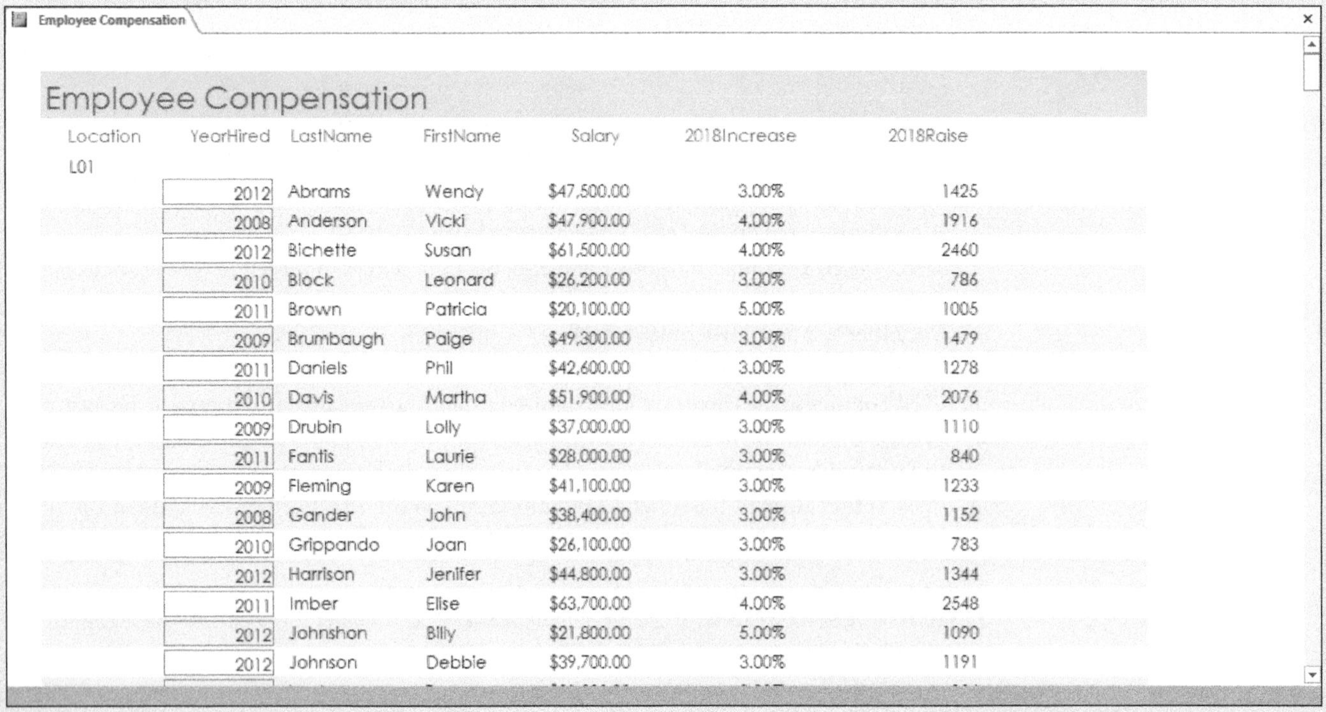

Employee Compensation

Employee Compensation

Location	YearHired	LastName	FirstName	Salary	2018Increase	2018Raise
L01						
	2012	Abrams	Wendy	$47,500.00	3.00%	1425
	2008	Anderson	Vicki	$47,900.00	4.00%	1916
	2012	Bichette	Susan	$61,500.00	4.00%	2460
	2010	Block	Leonard	$26,200.00	3.00%	786
	2011	Brown	Patricia	$20,100.00	5.00%	1005
	2009	Brumbaugh	Paige	$49,300.00	3.00%	1479
	2011	Daniels	Phil	$42,600.00	3.00%	1278
	2010	Davis	Martha	$51,900.00	4.00%	2076
	2009	Drubin	Lolly	$37,000.00	3.00%	1110
	2011	Fantis	Laurie	$28,000.00	3.00%	840
	2009	Fleming	Karen	$41,100.00	3.00%	1233
	2008	Gander	John	$38,400.00	3.00%	1152
	2010	Grippando	Joan	$26,100.00	3.00%	783
	2012	Harrison	Jenifer	$44,800.00	3.00%	1344
	2011	Imber	Elise	$63,700.00	4.00%	2548
	2012	Johnshon	Billy	$21,800.00	5.00%	1090
	2012	Johnson	Debbie	$39,700.00	3.00%	1191

FIGURE 4.40 Employee Compensation Report

a. Open *a04p2Insurance*. Save the database as **a04p2Insurance_LastFirst**.

b. Click the **Locations table** in the Navigation Pane. Click the **Create tab,** and click **Form** in the Forms group.

c. Click the **View arrow** in the Views group on the Home tab, and select **Design View**. Click anywhere in the subform control, and press **Delete**. Switch to Layout view.

d. Ensure that the **LocationID text box** containing *L01* in Record 1 is selected. Drag the right border to the left to resize the column to approximately half of its original width. The other text boxes will resize as well.

e. Click **Themes** in the Themes group on the Design tab. Right-click the **Wisp theme,** and select **Apply Theme to This Object Only**.

f. Change the font size of the Location text box control (containing *Atlanta*) to **14**, and change the Background Color to **Green, Accent 6, Lighter 60%**.

g. Click **Select Row** in the Rows & Columns group on the Arrange tab. Click **Move Up** in the Move group until Location displays above LocationID.

h. Save the form as **Locations Data Entry**.

i. Click **Layout view**, and delete the **LocationID field**. Delete the **Office Phone label**. Move the **Office Phone field** to the row immediately below the Location field.

j. Add **LocationID** back to the form from the Field List, immediately below the Address field. Close the Field List pane.

k. Switch to Form view, and then save and close the form.

l. Click the **Locations table** in the Navigation Pane. Click the **Create tab,** and click **Report** in the Reports group.

m. Click the **LocationID label,** and drag the right border of the label to the left to reduce the size of the control to approximately half of its original size.

n. Repeat the sizing process with the **Zipcode label** and the **OfficePhone label**. Adjust the other column widths until there are no controls on the right side of the vertical dashed line (page break). Drag the control containing the page number to the left so that it is inside the page break.

o. Display the report in Report view. Verify that the report is only one page wide in Report view. Save the report as **Locations** and close the report.

p. Click the **Employees Query** in the Navigation Pane. Click the **Create tab,** and click **Report Wizard** in the Reports group. Respond to the prompts as follows:

- Add all the fields to the Selected Fields list. Click **HireDate,** and remove the field from the Selected Fields. Remove **YearHired** from the Selected Fields. Click **Next**.
- Accept grouping by Location. Click **Next**.
- Select **LastName** for the first sort order, and **FirstName** for the second (ascending order for both). Click **Summary Options**.
- Click **Sum** for Salary, **Avg** for 2018Increase, and **Avg** for YearsWorked. Click **OK**. Click **Next**.
- Accept the Stepped layout. Change Orientation to **Landscape**. Click **Next**.
- Type **Employee Compensation** for the title of the report. Click **Finish**.

q. Click **Close Print Preview**. Switch to Layout view.

r. Adjust the column widths so that all of the data values are visible and the columns all fit within the vertical dashed border (page break). Some of the text boxes and labels will need to be relocated; select the control to be moved and click and drag it to a new location.

s. Click **Themes** in the Themes group on the Design tab. Right-click the **Slice theme** and select **Apply Theme to This Object Only**. Adjust the label widths and report title so that they are fully visible. Scroll to the bottom of the report and move any text boxes, such as the page number control, so that they are inside the page break. Resize all text boxes and labels so that their values are fully visible.

t. Delete the **YearsWorked field** and **label**.

u. Click and drag **YearHired** from the Field List into the report layout. Drag and drop the column into the space immediately to the right of the Location column. Close the Field List. Display the report in Print Preview. Compare your report to Figure 4.40. Make adjustments as required.

v. Save the report as a PDF file named **a04p2Employee_Compensation_LastFirst**. Close the reader window.

w. Save and close the Employee Compensation report.

x. Create a Multiple Items form based on the Titles table. Resize the fields so that they are all visible onscreen without scrolling. Save the form as **Job Titles**. Close the form.

y. Close the database and exit Access. Based on your instructor's directions, submit the following:

a04p2Insurance_LastFirst

a04p2Employee Compensation_LastFirst

Mid-Level Exercises

1 Hotel Chain

ANALYSIS CASE

You are the general manager of a large hotel chain. You track revenue by categories, such as conference room rentals and weddings. You want to create a report that shows which locations are earning the most revenue in each category. You will also create a report to show you details of your three newest areas: St. Paul, St. Louis, and Seattle.

a. Open *a04m1Rewards*. Save the database as **a04m1Rewards_LastFirst**.

b. Select the **Members table**, and create a Multiple Items form. Save the form as **Maintain Members**.

c. Modify the form in Layout view as follows:
- Change the MemNumber label to **MemID**, and reduce the MemNumber column width.
- Adjust the column widths to eliminate extra white space.
- Delete the form icon (the picture next to the title of the form) in the Form Header.

d. Change the sorting on the MemberSince control so that the members who joined most recently are displayed first.

DISCOVER

e. Click the **LastName field**. Change the Control Padding to **Wide**. (Hint: Search **Control Padding** in the *Tell me what you want to do...* box).

f. Save and close the form.

g. Select the **Revenue query**, and create a report using the Report Wizard. Answer the wizard prompts as follows:
- Include all fields in the report.
- Add grouping first by **City** and then by **ServiceName**.
- Add a Sum to the Revenue field, and click the **Summary Only option**.
- Select **Outline Layout**.
- Name the report **Revenue by City and Service**.

h. Scroll through all the pages to check the layout of the report while in Print Preview mode.

i. Close Print Preview. Switch to Layout view, and delete the **NumInParty** and **PerPersonCharge** controls.

j. Change the font size, font color, and background color of the Sum control (found at the bottom of the report) so the control stands out from the other controls.

k. Change the font size, font color, and background color of the Grand Total control (found at the end of the report) so the control stands out as well.

l. Change the sort on the report, so that it sorts by city in descending order—that is, so that the last city alphabetically (St. Paul) is displayed first.

m. Examine the data in the report to determine and note which city (St. Paul, St. Louis, or Seattle) has the highest Sum of event revenue. You will use this information to modify a query. Save and close the report.

n. Modify the Totals by Service query so that the criteria for the City field is the city you determined had the highest sum of event revenue (St. Paul, St. Louis, or Seattle). Run, save, and close the query.

o. Create a report using the Report tool based on the Totals by Service query. Name the report **Targeted City**.

p. Close the report.

q. Close the database and exit Access. Based on your instructor's directions, submit a04m1Rewards_LastFirst.

2 Benefit Auction

FROM SCRATCH

You are helping to organize a benefit auction to raise money for families who lost their homes in a natural disaster. The information for the auction is currently stored in an Excel spreadsheet, but you have volunteered to import it into Access. You will create a database that will store the data from Excel in Access. You will create a form to manage the data-entry process. You also create two reports: one that lists the items collected in each category and one for labels so you can send the donors a thank-you letter after the auction.

a. Open Access, and create a new database named **a04m2Auction_LastFirst**.

A new table displays with an ID column.

b. Switch to Design view. Type **Items** in the **Save As dialog box**, and click **OK**.

c. Change the ID Field Name to **ItemID**. Type **Description** in the second row, and press **Tab**. Set **Short Text** as the Data Type. Type **50** in the **Field Size property** in Field Properties.

d. Type the remainder of the fields and adjust the data types as shown:

Field Name	Data Type
DateOfDonation	**Date/Time**
Category	**Short Text**
Price	**Currency**
DonorName	**Short Text**
DonorAddress1	**Short Text**
DonorAddress2	**Short Text**

e. Open Excel. Open the *a04m2Items* file. Examine the length of the Category, Donor Name, Donor Address 1, and Donor Address 2 columns. Determine how many characters are needed for each field based on the longest value in each column, and round that value up to the nearest 5. For example, if a field needs 23 characters, you would round up to 25. You will use this to change field sizes in the table.

f. Change the field sizes for Category, DonorName, DonorAddress1, and DonorAddress2 to the sizes you chose in Step e. Save the table.

g. Copy and paste the 26 rows from the Excel spreadsheet into the Items table. To paste the rows, locate the * to the left of the first blank row, click the Record Selector, right-click the Record Selector, and then from the shortcut menu, select Paste. Resize the columns so all data is visible. Close the table.

TROUBLESHOOTING: Once you have pasted the data, ensure that your chosen field sizes did not cause you to lose data. If so, update the field sizes, delete the records you pasted to the table, and then repeat Step g.

h. Verify that the Items table is selected in the Navigation Pane. Create a new form using the **Form** tool.

i. Change the layout of the form to **Tabular Layout**. Resize field widths to reduce extra space. It is acceptable for field values in the text boxes to display on two lines.

j. Change the title of the form to **Items for Auction**.

k. Add conditional formatting so that each Price that is greater than 90 has a text color of **Green** (seventh column, first row below Standard Colors).

l. Save the form as **Auction Items Form**.

m. Switch to Form view. Create a new record with the following data. Note that the form will automatically assign an ItemID for you.

Description	DateOfDonation	Category	Price	DonorName	DonorAddress1	DonorAddress2
iPad	**12/31/2018**	**House**	**$400**	**Staples**	**500 Market St.**	**Brick, NJ 08723**

n. Add a sort to the form, so that the lowest priced items display first. Save and close the form.

o. Select the **Items table** in the Navigation Pane, and create a report using the Report Wizard. Include all fields except the two donor address fields, group by Category, include the Sum of Price as a Summary Option, accept the default layout, and then save the report as **Auction Items by Category**.

p. Switch to Layout view, and adjust the controls so that all data is visible. Adjust the widths of the controls until there are no controls extending over the right side of the vertical dashed line (page break). Preview the report to verify that the column widths are correct.

q. Sort the report so the least expensive item is displayed first in each group. Save and close the report.

DISCOVER H

r. Create mailing labels based on the Avery 5660 template. Place the donor name on the first line, address (**DonorAddress1**) on the second, and city, state, and ZIP (**DonorAddress2**) on the third line. Sort the labels by **DonorName**. Name the report **Donor Labels**. After you create the labels, display them in Print Preview mode to verify that all values will fit onto the label template. Close the label report.

s. Close the database and exit Access. Based on your instructor's directions, submit a04m2Auction_LastFirst.

3 New Castle County Technical Services

RUNNING CASE

New Castle County Technical Services (NCCTS) provides technical support for a number of companies in the greater New Castle County, Delaware, area. Now that you have completed the database tables, set the appropriate relationships, and created queries, you are ready to create a form and a report.

a. Open the database *a03m3NCCTS_LastFirst* and save it as **a04m3NCCTS_LastFirst**.

> **TROUBLESHOOTING:** If you did not complete the Chapter 3 case, return to Chapter 3, complete the case, and then return to this exercise.

b. Create a split form based on the Calls table.

c. Apply the **Integral theme** to this form only.

d. Add the **Description field** by dragging and dropping it immediately below the CallTypeID (Hint: Click **Show all tables** in the Field List pane, and locate the field by expanding the **Call Types table**). Close the Field List pane. Switch to Form view and ensure that the records are sorted by CallID in ascending order.

e. Save the form as **Calls Data Entry**, and close the form.

f. Use the Report tool to create a basic report based on the Customer Happiness query.

g. Sort the records by the **Avg Rating field** in ascending order.

h. Apply the **Integral theme** to this report only.

i. Change the title of the report to **Customer Satisfaction Ratings**, and format the background color of the control to **Medium Gray** (under Standard Colors).

j. Set the font color of the title control to **Blue, Accent 2**, the font size to **20**, and the alignment to **Center**. Click the default logo in the report header and press **Delete**.

k. Switch to Report view. Save the report as **Customer Satisfaction Survey**, and close the report.

l. Close the database and exit Access. Based on your instructor's directions, submit a04m3NCCTS_LastFirst.

Beyond the Classroom

Create a Split Form

This chapter introduced you to Access forms, including the split form. It is possible to convert an existing form into a split form if you know how to modify form properties. First, create a new database and name the file **a04b1Split_LastFirst**. Next, import only the Books table and Books form from the *a04b1BooksImport* database. To import the objects, click the **External Data tab** and click **Access** in the Import & Link group. Perform an Internet search to find the steps to convert a form to a split form. Use the information from the Internet to convert the Books form into a split form. Make sure the datasheet is in the bottom pane of the form. Delete the AuthorCode text box and label from the top pane of the form. Change the form so that it sorts by Title in ascending order. Increase the font size of the Title control to **14**, and change its background color to **Medium Gray** (under Standard Colors). Apply the **Integral** theme to this form only. Save the form as **Split Form Books**. Switch to Form view, and then close the form. Close the database and exit Access. Based on your instructor's directions, submit a04b1Split_LastFirst.

Properties by City

DISASTER RECOVERY

A co-worker is having difficulty with an Access report and asked you for your assistance. He was trying to fix the report and seems to have made things worse. Open the *a04b2Sales* database and save the file as **a04b2Sales_LastFirst**. Open the Properties Report in Report view. The report columns do not fit across one page. In addition, there is a big gap between two fields, and he moved the Beds and Baths fields so they are basically on top of one another. Add all of the fields to a tabular layout. Group the records first by City, and then by Beds in descending order. Within each group, sort the report by ListPrice in descending order. Change the report to Landscape orientation and adjust the column widths so they all fit across one page (inside the dashed vertical page break). Apply the Organic theme to this report only, and switch to Report view. Save the new report as **Properties by City**, close the report, and then delete the original **Properties Report** from the database (right-click the report in the Navigation Pane, and from the shortcut menu, select **Delete**). Close the database and exit Access. Based on your instructor's directions, submit a04b2Sales_LastFirst.

Capstone Exercise

MyITLab® Grader

Your boss asked you to prepare a schedule for each speaker for the national conference being hosted next year on your campus. She wants to mail the schedules to the speakers so that they can provide feedback on the schedule prior to its publication. You assure her that you can accomplish this task with Access.

Database File Setup

You need to copy an original database file, rename the copied file, and then open the copied database to complete this Capstone exercise. After you open the copied database, you replace an existing employee's name with your name.

a. Open the *a04c1_NatConf* database, and save it as **a04c1NatConf_LastFirst**.

b. Open the Speakers table.

c. Find and replace *YourName* with your own first and last name. Close the table.

Create and Customize a Form

You want to create a form to add and update the Speakers table. Use the Form tool to create the form and modify the form as required. You will also add a layout to an existing form.

a. Select the **Speakers table** in the Navigation Pane as the record source for the form.

b. Use the **Form tool** to create a new form with a stacked layout.

c. Change the form's title to **Enter/Edit Speakers**.

d. Reduce the width of the text box controls to approximately half of their original size.

e. Delete the **Sessions subform** control from the form.

f. View the form and the data in Form view. Sort the records by **LastName** in ascending order.

g. Save the form as **Edit Speakers**. Close the form.

h. Open the Room Information form in Layout view. Select all controls in the form, and apply the **Stacked Layout**.

i. Switch to Form view, and then save and close the form.

Create a Report

You will create a report based on the Speaker and Room Schedule query. You decide to use the Report Wizard to accomplish this task. You will also email the schedule to the presenters, so you will save the report as a PDF file.

a. Select the **Speaker and Room Schedule query** in the Navigation Pane as the record source for the report.

b. Activate the **Report Wizard**,and use the following options as you proceed through the wizard steps:

- Select all of the available fields for the report.
- View the data by Speakers.
- Accept LastName and FirstName as the grouping levels.
- Use **Date** as the primary sort field in ascending order.
- Accept the Stepped and Portrait options.
- Save the report as **Speaker Schedule**.
- Switch to Layout view, and apply the **Organic theme** to this report only.

c. Switch to Report view to determine whether all of the columns fit across the page. Switch to Layout view, and ensure that the column widths are adjusted accordingly.

d. Switch to Print Preview, and save the report as a PDF named **a04c1Speaker_LastFirst**.

e. Close the reader program that displays the PDF report, and return to Access. Close Print Preview. Save and close the report.

Add an Additional Field to the Query and the Report

You realize that the session start times were not included in the query. You add the field to the query and then create a new report with the Report Wizard to include the missing field.

a. Open the Speaker and Room Schedule query in Design view.

b. Add the **StartingTime field** from the Sessions table to the design grid, after the Date field. Run the query.

c. Save and close the query.

d. Click the **Speaker and Room Schedule query**. Activate the Report Wizard again and use the following options:

- Select all of the available fields for the report.
- View the data by Speakers.
- Use the LastName and FirstName fields as the grouping levels.
- Use **Date** as the primary sort field in ascending order.
- Use **StartingTime** as the secondary sort field in ascending order.
- Select the **Stepped** and **Portrait options**.
- Name the report **Speaker Schedule Revised**.
- Switch to Layout view and apply the **Facet theme** to this report only.

e. Adjust the widths of the columns and other controls so that all the data is visible and fits across the page. Switch to Report view to ensure that the adjustments were appropriate. Return to Layout view, and make any required changes.

f. Add spaces to the column heading labels so that all values display as two words where appropriate, for example, the label *LastName* should read **Last Name**, *RoomID* as **Room ID**, etc.

g. Save and close the report.

h. Close the database and exit Access. Based on your instructor's directions, submit the following:

a04c1NatConf_LastFirst
a04c1Speaker_LastFirst

Access Application Capstone Exercise

You were recently hired by your local college to help with registering all transfer students. The college's Transfer Counseling Department is a one-stop location for transfer students to come with questions. They have been working with Excel spreadsheets generated by the Information Technology department, but they are hoping to do more with an Access database. They have had a number of problems, including employees putting information in the wrong fields, inputting information in the wrong format, and creating incorrect formulas. They are also hoping for more consistent ways of finding information, as well as being able to generate reports. Your tasks include importing an existing Excel worksheet as a table into your Access database; modifying the table; creating a relationship between two tables; creating queries with calculated fields, functions, and totals; creating a form for input; creating a report; and backing up the database.

Set Up the Database File and Import an Excel Worksheet

To start, you have been provided with a database the Information Technology department created. The database has one table and one form. You will be importing an Excel spreadsheet into a table and creating a primary key.

a. Open *aApp_Cap1_College* and save the database as **aApp_Cap1_College_LastFirst**.

b. Import the *aApp_Cap1_Transfer* Excel workbook into a new table named **Transfer Schools**. While importing the data, ensure that **StudentID** has a data type of **Short Text**, and select **StudentID** as the primary key.

Modify a Table

Now that you have imported the data from the spreadsheet, you will modify the field properties in the Transfer Schools table and demonstrate sorting.

a. Open the Transfer Schools table in Design view.

b. Set the StudentID field size to **10**.

c. Remove the @ symbol from the StudentID format property.

d. Change the AdmittingSchool field size to **75**.

e. Change the RegistrationFee and TuitionDue fields to have **0** decimal places.

f. Switch to Datasheet view. Resize the AdmittingSchool column by double-clicking on the border between AdmittingSchool and AdmissionDate.

g. Sort the Transfer Schools table on the CreditsTransferred field in ascending order.

h. Save and close the table.

Create Relationships

Now that the table is imported and modified, you will create a relationship between the Transfer Schools and Transfer Students tables.

a. Add the Transfer Schools and Transfer Students tables to the Relationships window.

b. Create a one-to-one relationship between the StudentID field in the Transfer Students table and the StudentID field in the Transfer Schools table. Enforce referential integrity between the two tables and cascade updates.

c. Save the changes and close the Relationships window.

Modify Data in a Form

You will demonstrate changing information in a form.

a. Open the Transfer Students Data Entry form.

b. Change the major for *Cornelius Kavanagh* to **Elementary Education**. Close the form.

Create a Query

Rey Rivera, a counselor in the center, would like your assistance in helping him find certain information. You will create a query for him and demonstrate how he can change information.

a. Create a new query using Design view. This query will access fields from both the Transfer Schools and Transfer Students tables. From the Transfer Students table, add the FirstName, LastName, Major, Class, and GPA fields. From the Transfer Schools table, add the AdmissionDate, TuitionDue, CreditsEarned, and CreditsTransferred fields.

b. Save the query as **Transfer Credits**.

c. Set the criteria in the AdmissionDate field to **8/1/2018**. Run the query (19 records will display).

d. Type **$1500** in the TuitionDue field for Diana Sullivan and type **3.51** as the GPA for Audrey Owen.

e. Save and close the query.

Create Calculated Fields

Now that you have created the query, you will create a second query for Rey that will calculate the number of credits students lost upon transfer, the tuition payments for which they will be responsible (assuming three payments per semester), and the due date of the first payment.

a. Create a copy of the Transfer Credits query. Name the copy **Transfer Credit Calculations**. Open the new query in Design view.

b. Remove the criteria from the AdmissionDate field.

c. Create a calculated field in the first empty field cell of the query named **LostCredits** that subtracts CreditsTransferred from CreditsEarned.

d. Create another calculated field named **TuitionPayments** that determines tuition paid in three installments. Using the Pmt function, replace the rate argument with **0.025/3**, the num_periods argument with **3**, and the present_value argument with the student's tuition payment. Use **0** for the future_value and type arguments. Ensure that the payment appears as a positive number.

e. Format the TuitionPayments calculated field as **Currency**.

f. Create another calculated field named **FirstPayment** after the TuitionPayments field. To calculate the due date, add **30** to their AdmissionDate. Run the query and verify that the three calculated fields have valid data.

g. Add a total row to the datasheet. Sum the TuitionDue column and average the TuitionPayment column. Save and close the query.

Create a Totals Query

Cala Hajjar, the director of the center, needs to summarize information about the transfer students for the 2018–2019 academic year to present to the College's Board of Trustees. You will create a totals query for her to summarize the number of transfer students, average number of credits earned and transferred, and total tuition earned by transfer institution.

a. Create a new query in Design view. Add the Transfer Schools table.

b. Add the AdmittingSchool, StudentID, CreditsEarned, CreditsTransferred, and TuitionDue fields.

c. Sort the query by AdmittingSchool in ascending order.

d. Show the Total row. Group by AdmittingSchool and show the count of StudentID, the average of CreditsEarned, the average of CreditsTransferred, and the sum of TuitionDue.

e. Format both average fields as **Standard**.

f. Change the caption for the StudentID field to **NumStudents**, the caption for the CreditsEarned average to **AvgCreditsEarned**, the caption for the CreditsTransferred average to **AvgCredits Transferred**, and the caption for the sum of TuitionDue to **TotalTuition**.
g. Run the query.
h. Save the query as **Transfer Summary**.
i. Close the query.

Create a Form

Hideo Sasaki, the department's administrative assistant, will handle data entry. He has asked you to simplify the way he inputs information into the new table. You will create a form based on the new Transfer Schools table.

a. Create a Split Form using the Transfer Schools table as the source.
b. Change the height of the AdmittingSchool field to be approximately half the current height.
c. Remove the layout from all the labels and fields. Shrink each field so it is approximately as large as it needs to be.
d. Click record **123455** in the bottom half of the split form. Make sure all values are still visible in the top half of the form. If not, adjust the controls so all values are visible.
e. Move the CreditsTransferred field so it is to the right of the CreditsEarned field on the same row.
f. Change the format of the TuitionDue field so the font size is **18** and the font color is **Red** (last row, second column in the Standard Colors section). Resize the field if necessary so the entire value displays.
g. Change the fill color of the StudentID field to be **Yellow** (last row, fourth column in the Standard Colors section).
h. Save the form as **Transfer Schools Form**. Save and close the form.

Create a Report

Cala is hoping you can create a more print-friendly version of the query you created earlier for her to distribute to the Board of Trustees. You will create a report based on the Transfer Credit Calculations query.

a. Create a report using the Report Wizard. Add the **Class**, **FirstName**, **LastName**, **Major**, **GPA**, and **LostCredits** fields from the Transfer Credit Calculations query. Do not add any grouping or sorting. Ensure that the report is in Landscape orientation.
b. Save the report as **Transfer Students Report** and view the report in Layout view.

Format a Report

Now that you have included the fields Cala has asked for, you will work to format the report to make the information more obvious.

a. Apply the **Wisp theme** (last row, first column) to this object only.
b. Group the report by the Class field. Sort the records within each group by LastName then by FirstName, both in ascending order.
c. Change the font size of the Class field to **16**.
d. Adjust the text boxes so the values for the Major field are completely visible.
e. Switch to Print Preview mode and verify that the report is only one page wide (Note: It may be a number of pages long).
f. Export the results as a PDF document using the file name **aApp_Cap1_Transfer_LastFirst**.
g. Save and close the report.

Close and Submit the Database

a. Create a backup of the database. Accept the default name for the backup.

b. Close all database objects and exit Access. Based on your instructor's directions, submit the following:

   aApp_Cap1_College_LastFirst

   aApp_Cap1_College_LastFirst_*CurrentDate*

   aApp_Cap1_Transfer_LastFirst

Glossary

100% stacked column chart A chart type that places (stacks) data in one column per category, with each column the same height of 100%.

Absolute cell reference A designation that indicates a constant reference to a specific cell location; the cell reference does not change when you copy the formula.

Access A relational database management system in which you can record and link data, query databases, and create forms and reports.

Accounting Number Format A number format that displays $ on the left side of a cell, formats a value with a comma for every three digits on the left side of the decimal point, and displays two digits to the right of the decimal point.

Action Center A location in Windows 10, accessed by an icon in the Notifications area on the taskbar, that provides status information, notifications, and recommended actions for various maintenance and security settings.

Active cell The current cell in a worksheet. It is indicated by a dark green border, and the Name Box shows the location of the active cell.

Add-in A custom program or additional command that extends the functionality of a Microsoft Office program.

Adjustment handle A yellow circle on a shape that is used to change the shape.

Aggregate function A calculation performed on an entire column of data that returns a single value. Includes functions such as Sum, Avg, and Count.

Align A feature that enables you to line up shapes and objects. You can align objects by lining up the sides, middles, or top/bottom edges of objects.

Alignment The placement of data within the boundaries of a cell. By default, text aligns on the left side, and values align on the right side of a cell.

Alignment guide A horizontal or vertical green bar that appears as you move an object, assisting with aligning the object with text or with another object.

Alt text An accessibility compliance feature where you enter text and a description for an objective, such as a table or a chart. A special reader can read the alt text to a user.

AND condition A condition in a query, returns only records that meet all criteria.

Animation A motion applied to text and objects.

Annotation A written note or drawing on a slide for additional commentary or explanation

APA (American Psychological Association) A writing style established by the American Psychological Association with rules and conventions for documenting sources and organizing a research paper (used primarily in business and the social sciences).

Application part A feature that enables you to add a set of common Access components to an existing database, such as a table, a form, and a report for a related task.

Area chart A chart type that emphasizes magnitude of changes over time by filling in the space between lines with a color.

Argument A positional reference contained within parentheses in a function such as a cell reference or value, required to complete a function and produce output.

Aspect Ratio The ratio of an object's width to its height.

Auto Fill A feature that helps you complete a sequence of months, abbreviated months, quarters, weekdays, weekday abbreviations, or values. Auto Fill also can be used to fill or copy a formula down a column or across a row.

AutoComplete A feature that searches for and automatically displays any other label in that column that matches the letters you type.

AutoNumber A number that automatically increments each time a record is added.

AutoRecover A feature that enables Word to recover a previous version of a document.

AVERAGE function A predefined formula that calculates the arithmetic mean, or average, of values in a range of cells.

Axis title A label that describes either the category axis or the value axis. Provides clarity, particularly in describing the value axis.

Back Up Database A utility that creates a duplicate copy of the entire database to protect from loss or damage.

Background The portion of a picture that can be deleted when removing the background of a picture.

Background Styles gallery A gallery providing both solid color and background styles for application to a theme.

Backstage view A component of Office that provides a concise collection of commands related to an open file.

Bar chart A chart type that compares values across categories using horizontal bars where the length represents the value; the longer the bar, the larger the value. In a bar chart, the horizontal axis displays values and the vertical axis displays categories.

Bibliography A list of works cited or consulted by an author in his or her work.

Bitmap image An image created by bits or pixels placed on a grid to form a picture.

Blog The chronological publication of personal thoughts and Web links.

Bookmark A method used to mark specific locations in a video.

Border A line that surrounds a paragraph, page, or a table or table element.

Border (Excel) A line that surrounds a cell or a range of cells to offset particular data from the rest of the data in a worksheet.

Border Painter A feature that enables you to choose border formatting and click on any table border to apply the formatting.

Breakpoint The lowest value for a category or in a series.

Brightness A picture correction that controls the lightness or darkness of a picture.

Bulleted list A graphic element that itemizes and separates paragraph text to increase readability; often used to identify lists.

Calculated field A field that displays the result of an expression rather than data stored in a field.

Callout A shape that be can used to add notes, often used in cartooning.

Cancel An icon between the Name Box and Formula Bar. When you enter or edit data, click Cancel to cancel the data entry or edit, and revert back to the previous data in the cell, if any. Cancel changes from gray to red when you position the pointer over it.

Caption A descriptive title for a table

Caption property A property that is used to create a more understandable label than a field name that displays in the top row in Datasheet view and in forms and reports.

Cascade Delete Related Records When the primary key value is deleted in a primary table, Access will automatically delete all records in related tables that contain values that match the primary key.

Cascade Update Related Fields An option that directs Access to automatically change all foreign key values in a related table when the primary key value is modified in a primary table.

Category axis The chart axis that displays descriptive labels for the data points plotted in a chart. The category axis labels are typically text contained in the first column of worksheet data (such as job titles) used to create the chart.

Cell The intersection of a column and row in a table, such as the intersection of column B and row 5.

Cell address The unique identifier of a cell, starting with the column letter and then the row number, such as C6.

Cell style A set of formatting applied to a cell to produce a consistent appearance for similar cells within a worksheet.

Center alignment Positions text horizontally in the center of a line, with an equal distance from both the left and right margins.

Chart A visual representation of numerical data.

Chart area A container for the entire chart and all of its elements, including the plot area, titles, legends, and labels.

Chart element A component of a chart that helps complete or clarify the chart.

Chart filter A setting that controls what data series and categories are displayed or hidden in a chart.

Chart sheet A sheet within a workbook that contains a single chart and no spreadsheet data.

Chart style A collection of formatting that controls the color of the chart area, plot area, and data series.

Chart title The label that describes the entire chart. The title is usually placed at the top of the chart area.

Chicago Manual of Style A writing style established by the University of Chicago with rules and conventions for preparing an academic paper for publication.

Citation A note recognizing a source of information or a quoted passage.

Clipboard An area of memory reserved to temporarily hold selections that have been cut or copied and allows you to paste the selections.

Cloud storage A technology used to store files and to work with programs that are stored in a central location on the Internet.

Clustered column chart A type of chart that groups, or clusters, columns set side by side to compare several data points among categories.

Codec (coder/decoder) A digital video compression scheme used to compress a video and decompress for playback.

Collapsed outline An Outline view that displays only the slide number, icon, and title of each slide in Outline view.

Color scale A conditional format that displays a particular color based on the relative value of the cell contents to the other selected cells.

Colors gallery A set of colors available for every theme.

Column A format that separates document text into side-by-side vertical blocks, often used in newsletters.

Column chart A type of chart that compares values vertically in columns where the height represents the value; the taller the column, the larger the value. In a column chart, the vertical axis displays values and the horizontal axis displays categories.

Column heading The alphabetical letter above a column in a worksheet. For example, B is the column heading for the second column.

Column index number The column number in the lookup table that contains the return values.

Column width The horizontal measurement of a column in a table or a worksheet. In Excel, it is measured by the number of characters or pixels.

Combo chart A chart that combines two chart types, such as column and line, to plot different types of data, such as quantities and percentages.

Comma Style A number format that formats a value with a comma for every three digits on the left side of the decimal point and displays two digits to the right of the decimal point.

Command A button or area within a group that you click to perform tasks.

Comment A note, annotation, or additional information to the author or another reader about the content of a document.

Comment balloon A small balloon that displays on the right side of a paragraph in which a comment has been made and provides access to the comment.

Compact and Repair Database A utility that reduces the size of a database and fixes any errors that may exist in the file.

Comparison Operator An operator such as greater than (>), less than (<), greater than or equal to (>=), and less than or equal to (<=), etc. used to limit query results that meet these criteria.

Compressed (zipped) folder A folder created with the Zip feature, contains a file or group of files. A compressed folder uses less drive space and can be transferred or shared with other users more quickly.

Compression A method applied to data to reduce the amount of space required for file storage.

Conditional formatting A set of rules that applies specific formatting to highlight or emphasize cells that meet specific conditions.

Connector A line with connection points at each end.

Constant A value that does not change.

Contextual tab A tab that contains a group of commands related to the selected object.

Contrast The difference between the darkest and lightest areas of a picture.

Control A text box, button, label, or other tool you use to add, edit, and display the data in a form or report.

Copy A command used to duplicate a selection from the original location and place a copy in the Office Clipboard.

Copyright The legal protection afforded to a written or artistic work.

Cortana Microsoft 10's personal assistant that helps search the Web and your PC, and can also assist with reminders, tasks, and other activities.

COUNT function A predefined formula that tallies the number of cells in a range that contain values you can use in calculations, such as numerical and date data, but excludes blank cells or text entries from the tally.

COUNTA function A predefined formula that tallies the number of cells in a range that are not blank, that is, cells that contain data, whether a value, text, or a formula.

COUNTBLANK function A predefined formula that tallies the number of cells in a range that are blank.

Cover page The first page of a report, including the report title, author or student, and other identifying information.

Criteria row A row in Query Design view that determines which records will be selected.

Crop The process of reducing an image size by eliminating unwanted portions of an image or other graphical object.

Current List A list that includes all citation sources you use in the current document.

Custom Web app A feature which enables users to create a database that you can build and then use and share with others through the Web.

Cut A command used to remove a selection from the original location and place it in the Office Clipboard.

Data bar Data bar formatting applies a gradient or solid fill bar in which the width of the bar represents the current cell's value compared relatively to other cells' values.

Data label An identifier that shows the exact value of a data point in a chart. Appears above or on a data point in a chart. May indicate percentage of a value to the whole on a pie chart.

Data point A numeric value that describes a single value in a chart or worksheet.

Data redundancy The unnecessary storing of duplicate data in two or more tables.

Data series A group of related data points that display in row(s) or column(s) in a worksheet.

Data source A list of information that is merged with a main document during a mail merge procedure.

Data structure The organization method used to manage multiple data points within a dataset.

Data table A grid that contains the data source values and labels to plot data in a chart. A data table may be placed below a chart or hidden from view.

Data type Determines the type of data that can be entered and the operations that can be performed on that data.

Database A collection of data organized as meaningful information that can be accessed, managed, stored, queried, sorted, and reported.

Database Management System (DBMS) A software system that provides the tools needed to create, maintain, and use a database.

Database Splitter A utility that puts the tables in one file (the back-end database), and the queries, forms, and reports in a second file (the front-end database).

Datasheet view A grid containing fields (columns) and records (rows) used to view, add, edit, and delete records.

Deck A collection of slides.

Design view A view which gives users a detailed view of the table's structure and is used to create and modify a table's design by specifying the fields it will contain, the fields' data types, and their associated properties.

Desktop The primary working area of Windows 10 that contains objects such as windows and icons.

Dialog box A box that provides access to more precise, but less frequently used, commands.

Dialog Box Launcher A button that when clicked opens a corresponding dialog box.

Disk Cleanup An administrative tool in Windows that is used to remove unnecessary files from the computer.

Distribute To divide or evenly spread selected shapes over a given area.

Document Inspector Checks for and removes certain hidden and personal information from a document.

Document properties Data elements that identify a document, such as author or comments.

Document theme A set of coordinating fonts, colors, and special effects that gives a stylish and professional look.

Draft view View that shows a great deal of document space, but no margins, headers, footers, or other special features.

Effects gallery A range of special effects for shapes used in the presentation.

Embed A method of storing an object from an external source within a presentation.

Endnote A citation that appears at the end of a document.

Enhanced ScreenTip A small message box that displays when you place the pointer over a command button. The purpose of the command, short descriptive text, or a keyboard shortcut if applicable will display in the box.

Enter An icon between the Name Box and Formula Bar. When you enter or edit data, click Enter to accept data typed in the active cell and keep the current cell active. Enter changes from gray to blue when you position the pointer over it.

Error bars Visual that indicates the standard error amount, a percentage, or a standard deviation for a data point or marker in a chart.

Excel An application that makes it easy to organize records, financial transactions, and business information in the form of worksheets.

Expanded outline An Outline view that displays the slide number, icon, title, and content of each slide in the Outline view.

Exploded pie chart A chart type in which one or more pie slices are separated from the rest of the pie chart for emphasis.

Expression A combination of elements that produce a value.

Expression Builder An Access tool that helps you create more complicated expressions.

Eyedropper tool A tool used to recreate an exact color.

Field The smallest data element contained in a table, such as first name, last name, address, and phone number.

Field property A characteristic of a field that determines how it will look and behave.

File Explorer The Windows app that is used to create folders and manage files and folders across various storage locations.

File History A utility in Windows that continuously makes copies of your important files so that you can recover them if you encounter a file problem.

File management The means of providing an organizational structure to file and folders.

Fill color The background color that displays behind the data in a cell so that the data stands out.

Fill handle A small green square at the bottom-right corner of the active cell. You can position the pointer on the fill handle and drag it to repeat the contents of the cell to other cells or to copy a formula in the active cell to adjacent cells down the column or across the row.

Filter A feature which allows users to specify conditions to display only those records that meet those conditions.

Filter By Form A more versatile method of selecting data, enabling users to display records based on multiple criteria.

Filtering The process of specifying conditions to display only those records that meet those conditions.

Firewall A software program included in Windows 10 that helps to protect against unauthorized access, or hacking, to your computer.

First line indent Marks the location to indent only the first line in a paragraph.

Flash Fill A feature that fills in data or values automatically based on one or two examples you enter using another part of data entered in a previous column in the dataset.

Flip To reverse the direction an object faces.

Flow chart An illustration showing the sequence of a project or plan containing steps.

Font A combination of typeface and type style.

Fonts gallery A gallery that pairs a title font with a body font.

Footer Information that displays at the bottom of a document page.

Footnote A citation that appears at the bottom of a page.

Foreground The portion of the picture that is kept when removing the background of a picture.

Foreign key A field in a related table that is the primary key of another table.

Form A database object that is used to add data into or edit data in a table.

Form letter A letter with standard information that you personalize with recipient information, which you might print or email to many people.

Form tool A tool used to create data entry forms for customers, employees, products, and other tables.

Form view A view that provides a simplified user interface primarily used for data entry; does not allow you to make changes to the layout.

Format Painter A feature that enables you to quickly and easily copy all formatting from one area to another in Word, PowerPoint, and Excel.

Formatting The process of modifying text by changing font and paragraph characteristics.

Formula A combination of cell references, operators, values, and/or functions used to perform a calculation.

Formula AutoComplete A feature that displays a list of functions and defined names that match letters as you type a formula.

Formula Bar An element located below the Ribbon and to the right of the Insert Function command. It shows the contents of the active cell. You enter or edit cell contents in the Formula Bar for the active cell.

Freeform shape A shape that combines both curved and straight-line segments.

Freezing The process of keeping rows and/or columns visible onscreen at all times even when you scroll through a large dataset.

Fully qualified structured reference A structured formula that contains the table name.

Function A predefined computation that simplifies creating a complex calculation and produces a result based on inputs known as arguments.

Function ScreenTip A small pop-up description that displays the function's arguments.

Gallery An area in Word which provides additional text styles. In Excel, the gallery provides a choice of chart styles, and in Power Point, the gallery provides transitions.

Gradient fill A fill that contains a blend of two or more colors or shades.

Grid Intersecting lines on a slide that enable you to align objects.

Gridline A horizontal or vertical line that extends from the horizontal or vertical axis through the plot area to guide the reader's eyes across the chart to identify values.

Group A subset of a tab that organizes similar tasks together.

Group (PowerPoint) Multiple objects connected so they are able to move as though they are a single object.

Grouping A method of summarizing data by the values of a field.

Guide A nonprinting, temporary vertical or horizontal line placed on a slide to enable you align objects or determine regions of the slide.

Hanging indent Aligns the first line of a paragraph at the left margin, indenting remaining lines in the paragraph.

Header An area with one or more lines of information at the top of each page.

Header row The first row in a data source, which contains labels describing the data in rows beneath.

Hierarchy A method used to organize text into levels of importance in a structure.

Histogram A chart that is similar to a column chart. The category axis shows bin ranges (intervals) where data is aggregated into bins, and the vertical axis shows frequencies.

HLOOKUP function A function that looks for a value in the top row of a specified table array and returns another value located in the same column from a specified row.

Horizontal alignment The placement of cell data between the left and right cell margins. By default, text is left-aligned, and values are right-aligned.

Icon A graphical link to a program, file, folder, or other item related to your computer.

Icon set Symbols or signs that classify data into three, four, or five categories, based on values in a range.

IF function A predefined formula that evaluates a condition and returns one value if the condition is true and a different value if the condition is false.

Indent A format that offsets data from its default alignment. For example, if text is left-aligned, the text may be indented or offset from the left side to stand out. If a value is right-aligned, it can be indented or offset from the right side of the cell.

Index An alphabetical listing of topics covered in a document, along with the page numbers on which the topic is discussed.

Infographic Informational graphic that is a visual representation of data or knowledge.

Infringement of copyright A situation that occurs when a right of the copyright owner is violated.

Input area A range of cells in a worksheet used to store and change the variables used in calculations.

Insert control An indicator that displays between rows or columns in a table; click the indicator to insert one or more rows or columns.

Insert Function An icon between the Name Box and Formula Bar. Click Insert Function to open the Insertion Function dialog box to search for and insert a particular function.

Insertion point Blinking bar that indicates where text that you next type will appear.

Insights A pane that presents outside resources, such as images, definitions, and other references.

Jump List List of program-specific shortcuts to recently opened files, the program name, an option to pin or unpin the program, and a close window option.

Justified alignment Spreads text evenly between the left and right margins, so that text begins at the left margin and ends uniformly at the right margin.

Kelvin The unit of measurement for absolute temperature used to measure the tone of an image.

Label Wizard A feature that enables you to easily create mailing labels, name tags, and other specialized tags.

Landscape orientation A document layout when a page is wider than it is tall.

Layout Determines the position of the objects or content on a slide.

Layout control A tool that provides guides to help keep controls aligned horizontally and vertically and give your form a uniform appearance.

Layout view A view that enables users to make changes to a layout while viewing the data in the form or report.

Left alignment Begins text evenly at the left margin, with a ragged right edge.

Left indent A setting that positions all text in a paragraph an equal distance from the left margin.

Legend A key that identifies the color, gradient, picture, texture, or pattern assigned to each data series in a chart.

Line chart A chart type that displays lines connecting data points to show trends over equal time periods, such as months, quarters, years, or decades.

Line spacing The vertical spacing between lines in a paragraph.

Line weight The width or thickness of a shape's outline.

Link A connection from the presentation to another location such as a storage device or website.

Live Layout Feature that enables you to watch text flow around an object as you move it, so you can position the object exactly as you want it.

Live Preview An Office feature that provides a preview of the results of a selection when you point to an option in a list or gallery. Using Live Preview, you can experiment with settings before making a final choice.

Lock Drawing Mode Enables the creation of multiple shapes of the same type.

Logical test An expression that evaluates to true or false.

Lookup table A range that contains data for the basis of the lookup and data to be retrieved.

Lookup value The cell reference of the cell that contains the value to look up.

Macro A stored series of commands that carry out an action; often used to automate simple tasks.

Mail Merge A process that combines content from a main document and a data source.

Main document A document that contains the information that stays the same for all recipients in a mail merge.

Margin The area of blank space that displays to the left, right, top, and bottom of a document or worksheet.

Markup A feature to help customize how tracked changes are displayed in a document.

Marquee A selection of multiple objects created by dragging a rectangle around all of the objects you want to select.

Master A slide view where the control of the layouts, background designs, and color combinations for handouts, notes pages, and slides can be set giving a presentation a consistent appearance.

Master List A database of all citation sources created in Word on a particular computer.

MAX function A predefined formula that identifies the highest value in a range.

MEDIAN function A predefined formula that identifies the midpoint value in a set of values.

Merge field An item that serves as a placeholder for the variable data that will be inserted into the main document during a mail merge procedure.

Microsoft Office A productivity software suite including a set of software applications, each one specializing in a particular type of output.

Microsoft Word A word processing software application used to produce all sorts of documents, including memos, newsletters, forms, tables, and brochures.

MIN function A predefined formula that displays the lowest value in a range.

Mini toolbar A toolbar that provides access to the most common formatting selections, such as adding bold or italic, or changing font type or color. Unlike the Quick Access Toolbar, the Mini toolbar is not customizable.

Mixed cell reference A designation that combines an absolute cell reference with a relative cell reference. The absolute part does not change but the relative part does when you copy the formula.

MLA (Modern Language Association) A writing style established by the Modern Language Association, with rules and conventions for preparing research papers (used primarily in the area of humanities).

Module An advanced object written using the VBA (Visual Basic for Applications) programming language.

Multimedia Various forms of media used to entertain or inform an audience.

Multiple Items form A form that displays multiple records in a tabular layout similar to a table's Datasheet view, with more customization options than a datasheet.

Multitable query Results contain fields from two or more tables, enabling you to take advantage of the relationships that have been set in your database.

Name Box An element located below the Ribbon, which displays the address of the active cell.

Narration Spoken commentary that is added to a presentation.

Navigation Pane An Access interface element that organizes and lists the objects in an Access database.

Nested function A function that contains another function embedded inside one or more of it's arguments.

New sheet An icon that, when clicked, inserts a new worksheet in the workbook.

Nonadjacent range A collection of multiple ranges (such as D5:D10 and F5:F10) that are not positioned in a contiguous cluster in an Excel worksheet.

Normal view (Excel) The default view of a worksheet that shows worksheet data but not margins, headers, footers, or page breaks.

Normal view (PowerPoint) The default PowerPoint workspace.

Notes Page view Used for entering and editing large amounts of text to which the speaker can refer when presenting.

Notification area An area on the far right of the taskbar, that includes the clock and a group of icons that relate to the status of a setting or program.

NOW function A predefined formula that calculates the current date and military time that you last opened the workbook using the computer's clock.

Nper Total number of payment periods.

Null The term Access uses to describe a blank field value.

Number format A setting that controls how a value appears in a cell.

Numbered list Sequences items in a list by displaying a successive number beside each item.

Object An item, such as a picture or text box, that can be individually selected and manipulated in a document.

Object (Access) A component created and used to make the database function (such as a table, query, form, or report).

One-to-many relationship When the primary key value in the primary table can match many of the foreign key values in the related table.

OneDrive Microsoft's cloud storage system. Saving files to OneDrive enables them to sync across all Windows devices and to be accessible from any Internet-connected device.

Opaque A solid fill, one with no transparency.

OR condition In a query, returns records meeting any of the specified criteria.

Order of operations A rule that controls the sequence in which arithmetic operations are performed. Also called the *order of precedence*.

Outline A method of organizing text in a hierarchy to depict relationships.

Outline view A structural view of a document that can be collapsed or expanded as necessary.

Outline view (PowerPoint) A view showing the presentation in an outline format displayed in levels according to the points and any subpoints on each slide.

Output area The range of cells in an Excel worksheet that contain formulas dependent on the values in the input area.

Page break An indication of where data will start on another printed page.

Page Break Preview A view setting that displays the worksheet data and page breaks within the worksheet.

Page Layout view A view setting that displays the worksheet data, margins, headers, and footers.

Paragraph spacing The amount of space before or after a paragraph.

Paste A command used to place a cut or copied selection into another location.

Paste Options button An icon that displays in the bottom-right corner immediately after using the Paste command. It enables the user to apply different paste options.

PDF (Portable Document Format) A file type that was created for exchanging documents independent of software applications and operating system environments.

PDF Reflow A Word feature that converts a PDF document into an editable Word document.

Percent Style A number format that displays a value as if it was multiplied by 100 and with the % symbol. The default number of decimal places is zero if you click Percent Style in the Number group or two decimal places if you use the Format Cells dialog box.

Photo Album A presentation containing multiple pictures organized into album pages.

Picture A graphic file that is retrieved from storage media or the Internet and placed in an Office project.

Picture fill Inserts an image from a file into a shape.

Pie chart A chart type that shows each data point in proportion to the whole data series as a slice in a circle. A pie chart depicts only one data series.

Pin A process to add a tile to the Start menu or icon to the taskbar.

Placeholder A container that holds text, images, graphs, or other objects to be used in a presentation.

Plagiarizing The act of using and documenting the works of another as one's own.

Plain text format (.txt) A file format that retains only text but no formatting when you transfer documents between applications or platforms.

Plot area The region of a chart containing the graphical representation of the values in one or more data series. Two axes form a border around the plot area.

Pmt function A function that calculates the periodic loan payment given a fixed rate, number of periods (also known as term), and the present value of the loan (the principal).

Point The smallest unit of measurement used in typography, 1/72 of an inch.

Pointing The process of using the pointer to select cells while building a formula. Also known as *semi-selection*.

Portable Document Format (PDF) A file type that was created for exchanging documents independent of software applications and operating system environment.

Portrait orientation A document layout when a page is taller than it is wide.

Poster Frame The image that displays on a slide when a video is not playing.

PowerPoint An application that enables you to create dynamic presentations to inform groups and persuade audiences.

PowerPoint presentation An electronic slide show that can be edited or delivered in a variety of ways.

PowerPoint show An unchangeable electronic slide show format used for distribution.

Presenter view Specialty view that delivers a presentation on two monitors simultaneously.

Primary key The field (or combination of fields) that uniquely identifies each record in a table.

Print area The range of cells within a worksheet that will print.

Print Layout view View that closely resembles the way a document will look when printed.

Print order The sequence in which the pages are printed.

Print Preview A view that enables you to see exactly what the report will look like when it is printed.

Property Sheet The location where you change settings such as number format and number of decimal places.

Public domain The rights to a literary work or property owned by the public at large.

PV A predefined formula that calculates the present value of a loan.

Query A question about the data stored in a database answers provided in a datasheet.

Quick access A component of File Explorer that contains shortcuts to the most frequently used folders. Folders can be pinned and removed from Quick access.

Quick Access Toolbar A toolbar located at the top-left corner of any Office application window, this provides fast access to commonly executed tasks such as saving a file and undoing recent actions.

Quick Analysis A set of analytical tools you can use to apply formatting, create charts or tables, and insert basic functions.

Quick Style A combination of formatting options that can be applied to a shape or graphic.

Radar chart A chart type that compares aggregate values of three or more variables represented on axes starting from the same point.

Range A group of adjacent or contiguous cells in a worksheet. A range can be adjacent cells in a column (such as C5:C10), in a row (such as A6:H6), or a rectangular group of cells (such as G5:H10).

Range_lookup An argument that determines how the VLOOKUP and HLOOKUP function handle lookup values that are not an exact match for the data in the lookup table.

Rate The periodic interest rate; the percentage of interest paid for each payment period; the first argument in the PMT function.

Read Mode View in which text reflows automatically between columns to make it easier to read.

Reading View Displays the slide show full screen, one slide at a time, complete with animations and transitions.

Real Time Typing A Word feature that shows where co-authors are working, and what their contributions are as they type.

Real-time co-authoring A Word feature that shows several authors simultaneously editing the document in Word or Word Online.

Recolor The process of changing a picture by adjusting the image's colors.

Record A group of related fields representing one entity, such as data for one person, place, event, or concept.

Record source The table or query that supplies the records for a form or report.

Recycle Bin Temporary storage for files deleted from the computer's hard drive or OneDrive.

Referential Integrity Rules in a database that are used to preserve relationships between tables when records are changed.

Relationship A connection between two tables using a common field.

Relative cell reference A designation that indicates a cell's relative location from the original cell containing the formula; the cell reference changes when the formula is copied.

Report A database document that outputs meaningful, professional-looking, formatted information from underlying tables or queries.

Report tool A tool used to instantly create a tabular report based on the table or query currently selected.

Report view A view that enables you to determine what a printed report will look like in a continuous onscreen page layout.

Report Wizard A feature that prompts you for input and then uses your answers to generate a customized report.

Resource Monitor A feature that displays how the computer is using its key resources such as the CPU and RAM.

Revision mark Markings that indicate where text is added, deleted, or formatted while the Track Changes feature is active.

Ribbon The command center of Office applications. It is the long bar located just beneath the title bar, containing tabs, groups, and commands.

Rich Text Format (.rtf) A file format that retains structure and most text formatting when transferring documents between applications or platforms.

Right alignment Begins text evenly at the right margin, with a ragged left edge.

Right indent A setting that positions all text in a paragraph an equal distance from the right margin.

Rotate To move an object around its axis.

Row heading A number to the left side of a row in a worksheet. For example, 3 is the row heading for the third row.

Row height The vertical measurement of the row in a worksheet.

Sans serif font A font that does not contain a thin line or extension at the top and bottom of the primary strokes on characters.

Saturation A characteristic of color that controls its intensity.

Search box A feature located on the taskbar. Combined with Cortana, or used alone, it provides a convenient way to search your computer or the Web.

Section A division to presentation content that groups slides meaningfully.

Section break An indicator that divides a document into parts, enabling different formatting for each section.

Select All The triangle at the intersection of the row and column headings in the top-left corner of the worksheet. Click it to select everything contained in the active worksheet.

Selection Filter A method of selecting that displays only the records that match a criterion you select.

Selection net A selection of multiple objects created by dragging a rectangle around all of the objects you wish to select.

Selection pane A pane designed to help select objects.

Semi-selection The process of using the pointer to select cells while building a formula. Also known as *pointing*.

Serif font A font that contains a thin line or extension at the top and bottom of the primary strokes on characters.

Shading A background color that appears behind text in a paragraph, page, or table element.

Shape A geometric or non-geometric object, such as a rectangle or an arrow, used to create an illustration or highlight information.

Sharpening A technique that enhances the edges of the content in a picture to make the boundaries more prominent.

Sheet tab A visual label that looks like a file folder tab. In Excel, a sheet tab shows the name of a worksheet contained in the workbook.

Sheet tab navigation Visual elements that help you navigate to the first, previous, next, or last sheet within a workbook.

Shortcut An icon on the desktop designated with a small arrow in the bottom-left corner, that provides a link a program.

Shortcut menu A menu that provides choices related to the selection or area at which you right-click.

Simple Markup A Word feature that simplifies the display of comments and revision marks, resulting in a clean, uncluttered look.

Simple Query Wizard Provides a step-by-step guide to help you through the query design process.

Sizing handle A series of faint dots on the outside border of a selected object; enables the user to adjust the height and width of the object.

Sizing handles (Excel) Eight circles that display on the outside border of a chart—one on each corner and one on each middle side—when the chart is selected; enables the user to adjust the height and width of the chart.

Sleep A power saving state that puts work and settings in memory and draws a small amount of power to allow the computer to resume full-power operation quickly.

Slide The most basic element of PowerPoint, similar to a page in Word.

Slide master The top slide in a hierarchy of slides based on the master.

Slide show A series of slides displayed onscreen for an audience.

Slide Show view Displays the completed presentation full screen to an audience as an electronic presentation.

Slide Sorter view Displays thumbnails of presentation slides enabling a view of multiple slides.

Slide pane The main workspace in PowerPoint, that displays the currently selected slide.

Slides pane Pane on the left side of Normal view that shows the slide deck with thumbnails.

Smart Lookup A feature that provides information about tasks or commands in Office, and can also be used to search for general information on a topic such as *President George Washington*.

SmartArt A diagram that presents information visually to effectively communicate a message.

SmartGuide A guide that displays when an object is moved that helps align objects in relation to other objects.

Snip A screenshot taken with the Snipping Tool accessory application in Windows.

Softening A technique that blurs the edges of the content in a picture to make the boundaries less prominent.

Sort A feature which lists records in a specific sequence.

Sorting The process of arranging records by the value of one or more fields within a table or data range.

Source A publication, person, or media item that is consulted in the preparation of a paper and given credit.

Sparkline A small line, column, or win/loss chart contained in a single cell to provide a simple visual illustrating one data series.

Split form A form that combines two views of the same record source—one section is displayed in a stacked layout and the other section is displayed in a tabular layout.

Spreadsheet An electronic file that contains a grid of columns and rows used to organize related data and to display results of calculations, enabling interpretation of quantitative data for decision making.

Stacked column chart A chart type that places stacks of data in segments on top of each other in one column, with each category in the data series represented by a different color.

Stacked layout A layout that displays fields in a vertical column.

Stacking order The order of objects placed on top of one another.

Start menu A feature that provides the main access to all programs on your computer.

Status bar A bar located at the bottom of the program window that contains information relative to the open file. It also includes tools for changing the view of the file and for changing the zoom size of onscreen file contents.

Status bar (Excel) The row at the bottom of the Excel window that displays instructions and other details about the status of a worksheet.

Stock chart A chart type that shows fluctuation in stock prices.

Storyboard A visual plan of a presentation that displays the content of each slide in the slide show.

Structured reference A tag or use of a table element, such as a field label, as a reference in a formula. Field labels are enclosed in square brackets, such as [Amount] within the formula.

Style A named collection of formatting characteristics that can be applied to text or paragraphs.

Style manual A guide to a particular writing style outlining required rules and conventions related to the preparation of papers.

Style set A combination of title, heading, and paragraph styles that can be used to format all of those elements in a document at one time.

SUBTOTAL function A predefined formula that calculates an aggregate value, such as totals, for displayed values in a range, a table, or a database.

SUM function A predefined formula that calculates the total of values contained in one or more cells.

Surface chart A chart type that displays trends using two dimensions on a continuous curve.

Symbol A character or graphic not normally included on a keyboard.

Syntax A set of rules that governs the structure and components for properly entering a function.

Tab Located on the Ribbon, each tab is designed to appear much like a tab on a file folder, with the active tab highlighted.

Tab stop A marker that specifies the position for aligning text in a column arrangement, often including a dot leader.

Table (Access) The location where all data is stored in a database; organizes data into columns and rows.

Table (Excel) A structured range that contains related data organized in a method that increases the capability to manage and analyze information.

Table alignment The horizontal position of a table between the left and right margins.

Table array The range that contains the lookup table.

Table of contents A page that lists headings in the order in which they appear in a document and the page numbers on which the entries begin.

Table style A named collection of color, font, and border designs that can be applied to a table.

Tabular layout A layout that displays fields horizontally.

Task Manager A tool that displays the programs and processes that are running on your computer. It is also used to close a non-responding program.

Task pane A window of options to format and customize chart elements. The task pane name and options change based on the selected chart element.

Task view A button on the taskbar that enables the user to view thumbnail previews of all open tasks in one glance.

Taskbar The horizontal bar at the bottom of the desktop that displays open applications, the Notification area, the Search box, and pinned apps or programs.

***Tell me what you want to do* box** Located to the right of the last tab, this box enables you to search for help and information about a command or task you want to perform and also presents you with a shortcut directly to that command.

Template A predesigned file that incorporates formatting elements, such as a theme and layouts, and may include content that can be modified.

Template (Access) A predefined database that includes professionally designed tables, forms, reports, and other objects that you can use to jumpstart the creation of your database.

Text Any combination of letters, numbers, symbols, and spaces not used in Excel calculations.

Text box A graphical object that contains text.

Text box (PowerPoint) An object that provides space for text anywhere on a slide; it can be formatted with a border, shading, and other characteristics.

Text pane A pane for text entry used for a SmartArt diagram.

Texture fill Inserts a texture such as canvas, denim, marble, or cork into a shape.

Theme A collection of design choices that includes colors, fonts, and special effects used to give a consistent look to a document, workbook, presentation, or database form or report.

Thesaurus A tool used to quickly find a synonym (a word with the same meaning as another).

Thumbnail A miniature view of a slide that appears in the Slidespane and Slide Sorter view.

Tile A rectangular icon on the Start menu that allow you to access programs and apps.

Title bar The long bar at the top of each window that displays the name of the folder, file, or program displayed in the open window and the application in which you are working.

TODAY function A predefined formula that displays the current date.

Toggle commands A button that acts somewhat like light switches that you can turn on and off. You select the command to turn it on, then select it again to turn it off.

Tone A characteristic of lighting that controls the temperature of a color. See also *Kelvin*.

Total row (Access) A method to display aggregate function results as the last row in Datasheet view of a table or query.

Total row (Excel) A table row that appears below the last row of records in an Excel table and displays summary or aggregate statistics, such as a sum or an average.

Totals query A way to display aggregate data when a query is run.

Track Changes A word feature that monitors all additions, deletions, and formatting changes you make in a document.

Transition A specific animation that is applied as na previous slide is repladed by a new slide while displayed in Slide Show view or Reading view.

Transparency The visibility of fill.

Trendline A line that depicts trends or helps forecast future data in a chart. For example, if the plotted data includes 2005, 2010, and 2015, a trendline can help forecast values for 2020 and beyond.

Ungroup To break a combined grouped object into individual objects.

Unqualified reference The use of field headings without row references in a structured formula.

Value A number that represents a quantity or a measurable amount.

Value axis The chart axis that displays incremental numbers to identify approximate values, such as dollars or units, of data points in a chart.

Variant A variation on a chosen design theme.

Vector graphic An image created by a mathematical statement.

Vertex The point where a curve ends or the point where two line segments meet in a shape.

Vertical alignment The placement of cell data between the top and bottom cell margins.

View The various ways a file can appear on the screen.

View controls Icons on the right side of the status bar that enable you to change to Normal, Page Layout, or Page Break view to display the worksheet.

Virtual desktop A way to organize and access groups of windows for different purposes.

VLOOKUP function A predefined formula that accepts a value, looks the value up in a vertical lookup table with data organized in columns, and returns a result.

Watermark Text or graphics that display behind text.

Web Layout view View that displays the way a document will look when posted on the Internet.

Wildcard A special character that can represent one or more characters in the criterion of a query.

Windows app A program that displays full screen without any borders or many controls. It is designed to be best viewed and used on smaller screens such as those on smartphone and tablets.

Windows Defender Antispyware and antivirus software included in Windows 10.

Windows Update A utility in Windows that provides a means to initiate updates and modifications pushed to the user that enhances Windows security or fixes problems.

Word An application that can produce all sorts of documents, including memos, newsletters, forms, tables, and brochures.

Word Online An online component of Office Online, it is a Web-based version of Word with sufficient capabilities to enable you to edit and format a document online.

Word processing software A computer application, such as Microsoft Word, used primarily with text to create, edit, and format documents.

Word wrap The feature that automatically moves words to the next line if they do not fit on the current line.

WordArt A feature that modifies text to include special effects, such as color, shadow, gradient, and 3-D appearance.

Workbook A collection of one or more related worksheets contained within a single file.

Works Cited A list of works cited or consulted by an author in his or her work; the list is titled Works Cited.

Worksheet A single spreadsheet that typically contains descriptive labels, numeric values, formulas, functions, and graphical representations of data.

Wrap text An Excel feature that makes data appear on multiple lines by adjusting the row height to fit the cell contents within the column width.

Writing style Writing a paper as directed by a style manual such as MLA or APA.

X Y (scatter) chart A chart type that shows a relationship between two variables using their X and Y coordinates. Excel plots one coordinate on the horizontal X-axis and the other variable on the vertical Y-axis. Scatter charts are often used to represent data in education, scientific, and medical experiments.

X-axis The horizontal border that provides a frame of reference for measuring data left to right on a chart.

Y-axis The vertical border that provides a frame of reference for measuring data up and down on a chart.

Zoom control A control that enables you to increase or decrease the size of the worksheet data onscreen.

Zoom slider A feature that displays at the far right side of the status bar. It is used to increase or decrease the magnification of the file.

Index

N

O

P

S

T

U

V

W

X

Y

Z

Go Beyond the Point & Click

The ***Exploring*** Series charts your learning beyond the "point and click," helping you understand WHY you use Microsoft Office skills along with HOW you perform them. The latest edition provides an easy-to-follow map to achieve the outcomes identified in each chapter, based on how you already use your materials, to help you learn, study, and review efficiently to be successful in this class and beyond.

Student Textbook

Exploring is a tool built to match the way you use your materials: Your first stop is what you are required to do, your second stop is referencing important background information to help you better understand what you need to do. This edition has been set up to help you easily navigate between the two.

- Outcomes, Objectives, and Skills are laid out for you at the beginning of each chapter so you know exactly what you will learn.
- Hands-On Exercises (yellow pages) appear throughout each chapter, allowing you to apply Microsoft skills in an active, hands-on way.
- Enhanced Objective Mapping enables you to efficiently navigate the theory (white pages) to get the answers you need to move forward.
- Step icons help you navigate back to the concepts in the white pages.
- Quick Concept Checks are included at the end of every white page section to help you confirm your understanding of key objectives.
- End of Chapter Exercises allow you to test your knowledge of Key Terms, create projects From Scratch, learn how to Collaborate with others, and be both Analytical and Creative when approaching your data.

Student Data Files

Access your student data files needed to complete the exercises in this textbook at www.pearsonhighered.com/exploring.

MyITLab and Premium Media

www.myitlab.com

MyITLab is your one-stop-shop for interactive simulated and auto-graded homework featuring immediate feedback as well as self-study tools to help you succeed in this course.

- **Hands-On Exercise Videos** allow you to review and study the concepts taught in the Hands-On Exercises.
- **Multiple Choice quizzes** enable you to test concepts you have learned by answering auto-graded questions.
- **MOS Certification Map** provides a clear guide for you to get everything you can out of the series resources to prepare to pass the MOS Certification tests of your choice.
- **Audio PowerPoints** turn the chapter PowerPoints into lectures with narration that students can pause, rewind, and view as much as they like.